Perception Metaphors

Converging Evidence in Language and Communication Research (CELCR)

ISSN 1566-7774

Over the past decades, linguists have taken a broader view of language and are borrowing methods and findings from other disciplines such as cognition and computer sciences, neurology, biology, sociology, psychology, and anthropology. This development has enriched our knowledge of language and communication, but at the same time it has made it difficult for researchers in a particular field of language studies to be aware of how their findings might relate to those in other (sub-)disciplines.

CELCR seeks to address this problem by taking a cross-disciplinary approach to the study of language and communication. The books in the series focus on a specific linguistic topic and offer studies pertaining to this topic from different disciplinary angles, thus taking converging evidence in language and communication research as its basic methodology.

For an overview of all books published in this series, please see
http://benjamins.com/catalog/celcr

Editors

Kris Heylen
KU Leuven

Ninke Stukker
University of Groningen

Advisory Board

Walter Daelemans
University of Antwerp

Martin Pütz
University of Koblenz-Landau

Cliff Goddard
University of New England

Wilbert Spooren
RU Nijmegen

Roeland van Hout
Radboud University Nijmegen

Marjolijn H. Verspoor
University of Groningen

Leo Noordman
Tilburg University

Volume 19

Perception Metaphors
Edited by Laura J. Speed, Carolyn O'Meara, Lila San Roque and Asifa Majid

Perception Metaphors

Edited by

Laura J. Speed
University of York and Radboud University

Carolyn O'Meara
National Autonomous University of Mexico and Radboud University

Lila San Roque
National Autonomous University of Mexico and Radboud University

Asifa Majid
University of York and Radboud University

John Benjamins Publishing Company

Amsterdam / Philadelphia

The paper used in this publication meets the minimum requirements of the American National Standard for Information Sciences – Permanence of Paper for Printed Library Materials, ANSI Z39.48-1984.

DOI 10.1075/celcr.19

Cataloging-in-Publication Data available from Library of Congress:
LCCN 2018045420 (PRINT) / 2018058351 (E-BOOK)

ISBN 978 90 272 0200 0 (HB)
ISBN 978 90 272 6304 9 (E-BOOK)

John Benjamins Publishing Company · https://benjamins.com

Table of contents

Preface

Asifa Majid
University of York and Radboud University

The impetus for this volume came from a workshop – *Perception Metaphor* – organised by the editors in 2016, and held at the Max Planck Institute for Psycholinguistics, Nijmegen, The Netherlands. The workshop explored the myriad ways perceptual language serves as the basis of, or target for, metaphorical extension. Despite the fact that sensory domains have been characterised as physical and relatively concrete, making for potential source domains in metaphorical mapping, closer examination shows that perceptual language itself is rife with complexity that calls for closer scrutiny. As such, this volume builds on an emerging literature in linguistics that seeks to understand perceptual language itself, following in the wake of a special issue edited by Majid and Levinson (2011) published in *The Senses and Society* entitled "The Senses in Language and Culture", and the edited collection of Caballero and Diaz-Vera (2013) titled *Sensuous Cognition*.

The volume brings together a wide variety of approaches – historical, typological, corpus, experimental, and developmental – all providing diverse perspectives on perceptual language and its role in metaphor. It also brings together voices from both established and emerging scholars from across the globe. Aside from the wonderful contributions from the workshop attendees, we are delighted to be able to include three additional contributions by Constance Classen, Kobin Kendrick and Marcin Trojszczak which add further dimensions to the volume. The Constance Classen contribution is a reprint of Chapter 3 (pp. 50–76) from her 1993 book *Worlds of Sense: Exploring the Senses in History and Across Cultures*, kindly reprinted with permission from Routledge. In this chapter, Classen makes a number of insightful observations that are as relevant today as they were 25 years ago.

To round off, we would like to thank all the attendees of the Perception Metaphor Workshop, especially Vicky Fisher, Ad Foolen, Ulrike Nederstigt, Margot van Mulken, and Andreu van Hooft, for the lively discussions which enriched the current volume. Thanks also to Martine Vanhove, David Howes, and Steve Levinson for their encouragement along the way, and Josje de Valk and Patricia Manko and other members of the Meaning, Culture, & Cognition group for their assistance

https://doi.org/10.1075/celcr.19.pre

with the many things that enable a project like this to be completed. Thanks finally to the Netherlands Organisation for Scientific Research whose generous support allowed this workshop and book to happen.

CHAPTER 1

Perception metaphors

A view from diversity

Carolyn O'Meara[i,ii], Laura J. Speed[ii,iii], Lila San Roque[ii]
and Asifa Majid[ii,iii]
[i]National Autonomous University of Mexico / [ii]Radboud University /
[iii]University of York

Our bodily experiences play an important role in the way that we think
and speak. Abstract language is, however, difficult to reconcile with this
body-centred view, unless we appreciate the role metaphors play. To explore
the role of the senses across semantic domains, we focus on perception metaphors, and examine their realisation across diverse languages, methods, and
approaches. To what extent do mappings in perception metaphor adhere to predictions based on our biological propensities; and to what extent is there space
for cross-linguistic and cross-cultural variation? We find that while some metaphors have widespread commonality, there is more diversity attested than should
be comfortable for universalist accounts.

Keywords: metaphor, abstract concepts, embodiment, sensory perception, hierarchy

1.   Metaphor and perception

Metaphor has been characterised as a mechanism that allows us to think and talk
about one thing in terms of another, ratcheting up the cognitive and expressive
capacity of humankind. For example, a common way to talk about time is in terms
of space, as seen in such expressions as *Halloween is just around the corner* or *the
day before yesterday* (Boroditsky, 2000; Casasanto & Boroditsky, 2008; see Clark,
1973 and Traugott, 1975 for some early discussions). Decades of work on dozens of
languages has identified a range of metaphors (e.g., Gibbs, 1994; Lakoff & Johnson,
1980; Lakoff & Turner, 1989), and further demonstrated how linguistic metaphor
affects thought (e.g., Boroditsky, 2000; Dolscheid et al., 2013).
     Lakoff and Johnson (1980) proposed that metaphor involves grounding ab-
stract concepts in more concrete concepts. This idea is in line with more recent
research in the area of embodied cognition: the claim that language and thought
are grounded in bodily interactions with the environment (Pecher & Zwaan, 2005),

https://doi.org/10.1075/celcr.19.010me

and that meaning is instantiated through recourse to sensory and motor representations (Barsalou, 1999). Embodied theories are supported by neuroimaging studies showing that sensory language activates perceptual systems. For example, auditory, gustatory, tactile and visual semantic processing has been shown to activate regions of the brain responsible for the encoding of the corresponding percepts (Goldberg, Perfetti & Schneider, 2006a, 2006b). Such studies have highlighted the way our sensorimotor experiences are heavily intertwined with the way we think and talk. Thus, one starting point for the study of metaphor is the language of perception itself. How do we communicate sensations, and how do such expressions interface with practices of linguistic metaphor?

Perceptual language is an area that has continued to confound expectations concerning linguistic universals and the limits of semantic systems (Levinson & Majid, 2014; Majid & Levinson, 2011; Majid et al., in press). It turns out that even if meaning is grounded in perception and action systems, as suggested by embodiment perspectives, perceptuo-motor systems still radically under-determine the possibilities for meaning (Majid, 2013). There is startling non-conformity of colour-naming exhibited by certain languages (e.g., Levinson, 2000; Surrallés, 2016) that continue to challenge universalist accounts (e.g., Berlin & Kay, 1964; Kay et al., 2009). Some languages have honed vocabularies for texture distinctions (e.g., Dingemanse, 2011; Dingemanse & Majid, 2012; Le Guen, 2011), while others treat the supposedly ineffable world of odour as something that is, in fact, highly codable (Majid & Burenhult, 2014). It has, furthermore, been proposed that metaphors relating to the perceptual senses are culturally successful and more memorable than their semantic equivalents (Akpinar & Berger, 2015). By investigating perception metaphors, we gain further insights into the structure of the semantic domains of perception, and our capacity (and proclivity) for figurative language.

This volume presents empirical studies that test different theories and approaches to the study of metaphor and perceptual language, as well as essays that comment more broadly on how perception metaphor can be (or has been) studied and conceptualised. The contributions investigate three kinds of metaphors of perception (summarised in Table 1): those that use the language of perception to express phenomena that are not directly part of the perceptual semantic domain (in Matisoff's 1978 terms, "transfield" extensions, such as using the verb *see* to mean 'understand'; we call these *Transfield I*); those that express sensory experiences using language that is "borrowed in" from a different domain (as in the use of the spatial terms *high* and *low* to talk about the auditory sensation of relative pitch, another kind of transfield extension termed here *Transfield II*); and those that are a combination of the two, where the language of one perceptual modality is used to describe the experience in another, such as a *bright sound* or *sharp taste* (so-called "intrafield" metaphor, or, more controversially, "synaesthetic" metaphor).

Table 1. Types of perception metaphor

	Source domain	Target domain	Example
Transfield I	perception	other	*jangling nerves*
Transfield II	other	perception	*high voice*
Intrafield	perception	perception	*sour note*

With regards to the senses, in general, the authors in this volume adopt what is largely common practice by following a "five-senses" model of sensory perception: vision, audition, taste, smell, and touch. Thus, the senses are identified by canonical sense organs – eyes, ears, mouth, nose, and hands – as conceptualised in Western folk theory. There are, of course, other ways to carve up the senses. We could distinguish three senses based on the type of stimulus – light (vision), chemical (smell, taste, internal sensors), and mechanical (touch and hearing); or we could split them in two: distal (vision, hearing) and proximal (touch, taste, smell). At the other end, we could identify up to 33 senses, if we identify them by receptors. For example, the eye has two different types of light sensors – rods, which register light intensity (and give us the perception of form), and (three types of) cones, which sense colour; the inner ear has sound sensors, but also distinct sensors for the sense of balance; and so forth. If we look at the senses physiologically, they could even be considered continuous (see Winter, this volume). Although many have pointed to the limitations of the five-senses model (e.g., Evan & Wilkins, 2000; Geurts, 2002), an alternative framework has yet to present itself. Nevertheless, while only touched upon in this volume, we recognise that there are many metaphorical riches to be uncovered in areas that fall somewhat outside the five senses model. A standout example here is the language of temperature (see Koptjevskaja-Tamm, 2015), as incorporated into expressions about emotion such as *hot anger* (see, for example, Lakoff & Kövecses, 1987; Yu, 1995).

Another wrinkle in the literature is the unspoken assumption of sensory apartheid, with each word assigned to a single perceptual modality. However, this assumption may be more problematic than it appears. For example, Lynott & Connell's (2009) study of 423 English adjectives showed that adjectives tend to be multimodal, i.e., referring to multiple modalities at once. Participants rated adjectives on the extent to which they were related to vision, audition, touch, taste and smell. Based on these ratings, modality exclusivity scores were calculated, reflecting the extent to which a property could be considered unimodal (0%) to fully multimodal (100%). Although adjectives were typically rated dominant in one modality, they were rated on average 46.1% on the modality exclusivity scale, somewhere between unimodal and multimodal (Lynott & Connell 2009). Similar ratings of modality exclusivity have been found for nouns (Lynott & Connell, 2013; Speed &

Majid, 2017). In line with these findings, Winter (this volume) argues that many expressions thought to be metaphorical (e.g., *sweet fragrance*) should instead be considered to have meanings that encompass multiple senses, rather than involving metaphorical extension across perceptual modalities.

Our exploration of perception metaphors in this volume reveals how we conceptualise and talk about perceptual experience that is, to a large degree, universal (based on our biological propensities), but at the same time, utterly subjective (Majid & Levinson, 2011). In the following two sections, we discuss the contributions of this volume in relation to two aspects of perception metaphor that shed light on the extent to which perceptual experience and thought may be universal: (i) whether perception metaphor follows rigid patterns of directionality of metaphoric extension in line with predictions from embodiment theories and cross-linguistic work on intrafield metaphor; and (ii) the extent to which cross-linguistic and cross-cultural differences manifest themselves in perception metaphor, and how diversity more generally features in studies of perception metaphor.

2. Perception metaphor and directionality

Theories of embodiment often face problems when it comes to explaining abstract concepts (e.g., Mahon & Caramazza, 2008). How can notions like *judgement* or *confusion* be explained in terms of sensorimotor systems? There is some evidence that the action system is involved in representing some abstract meanings specifically related to emotion, such as words that denote internal states, like *dread* and *spite* (Moseley et al. 2012). Others have argued that abstract meaning is grounded in emotional, rather than perceptual, experience (Kousta et al., 2011; Vigliocco et al., 2013). Beyond emotional concepts that may be highly tied to action experience, metaphor may be the best mechanism for grounding other abstract concepts (Jamrozik et al., 2016). Examples of metaphoric grounding across sensory modalities include: experience of interpersonal 'warmth' (e.g., IJzerman & Semin, 2009) and anger (Wilkowski et al., 2009) as physical warmth; 'suspicion' based on smell (i.e., suspicion is expressed as something smelling fishy; Lee & Schwarz, 2012); textural metaphor (e.g., *She had a rough day*) being grounded in texture-selective somatosensory cortex (Lacey, Stilla, & Sathian, 2012; Schaefer, Denke, Heinze, & Rotte, 2013); and auditory metaphors (e.g., *His memoirs were a toilet flush*) leading to similar brain responses as sentences about literal sounds (Schmidt-Snoek, Drew, Barile, & Agauas, 2015).

Given this evidence, sensory perception – which is considered concrete and based in the body – should be an ideal source for metaphorical extension; and should be unlikely to feature as a target domain. Conversely, since abstract concepts need to be grounded, they should be more likely to be the target of metaphor, not the source. In other words, we would expect a general directionality to metaphorical extension, where abstract concepts are metaphorically grounded in perceptual systems, but not vice versa. The studies in this volume provide many examples to confirm this view, but also give evidence of linguistic practices that raise questions for straightforward accounts of metaphorical extension from concrete to abstract domains. As we shall see below, these questions concern, among other things, the possibility for differential treatment of sensory modalities in regard to perception metaphor; the related issue of how perception can serve as a target – rather than a source – of both transfield and intrafield metaphor; and even the contention that intrafield polysemies do not represent any kind of directional transfer at all.

Within the chapters that follow, findings from a range of languages support the idea that we use perception metaphor to express more abstract or ineffable ideas. This is seen first of all in verbs of vision – one of the classic areas of investigation for perception metaphor. Using a combination of corpus and psycholinguistic methods, Proos (Chapter 12) shows that the basic vision verb *nägema* in Estonian extends to the abstract domain of intellection and knowledge, as has been shown in other languages, but also to states of mind and feelings, meaning something like 'experience'. Interestingly, Proos shows that distinctions between concrete and abstract semantic domains may remain invisible as regards the structural collocates of the different senses of the verb in a corpus (i.e., according to a Behavioural Profile Analysis), but remain important for speakers making metalinguistic judgments about sense similarity. Kendrick (Chapter 13) demonstrates further how the journey from concrete to abstract can encompass the development of discourse functions, describing the special use of the form *"See?"* in English (pronounced with rising intonation) to invite the interlocutor to consider prior discourse as evidence for a previously made assertion, without an entailment of literal visual perception. Zeshan and Palfreyman (Chapter 14) discuss different signs articulated around the eyes and the non-perceptual meanings they can have, specifically meanings related to knowledge. For example, in Chinese Sign Language and South Korean Sign Language the sign that literally means 'blind' – signed by covering one's eyes – is also used to mean 'not want to know about something'. Similarly, in Indian Sign Language a sign articulated around the eyes to mean 'wink' can also mean 'a secret understanding or tip'. San Roque and Schieffelin (Chapter 17) discuss some of the ways that children may encounter a verb of seeing in relation to more abstract notions like knowing and attempting. At the same time, they note that for a first language learner it may not be so clear that the concrete sense precedes the abstract one, as it is possible that these are bundled together as part of interactional experience (as per Johnson, 1999).

While it has often dominated our understanding of the language of perception, sight is not the only sense that shows support for a dominant concrete > abstract directionality for metaphor. In both Polish and English, tactile properties are used to talk about mind and thought (Trojszczak, Chapter 11); for example, thoughts are conceived of as physical objects involving properties like density (*hard thought*), weight (*unbearable thought*), size (*big thought*), and temperature (*warm thought*). The use of corpus data reveals new metaphors in the area of mind and thought and at the same time highlights similarities in metaphorical extension between two unrelated languages, suggesting that embodied experiences could be the basis for these metaphorical extensions. From a historical perspective, Anderson (Chapter 4) notes the prevalence of touch as a source domain for concepts related to understanding. Ryzhova, Rakhilina and Kholkina (Chapter 10) also discuss how the concept 'heavy', a complex perceptual experience that involves touch, is extended to evaluation in several diverse languages. Beyond touch, Steinbach-Eicke (Chapter 8) explores the metaphorical mapping of taste in Ancient Egyptian, for example to the domains of emotion and cognition, as in EMOTIONAL FEELING IS TASTING and KNOWING IS TASTING.

The unprecedented historical depth and breadth of the Mapping Metaphor project, presented by Anderson (Chapter 4), reveals smell as a rich source domain for metaphorical extension, also discussed by Ibarretxe-Antuñano (Chapter 3; see also Ibarretxe-Antuñano, 1999). Kövesces (Chapter 16) also explicates this theme, noting not only the previously discussed metaphors BAD IS SMELLY and SUSPICION IS SMELLING, but also THE GENERAL ATMOSPHERE IS AN OLFACTORY PERCEPT, as in *It had the smell of treason* –a metaphor not commonly discussed. However, the chapters also uncover examples where it seems metaphoric extensions do not follow the expected directional mapping, but rather map from a concrete domain to another concrete domain, e.g., smell to quantity (Anderson, Chapter 4).

Evidence that complicates the notion of universal concrete > abstract directionality is also seen in situations where sensory perception is the target, rather than the source, in transfield metaphor (*Transfield II* type). Kövesces (Chapter 16) explores some of the ways smell serves as a target domain in English data. For instance, the adjectives *sharp* and *pungent* project the sharpness of an object to describe smells, particularly the intensity of a smell. Julich (Chapter 9) explores the way music critics have a strong tendency to describe music as moving or as having a location in space. For instance, a rhythm can be accelerated or slowed down, and musical events can follow each other or traverse space. These cases of perception as the target of metaphor bring into question some of the common assumptions regarding the role of sensory perception as an ideal source domain.

The work in this volume also informs us about another important aspect of directionality in perception metaphor, that is, whether intrafield extensions (from one perceptual modality to another) follow a universal hierarchy. In particular, previous studies have proposed universal patterns in the way different sensory perception verbs can be extended to describe other sensory modalities (Viberg, 1983). For example, patterns of semantic extension reveal that vision verbs can be used to talk about audition, but not vice versa (Viberg, 1983). Vision ends up being the most extendable, followed by audition, whereas the proximal senses (touch, taste and smell) figure lower in the hierarchy. This hierarchy has been confirmed cross-linguistically, for instance, in around 60 indigenous languages of Australia (Evans & Wilkins, 2000), although some exceptions have been described (e.g., Nakagawa, 2012). However, it has also been proposed that in regard to the extension of adjectives (as opposed to verbs) the hierarchy moves in the opposite direction (Williams 1976; see also Levinson, Majid & Enfield, 2007, concerning word class and the language of perception more generally).

Strik Lievers and De Felice's chapter (Chapter 5) puts patterns of intrafield and transfield polysemy found in synchronic data to the test by analysing data from Classical Latin up to Contemporary Italian. Their findings confirm the general patterns found in previous studies of intrafield extensions going from the "lower" (touch, taste, and smell) to "higher" (seeing and hearing) senses. More specifically, the adjectives they look at from a diachronic perspective confirm a hierarchy of semantic extension as follows: touch > taste/smell > seeing/hearing). For example, the Latin word *asper* has a primary meaning related to touch ('sharp, stinging'), but in contemporary Italian, the meaning has been extended, primarily relating to taste ('sour'). So when sensory adjectives acquire new meaning, the meaning relates to a higher sensory domain in the hierarchy.

Finally, Ryzhova, Rakhilina, and Kholkina's work (Chapter 10) uses a rather different, methodological approach to reveal directionality in perception metaphor. The contexts in which a lexeme is used in metaphorical extensions is compared in order to inform about the structure of a semantic domain. Using this methodology, metaphorical mappings from the touch-related sense of haptics to the auditory and visual domain were found for the concept HEAVY.

Yet directionality may not be the driving force of perceptual metaphors, as certain kinds of perceptual adjectives have been claimed to not involve metaphor. For instance, Winter (this volume) argues that examples like *sweet fragrance* do not involve perception metaphor. At first glance we think of *sweet* as inherently referring to taste, but under Winter's analysis, *sweet* has both a taste- and a smell-related meaning, related to the fact that smells and flavours are tightly linked in terms of the way we perceive them. If this is the case, there is no need to analyse *sweet* in the context of smells as involving metaphor. What might appear to be intrafield or transfield metaphor can also be analysed as a case of multisensory meanings within one lexical item. According to Winter, patterns of perceptual metaphors are not driven by any kind of directionality, but instead are due to either the integrated nature of perceptual modalities in experience, or the evaluative qualities of certain senses.

Caballero (Chapter 7) also makes a case for looking at perception metaphors in a more holistic cross-modal manner, as opposed to a monosensory one, specifically in winespeak: tasting wine is a holistic experience across vision, smell, touch and taste. Our everyday perceptual experiences are rarely monosensory, but instead involve multiple sensory modalities together. Yet, in contrast to Winter, Caballero considers metaphors that map sensory information across domains (as in *a loud colour*) as cases of *synaesthetic* metaphor. Winter instead views such cases as examples of the broad referential scope of sensory adjectives. This theoretical tension requires further empirical investigation in order to be resolved in a satisfactory manner.

Returning to the perspective of embodiment, there may be differences between sensory systems that are reflected in how those senses are extended metaphorically. Language may be more or less connected with some senses rather than others. For example, previous research has suggested that language is weakly linked with the olfactory system (Engen, 1987; Oloffson & Gottfried, 2015), and that odour language may not be strongly grounded in perception (Speed & Majid, 2018). It could be predicted, then, that odour is in fact more likely to be the target of a metaphor, rather than the source. However, as already discussed, Kövecses (Chapter 16) provides evidence that odour acts as both a target and a source domain of metaphor, suggesting grounding of sensory language is not the only factor at play. Both linguistic structure (for example, as regards word class), and culture (e.g., O'Meara & Majid, submitted), also have important roles to play. Debates about embodied and hierarchical approaches thus need to be further explored in relation to the linguistic and cultural diversity found around the globe.

As suggested earlier, embodied approaches would predict we all experience sensory metaphors in a similar way (if we have similar bodies), yet there is evidence that the experience of metaphor differs across cultures and languages. For example, Gilead, Gal, Polak, and Cholow (2015) found that contrary to the positive hedonic associations to sweetness and negative hedonic associations to spiciness, Israeli participants rated a social target as more intellectually competent, authentic, and overall more positive when primed with spicy tastes compared to sweet tastes. This example highlights why it is crucial – not just optional – to examine perception metaphor across diverse languages, as well as in relation to other aspects of diversity.

3. Perception metaphor and diversity

While metaphor is assumed to be a universal feature of human language, there is ongoing debate as to the (possibly competing) roles of cognition and culture in the development of metaphorical correspondences. Work on under-studied languages continues to support the discovery of unique or lesser-documented metaphors that call into question what we might think of as "natural" ways of relating one category to another (Idström & Piirainen, 2012).

Sweetser's (1990) seminal study of English and other Indo-European languages showed there is a tendency for vision verbs to be metaphorically extended to meanings relating to mental activity and knowledge (e.g., using *I see* to mean *I understand*), and argued for a possible universal identification of vision with the objective intellect (Sweetser, 1990, p. 33–35). However, subsequently Evans and Wilkins (2000) demonstrated that many languages of Australia do not follow this supposedly universal pattern, in that it is commonly hearing verbs – rather than sight verbs – that extend to mean 'think' or 'know'. Examples of *Transfield II* type metaphors that describe the domain of pitch have given us another glimpse of how different metaphors can be in different languages. For example, where English speakers describe pitch as being *high* or *low*, Farsi speakers describe high pitch as 'thin' and low pitch as 'thick' (Shayan et al., 2011); the Kpelle use 'light' and 'heavy' (Stone, 1981); Suyá 'young' and 'old' (Zbikowski, 1998); and Shona includes an opposition between 'crocodile' (low pitch) and 'those who follow crocodiles' (high pitch) (Ashley, 2004). Each language studied opens up new vistas for conceptualisation.

Adding to our knowledge of perception metaphor around the globe, this volume includes a diverse sample of languages, time periods, and genres, totalling 43 different languages. This includes 15 contemporary spoken languages (Arabic, Armenian, Basque, Besleney Kabardian, Bosavi, Chinese, English, Estonian, French, Italian, Japanese, Polish, Russian, Serbian, Spanish), historical data from 4 languages at different periods of time (English, Ancient Egyptian, pre-Contemporary Italian and Latin), as well as Japanese Sign Language (JSL) and 23 other sign languages (see Table 2 in Zeshan & Palfreyman, this volume, for a detailed list of the sign languages surveyed). The broad scope of both spoken and signed languages from various parts of the world and from different language families allows us to gain a more comprehensive understanding of shared tendencies in perception metaphor and diversity across different speech communities.

Sign languages offer compelling insights regarding the possibilities of semantic extension to and from perceptual domains, specifically when we consider the different parameters that are at play in signs. While in spoken languages places of articulation are found within the vocal tract, signs are articulated on the body or in what is known as "signing space". For example, signers can produce signs on or near the nose or the eyes. Additionally, signers can make use of non-manual signals in systematic ways, such as movement of the eyes, eyebrows, and nose. The nature of sign languages then allows us to investigate which signs are articulated on or around the organs of perception and to contrastively look at basic perception meanings to see if they are systematically articulated on or around eyes, nose, mouth or ears. One situation that mirrors this facility of sign languages to some degree is the use of classifiers in Hieroglyphic Egyptian (Steinbach-Eicke, Chapter 8).

Meanings found in signed language can also help us understand extensions from the perceptual domain to other conceptual domains. For instance, in many communities where Australian Aboriginal languages are spoken, there are also (auxiliary) sign languages used by both deaf and hearing individuals. In many of these systems a sign made in the region of the ear corresponds to a meaning of basic cognition, coinciding with the polysemous meaning of verbs of hearing in Australian languages used to mean 'know', think', remember', understand' and even 'obey' (Evans & Wilkins, 2000). We gain new insights on perception metaphors in sign from Zeshan and Palfreyman (Chapter 14) who explore cross-linguistic perception metaphors in a range of sign languages, and Takashima (Chapter 15) who compares perception metaphors in JSL with similar expressions in spoken Japanese.

Co-speech gesture is another window to investigate perception metaphor. For example, in her overview of perception metaphor Ibarretxte-Antuñano (Chapter 3) presents gestures made on the nose that manifest the same conceptual metaphor, SUSPECTING IS SMELLING, but in different languages. However, similar gestures can fail to instantiate the same metaphor cross-linguistically. For example, tapping one's finger against a nostril is used to convey suspicion in European Spanish, but not in Mexican Spanish where it means that someone was sniffing illicit drugs. This illustrates the additional point that different varieties of the "same" language may have different metaphorical codes (see also Takashima, Chapter 15, regarding the related point as to whether signed languages share metaphors with the surrounding community of spoken language users).

[As well as diverse languages and language varieties, the volume represents diversity in registers, including work that draws on general written material, adult conversation, interaction involving children, esoteric texts, and the specialist genres of wine and music reviews. These corpus data give a richly varied picture of perception metaphors as used in different modes and contexts, in some cases even within the same languages.]

Face-to-face interaction in spontaneous conversation is potentially one of the most basic ways that speakers of almost all languages of the world communicate. Yet, very few studies have looked at perceptual language use cross-linguistically using conversational data (see also San Roque et al., 2015; 2018), let alone perception metaphor in conversation. Kendrick's work (Chapter 13) reveals special discourse functions of the perception verb *see* that cannot be explored using standard written corpus data. San Roque and Schieffelin (Chapter 17) engage with the challenge of identifying possible "bridging contexts" in examining extended meanings of perception verbs in conversation between children and their caregivers, as well as commenting on the use of perception verbs in religious discourse and missionisation.

The creation and exploration of corpus data is also a means to study how perceptual language is used by members of expert communities. On the one hand, a naïve perspective might expect experts in a particular domain to talk about their area of expertise with precise language such that it conveys factual, objective information, especially if the goal is to disseminate information to non-experts (Croijmans & Majid, 2016). However, corpus data from experts in different domains reveal a plethora of figurative language. Caballero (Chapter 7) looks at a corpus of wine-speak, composed of wine tasting notes and other sources of wine experts talking about wine in English. The data illustrate sophisticated variation and combinations of much of the language we already use to describe everyday sensory experiences, with a high frequency of cross-modal metaphors. This suggests that we should take a more holistic approach to sensory perception, as opposed to a monosensory one.

Finally, another expert domain featured in this volume can be found in the work of Julich (Chapter 9) regarding the way classical music critics talk about musical structure in English by construing music as motion. The basis for conceptualising music in terms of motion in English may have to do with musical pitch being thought of as low or high, where melodies can go up or down. This is reflected in the general conceptual metaphors at play in the perception of musical structure, TIME IS MOTION and CHANGE IS MOTION. However, classical music critics tend to use more diverse figurative language involving fictive motion as a result of their tendency to "scan" the music mentally as it progresses in time, indicating a close relationship between fictive motion and metaphorical motion.

4. Concluding remarks

The chapters in this volume provide diverse perspectives on perception metaphor in various unrelated spoken and sign languages, using a variety of methods, as well as different theoretical approaches. We find that while intrafield metaphors tend to follow the predicted directionality observed in previous studies (e.g., Viberg 1983; Evans & Wilkins 2000), cross-linguistic studies reveal more diversity with respect to the specific linguistic expressions that involve transfield metaphors. Additionally, the embodied nature of sensory perception proves relevant in terms of the role of the different perceptual senses as the targets of metaphorical extension. At the same time, the studies presented here highlight the fact that sensory domains also serve as targets of metaphor, putting into question the status of the sensory domains as inherently concrete, and the assumption that metaphorical extension always goes from the abstract to the concrete. The way to provide definitive answers to such open questions is to continue to study metaphor in lesser-studied languages and use diverse data sources, including natural language corpora and experimental methods.

Many of the studies presented here give in-depth accounts of perception verbs and adjectives related to perceptual experiences, as well as larger constructions that instantiate perception metaphors. Chapters such as those by Anderson, Kövecses, Zeshan and Palfreyman, and Takashima hint at the issue of how perception metaphor plays out in word classes other than verbs and adjectives, pointing to further questions that need to be explored (cf., Levinson, Majid & Enfield, 2007). Adjectives and verbs appear to follow different directions in regard to the most typical intrafield metaphors they engender, but how might "perceptual nouns" and other highly relevant word classes such as ideophones fit into patterns of directionality? And what about metaphor in languages for which definitions of word classes may be problematic or under-developed (cf., Schwager & Zeshan, 2008)? We look forward to learning more about these and other questions – and other languages – in future studies.

Acknowledgements

This research was supported primarily by the Netherlands Organisation for Scientific Research, NWO project 277-70-011, with San Roque supported by NWO project 275-89-024.

References

Akpinar, E. & Berger, J. (2015). Drivers of cultural success: The case of sensory metaphors. *Journal of Personality and Social Psychology*, 109(1), 20–34. https://doi.org/10.1037/pspa0000025

Ashley, R. (2004). Musical pitch space across modalities: Spatial and other mappings through language and culture. In *Proceedings of the 8th International Conference on Music Perception and Cognition* (Vol. 72). Adelaide, Australia: Causal Productions.

Barsalou, L. W. (1999). Perceptual Perceptual symbol systems. *Brain and Behavioral Science*, 22(4), 577–609.

Berlin, B., & Kay, P. (1964). *Basic color terms: Their universality and evolution*. Berkeley, CA: University of California Press.

Boroditsky, L. (2000). Metaphoric structuring: Understanding time through spatial metaphors. *Cognition*, 75(1), 1–28. https://doi.org/10.1016/S0010-0277(99)00073-6

Casasanto, D., & Boroditsky, L. (2008). Time in the mind: Using space to think about time. *Cognition*, 106, 579–593. https://doi.org/10.1016/j.cognition.2007.03.004

Clark, H. H. (1973). Space, time, semantics, and the child. In T. E. Moore (Ed.), *Cognitive development and the acquisition of language* (pp. 27–63). New York: Academic Press. https://doi.org/10.1016/B978-0-12-505850-6.50008-6

Croijmans, I. & Majid, A. (2016). Not all flavor expertise is equal: The language of wine and coffee experts. *PLoS ONE* 5(5): e0155845. https://doi.org/10.1371/journal.pone.0155845

Dingemanse, M. (2011). The meaning and use of ideophones in Siwu. Ph.D. Thesis, Radboud University Nijmegen, Nijmegen.

Dingemanse, M., & Majid, A. (2012). The semantic structure of sensory vocabulary in an African language. In N. Miyake, D. Peebles, & R. P. Cooper (Eds.), *Proceedings of the 34th Annual Meeting of the Cognitive Science Society (CogSci 2012)* (pp. 300–305). Austin, TX: Cognitive Science Society.

Dolscheid, S., Shayan, S., Majid, A., & Casasanto, D. (2013). The thickness of musical pitch: Psychophysical evidence for linguistic relativity. *Psychological Science*, 24(5), 613–621. https://doi.org/10.1177/0956797612457374

Engen, T. (1987). Remembering odors and their names. *American Scientist*, 497–503.

Evans, N. & Wilkins, D. (2000). In the mind's ear: The semantic extensions of perception verbs in Australian languages. *Language*, 76(3), 546–592. https://doi.org/10.2307/417135

Geurts, K. L. (2002) *Culture and the senses: Bodily ways of knowing in an African community*. Berkeley, CA: University of California Press.

Gibbs, R. W. (1994). *The poetics of mind: Figurative thought, language and understanding*. Cambridge: Cambridge University Press.

Gilead, M., Gal, O., Polak, M., & Cholow, Y. (2015). The role of nature and nurture in conceptual metaphors: The case of gustatory priming. *Social Psychology*, 46, 167–173. https://doi.org/10.1027/1864-9335/a000238

Goldberg, R. F., Perfetti, C. A. & Schneider, W. (2006a). Perceptual knowledge retrieval activates sensory brain regions. *Journal of Neuroscience*, 26(18), 4917–4921. https://doi.org/10.1523/JNEUROSCI.5389-05.2006

Goldberg, R. F., Perfetti, C. A., & Schneider, W. (2006b). Distinct and common cortical activations for multimodal semantic categories. *Cognitive, Affective, & Behavioral Neuroscience*, 6(3), 214–222. https://doi.org/10.3758/CABN.6.3.214

Ibarretxe-Antuñano, I. (1999). Polysemy and metaphor in perception verbs: A cross-linguistic study. PhD Thesis. University of Edinburgh.

Idström, A. & Piirainen, E. (2012). *Endangered metaphors*. Amsterdam/Philadelphia: John Benjamins. https://doi.org/10.1075/clscc.2

IJzerman, H., & Semin, G. R. (2009). The thermometer of social relations: Mapping social proximity on temperature. *Psychological Science*, 20(10), 1214–1220. https://doi.org/10.1111/j.1467-9280.2009.02434.x

Jamrozik, A., McQuire, M., Cardillo, E. R., Chatterjee, A. (2016). Metaphor: Bridging embodiment to abstraction. *Psychonomic Bulletin & Review* 23(4): 1080–1089. https://doi.org/10.3758/s13423-015-0861-0

Johnson, C. (1999). Metaphor vs. conflation in the acquisition of polysemy: The case of *see*. In M. K. Hiraga, C. Sinha & S. Wilcox (Eds.), *Cultural, psychological and typological issues in cognitive linguistics: Selected papers of the bi-annual ICLA meeting in Albuquerque, July 1995* (pp.155–170). https://doi.org/10.1075/cilt.152.12joh

Kay, P., Berlin, B., Maffi, L., Merrifield, W. R., & Cook, R. (2009). *The world color survey*. Stanford: Center for the Study of Language and Information.

Koptjevskaja-Tamm, M. (Ed.). (2015). *The linguistics of temperature*. Amsterdam/Philadelphia: John Benjamins. https://doi.org/10.1075/tsl.107

Kousta, S. T., Vigliocco, G., Vinson, D. P., Andrews, M., & Del Campo, E. (2011). The representation of abstract words: why emotion matters. *Journal of Experimental Psychology: General*, 140(1), 14–34. https://doi.org/10.1037/a0021446

Lacey, S., Stilla, R., & Sathian, K. (2012). Metaphorically feeling: comprehending textural metaphors activates somatosensory cortex. *Brain and language*, 120(3), 416–421. https://doi.org/10.1016/j.bandl.2011.12.016

Lakoff, G. & Johnson, M. (1980). *Metaphors we live by*. Chicago: The University of Chicago Press.

Lakoff, G., & Kövecses, Z. (1987). The cognitive model of anger inherent in American English. In D. Holland & N. Quinn (Eds.), *Cultural models in language and thought* (pp. 195–221). Cambridge: Cambridge University Press. https://doi.org/10.1017/CBO9780511607660.009

Lakoff, G. & Turner, M. (1989). *More than cool reason: A field guide to poetic metaphor*. Chicago: The University of Chicago Press. https://doi.org/10.7208/chicago/9780226470986.001.0001

Le Guen, O. (2011) Materiality vs. expressivity: The use of sensory vocabulary in Yucatec Maya. *Senses & Society* 6(1), pp. 117–125. https://doi.org/10.2752/174589311X12893982233993

Lee, S. W., & Schwarz, N. (2012). Bidirectionality, mediation, and moderation of metaphorical effects: The embodiment of social suspicion and fishy smells. *Journal of Personality and Social Psychology*, 103(5), 737–749. https://doi.org/10.1037/a0029708

Levinson, S. C. (2000). Yélî Dnye and the theory of basic color terms. *Journal of Linguistic Anthropology*, 10(1), 3–55. https://doi.org/10.1525/jlin.2000.10.1.3

Levinson, S. C., Majid, A., & Enfield, N. J. (2007). Language of perception: The view from language and culture. In A. Majid (Ed.), *Field Manual* Volume 10 (pp. 10–21). Nijmegen: Max Planck Institute for Psycholinguistics.

Levinson, S. C., & Majid, A. (2014). Differential ineffability and the senses. *Mind & Language*, 29(4), 407–427. https://doi.org/10.1111/mila.12057

Lynott, D., & Connell, L. (2009). Modality exclusivity norms for 423 object properties. *Behavior Research Methods*, 41(2), 558–564. https://doi.org/10.3758/BRM.41.2.558

Lynott, D., & Connell, L. (2013). Modality exclusivity norms for 400 nouns: The relationship between perceptual experience and surface word form. *Behavior Research Methods*, 45(2), 516–526. https://doi.org/10.3758/s13428-012-0267-0

Mahon, B. Z., & Caramazza, A. (2008). A critical look at the embodied cognition hypothesis and a new proposal for grounding conceptual content. *Journal of Physiology-Paris*, 102(1), 59–70. https://doi.org/10.1016/j.jphysparis.2008.03.004

Majid, A. (2013). Making semantics and pragmatics "sensory". *Journal of Pragmatics*, 58, 48–51. https://doi.org/10.1016/j.pragma.2013.09.019

Majid, A., & Burenhult, N. (2014). Odors are expressible in language, as long as you speak the right language. *Cognition*, 130(2), 266–270. https://doi.org/10.1016/j.cognition.2013.11.004

Majid, A. & Levinson, S. C. (2011). The senses in language and culture. *Senses & Society*, 6(1), 5–18. https://doi.org/10.2752/174589311X12893982233551

Majid, A., Roberts, S. G., Cilissen, L., Emmorey, K., Nicodemus, B., O'Grady, L., Woll, B., LeLan, B., de Sousa, H., Cansler, B. L., Shayan, S., de Vos, C., Senft, G., Enfield, N. J., Razak, R. A., Fedden, S., Tufvesson, S., Dingemanse, M., Oztürk, O., Brown, P., Hill, C., Le Guen, O., Hirtzel, V., van Gijn, R., Sicoli, M. A., & Levinson, S. C. (in press). The differential coding of perception in the world's languages. *Proceedings of the National Academy of Sciences*.

Matissof, J. A. (1978). Variational semantics in Tibeto-Burman: The 'organic' approach to linguistic comparison. *Occasional Papers of the Wolfenden Society on Tibeto-Burman Linguistics*, Volume VI. Philadelphia, PA: Institute for the Study of Human Issues (ISHI).

Moseley, R., Carota, F., Hauk, O., Mohr, B., Pulvermüller, F. (2012). A rol for the motor system in binding abstract emotional meaning. *Cerebral Cortex*, 22(7): 1634–1647.

Nakagawa, H. 2012. The importance of taste verbs in some Khoe languages. *Linguistics* 50(3), 395–420. https://doi.org/10.1515/ling-2012-0014

Olofsson, J. K., & Gottfried, J. A. (2015). The muted sense: Neurocognitive limitations of olfactory language. *Trends in Cognitive Sciences*, 19(6), 314–321. https://doi.org/10.1016/j.tics.2015.04.007

O'Meara, C. & Majid, A. (submitted). Anger stinks in Seri: Olfactory metaphor in a lesser-described language.

Pecher, D., & Zwaan, R. A. (Eds.) (2005). *The grounding of cognition: The role of perception and action in memory, language, and thinking.* Cambridge: Cambridge University Press. https://doi.org/10.1017/CBO9780511499968

San Roque, L., Kendrick, K. H., Norcliffe, E., Brown, P., Defina, R., Dingemanse, M., Dirksmeyer, T., Enfield, N. J., Floyd, S., Hammond, J., Rossi, G., Tufvesson, S., Van Putten, S., & Majid, A. (2015). Vision verbs dominate in conversation across cultures, but the ranking of non-visual verbs varies. *Cognitive Linguistics*, 26(1), 31–60. https://doi.org/10.1515/cog-2014-0089

San Roque, L., Kendrick, K. H., Norcliffe, E. & Majid, A. (2018). Universal meaning extensions of perception verbs are grounded in interaction. *Cognitive Linguistics*, 29(3), 371–406. https://doi.org/10.1515/cog-2017-0034

Schaefer, M., Denke, C., Heinze, H. J., & Rotte, M. (2013). Rough primes and rough conversations: Evidence for a modality-specific basis to mental metaphors. *Social Cognitive and Affective Neuroscience*, 9(11), 1653–1659. https://doi.org/10.1093/scan/nst163

Schmidt-Snoek, G. L., Drew, A. R., Barile, E. C., & Agauas, S. J. (2015). Auditory and motion metaphors have different scalp distributions: an ERP study. *Frontiers in Human Neuroscience*, 9, 126. https://doi.org/10.3389/fnhum.2015.00126

Schwager, W., & Zeshan, U. (2008). Word classes in sign languages: Criteria and classifications. *Studies in Language*, 32(3), 509–545. https://doi.org/10.1075/sl.32.3.03sch

Shayan, S., Ozturk, O., & Sicoli, M. A. (2011). The Thickness of pitch: Crossmodal metaphors in Farsi, Turkish, and Zapotec. *Senses & Society*, 6(1), 96–105. https://doi.org/10.2752/174589311X12893982233911

Speed, L. J., & Majid, A. (2018). An exception to mental simulation: No evidence for embodied odor language. *Cognitive Science*, 42(4), 1146–1178. https://doi.org/10.1111/cogs.12593

Speed, L. J., & Majid, A. (2017). Dutch modality exclusivity norms: Simulating perceptual modality in space. *Behavior Research Methods*, 49(6), 2204–2218. https://doi.org/10.3758/s13428-017-0852-3

Stone, R. M. (1981). Toward a Kpelle conceptualization of music performance. *The Journal of American Folklore*, 94(372), 188–206. https://doi.org/10.2307/540124

Surrallés, A. (2016). On contrastive perception and ineffability: assessing sensory experience without colour terms in an Amazonian society. *Journal of the Royal Anthropological Institute*, 22(4), 962–979. https://doi.org/10.1111/1467-9655.12499

Sweetser, E. (1990). *From etymology to pragmatics.* New York: Cambridge University Press. https://doi.org/10.1017/CBO9780511620904

Traugott, E. L. (1975). Spatial expressions of tense and temporal sequencing: A contribution to the study of semantic fields. *Semiotica*, 15(3), 207–230. https://doi.org/10.1515/semi.1975.15.3.207

Viberg, Å. (1983). The verbs of perception: A typological study. *Linguistics* 21(1), 123–162. https://doi.org/10.1515/ling.1983.21.1.123

Vigliocco, G., Kousta, S. T., Della Rosa, P. A., Vinson, D. P., Tettamanti, M., Devlin, J. T., & Cappa, S. F. (2013). The neural representation of abstract words: the role of emotion. *Cerebral Cortex*, 24(7), 1767–1777. https://doi.org/10.1093/cercor/bht025

Wilkowski, B. M., Meier, B. P., Robinson, M. D., Carter, M. S., & Feltman, R. (2009). "Hot-headed" is more than an expression: The embodied representation of anger in terms of heat. *Emotion*, 9(4), 464–477. https://doi.org/10.1037/a0015764

Williams, J. M. (1976). Synaesthetic adjectives: A possible law of semantic change. *Language*, 52(2), 461–478. https://doi.org/10.2307/412571

Yu, N. (1995). Metaphorical expressions of anger and happiness in English and Chinese. *Metaphor and Symbol*, 10(2), 59–92. https://doi.org/10.1207/s15327868ms1002_1

Zbikowski, L. (1998). Metaphor and music theory: Reflections from cognitive science. *Music Theory Online*, 4(1), 1–11.

CHAPTER 2

Words of sense

Constance Classen
Concordia University

We are accustomed to thinking of language, in its spoken and written forms, as an auditory and visual phenomenon. However, language, in fact, can be said to involve all the senses. Writing is tactile as well as visual, requiring the touch of one's hand. Speech is not only auditory, but also kinaesthetic, olfactory (speech is carried on the breath), and even gustatory, as we shall see in the linguistic theories of Jacob Boehme. At the same time, language expresses sensory phenomena. The word 'blue' expresses a colour category, 'sweet', a flavour category, and so on.

In the ancient world it was believed that there was an intrinsic relationship between words and their referents, even to the extent of the former giving rise to the latter. Thus, in the Bible, for example, the word for light precedes and creates light itself. For the ancients, in an essential fashion, words *were* what they represented.

The idea that language, or at least some hypothetical ideal language, has a direct relationship with the world it describes was popular in the West up until the time of the Enlightenment. The seventeenth-century mystic and philosopher Jacob Boehme, for example, held that words express their meaning through the kinaesthesis and 'gustation' of speech. He explains the German word *barmhertzig*, warm-hearted, for instance as consisting of a combination of sour and sweet attributes:

> When thou pronouncest BARM- then thou shuttest thy mouth, and snarlest in the hinder part of the mouth; and this is the astringent quality … But when a man saith BARM-HERTZ, he fetcheth or presseth the second syllable out from the deep of the body, out from the heart … The spirit in the word -HERTZ – [heart] goeth forth *suddenly*, [producing a sweet quality] and giveth the distinction and understanding of the word…   (Boehme, 1960)

Written words could also be thought to contain the significance of their referents within themselves. Thus in the medieval cabalistic text *The Zohar*, for instance, we read that humans were created by the written word as well as the spoken word: 'The word *vayizer* (and he formed) implies that God brought [humans] under the aegis of his own name [YHVH] by shaping the two eyes like the letter *Yod* and the nose between like the letter *Vau*.' (Sperling & Simon, 1949: 101)

https://doi.org/10.1075/celcr.19.02cla

In the modern West we no longer believe there to be any intrinsic connection between words and their referents. There is no particular 'tree-ness' to the word *tree*, or 'blueness' to the word *blue*. Language is an abstract conceptual system, closed in within itself. This removal of language from the world to the mind, has led us to develop a rather de-sensualized understanding of language and to be inattentive to the sensory content of the words we speak and think with. The purpose of this chapter, therefore, is to bring to light some of the sensory bases and biases of English through an etymological exploration of a selection of words with sensory connotations. We shall look at how the meanings of different sensory terms have shifted with time, how relationships among the senses are expressed through language, how sensory metaphors are used to stand for non-sensory qualities, and how many of our terms for thought processes have sensory etymological roots.[1]

Boehme's idea of words as embodying the essence of what they stand for may seem rather far-fetched to us moderns. Nonetheless some words are imitative of the phenomena they represent. This is especially true of onomatopoeic words, such as *thud* and *bang*, but also of words dealing with tactile and kinaesthetic sensations. *Mushy*, and *slip*, for example, convey, through the sound and kinaesthesis of speech, the tactile sensation of mushiness and the kinaesthetic sensation of slipping. Such associations possibly extend to words dealing with other sensory phenomena as well. For instance, cross-cultural studies have shown that different vowel sounds are associated with different degrees of size and brightness. Thus in one study of English and Chinese speakers, in which the made-up words *mal* and *mil* were said to mean 'table', both groups agreed that *mal* suggested a larger table than *mil* (Marks, 1978: 77–80; Sapir, 1929).

In certain cases, what started off as an echoic word had its meaning transferred from the auditory to another sensory modality. *Crack*, for instance, meaning a breaking noise, came to signify the action and result of breaking as well. *Bound*, from the Latin *bombire*, 'to resound', apparently went from meaning an echo to meaning a leap. *Touch* is based on the Latin *toccare*, 'to knock', derived from *tok*, echoic of a light blow. *Flash*, meaning a burst of light, is based on *plash*, imitative of a splash of water. *Raven*, originally imitative of a raven's call (making it similar to *crow*, another echoic word) now is also used as a colour term. Likewise *blatant*, once meaning 'babbling, noisy', is now more likely to be applied to visual showiness.

Some words which now have predominantly auditory meanings, on the other hand, once referred to one of the other senses. *Noise*, for example, appears to be based on the Latin *nausea*, 'sea-sickness'. *Mellifluous* once meant 'honeyed in taste',

---

1. The sources used for this exploration are Klein (1966); Simpson and Weiner (1989); Skeat (1989); and Guralnik (1968). The examples of historical usage of words are all from Simpson and Weiner (1989).

but is now used to mean 'honeyed in sound'. *Tone*, meaning a sound, is derived from the Greek verb *tenein*, 'to stretch'. *Boisterous* originally meant 'rough', but has had its sensory balance tipped in favour of 'loud'. Similarly, *quiet* has gone from meaning primarily 'still' to meaning primarily 'soundless'. The word *hear*, interestingly, is itself a sensory transposition, as it developed from the Indo-European base *qeu-*, meaning 'to look at, perceive'.

It is remarkable, indeed, how many words dealing with the senses have undergone sensory shifts. This is particularly true of gustatory terms, most of which are tactile in origin. *Bitter, tangy, piquant, pungent, tart, acid*, and *acrid* are all based on words meaning 'sharp'. *Cloying*, meaning 'overly sweet', originally meant 'to lame a horse with a nail'. The word *taste* itself originally meant 'touch'. The fact that these gustatory terms have their origin in the sense of touch illustrates the importance of the tactile component of gustation, and also suggests that touch serves as a model for taste in Western thought. Other gustatory terms which have shifted their sensory meaning include *flavour*, which once meant 'an odour', and *spicy*, which has a visual basis, being derived from the Latin *species*, meaning 'appearance'.

Gustatory terms, such as *sour, sweet*, or *pungent*, usually double for olfactory terms. Olfactory terms themselves often derive from words referring to fire or smoke. *Smell, reek, perfume* and *incense*, for example, all have bases meaning 'to burn' or 'smoke'. *Breath* originally meant the smell of anything cooking or burning, and is derived from an Indo-European base meaning 'to boil'. This suggests that odours produced through burning were the archetypical smell for our linguistic ancestors who, of course, attached far more practical and symbolic significance to fire than we do.

In fact, conditions of smokiness and dustiness apparently made quite an impression on our forebears, as many of our present sensory terms are developed from roots meaning 'smoky' or 'dusty'. The Indo-European base, *dheu* 'to fly about like dust, to smoke', is at the root of words such as *dizzy, dim, dull, dun, dust, dusk, fume*, and *tumble*. *Deaf, dumb*, and *dead* are derived from *dheu-* as well, evoking the deadening of the senses that occurs in a dust storm. *Blind*, apparently from another Indo-European base, *blendh-*, 'to mix', also suggests the sensory confusion of blurred boundaries. Indeed, the Greek word for 'blind', *typhlos*, is derived from the same *dheu-* base as our *deaf* and *dumb*. The tactile dimension of *dheu-* can be seen in another of its offspring, *down*, meaning 'soft feathers', and its olfactory dimension in the Sanskrit *dhup*, 'to burn incense'. The Indo-European word for 'breath', *dhewes*, in turn, is based on *dheu-* as well, perhaps due to the smoke-like nature of breath. Finally, the word *stink* is derived from the Indo-European *steu-*, like *dheu-*, meaning 'to rise up like dust'. Thus the experience of blowing dust and smoke has given rise to a whole multi-sensory complex of words.

Returning now to <u>olfaction,</u> *scent* is an interesting word in that it is based on the Latin *sentire*, meaning 'to feel, to perceive in general'. Our English word *scent* comes by way of the French *sentir*, which carries the double meaning of 'to feel' and 'to smell'. This association between smell and perception in general might have occurred because of a certain primacy accorded to the role of smell in sense experience, or equally, because smell was such a difficult sense to pin down that it ended up being expressed simply as 'feeling'. There are relatively few olfactory terms in English and of these many more refer to bad smells – *fetor, foulness, fustiness, malodour, rankness, reek, stench, stink* – than to good smells – *aroma, fragrance, perfume, redolence*. In fact, there is a tendency for smell words to acquire negative connotations in English. To *stink*, for example, once meant to emit any odour, bad or good, and now means only to emit a bad odour. To *smell*, in the sense of giving off an odour, seems to be going the same route. It *smells* means 'it smells bad'. Why should this be so? Why should the connotation of *smelly* be negative, while that of *tasty* is positive? The answer may be in part that we are confronted with foul smells more often than we are confronted by foul tastes. We can choose our food, but we cannot as readily close our noses to bad smells.

Moving on to touch, tactile terms with non-tactile roots usually have echoic bases, such as *slap*, imitative of the sound produced by a slap. As regards sight, relatively few visual terms have non-visual roots. Exceptions include *see*, derived from an Indo-European root meaning both 'to see' and 'say', and *scan*, derived from the Latin 'to climb'. A tactile word may develop into an auditory, gustatory or olfactory term, for instance, but it is unlikely to develop into a visual term. Nor do visual terms develop into non-visual terms. Just as *sharp* does not come to mean 'bright', *bright* does not come to mean 'sweet'. This suggests a certain cordoning off of sight from the other senses, an assertion of the distinctness of the visual experience.

While non-visual words usually do not develop into visual words, they are, however, widely used to qualify visual experience. For instance, one can speak of a *sweet, rough,* or *loud* appearance. Tactile terms are especially likely to be used to characterize visual and other sensory experience. Tactile adjectives such as *sharp, smooth, harsh* and *heavy*, for instance, can be used with all the senses. However, tactile terms cannot themselves usually be qualified by adjectives from any of the other senses.[2]

Gustatory adjectives can also be applied across the senses, with the exclusion of touch. One can speak of a *sour* appearance, smell or sound, for example, but not a *sour* touch. Similarly, it is not difficult to conceive of a *spicy* piece of music, but what would a *spicy* texture be like? An exception to this rule is *sweet*, which can, in certain cases, be applied to touch; for example, a *sweet caress*. *Suave* is also

---

2.   Williams (1976) postulates a law of semantic change based on the patterns of transfer of adjectives from one sensory modality to another.

interesting in this regard in that it went from meaning 'sweet' to meaning, albeit in a predominantly figurative sense, 'smooth'.

Taste itself can usually only be qualified by sensory adjectives that are tactile, for example, *hot* and *sharp*. In general, olfactory terms cannot be figuratively applied to taste terms. Exceptions are *foul* which can be used with taste, and *flavour*, which was originally a smell word. Thus, while to speak of a *bitter* smell makes sense, to speak of a *stinking* taste does not.

Visual adjectives can often be applied to auditory terms, but not usually to other sensory terms. One can refer to a *bright* sound, for instance, but not a *bright* touch, taste or smell; to tone *colour*, but not touch, taste or smell *colour*. To a much lesser extent auditory adjectives can be applied to visual terms (and not to other sensory words), for example, *screaming pink*.

Visual terms can be characterized by adjectives derived from any of the senses but smell. A colour can be *sweet, sharp* or *loud*, but not *fragrant*. Auditory terms, on the other hand, come close to being able to be qualified by olfactory adjectives, as well as by adjectives from the other senses. A *fragrant melody*, for example, makes sense in a poetic sort of way.

Smell, indeed, is curious in that it is so resistant to cross-sensory application. Basic olfactory terms such as *stinking* and *aromatic* simply cannot be applied to any other sensory experience. Few of them as there are, smell terms are apparently too strongly olfactory in nature to lend themselves to other sensory usages. (Although they can have figurative meanings – *foul*, for example, can be used to mean 'evil'.)

A certain rule of sensory interaction seems to be at work here. Touch appears to be the most basic and diffuse sense in English, providing terms applicable to all the senses. This may be because all the senses are experienced as being quasi-tactile in nature. This primacy of touch, however, generally makes it unable to be qualified by terms from the more specialized senses.

Taste is the next most basic sense. Its ability to characterize a variety of other sensory terms may be due to the strongly tactile component of gustation. It is perhaps the case that sensations of taste and touch – the sweetness of honey, the stab of a knife – are experienced so intensely that they tend to 'colour' other sensations. In turn, taste, like touch, resists being qualified by the more specialized visual, auditory and olfactory terms.

Sight provides adjectives that can qualify auditory terms but, in general, not those of any of the other senses (i.e. *bright, dim, blurred, blue*). The perceived likeness of sound to light is perhaps due in part to both sight and hearing being experienced as distance senses. Touch, taste and smell are perceived as too internal to the body to be qualified by visual terms. They are metaphorically 'dark' senses. Sound is more likely to be conceived of as taking place outside the body and, therefore, as figuratively accessible to sight.

Whereas visual terms can qualify auditory terms, the reverse is less true. This may be because hearing is considered to be more a specialized or complex sense than sight. The general rule at work here would be that a particular sense can be qualified by terms from senses deemed more basic, but can itself only be used to qualify senses deemed more specialized. Therefore, as a more specialized sense than sight, taste or touch, hearing can be qualified by adjectives belonging to these senses but cannot itself provide many adjectives that will qualify them in return.

Hearing, of course, is unique among the senses in that its medium is also the medium of language. Thus it may be that most auditory terms are too echoic or suggestive of the sounds they represent to be used to characterize other sensory phenomena. An exception to this is the use of echoic words to represent actions that accompany particular sounds. As mentioned earlier, the verb to *crack* is based on the echoic term *crack*.

Smell is the one sense to elude inclusion under the rule postulated above. Theoretically, it should fall in between taste and sight. Olfactory terms can be qualified by tactile and gustatory terms but usually not by visual or auditory terms. They should therefore, according to the rule, be able to qualify the latter terms and unable to qualify the former. Instead, they are unable to do either. One can no more speak of a *fragrant* or *fetid* colour than one can of a *fragrant* or *fetid* texture. Hearing indeed, as was noted, is the only sense that can be somewhat character-ized by smell. Smell, in turn, can be somewhat characterized by auditory terms. Perfumers, for example, speak of different scents as *notes*. This perceived similarity of sound and scent probably has to do with the fact that both are experienced as carried on the air.

Why smell, which, in fact, constitutes a large part of taste, should produce fewer linguistic terms than taste, and why those terms it does produce should be unable to qualify other sensory experiences, are open questions. It would be informative to see if the linguistic expression of smell has similar characteristics in other cultures, particularly non-Western cultures. If so it might point to an essential resistance of olfaction to verbalization.

Such a resistance has been suggested by the results of experiments in which subjects who are asked to classify odours by language have difficulty in recalling the names of even familiar smells. One possible reason for it is that the location of smell – in the most primitive, 'reptilian' part of the brain – renders it inaccessible to the much later-developing language centres of the brain (Rivlin & Gravelle, 1984, p. 88–89).

The case of smell apart, it is evident from what we have seen that the senses are closely interrelated in language, so closely, indeed, that a term expressive of one sense can, in time, transfer its meaning to another sense. Prime examples of this are the verbs for the senses themselves: *hear* is based on a root meaning 'to look';

see is based on a root that means both 'to see' and 'say', *touch* is based on the echoic representation of a knock, and *taste* originally meant 'to touch'. This interchangeability of sensory meaning suggests that sensory perception was once conceived of in a more fluid fashion than nowadays, with less rigid distinctions between senses.

Interestingly, such sensory mingling appears to be the natural sensory state of newborn humans. Studies with newborns have shown, for instance, that babies will both turn to look at and try to grab a sound in a dark room. Even blind babies turn their eyes towards the source of a sound at the same time as they try to grab it. It is only after a few months of growth and experience that babies learn to differentiate between senses. Such data have been interpreted to mean that there is a basic unity of sensory experience in newborns (Rivlin & Gravelle, p. 85–86). Perhaps something of these early experiences of sensory integration finds expression in the shifting of meaning in sensory terms from one sense to another.

Sensory terms, of course, are used to characterize not only sensory experience, but also more abstract states. *Blue* can mean 'sad', and *green*, 'envious'; *hard* can mean 'difficult', and *soft*, 'easy', and so on. Such figurative uses of sensory terms are revealing of the values we assign to different sensations. In the case of taste, for example, it is evident from the figurative ways in which *sweet* and *bitter* are used that the former is deemed to be a very pleasant sensation and the latter very unpleasant. On a more abstract level, taste terms are often used to mean 'risqué' or 'daring'. Examples of this are *piquant, racy, salty, saucy* (from the Latin *sal*, 'salt'), and *spicy*. In the case of *racy*, this secondary meaning has completely overshadowed the original meaning of 'flavourful'. The inference in these cases is that risqué material affects one in a way similar to a stimulating flavour.

Taste itself figuratively means 'judgement of what is beautiful'. Taste is therefore characterized as a sense of discrimination, and specifically, aesthetic discrimination. Good taste decrees what is aesthetically right and proper. Something is in bad taste when it violates this decree, causing disgust – distaste.

All of the senses, except for hearing, have metaphorical meanings similar to that of taste. *Flair* literally means 'a keen sense of smell', and, metaphorically, 'talent' or 'style'. *Tact* – touch – is the sense of knowing how to 'handle' people in order to avoid giving offence. To *have vision* is to see beyond what is immediately apparent to what could be.

These metaphors point to the extent to which our understanding of character traits is shaped by our understanding of sensory perception. This is further revealed by the number of non-sensory terms with sensory bases. Examples are *absurd*, originally meaning 'inharmonious'; *splendid*, originally meaning 'shining'; and *austere*, originally meaning 'dry'. Such sensory bases are especially found in words dealing with emotions. Thus to be *exasperated* is to be 'roughened', to be *angry* is to be 'constricted', to be *glad* is to be 'shining', to be *eager* is to be 'sharp', to be *rancorous* is to be 'rancid', and so on. The expression of emotional feeling in terms corresponding to physical feeling brings out the experiential intermingling of sense and emotion.

Sometimes a similar sensation can give rise to words with very different meanings. Both *sad* and *content*, for example, arise from terms meaning to 'be satisfied'. While to be *sad*, however, in its original sense, is to be 'sated to the point of being fed up', to be *content* is to be 'contained' and therefore fulfilled. Similarly both *sage* and *sap*, 'wise person' and 'fool', are derived from a base meaning 'to taste'. A *sage* is someone who discerns wisely as through the sense of taste. A *sap* is someone who is full of taste or juice, and therefore 'wet'. Even *black* and *white*, that classic pair of opposites, are based on a similar sensation, as both are derived from roots meaning 'to gleam'. In the case of *white*, it is the paleness of light which is emphasized: in the case of *black*, the soot of the flame. These divergences show the different paths of meaning that terms originating in similar physical sensations can take.

Of particular interest is the sensory terminology used to convey mental processes. In the West we rely heavily on visual terms for this purpose, a tendency which has been noted and analysed by a number of scholars.[3] Common examples of such terms are: *point of view*, *overview*, *observation*, *enlighten*, and *focus*. Indeed, we say *I see* to mean 'I understand'.

Some of our terms for thought – for example, *consider*, *speculate*, *idea*, *theory*, and *wit* – are also based on visual roots. Many more, however are tactile or kinaesthetic in basis.[4] These include *apprehend*, *brood*, *cogitate*, *comprehend*, *conceive*, *grasp*, *mull*, *perceive*, *ponder*, *ruminate* and *understand*. The predominance of tactile images in words dealing with intellectual functions indicates that thought is, or was, experienced primarily in terms of touch. Thinking was therefore less like looking than like weighing or grinding, and knowing was less like seeing than like holding.

The use of tactile and kinaesthetic terms for thought expresses a more active involvement with the subject matter than visual terms do. To *understand* is to stand under or among, to be part of the picture, whereas to *see* is to view the picture from without. In light of this it seems possible that an emphasis on visual metaphors for intellectual functions, such as one finds in scholarly writing, for example, has to do in part with a desire to have or convey a certain detachment from the subject under consideration: to be objective. At the same time, visual metaphors for thought convey an accessibility of meaning, which tactile metaphors do not. There is a great deal more tension involved in grasping or weighing a subject than in looking it

---

3.   For example, Ong (1977, Chapter 5); Danesi (1990); Tyler (1984).

4.   It is notable that the terms *read*, *write*, and *text*, which we now think of as models of visualism, all have non-visual bases. To *read* originally meant to 'counsel' and 'interpret', to *write* meant to 'scratch or score', and a *text* was a woven fabric.

over. Thus, by using visual metaphors for thought, one can mask the tensions that touch-based terms – such as comprehend and ponder – indicate are involved in intellectual processes, and present knowledge as readily and easily apparent.

With terms of intelligence, we again find touch-based words such as *acumen*, *acute, keen, sharp, smart, clever*, and *penetrating*, outnumbering sight-based words such as *wise, bright, brilliant*, and *lucid*. It was only in the Enlightenment period, indeed, that these last three words began being used to mean 'intelligent', perhaps in consequence of the general rise of visualism at that time. Knowledge, therefore, was conceived of not so much as sight or light, but as sharpness. A knowledgeable person does not simply illuminate a subject, but cuts into it. Likewise, difficult subject matter is characterized as *hard* or *complicated* ('twisted together'), resisting being cut or penetrated. *Intelligence* itself, along with *intellect*, is a tactile-visual metaphor, as its basic meaning is 'to pick between'.[5]

Taste and smell furnish two basic terms of intelligence: *sapience* and *sagacious*. In Latin, taste did not merely stand for a sense of aesthetic discrimination, as in English, but for the faculty of intelligence. The verb 'to taste', *sapere*, also meant 'to know', giving us our *sapience* – 'wisdom' – and *sage* – 'wise person'. Thus *homo sapiens* is not only 'knowing man', but also 'tasting man'. *Sagacious*, on the other hand, comes from the Latin *sagacis*, meaning 'keen-scented' and therefore perceptive and wise. Similarly, *nose-wise*, a now obsolete word, could mean either 'clever' or 'keen-scented.' Thus, even the supposedly lower senses of taste and smell can stand for intellectual processes.

Significantly, auditory terms rarely serve as metaphors for thought or intelligence in English. An exception is *logical*, derived from Greek *logos*, 'word' (although even this term has more to do with speaking than with hearing). This is perhaps because hearing is conceived of as a passive sense, receiving information but not probing it. Therefore, rather than being associated with intelligence, hearing is associated with obedience. The word *obedience*, indeed, is derived from the Latin *audire*, 'to hear'. So if to hear is to obey, to obey is also to hear.

There are, of course, non-sensory terms of thought and intelligence, such as *know, think, mind*, and *memory* (although even these we cannot be sure did not once have a sensory base unknown to us now). What is notable, however, is the extent to which sensory terms *are* used to stand for processes of thought, so that, far from standing apart from sensory experience, thought is conceptualised in terms of sensory experience.

This is not to say that thought is limited to language or that all sensory experience is well expressed by language. The fact that there are few words dealing with

---

5.   Tactile and kinaesthetic terms such as *slow, dense, soft, wet, cracked, crazy, unbalanced*, and *unstable*, also serve to characterize a lack of intelligence or sanity.

smell, for example, does not necessarily mean that smell is a relatively unimportant sense, but rather that, for one reason or another, it has eluded linguistic expression. Indeed, as we shall see in Chapter 4,[6] olfaction *does* form the basis for important symbolic codes in the West and elsewhere.

Nonetheless, the way we feel and think is obviously deeply influenced by the language we speak and vice versa. To the extent that words express sensory experience and condition thought, consequently, the sensory basis of much of our vocabulary, and particularly of our intellectual vocabulary, indicates that we think through our senses. The exploration of how we grope to express sensory experience through language, and to convey non-sensory experiences through sensory metaphors, is revealing not only of how we process and organize sensory data, but also of the sensory underpinnings of our culture.

In the days when Latin was widely known, and words less divorced from their original sense, the sensory basis of many of our words would have been much more evident than today. It is in order to help recover this sensual dimension of language and thought, and raise questions about the cultural and physical norms operating through it, that the following vocabulary of 'words of sense' has been compiled.

Acerbity From the Latin *acerb*, meaning harsh to the taste. First used to refer to bitter, unripe tastes, and then extended to mean harsh and bitter character or words.

Acid From the Latin *acidus*, sour, based on the root *ac-*, sharp. Acid means sour to the taste, and, when applied to speech or manner, sharp and unpleasant.

Acrid From the Latin *acris*, meaning sharp, pungent and related to *acus*, needle. Acrid means bitter and slinging to the taste, as does acrimony. By extension both these words are used to mean bitterness of manner.

Acumen From the Latin *acumen*, meaning anything sharp, which, in turn, is derived from *acuere*, to sharpen, and *acus*, needle. Acumen conveys the meaning of sharp wits, as does acute, also derived from *acuere*.

Aesthetic From the Greek *aisihetikos*, meaning what is perceived by the senses, that is, things material as opposed to things thinkable or immaterial. The term was applied in German by the philosopher Baumgarten in the 1750s to refer to the philosophy of 'taste' or beauty. It was adopted into English with this meaning in 1830.

Apprehend From the Latin *adprehendere*, to seize. Apprehend means to lay hold of and, figuratively, to lay hold of with the mind, to learn, understand.

---

6. Editors' note: This refers to Chapter 4 of Classen's 1993 book, *Worlds of Sense: Exploring the Senses in History and Across Cultures*, and not to Chapter 4 of the present volume.

Astringent From the Latin *astringere*, to draw together. Astringent means causing to contract. Figuratively it conveys the meaning of stem. It is used with tastes to mean sour, harsh.

Austere From the Latin *austerus,* meaning dry, harsh, sour, in turn derived from the Greek *austeros*, meaning to make the tongue dry and rough. In the sense of harsh taste it was used up until the second half of the nineteenth century after which its metaphorical meaning of stem and severe became dominant.

Bitter From the Old English *biter*, meaning biting. Bitter once meant a sharp, biting taste, but in modern usage means the unpleasant taste of substances such as quinine and bitter aloes. By extension, bitter means painful and hard to endure. The first recorded application of bitter to cold occurs in 1600 in Shakespeare's *As You Like It*: 'Freize, freize thou bitter skie.'

Black From the Old English *blaec*, derived from the Indo-European base *bhleg-*, shine, gleam. The original sense was smoke-black from fire. Black has the figurative meanings of sad and evil.

Bland From the Latin *blandus*, meaning soft, smooth, and used to mean pleasing of manner or to the senses. Keats, for example, writes in 1820 of 'the sound of merriment and chorus bland' (*St Agnes*). It acquired its meaning of mild with regard to food in the nineteenth century. This usage, in turn, led to its present figurative meaning of not stimulating.

Blatant This word was apparently coined by Edmund Spenser in his *Faerie Queene* of 1596 to mean noisy, clamorous. An example of this usage is the phrase 'patent to the eye and blatant to the ear' from a work of 1867 (J. MacGregor, *Voyage Alone*). In its present sense it means showy, gaudy, obvious, unashamed. Thus in a letter of 1912, G. B. Shaw writes of the 'blatant picturesqueness' of the scenery.

Blind Probably derived from the Indo-European base *bhlendh-*, meaning to be indistinct, to confuse, and thus related to blend. The sense would be that of blurred vision. Blind is used metaphorically from an early period to mean lacking intelligence.

Blue From Middle English *bleu*, influenced by the Old French *bleu*, blue, and the Middle English *blo*, livid, said of bruised skin. The first recorded use of blue to mean depressed occurs in the sixteenth century, and to mean indecent, in the nineteenth century.

Blunt Probably related to the Old Norse *blunda*, meaning to shut the eyes, derived from the Indo-European base *bhlendh-*, to be indistinct, to confuse. Blunt, meaning dull, insensitive, is originally applied to sight and then extended to the other senses and the intellect. Spenser in the *Faerie Queene*, for example, describes sightless eyes as being 'blunt and bad'. The meaning of not sharp, now the primary sense of blunt, was developed in the fourteenth century. In the sixteenth century blunt came to be applied to speech to mean abrupt, plain-spoken.

Boisterous From the Middle English *boistous*, meaning rough. The modern sense is loud, turbulent and exuberant.

Breath From the Old English *brep*, meaning odour, smell, exhalation, as of anything cooking or burning. The Indo-European base is *bher-*, to boil. The sense passed into English through that of heated air expired from the lungs and manifest to the sense of smell. Breath was originally used to mean an odour but in its modern senses means the air taken into and let out of the lungs.

Bright From the Indo-European base *bhereg-*, to gleam, white. Bright means shining or vivid, and, when applied to sounds, clear or shrill. When applied to a person, bright originally meant cheerful and lively. Shakespeare, for example, writes, 'Be bright and jovial among your guests' (*Macbeth*). Beginning in the early eighteenth century, bright was used to mean clever.

Brilliant Adopted from the French *brillant*, shining, taken in turn from the Latin *beryllus*, beryl, in the seventeenth century. Originally meaning bright and sparkling, brilliant came to mean splendid, and then in the nineteenth century, the meaning of clever and distinguished was added.

Brood From the Old English *brod*, derived from the Indo-European base *bhre-*, to warm. To brood means to sit on and hatch eggs, and thus, figuratively, to think deeply about something, usually with anxiety.

Calm From the Greek *kauma*, meaning burning heat of the sun. The likely development in meaning is from heat of the day, to rest during the heat of the day, to stillness.

Clear From the Latin *clarus*, originally meaning clear-sounding, and then visually bright, derived from the Indo-European base *kel-*, to cry out, sound loudly. Clear was first used in English to express an intensity of light and colour. From this the meaning of transparent and unobscured, and figuratively, intelligible, was derived. The first recorded use of clear with sound to mean well-defined occurs in 1300.

Clever From the Middle English *cliver*, meaning nimble-handed and possibly related to the Old English *clifian*, to stick, cling. The current tense of clever as talented, intelligent came into use in the eighteenth century.

Cloy From the Middle English *acloien*, meaning to lame a horse with a nail, hence stop up. This meaning became obsolete in the seventeenth century. From the sixteenth century on cloy has been used to mean to glut with food so as to cause disgust. The term cloying in modern usage conveys the meaning of overly sweet and rich foods.

Cogitate From the Latin *cogitare*, literally meaning to put in motion together. Cogitate means to think seriously.

Cold From the Old English *cald*, meaning cold. Cold is used metaphorically to mean unfriendly, unfeeling, indifferent. With regard to sensory properties, when applied to scent, cold means faint, and when applied to light and colour, it means pale, blue, or lacking red and yellow tints. In the sixteenth and seventeenth centuries cold was used with taste to mean unstimulating.

Colour From the Latin *color*, meaning colour, outward show, and related to *celare*, to hide. Among the figurative meanings of colour are: type, specious appearance, shade of meaning and expressiveness. It is used in music from the sixteenth century on to mean timbre and variety of expression.

Common sense From the Latin *sensus communis*. Common sense was a notion developed by Aristotle to mean an internal sense which served to unite and interpret the impressions of the five senses. Burton writes in *The Anatomy of Melancholy* (1621), for example, that the 'common sense is the judge or moderator of the rest'. The meaning we associate with common sense today, that of practical judgement, was first recorded in the eighteenth century.

Comprehend From the Latin *comprehendere*, to grasp. From the fourteenth century comprehend has been used in English to mean to grasp with the mind.

Conceive From the Latin *concipere*, meaning to take and hold, and hence to receive and to perceive. Conceive means to become pregnant, to beget, and figuratively to take into or form in the mind, to formulate an idea.

Consider From the Latin *considerare*, literally meaning 'with a star', and figuratively to look at closely. Consider means both to look at carefully and to think carefully.

Contemplate From the Latin *contemplari*, meaning literally to mark out an augural temple, and figuratively, to gaze attentively. Contemplate means to gaze at, and hence to consider and to look forward to.

Cracked From the Middle English *cracken*, to make a sharp noise. The Indo-European base is *ger-*, to cry hoarsely. The primary meaning of crack is the noise of something breaking; the secondary meaning, derived from this, is a break, a fissure. From this second sense comes the term cracked, used figuratively to mean unsound in mind.

Crazy From the Middle English *crasen*, to break in pieces. Crazy retained the meaning of full of cracks into the nineteenth century. In a letter of 1844, Dickens, for example, writes that 'the court was full of crazy coaches'. Figuratively, crazy could once mean either physically or mentally impaired. Now only the latter meaning remains.

Deaf From the Old English *deaf*, cognate with the Old Irish *dub*, black, and the Greek *typhlos*, blind. The Indo-European base of deaf is *dheubh-*, meaning to fly about like dust, to smoke, and thus misty or obscured. *Dheubh-* was used in pre-Teutonic to mean dull of perception, from which the more specific meaning of unable to hear developed. Deaf once had several figurative meanings. In the fifteenth and sixteenth centuries it was used to mean stupid, and in the seventeenth and eighteenth centuries, to mean indistinctly heard as, for example, in a 'deaf murmur'. Up until the late nineteenth century deaf could mean barren or empty, particularly in connection with fruits and vegetables; for example, a deaf nut, or a deaf ear of corn. The one figurative meaning of deaf which has survived to the present day is that of inattentive or unwilling to hear.

Delicate From the Latin *delicatus*, meaning luxurious, dainty. Delicate is first applied to foods in the fourteenth century to mean pleasing. In the sixteenth century it is applied to textures to mean fine, not coarse, and in the nineteenth century to colour to mean soft, subdued. From the sixteenth century on delicate is also used to mean very sensitive, very fine in power of perception, e.g. a delicate ear.

Dim From the Indo-European base *dhem-*, to be dusty, smoky, misty. Dim means not bright, not clear to the sight, and figuratively, not clear to the understanding. The first recorded application of dim to sound occurs in 1386 in Chaucer's *Knights Tale*: 'He herde a murmurynge ful lowe and dym'. In the eighteenth century the meaning of dull of apprehension was added, for example, in the following sentence taken from a sermon written in 1729: 'The understanding is dim, and cannot by its natural light discover spiritual truth' (J. Rogers, *Sermons*).

Dry From the Old English *dryge*, derived from the Indo-European base *dher-*, to hold fast. Dry means free from moisture. With reference to taste, it means not sweet, said of wines, a usage introduced in the seventeenth century. Figuratively, dry is used to mean showing no emotion, reserved, ironical.

Dull From the Old English *dol*, meaning foolish, based on the Indo-European base *dhwel-*, muddy, dim, derived in turn from *dheubh-*, to fly about like dust. Beginning in the fourteenth century dull acquired a wide range of figurative meanings: lacking sensibility, slow, indistinctly felt, uninteresting, dismal, and blunt, while retaining its original meaning of foolish. Dull is applied to texture, colour, sound, and taste to mean indistinct, muffled, not sharp.

Dumb From the Indo-European base *dheubh-*, to fly about like dust, to smoke, to darken. In Old English dumb meant only mute, lacking speech. However in related languages, such as Old High German, it carried the sense of stupid as well. Dumb was used in the sense of 'meaningless' in English (e.g. 'dumb traditions') in the sixteenth century. In modem colloquial usage it means stupid, silly.

Eager From the Old French *aigre*, sharp, keen, sour, derived in turn from the Latin *acreus*, sharp, pungent. Eager was used to mean sharp, pungent until the eighteenth century. For example, in 1600 Shakespeare writes, 'To make our appetites more keene, with eager compounds we our pallat urge' (*Sonnets*). During the same period it was used to mean figuratively sharp and biting. Thus in 1386 Chaucer warns us to rather 'flee fro the sweete wordes of flaterynge preiseres [praisers] than fro the egre words of thy freend' (*Melibeus*). In the fifteenth century the modem meaning of 'full of keen desire' came into use.

Flair From the Old French *flair*, odour, derived in turn from the Vulgar Latin *flagrare*, to emit an odour. Originally used to mean an odour, in the nineteenth century, influenced by the French *flairer*, to smell, to detect, it came to mean instinctive discernment.

Flash From the Middle English *flasken*, to splash, an onomatopoeic word based on plash, a splashing sound. Flash was used to mean a pool or a marsh until the late nineteenth century. Its present meaning of a burst of light came into use in the sixteenth century.

Flat From the Middle English *flatte*, derived from the Indo-European base *plet-*, meaning wide and level. In the sixteenth century flat acquired various figurative meanings. It can be used with sound to mean either not clear or relatively low in pitch. Bacon writes in 1626, for example, 'If you stop the Holes of a Hawkes Bell, it will make no Ring, but a flat noise, or Rattle' (*Sylva*). When said of taste, flat refers to a liquid that has lost its flavour or effervescence. With reference to colour, flat means uniform in tint or without gloss. Flat also has the figurative meanings of unqualified (e.g. a flat lie), stupid, and wanting in spirit.

Flavour From the Old French *flaor*, smell, based on the Vulgar Latin *flator*, that which blows. Originally flavour meant a smell. Dickens, for example, writes in 1870 of a 'city, deriving an earthy flavour throughout from its cathedral crypt' (*Edwin Drood*). From the seventeenth century on flavour could be used to mean a taste, the meaning that predominates today.

Foul From the Middle English *ful*, derived from the Indo-European base *pu-*, to stink, perhaps an exclamation of disgust. This base is also found in putrid. The primary meaning of foul is stinking, disgusting, from which the figurative meaning of morally corrupt, evil, is derived.

Fusty From the Old French *fust*, cask, derived from the Latin *fustis*, stick. Fusty was first applied to wine which had taken the odour and taste of the cask in which it was stored. From this definition it acquired the meaning of mouldy or stale-smelling and the figurative meaning of stale and old-fashioned.

Grasp From the Old English *grespan*, to grab. The use of grasp to mean intellectual mastery is first recorded in the seventeenth century.

Green From the Old English *grene*, derived from the Indo-European base *ghro-*, from which grow and grass are also derived. Green refers to the characteristic colour of growing plants. Figuratively, it can mean young, inexperienced, envious.

Hard From the Indo-European base *qar-*, hard. The basic sense of hard is unyielding to the touch. Figuratively it means callous, severe. In the fourteenth century hard acquired the meaning of difficult to penetrate with the understanding and, hence, difficult in general.

Harsh From the Middle English *harsk*, possibly related to the Old Swedish *härsk* meaning rancid. Harsh means rough to the touch and, figuratively, stem, severe. The use of harsh with taste to mean astringent is first recorded in 1440, with sound to mean discordant, in 1530, and with visual appearance to mean of rough aspect, glaring, in 1774.

Hear From the Old English *heran*, to hear, derived from the Indo-European base *qeu-*, to look at, perceive. In Old and Middle English to hear could also mean to obey. To hear has the figurative meaning of to assent, as, for example, in 'my prayer has been heard'. Refusing to hear, on the other hand has the figurative meaning of refusing to assent, as in 'she would not hear of it'.

Heavy From the Old English *hefig*, meaning of concentrated weight for its size. Heavy can be used with touch, heat, colour, sound, smell and taste to mean forceful, oppressive.

High From the Middle English *heigh*, derived from the Indo-European base *qeu-*, to curve. High means elevated and is used with physical qualities to mean intense, for example 'high wind'. High is first recorded to mean rich in flavour in 1384. As an example of this usage Bacon writes in 1626 of 'Almonds that are not of so high a taste as Flesh' (*Sylva*). It is first recorded used with sound to mean acute in pitch in 1390, and was also used into the eighteenth century to mean loud. In the nineteenth century high began to be used with odour to mean smelling tainted or putrid. When applied to light, high means brighter than the surrounding light. High also has the figurative meanings of exalted in rank or quality, important, intoxicated.

Hot From the Old English *hat*, meaning hot, derived from the Indo-European base *qai-*, heat. Hot is used figuratively to mean excited, passionate. It is first used with taste to mean pungent in the sixteenth century. In the seventeenth century it begins to be used with scent to mean strong. In the nineteenth century hot is applied to colour to mean intense, while in current usage hot is applied to music to mean lively, syncopated.

Idea From the Greek *idea*, meaning appearance, form, kind, and based on *idein*, to see. In Platonic philosophy idea was used to mean an archetype and it was in this sense that it was adopted into English. In the seventeenth century the current sense of an idea being a thought, a conception, came into use.

Incense From the Latin *incendere*, to set on fire. Incense can mean both to inflame with anger and to burn fragrant gums and spices, fumigate.

Intelligent From the Latin *intelligere*, to see into, perceive, understand, composed of *inter-*, between, and *legere*, to pick, catch with the eye, read. Intelligent is used in English to mean having the faculty of understanding.

Keen From the Old English *cene*, meaning bold, brave, clever, from which the current meaning of sharp-edged was apparently derived. Keen is used from the fourteenth century onwards to mean affecting the senses like a sharp edge: with touch it means smarting; with taste, pungent; with cold or heat, piercing, intense; with sound, shrill; with light, vivid; with scent, strong. From the fourteenth century on keen also means eager and full of desire. Beginning in the eighteenth century, keen is used to mean acute or highly sensitive, with regard to the sensory faculties and to the intellect.

Light From the Old English *leoht*, meaning luminous, based on the Indo-European *leuk-*, to shine, to see. The use of light to mean mental enlightenment is first recorded in the fifteenth century.

Light From the Old English *leoht*, meaning of little weight based on the Indo-European *legwh-*, light in weight or motion. Light can be used with visual appearance, sound, smell, taste or touch to mean soft, slight, not intense.

Logical From the Greek *logos*, signifying reason, word, and derived from *legein*, to speak. Logical has the meaning of reasonable.

Loud From the Old English *hlud*, meaning sonorous, based on the Indo-European root *kleu-*, to hear. Beginning in the seventeenth century, loud is used with scent to mean strong. In 1641, Milton, for example, speaks of the 'loud stench of avarice' (*Of Reformation in England*). In the nineteenth century loud begins to be applied to colours and patterns to mean gaudy or strong.

Low From the Middle English *lowe*, derived from the Indo-European base *legh-*, to lie down. Low means of little height. It is first recorded used with sound to mean of deep pitch in 1422, and to mean not loud in 1440. Low also has the figurative meanings of humble in rank, inferior, vulgar, wanting in strength, and emotionally depressed.

Lucid From the Latin *lucidus*, meaning shining. Lucid was originally used to mean bright or translucent, and figuratively to describe an interval of sanity between attacks of lunacy. In the eighteenth century lucid is first used to mean easily intelligible, and in the nineteenth century to mean rational and sane.

Meditate From the Latin *meditari*, to meditate, derived from the Indo-European base *med-*, to measure, consider. Meditate means to plan or think deeply.

Mellifluous From the Latin *mellifluus*, meaning flowing with honey. From the fifteenth to the nineteenth centuries, mellifluous was used to mean honeyed, sweet. This meaning is now rare; however, the figurative usage of mellifluous with sound and speech to mean pleasant and smooth, also in use since the fifteenth century, is still current.

Mellow From the Middle English *melwe*, ripe, possibly derived from the Indo-European *mel-*, to grind. Mellow refers primarily to the softness and juiciness of ripe fruit and secondarily to the flavour, scent and colour of ripe fruit. From this basis, the meaning of mellow is broadened in the seventeenth and eighteenth centuries to convey softness and smoothness in general with regard to sensations of sound (1668), taste (1700), colour (1706) and texture (1797); and geniality with regard to character.

Mild From the Middle English *milde*, possibly derived from the Indo-European *mel-*, to grind. Mild means of a kind and gentle disposition, not harsh. In the twelfth century it is first applied to looks and language. In the sixteenth century it is applied to weather and temperature to mean calm, moderate, and in the seventeenth century to light to mean soft, and to beer to mean not acid, not strongly flavoured. In the nineteenth century it is applied to soil, wood, and other material to mean soft and easy to work with.

Mull From the Middle English *mullen*, to grind, probably derived from the Indo-European *me-*, to grind. Mull is used to mean to consider or ponder.

Muse From the Old French *muser*, meaning to gaze at, to ponder. Muse means to think deeply, to contemplate.

Musty Of obscure origin, probably related to moist, musty means mouldy, spoiled with damp and hence, having a mouldy or decayed smell or taste.

Noise Probably from the Latin *nausea*, meaning sea-sickness.

Nose-wise Compounded from 'nose' and 'wise', nose-wise was used from the sixteenth to the eighteenth centuries to mean clever, conceited, or keen-scented.

Pensive From the Latin *pensare,* meaning to weigh and hence to ponder, consider.

Perceive From the Latin *percipere,* meaning to seize, and hence to observe, to apprehend.

Perfume From the Latin *per-*, through, and *fumare*, to smoke. The primary meaning of perfume when it came into use in the sixteenth century was to fumigate, to cense. From this meaning the sense of imparting a pleasant odour is derived.

Piquant From the French *piquer*, to prick, sting. Piquant originally meant piercing or stinging. In the seventeenth century it developed the meaning of agreeably pungent to the taste. Figuratively, piquant means exciting interest, provocative.

Poignant From the Old French *poignant*, pricking, derived from the Latin *pungere*, to prick. Poignant once meant sharp to the touch, sharp to the taste or smell, and figuratively sharp to the feelings. Now only the last meaning remains.

Ponder From the Latin *ponderare*, meaning to weigh. Ponder means to weigh mentally, consider carefully.

Pungent From the Latin *pungere*, to prick, derived from the Indo-European base *peug-*, to stab. Pungent was originally used to mean sharp. The first recorded use of pungent to mean a sharp taste or smell occurs in 1668, and to mean mentally stimulating, in 1850.

Quiet From the Latin *quies*, rest. Quiet was first used to mean peaceful, from which the meanings of still and noiseless were derived.

Racy A seventeenth-century formation based on 'race', meaning a particular class or flavour of wine. The primary meaning of racy is having a characteristically excellent taste. From this the metaphorical meaning of lively, risqué is derived.

Read From the Middle English *reden*, to explain, hence to read, developed from the Old English *raedan*, to counsel, interpret, derived, in turn, from the Indo-European base *(a)re-*, to join, fit.

Red From the Old English *read,* derived from the Indo-European base *reudh-*, red and perhaps bloody.

Reek From the Old English *rec*, meaning smoke or vapour. Reek was originally used to mean smoke or vapour, and therefore also blowing dust or snow. This meaning was retained into the nineteenth century. In 1854, Dickens, for example, writes of 'the reek of her own tread in the thick dust' (*Hard Times*). Reek is first used to mean a strong smell, the predominant meaning today, in the seventeenth century.

Reflect From the Latin *reflectere*, to bend back. Reflect was first used to mean to divert, deflect. In the seventeenth century it acquired the meanings of to cast back light and to turn something over in one's mind.

Rough From the Middle English *rugh*, derived from the Indo-European *reu-*, to tear. Rough means having an uneven surface and, figuratively, disorderly, violent, crude. The first use of rough applied to sounds to mean discordant is recorded in 1400; of taste to mean astringent, in 1545; and of appearance to mean coarse, in 1595.

Ruminate From the Latin *ruminare*, to chew the cud. Ruminate means to ponder, to turn over in the mind.

Sagacious From the Latin *sagire*, meaning to smell, to perceive acutely. Sagacious once meant acute in perception, particularly smell. Now only the meaning of acuteness of mental discernment is retained.

Sage From the Latin *sapere*, to taste, know, derived from the Indo-European base *sap-*, to taste, perceive. Sage means wise.

Salty From the Old English *sealt*, salt. Salty developed the figurative meanings of witty and somewhat improper in the nineteenth century.

Sappy From the Old English *saepig*, derived from the Indo-European base *sap-*, to taste. The primary meaning of sappy is full of sap, juice. The figurative meaning of foolish, first recorded in the seventeenth century, is based on the association of foolishness with wetness.

Sapient From the Latin *sapiens*, wise, derived from *sapere*, to taste, know. Sapient means wise.

Scan From the Latin *scandere*, to climb. Scan can mean either to look at closely or to glance at quickly.

Scent From the Old French *sentir*, to feel, smell, based on the Latin *sentire*, to feel, perceive. Scent means both to smell, especially at a distance, and a smell. Scent is used figuratively to mean to find out instinctively, to detect.

See From the Old English *seon*, derived from the Indo-European *seqw-*, to see, to say. The first recorded use of see to mean to perceive mentally, to understand, occurs in 1200. In 1300 see is first used to mean to read. See also has the figurative meanings of to find out (e.g. to see what can be done), to take care of (e.g. to see to one's affairs), to accompany (e.g. to see a person off), to know by observation (e.g.

to see the world), and to allow (e.g. to be willing to see something take place). The expression 'let me see' is used to mean let me think, remember, find out.

Sense From the Latin *sensus*, meaning sense, feeling, based on the Indo-European root *sent-*, to go, find out. The primary meaning of sense is 'faculty of perception'. In the sixteenth century, sense also comes to mean instinctive knowledge, sensation, signification, and the mental and moral faculties, often expressed as 'interior senses'. In the seventeenth century sense acquires the meaning of judgement.

Sensible From the Latin *sensibilis*, derived from *sentire*, to feel, perceive. The original meaning of sensible was perceptible by the senses and endowed with the faculty of sensation. From the sixteenth into the nineteenth centuries sensible was used to mean having an acute power of sensation and in the seventeenth and eighteenth, capable of delicate and tender feelings, sensitive. In Jane Austen's *Sense and Sensibility*, for example, sense, meaning good judgement, is contrasted with sensibility, meaning an acute responsiveness to aesthetic and intellectual values. The meaning of sensible predominant today, that of reasonable, judicious, came into use in the sixteenth century. This meaning was stigmatized by Johnson in 1755 as used only 'in low conversation'.

Sensitive From the Latin *sensitivus*, derived from *sentire*, to feel, perceive. Like sensible, sensitive means perceptible by the senses and having the faculty of sensation. Sensitive was often used to refer in general to sentient beings. Swift, for example, writes in *Gulliver's Travels*, 'As to those Filthy Yahoos... I confess I never saw any sensitive being so detestable on all accounts'. In the nineteenth century the current meaning of having acute perception, impressionable, very responsive, came into use.

Sharp From the Old English *scearp*, cutting, based on the Indo- European (s)qereb-, to cut. The primary meaning of sharp is having a keen, cutting edge. From this the figurative sense of acute intelligence and sensory powers is derived. Sharp is first recorded used with form to mean tapering to a point in 825, with taste and smell to mean pungent or sour in 1000, with sound to mean shrill, high-pitched in 1390, and with movement to mean quick (e.g. a sharp gallop) in 1440. Sharp can also be used with colour to mean vivid.

Smart From the Old English *smeortan*, to be painful, based on the Indo- European *mer-*, to rub, wear away. In the fourteenth century smart acquires the meaning of vigorous and brisk (e.g. a smart pace), in the seventeenth century, that of quick at learning, and in the eighteenth, that of stylish.

Smell From the Middle English *smellen*, to emit or perceive an odour, derived from the Indo-European base *smul-*, to give off smoke. The first use of smell to mean to detect is recorded in the fourteenth century. In that century smell is also first used to mean to emit an offensive odour. Figuratively, to smell can mean to suggest something, as in 'to smell of trouble'. In modern slang 'to smell' means to lack worth.

Smooth From the Middle English *smothe*. Smooth means presenting an even surface to the touch or sight and, figuratively, pleasant, affable, or having a show of affability. Smooth is first applied to taste to mean soft and pleasing in the eighteenth century, and to sounds to mean soft, flowing, in the nineteenth.

Soft From the Old English *softe*, meaning meek, mild, quiet, based on the Indo-European *sem-*, together, and therefore fitting, suited to. Soft is first recorded used with texture, to mean not hard, yielding, in 1200; with sound to mean not loud, melodious, in 1250; with movement to mean gentle, in 1290; with taste and smell to mean not pungent, pleasing, in 1398; and with colour and visual appearance to mean subdued, pleasing, in 1702.

Sour From the Middle English *sur*, based on the Indo-European *suro-s*, salty, bitter. The primary meaning of sour is a sharp, acid taste. This meaning was later extended to apply to smell as well. Figuratively sour means disagreeable, bad-tempered.

Speculate From the Latin *speculari*, to view. Speculate means to ponder, to conjecture, and therefore to take part in a business venture on the chance of making huge profits.

Spicy From the Latin *species*, appearance, kind, derived from *specere*, to look. In late Latin *species* came to mean assorted goods, and particularly spices and drugs. Spicy means having the taste or fragrance of spice. In the nineteenth century it acquired the figurative meanings of smart-looking, full of spirit, and somewhat improper.

Stink From the Old English *stincan*, to emit a smell, good or bad. derived from the Indo-European *steu-*, to rise up like dust, to rise. Stink is first used to mean an offensive smell in the eleventh century. In modern slang to stink means to be no good.

Stupid From the Latin *stupidus*, meaning struck senseless, stunned. Stupid originally meant insensible and then came to mean slow-witted.

Suave From the Latin *suavis*, sweet, agreeable. Suave was originally used to mean pleasing to the senses or mind, sweet. In 1849, Charlotte Brontë, for example, writes of oat cakes tasting as 'suave as manna' (*Shirley*). Suave is now used to mean smoothly gracious, urbane.

Sweet From the Old English *swete*, derived from the Indo-European *swad-*, pleasing to the taste. Meaning primarily tasting of sugar, pleasing to the taste, sweet developed the related meanings of pleasing to the senses of smell and hearing very early on. The use of sweet to mean pleasing to the sight is a later development, occurring in the fourteenth century.

Tact From the Latin *tactus*, meaning the sense of touch. Tact was originally used to mean the sense of touch. In the eighteenth century the figurative meaning of having a delicate sense of the proper thing to do or say came into use.

Tang From the Middle English *tange*, meaning a sharp point, stinging. From this sense the meaning of a penetrating taste developed in the fifteenth century. Tang was first applied to odour to mean sharp, strong, in the nineteenth century.

Tart From the Old English *teart*, meaning painful, sharp, derived from the Indo-European base *der-*, to flay, split. Tart means sharp in taste and. figuratively, sharp in meaning.

Taste From the Middle English *tasten*, to feel, derived from the Latin *taxare*, to feel, touch sharply, judge. Taste could refer to the sense of touch into the fifteenth century, and also had the meaning of a trial, test. The first recorded use of taste to mean savour occurs in the fourteenth century. In the fifteenth century taste acquired the figurative meaning of a preference, a mental sense of discrimination. In the seventeenth century, taste also came to mean an aesthetic sense capable of discerning the beautiful (i.e. good taste).

Theory From the Greek *theoria*, meaning contemplation, a thing looked at, derived from *theorein*, to look at, speculate. Theory originally meant a mental viewing, contemplation. From this arose the meaning of a mental plan and hence a formulation of underlying principles.

Tone From the Latin *tonus*, a sound, derived from the Greek *tonos* meaning a stretching. Tone is used primarily to mean a modulation of sound. It can also mean normal resiliency, as in muscle tone, and in painting, the effect produced by combined light, shade and colour.

Touch From the Late Latin *toccare*, meaning to knock, derived from *tok*, a light blow, of echoic origin. Touch means both to perceive by the sense of feeling and to bring something into contact with something else. Figuratively, touch can mean to draw, colour (e.g. to touch a sky with red), to compare with (e.g. my drawings can't touch hers), to concern (e.g. a matter that touches us), to arouse sympathy in (e.g. she was touched by his plea), and to mention (e.g. to touch on a subject).

Understand From the Middle English *understanden*. Understand literally means to stand under or among, and hence to know thoroughly, to perceive the meaning of something.

Warm From the Middle English *wearm*, derived from the Indo-European base *gwher-*, hot. From its basic meaning of having a moderate degree of heat, warm can figuratively mean both angry, characterized by disagreement, as in a 'warm argument', and cordial, enthusiastic, as in a 'warm welcome'. In the eighteenth century warm is first applied to scent to mean strong, and to colour to mean having a red or yellow hue.

White From the Old English *hwit*, derived from the Indo-European base *kweit-*, to gleam, be pale. White has the figurative meaning of innocent (e.g. a white lie).

Wise From the Middle English *wis*, derived from the Indo-European base *weid-*, to see, know. Wise conveys the meaning of judicious, knowledgeable.

Wit From the Middle English *witte*, derived from the Indo-European base *weid-*, to see, know. Wit originally meant the mind and the faculty of thought, and then was applied to the senses, called the five wits. Its current meaning is the ability to make clever, ironical remarks.

Write From the Old English *writan*, meaning to scratch, score, hence to write, derived from the Indo-European base *wer-*, to tear off, scratch.

Yellow From the Old English *geolo*, derived from the Indo-European base *ghel-*, to gleam, to be green or yellow. Yellow has the figurative meanings of cowardly and sensationalistic.

Acknowledgements

This is a reprint of Chapter 3 pp. 50–76 from Constance Classen's (1993) book *Worlds of Sense: Exploring the Senses in History and Across Cultures*, kindly reprinted with permission from Routledge.

References

Boehme, J. (1960). *The Aurora* [J. Sparrow, trans.]. London: John M. Watkins and James Clark & Co.

Danesi, M. (1990). Thinking is seeing: Visual metaphors and the nature of abstract thought. *Semiotica*, 80(3/4): 221–37.

Guralnik, D. B. (Ed.). (1968). *Webster's New World Dictionary*. Springfield, MA: Merriam-Webster.

Klein, E. (1966). *A comprehensive etymological dictionary of the English language*. New York: Elsevier.

Marks, L. (1978). *The unity of the senses: Interrelations across the modalities*. New York: Academic Press. https://doi.org/10.1016/B978-0-12-472960-5.50011-1

Ong, W. (1977). *Interfaces of the word: Studies in the evolution of consciousness and culture*. Ithaca, N.Y.: Cornell University Press.

Rivlin, R. & Gravelle, K. (1984). *Deciphering the senses: The expanding world of human perception*. New York: Simon and Schuster.

Sapir, E. (1929). A study of phonetic symbolism. *Journal of Experimental Psychology*, 12, 225–39. https://doi.org/10.1037/h0070931

Simpson, J. & Wiener, E. (Eds.). (1989). *The Oxford English dictionary* [2nd edition]. Oxford: Clarendon Press.

Skeat, W. (1898). *An etymological dictionary of the English language*. Oxford: Clarendon Press.

Sperling, H. & Simon, M. [trans.]. (1949). *The Zohar*. London: The Soncino Press.

Tyler, S. (1984). The vision quest in the West, or what the mind's eye sees. *Journal of Anthropological Research* 40(23): 23–40. https://doi.org/10.1086/jar.40.1.3629688

Williams, J. M. (1976). Synaesthetic adjectives: A possible law of semantic change. *Language*, 52(2), 461–78. https://doi.org/10.2307/412571

CHAPTER 3

Perception metaphors in cognitive linguistics
Scope, motivation, and lexicalisation

Iraide Ibarretxe-Antuñano
University of Zaragoza

This chapter presents an up-to-date retrospective on the study of perception metaphors in cognitive linguistics. After a brief introduction to some of the main theoretical tools for the analysis of conceptual metaphor, three main areas are discussed: the scope of perception metaphors, the motivation for perception metaphors, and the lexicalisation of perception metaphors. The chapter ends with some indications for future work in this area.

Keywords: perception metaphors, scope, embodiment, multimodal, cross-linguistic

1. Perception metaphors ahoy!

It is not difficult to find expressions with perception words. We constantly use words related to see, hear, touch, smell, and taste to describe how the world is and how we perceive it. However, what is strikingly interesting is that often these words go beyond the physical world. They do not only refer to 'shapes and colours', 'sounds', 'odours', 'textures' or 'flavours' but also to 'knowledge', 'gossip', 'suspicions', 'feelings', and 'preferences'. That is, these words are used metaphorically, and what is more, they turn up in all sorts of discourse contexts to fullfil different functions as shown in the examples compiled in Figure 1.

What this selection of heterogeneous examples demonstrates is that perception metaphors are ubiquitous. The senses are not just our channels to gather information about the physical world; they provide us with the necessary information to talk about things that cannot be apprehended in a physical way. Two questions immediately arise: why? and how?

The senses have been studied from a wide variety of fields. For instance, physiology and psychology (Blake & Sekuler, 2005; Goldstein, 2005, 2010; Rouby, Schaal, Dubois, Gervais & Holley, 2002), philosophy (Matthen, 2015; Stokes, Matthen &

https://doi.org/10.1075/celcr.19.03iba

Biggs, 2015), arts (Bacci & Melcher, 2013), anthropology (Classen, 1997; Howes, 1991, 2003, 2004; Majid & Levinson, 2011; Serres, 2008), and of course, linguistics. In the latter, perception words and structures have been attractive for linguists working from different perspectives and frameworks, since they often show complex syntactic relations (e.g., complementation, Gisborne, 2010), are the source of special word classes (e.g., evidentials, Aikhenvald & Storch, 2013), lexicalise a wide variety of polysemous senses (Vanhove, 2008), and are used in specialised discourse contexts (e.g., wine, Lehrer, 2009; Caballero, this volume; cf. Caballero, Suárez-Toste & Paradis, in press).

Figure 1. Perception everywhere

This chapter focuses on one of these linguistic areas: the polysemy of perception words. More concretely, it provides an up-to-date retrospective on some of my work on the study of metaphorical meanings in perception words from a cognitive linguistics perspective. The paper is organised as follows. After a brief description of some basics in the study of metaphor in cognitive linguistics, the paper revolves around three main issues that will explain why and how the physical domain of perception provides conceptual material to talk about unrelated abstract domains: the scope of perception metaphors (Section 3), the motivation of perception metaphors (Section 4), and the lexicalisation of perception metaphors (Section 5).[1]

---

1. Since this is an up-to-date retrospective on my research in perception, some parts in this chapter have been discussed in some of my previous work (Ibarretxe-Antuñano, 1999a, b, 2002, 2006, 2008, 2013a, 2015). This is, however, the first time that I discuss them all as a whole.

2. Some notes on how to deal with conceptual metaphors in cognitive linguistics

Metaphor is one of the flagship research areas in cognitive linguistics. Since Lakoff and Johnson published their, now classic, *Metaphors We Live By* in 1980, the theory of conceptual metaphor (CMT) has been continuously growing and applied to a wide range of areas and fields (for an overview see Gibbs, 2008; Semino & Demjén, 2017). It is impossible to summarise in just a few paragraphs all we know about conceptual metaphor (for an introduction see Kövecses, 2002). However, for the purpose of this chapter, it is crucial to bear in mind three key aspects of CMT.

First, conceptual metaphors are considered mappings between two unrelated conceptual domains: the SOURCE and the TARGET. For example, in LOVE IS A JOURNEY, the source domain (JOURNEY) provides the necessary conceptual information and structure to conceptualise the TARGET domain (LOVE). In CMT, the same target domain can be conceptualised in terms of different types of source domains. For example, LOVE can be understood as a JOURNEY (*Their relationship is at the crossroads*), as MADNESS (*I'm crazy about you*), etc. This is known as the scope of metaphor, that is, "the range of cases, that is, the target domains, to which a source concept applies" (Kövecses 2002, p. 108). On the other hand, the same source domain could be the donor of conceptual structure for other target domains. For example, a JOURNEY can be the source of LIFE (*His life wasn't easy, he trudged along year by year*), a CAREER (*Peter reached the highest point in this career*), etc.

The fact that the same metaphor can turn up in different languages is just a first step. Research in CMT in its initial stages provided lists of the different conceptual metaphors that were used to conceptualise a specific target domain. However, this is not enough. A second step in metaphor research should establish its distribution. Distribution is understood in three complementary ways (see Caballero & Ibarretxe-Antuñano, 2014; Ibarretxe-Antuñano, 2013a). One way to interpret this concept of distribution relates to the salience of the conceptual metaphor in a language; that is, how prominent a given conceptual metaphor is to conceptualise a target domain. As mentioned above, a target domain can be structured by means of different sources but, are all these sources equally prominent in the conceptualisation of the target domain or is there a particular source domain that stands out as the most pervasive when it comes to a particular domain? A second way to understand distribution is in terms of the frequency of the conceptual metaphor; that is, how often the conceptual metaphor is used in language. Finally, another possible interpretation of distribution is the situatedness of the conceptual metaphor; in other words, the contexts and genres, as well as the (discourse) functions the conceptual metaphor is used in and for.

The distribution of a conceptual metaphor becomes even more crucial when it is studied from a cross-linguistic perspective. It may not be difficult to find coincidences in the 'types' of members that integrate the lists of conceptual metaphors. However, what is indeed not that easy is to find the same 'tokens', that is, the same degree of coincidence in their distribution; the latter is understood as a cover term for salience, frequency, and situatedness.

Another key aspect of CMT is the motivation of conceptual metaphors. Meaning in cognitive linguistics is taken as grounded in our experience. One of the main groundbreaking ideas in Lakoff and Johnson's (1980) book was precisely to claim that the experiential basis of conceptual metaphors is embodied, that is, based on our interaction with the physical, social, and cultural dimensions of the world around us (see also Johnson, 1987). In other words, the mappings that take place between the source and target domains are not whimsical or ad-hoc, but based on our own experience. The concept of embodiment is one of the main tenets in cognitive linguistics, and as such it has been reinterpreted in many ways (Bergen, 2015; Rohrer, 2007). Although Johnson (1987) in his original discussion about embodiment was clear that it referred to both our sensorimotor as well as sociocultural experience, not all CMT researchers have actually focused on these two complementary sides in the same way. Some have given priority to the biological (sensorimotor) side and thus, heading towards a more universalist account of conceptual metaphor. A case in point is Grady's (1997, 2007) primary metaphors. Others have argued for a more culture-oriented perspective that also takes into account the role of sociocultural factors in the grounding of metaphors. This position defends that all human beings may share the same biological grounding but that the way they use this bodily-based experience may not be universal but culture-specific. Therefore, this bodily-based experience has to be purged, adapted, and modified by the sociocultural information available; in other words, it has to be filtered through a culture-specific sieve (Ibarretxe-Antuñano, 2013b; Yu, 2008).

Finally, the third issue of CMT is a methodological one, but it is sometimes overlooked by some metaphor researchers outside cognitive linguistics. In this framework, form (multimodal) and concept (meaning) are differentiated. This distinction, which resembles the traditional Saussurean signifier (*signifiant*) and the signified (*signifié*) in the linguistic sign, is also reflected in metaphor theory. There is a paramount difference between conceptual metaphor and the metaphorical expression. The former is the actual conceptual mapping that could occur in different languages, whereas the latter is the (multimodal) linguistic expression that each language uses to lexicalise the conceptual metaphor. Since each language has its own linguistic mechanisms to encode meaning, metaphorical expressions are not cross-linguistic but particular to each language. For instance, the conceptual metaphor LOVE IS A JOURNEY can be codified by means of the expression *Their relationship is at the crossroads* in English. The same metaphor exists in other languages but their expressions vary. For example, *Su relación estaba en punto muerto* (Lit. Their relationship was in neutral (gear)) in Spanish. This distinction is in fact one of the main advantages of CMT when it comes to deal with metaphor from an applied perspective (Rojo & Ibarretxe-Antuñano, 2013).

The remainder of this paper explores how these three key aspects in CMT apply to perception metaphors.

① scope ② motivation, ③ lexicalization

3. The scope of perception metaphors

It is well known that perception words are a rich source for polysemous meaning across languages. Traditional lexicographic work such as Buck's (1949) dictionary already included a whole chapter devoted to perception. In cognitive linguistics, the work of Eve Sweetser in 1990 was the starting point for a series of studies on the different meanings, literal and figurative, that these words may convey. Based on Lakoff and Johnson's (1980) work, Sweetser proposed the MIND-AS-BODY metaphor to comprise all the metaphors where the body was used to conceptualise aspects related to the mind, understood in a very broad sense. This general category includes perception-related metaphors such as UNDERSTANDING IS SEEING or UNDERSTANDING IS GRASPING. Over the years, the list of cross-linguistic perception metaphors has been expanded. Table 1 summarises some of the perception-related metaphors mentioned in the literature.

Table 1. Perception metaphors (adapted and expanded from Ibarretxe-Antuñano, 2013a)

Vision	UNDERSTANDING / KNOWING IS SEEING
	FORESEEING IS SEEING
	AN AID TO KNOWING IS A LIGHT SOURCE
	IMPEDIMENTS TO KNOWLEDGE ARE IMPEDIMENTS TO VISION
	KNOWING FROM A 'PERSPECTIVE' IS SEEING FROM A POINT OF VIEW
	IMAGINING IS SEEING
	CONSIDERING IS SEEING
	STUDYING / EXAMINING IS SEEING
	FINDING OUT IS SEEING
	MAKING SURE IS SEEING
	HAVING A RELATIONSHIP IS SEEING SOMEBODY
	MEETING WITH SOMEBODY IS SEEING SOMEBODY
	PAYING A VISIT IS SEEING SOMEBODY
	ESCORTING IS SEEING
	GETTING ON BADLY WITH SOMEBODY IS BEING UNABLE TO SEE
	TAKING CARE IS SEEING / LOOKING AFTER

(continued)

Table 1. (*continued*)

	DECEPTION IS PURPOSEFULLY IMPEDING VISION
	WITNESSING IS SEEING
	SUFFERING IS SEEING
	OBEYING IS SEEING
	REFRAINING IS SEEING
	BEING INVOLVED IS HAVING TO SEE
	COMMUNICATING IS SHOWING
	DOMAIN OF CONTROL IS RANGE OF VISION
	PAYING ATTENTION IS LOOKING AT
Hearing	PAYING ATTENTION / HEEDING IS HEARING
	OBEYING IS HEARING
	BEING TOLD / KNOWING IS HEARING
	BEING RECEPTIVE IS HEARING
	TAKING SOMETHING SERIOUSLY IS LISTENING
	UNDERSTANDING IS HEARING
	NOTICING IS HEARING
	BEING TRAINED IS BEING HEARD
	HAVING AN AGREEMENT IS HEARING
Touch	AFFECTING IS TOUCHING
	DEALING WITH IS TOUCHING
	REACHING IS TOUCHING
	ASKING FOR A LOAN IS TOUCHING
	CONSIDERING IS TOUCHING
	BEING A RELATIVE IS BEING TOUCHED BY SOMEBODY
	FALLING TO SOMEBODY TO DO SOMETHING IS BEING TOUCHED
	PERSUADING IS TOUCHING
Smell	SUSPECTING IS SMELLING
	SENSING (KNOWING INTUITIVELY) IS SMELLING
	GUESSING (REALISING) IS SMELLING
	INVESTIGATING (SEARCHING) IS SMELLING/SNIFFING AROUND
	SHOWING CONTEMPT IS SNIFFING
	BECOMING BAD (SPOILING, CORRUPTING) IS SMELLING
	BEING OBLIVIOUS IS NOT TO SMELL
	HAVING NEGATIVE FEELINGS IS SMELLING
	THE GENERAL ATMOSPHERE OF SOMETHING IS AN OLFACTORY PERCEPTION
	EVALUATION IS SMELL
	PROPHESYING IS SMELLING
Taste	EXPERIENCING SOMETHING IS TASTING
	PRODUCING A FEELING IS TASTING (ENJOYING/DISLIKING)
	PERSONAL PREFERENCE IS TASTE
	KNOWING IS TASTING

Table 1 shows that perceptual modalities map onto a wide variety of general target domains such as intellect and mental activities (CONSIDERING IS TOUCHING), assurance and evidence (ASCERTAINING IS SEEING), discovery (INVESTIGATING IS SNIFFING AROUND), emotions (ENJOYING IS TASTING), social interpersonal relationships (HAVING A RELATIONSHIP IS SEEING SOMEBODY, OBEYING IS HEARING), among others.

Although the conceptual metaphors in Table 1 have been attested in different languages, there are two issues that should be kept in mind. One is the question of distribution. As discussed in Section 2, to be able to find a perception metaphor in a language does not necessarily entail that it is pervasively used by their speakers or that its prominence is the same across languages.

One way to test the distribution of conceptual metaphors is to use corpus data. In a previous study, I looked at the different meanings conveyed by the same linguistic expression in English (*I see*), Spanish (*veo* [see.1SG.PRES]), and Basque (*ikusten dut* [see.HAB AUX.3SG-ABS.1SG-ERG.PRES]) in a random sample extracted from contemporary corpora. I found that, while the type of vision-related meanings (physical and metaphorical) was very similar, their distribution uncovered quite a number of differences as illustrated in Table 2.

Table 2. Meanings in visual perception (adapted from Ibarretxe-Antuñano 2013a, p. 126)

Semantic extensions	English tokens	Spanish tokens	Basque tokens
Physical meaning	25	28	20
UNDERSTANDING IS SEEING	58	34	32
FORESEEING IS SEEING	–	2	3
IMAGINING IS SEEING	2	19	15
CONSIDERING IS SEEING	–	1	19
WITNESSING IS SEEING	2	15	9
SOCIALISING IS SEEING (visit, escort, etc.)	5	–	–
REFERRING TO IS SEEING	2	1	1
Not enough context	6	1	1
Total tokens	100	100	100

The most pervasive meaning in English, Spanish, and Basque was the metaphor UNDERSTANDING IS SEEING, followed by the meaning of physical visual perception. However, a closer look at token numbers reveals that the saliency of the metaphor UNDERSTANDING IS SEEING clearly stands out in English but not so much in the other two languages. This metaphor in English overrides the other semantic extensions in this language, but this is not the case for Spanish and Basque; other metaphors (IMAGINING IS SEEING and CONSIDERING IS SEEING) share this salience quota.

An even more interesting research pathway is to analyse parallel corpora. That is, to contrast how the same texts are being rendered in different languages. Viberg (2008) conducted such a study on vision in Swedish and English only to find that vision words were more often found in English than in Swedish and that frequently-used discourse markers such as *I see* and *see* in English were systematically translated into Swedish as *jaså* 'yes-so' and *förstå* 'understand' and never with the verb *se* 'see'.

Similarly interesting results can be found in other languages. For instance, a preliminary look at the use of the basic smell word *usain(du)* 'smell.n (v)' in a Basque-Spanish parallel corpus (Elhuyar Web Corpus Paraleloa [http://webcorpusak.elhuyar.eus]) reveals that smell in Basque covers areas where other languages such as Spanish prefer senses such as vision (*ver* 'see') or touch (*palpar* 'palpate').

In (1)–(3), smell is the only source domain used to convey the meanings 'look for, detect, investigate', 'realise, sense', and 'feel' in Basque. However, this is not the case in Spanish. Instead of using a smell verb such as *oler(se)*, different words (*acercamiento* 'approach', *intuir* 'sense', *palpar* 'palpate') are used to render these meanings instead. Compare these examples:

(1) a. *Eta zorionez, ezinezkoa dena **usainduz**, lortu egiten dugu Euskal Artzain txakurrarekin topo egitea*
        Lit. 'And fortunately, by smelling the impossible [investigating everything], we did manage to find a Basque shepherd dog'

     b. *Y, afortunadamente, en un **acercamiento** hacia lo inalcanzable, se cruza en nuestro camino el perro Pastor Vasco*
        Lit. 'And, fortunately, in an approach towards the unattainable, the Basque shepherd dog crosses our way'

(2) a. *Gurera etorrita, badira urte batzuk Josu Landak aldaketok **usaindu** zituela (2004: 411): "Internetek hedabideen mundura ekarri duen aldaketa pisuz-koenetako bat (…) mass media kontzeptua kolokan jartzen izan da*
        Lit. 'Back to ours, it has been a few years since Josu Landa smelled these changes (2004: 411): "Internet has brought to the media world an important change (…) it has cast doubts on the concept of mass media"'

     b. *Volviendo a nuestro entorno, hace ya varios años que Josu Landa **intuyó** estas transformaciones (2004: 411): "Uno de los cambios más importantes que ha producido Internet en el mundo mediático (…) ha sido el de poner en entredicho el concepto de mass media*
        Lit. 'Coming back to our field, Josu Landa already sensed these changes a few years ago (2004: 411): "One of the most important changes that Internet contributed to in media communication (…) has been to cast serious doubts on the concept of mass media"'

(3) a. *Kobazulo, leize eta trikuharriz betetako ingurunea dugu, beraz, Ataun,*
         *historiaurreko gizakiaren **usaina** dariona*
         Lit. 'We have an area full of caves, grottos and dolmens, therefore, Ataun,
         a place that emits the smell of the prehistoric human being'
     b. *Por lo tanto, Ataun es un enclave lleno de cuevas, grutas y dólmenes, se **palpa***
         la presencia del hombre prehistórico
         Lit. 'Therefore, Ataun is a settlement full of caves, grottos and dolmens, the
         presence of the prehistoric man can be palpated [touched]'

The final issue related to the scope of metaphors has to do with the target domain.
As discussed in Section 2, the same target domain can be structured by different
source domains. What Table 1 reveals is that the same target domain, COGNITION,
can be conceptualised by means of the five perceptual modalities. However, the type
of cognition does not seem to be exactly the same. It depends on the perceptual
modality; the way we gather information through the senses is not the same and,
consequently, the type of information also differs. It seems that each perceptual
modality offers a different kind of knowledge as summarised in (4).

(4) a. vision → reliable knowledge
     b. hear → indirect knowledge
     c. smell → intuitive knowledge
     d. touch, taste → experiential knowledge

If the 'knowledges' in (4) are correct, the next step should be to find evidence that
supports that this is the way we 'experience' the senses and that these metaphorical
extensions are actually motivated and grounded in this experience. The next section
deals with this issue.

4. The motivation of perception metaphors

The idea that conceptual metaphors are grounded in our experience is an attractive
one. Intuitively, it is not difficult to see why certain perceptual metaphors are related
to certain perceptual modalities. We trust the information we see with our own
eyes, we touch and immediately feel some sensation; therefore, it is only natural that
vision is related to knowing and touching with feelings. However, it is necessary to
find evidence to support these intuitions.

  One approach I developed to provide some evidence for these embodied mappings was the creation of an open-ended list of '<prototypical properties>' (see,
Ibarretxe-Antuñano, 1999a). These are shorthand ways of providing a characterisation of how perception and the senses prototypically work from both a physiological and psychological perspective. They are called 'prototypical' because they

are meant to capture the basic characteristics that describe the senses. The list of prototypical properties is neither closed nor restricted. If needed, more properties could be added to explain these metaphorical mappings; the only constraint is that these properties should be backed up by specialised literature on the senses. These properties are defined in accordance with the interrelations between the three elements involved in perceptual processes: Perceiver (PR), Object of Perception (OP), and Perception (P). Table 3 provides a definition for each property.

Table 3. Prototypical properties for perception. *PR* = Perceiver, *OP* = Object of Perception, *P* = Perception

<property>
<contact>
whether the PR must be in physical contact with the OP in order to be perceived
<closeness>
whether the OP must be in the vicinity of the PR to be perceived
<internal>
whether the OP must go inside the PR to be perceived
<limits>
whether the PR is aware of the boundaries imposed by the OP when perceived
<location>
whether the PR is aware of the situation of the OP when perceiving
<detection>
how the PR performs the P: how PR discloses the presence of an object, and distinguishes one object from another
<identification>
how well the PR can discern what she is perceiving, the OP
<voluntary>
whether the PR can choose when to perform a P
<directness>
whether the P depends on the PR directly, or is mediated by another element
<effects>
whether the P causes any change in the OP
<briefness>
how long the relation between P and OP should be in order for the perception to be successful
<evaluation>
whether the P assesses the OP
<correction-of-hypothesis>
how correct and accurate the hypotheses formulated about the OP in the P are in comparison with the real object of P
<subjectivity>
how much influence the PR has on the P

Each property takes a yes, no, or empty value depending on whether the property applies to each sense; this is because each sense has its own characteristics and its own way of processing information. This diversity is reflected in the distribution of both properties and values that take the citation form <property$_{yes}$> or <property$_{no}$>. Once again, if needed, some of these values could be modified and/or added in order to explain metaphorical mappings. There is one restriction: values should observe the characteristics described by specialised literature on the senses. Table 4 reproduces these prototypical properties with the values for each sense.

Table 4. Distribution of values for prototypical properties

<property>	Vision	Hearing	Touch	Smell	Taste
<contact>	no	no	yes	no	yes
<closeness>	no	no	yes	yes	yes
<internal>	no	yes	no	yes	yes
<limits>			yes		
<location>	yes	yes			
<detection>	yes	yes	yes	yes	yes
<identification>	yes	yes	yes	no	yes
<voluntary>	yes	no	yes/no	no/yes	yes
<directness>	yes	no	yes	yes	yes
<effects>			yes		
<briefness>			yes		yes
<evaluation>			yes		yes
<correction-of-hypothesis>	yes	yes		yes	
<subjectivity>			yes		yes

The rationale behind this list is simple. If it is true that meaning is embodied, then the biological and psychological characteristics of the senses should provide the sensorimotor grounding for these extended meanings. Therefore, all these properties are based on both the physiology of the senses as well as the psychology of the senses (folk models). There are two reasons that explain why both sources are necessary. On the one hand, the conceptualisers of these metaphors, i.e., the speakers, are not always aware of how perception really works from a physiological perspective. A case in point is the classical distinction between the distant senses (vision, hearing) and close senses (touch, taste). The former are believed to be more objective since we do not have to be very close to the object of perception to actually perceive it. However, this is a folk belief. Not only do light and sound physically touch our perceptual organs in order to be processed (that is, all senses should be 'close') but also these senses are often too ephemeral and unconscious to be trusted. As Hughes, Fendrich & Streeter (2015) argue, the human visual system is remarkable but it is also full of paradoxes. Phenomena such as change blindness (not to see a change in a scene even with careful and prolonged scrutiny), blindsight (to respond to visual stimuli with lesions in the striate cortex (V1)), or Anton-Babinski syndrome (visual anosognosia) are just a few examples that remind us that there is more to perception than just their neurophysiological conditions. On the other hand, the literature on perception has traditionally talked about perception phenomena as if each modality were independent from each other, as if they worked separatedly. Current literature in the field argues that perception is a more complex process; it is a multisensory activity (see, Nudds, 2015; O'Callaghan, 2015; Spence & Bayne, 2015).

Once the list of properties is ready, the next step is to select those propeties that apply to each metaphor (or semantic extension, figurative and physical, see Ibarretxe-Antuñano, 1999a, b, 2006 for an account of smell and touch meanings). This is possible thanks to the 'property selection processes'. I will use the COGNITION IS PERCEPTION metaphor as an illustrative example (see Steinbach-Eicke, this volume, for more examples). This metaphor could be explained by means of four prototypical properties: <detection>, <directness>, <identification>, and <contact>.[2] The values that these four properties take in the types of 'knowledge' in Example (4) in Section 3 justify why these are understood differently. Table 5 illustrates this distribution.

Table 5. Property selection processes in COGNITION IS PERCEPTION

Meanings		<Selected properties>			
COGNITION IS PERCEPTION		<detection>	<directness>	<identification>	<contact>
Vision	'reliable knowledge'	yes	yes	yes	no
Hear	'indirect knowledge'	yes	no	yes	no
Smell	'intuitive knowledge'	yes	yes	no	no
Touch	'experiential knowledge'	yes	yes	yes	yes
Taste	'experiential knowledge'	yes	yes	yes	yes

All senses coincide on the value for the property <detection> since they all are good at perceiving their own stimuli. However, there are differences in the values for the other properties and, as a result the type of knowledge is not the same. Hearing depends on the Object of Perception (OP). It is not possible to hear a sound unless it is produced by a third element, and therefore, hearing is a mediated perception (<directness$_{no}$>). Smell is good at detecting that something happens but bad at

2. In my previous accounts of this metaphor I compared vision and smell. Therefore, I only used the property <correction-of-hypothesis>, which is a second-order property composed of the first-order properties <directness> and <identification> (Ibarretxe-Antuñano, 1999a, 2013a). Here I expand this discussion to touch and taste, and thus include more properties to capture their similarities and differences.

identifying the type of stimulus, the type of OP (<identification$_{no}$>). Touch and taste require a direct physical contact with the OP (<contact$_{yes}$>).[3] Vision is good at detecting and identifying stimuli, independent from the OP and free of contact. The values in these four properties might explain the reason why vision is understood as the most reliable source of knowledge, but is this so for every culture?

It is indeed very tempting to believe that the distribution of these properties, and therefore, the sensorimotor explanation of this metaphor actually holds universally. This is an idea that has been lingering around in cognitive linguistics for a long time now (see, Ibarretxe-Antuñano, 2013b for a discussion). However, as I have argued before, the mappings between the senses and the specific types of knowledge are culture-specific (Ibarretxe-Antuñano, 2008, 2013a, b). These mappings are valid for western societies, but they do not necessarily work for other communities around the world such as the Australian aborigines (Evans & Wilkins, 2000) or the Ongee on the Andaman Islands (Pandya, 1993). For them, hearing and smelling are the perceptual modalities that render reliable knowledge and not vision. Therefore, hearing in the Australian model and smell in the Ongee model should be the senses with <detection$_{yes}$>, <directness$_{yes}$>, <identification$_{yes}$>, and <contact$_{no}$>.

Ultimately, embodiment is a biocultural phenomenon. In other words, the general conceptual metaphor COGNITION IS PERCEPTION might be well explained by the properties <detection>, <directness>, <identification>, and <contact>. However, the choice of a specific perceptual modality seems to be driven by each culture; therefore, the values that apply to these prototypical properties should be tuned accordingly.

5.   The lexicalisation of perception metaphors

The final issue of this chapter relates to the way perception metaphors are lexicalised in language, that is to say, which linguistic resources are characteristically used to codify perception metaphors. Here I will discuss three points: the link between a specific conceptual metaphor and a specific type of metaphorical expression, the role of the linguistic items in the metaphorical expression, and the use of multimodal expressions.

---

3.   In (4), touch and taste are both 'experiential knowledge', and therefore, they have the same distribution of properties and values here. However, the type of experiential knowledge might also differ given the differences that exist between these two senses. One of the main differences is the property <internal> which takes a negative value for touch but a positive value for taste. This might explain why, despite both rendering experiential knowledge, this is understood as less deep and more superficial in touch than in taste.

When we look at the lists of metaphorical mappings related to each of the senses, we only see that a certain conceptual metaphor is linked with a certain sense. For instance, if we look at the list of smell metaphors in Table 1, smell is related to sensing, suspecting, and investigating. However, it is necessary to have a closer look at the specific linguistic structures that codify these metaphorical mappings because it might be the case that certain mappings only occur with certain linguistic structures and not others. Let us illustrate this point with an example from Basque and its smell words (Ibarretxe-Antuñano, in press).

Basque has at least five etymologically different sources for smell related nouns as summarised in (5).

(5)   a.   *hats* (*kir-ats*; native; 'breath, whiff' > 'bad smell')
      b.   *lurrin, urrin* (native; 'smell' > 'scent (perfume)')
      c.   *kirats, kino, kindu, keru* (**ken-*; 'smell' > 'stench')
      d.   *usna, suma, sunda, susma, sumo, sunja, susmo, usmo, susna* (Greek *osmao-mai* > Romance *usmar*; 'smell', 'sense of smell')
      e.   *usain* (native?, basic word for everything)

All these nouns are related with smell in different ways. Nouns in (5b) used to refer to neutral, positive, and negative smells indistinctly, but they are becoming more and more specialised in present-day Basque as only good. Nouns in (5d) could be used either to describe the sense of smell or the active result of the perception. Finally, *usain* in (5e) is the main basic-level smell noun in Basque and covers all the abovementioned meanings ('smells', 'sense of smell').

What is interesting about these different words is that some olfactory conceptual metaphors are only lexicalised by some of these words (constructions) and not others. For example, the conceptual metaphors BECOMING BAD (SPOILING, CORRUPTING) IS SMELLING and HAVING NEGATIVE FEELINGS (RANCOUR, GET BITTER) IS SMELLING are only codified by means of the verbs derived from bad smell nouns (5a, c). Similarly, it is only those active nouns in (5d) and (5e) that codify metaphorical meanings related to intuition, sagacity, clue, and investigation. That is, conceptual metaphors related to cognition SENSING (KNOWING INTUITIVELY) IS SMELLING, GUESSING (REALISING) IS SMELLING and INVESTIGATING (SEARCHING) IS SMELLING.

Another related point is the role that the linguistic items in the perception construction play in triggering the conceptual metaphor. One of the major claims in cognitive semantics has been to show that meaning is not necessarily compositional, that is, that the meaning of the whole is not necessarily the sum of the meaning of its parts (Valenzuela, 2017). However, on some occasions, it is necessary to bear in mind that the role of some parts might be more prominent than the role of others, and that certain elements should be present in the metaphorical expression in order to actually convey the conceptual metaphor. An illustrative example that I have discussed elsewhere is that in (6).

(6) *John touched Mary*   (Ibarretxe-Antuñano, 2006, p. 245)

This is an example of the meaning 'to affect' in the sense of touch. Without any more context, this utterance is ambiguous because it could mean that John physically touched Mary (and this had a physical effect on her), or that John metaphorically touched Mary, in which case this will be a metaphorical expression of AFFECTING IS TOUCHING.[4] However, the same linguistic expression in Spanish is not ambiguous. It can only render the physical meaning.

(7) *Juan tocó a María*
     Lit. John (physically) touched to Mary

This is not to say that this metaphor does not happen in Spanish, it does. However, it is more 'compositional' than in English. It needs a complement that allows a metaphorical meaning such as *her feelings*, *her ego* or *deep inside*.

Finally, the last issue I will cover is the multimodal expression of perception metaphors in both oral and signed languages. So far, most literature on oral languages in this area has dealt with verbs and to a lesser extent with other categories such as adjectives, nouns, and ideophones. However, an open field for research is the use of different types of gestures in the expression of perception meanings. Here, I will mainly focus only on 'emblems', that is to say, conventionalised form-meaning pairs similar to words that do not have to necessarily occur with speech (see, Kendon, 2008; McNeill, 1992, 2005 among others, for a description of gesture types).

Let us look at the images in Figure 2.

(a) smell 'stink'   (b) hear 'can't hear'

Figure 2. Smell and hear gestures

---

4. Interestingly enough a Google image search of the word *touched* immediately shows that the preferred interpretation in English is the metaphorical one.

The two gestures in Figure 2 are easily recognisable for a (European) Spanish speaker. To pinch the nose is usually interpreted as a bad smell, 'it stinks', whereas the hand cupped behind the ear means '(cannot) hear, listen'. It is interesting to notice that similar gestures are used in signed language with similar meanings. As Zeshan and Palfreyman (this volume) explain, perceptual related meanings are usually signed near the place of articulation of the perception (see also Takashima, this volume). In Catalan Sign Language (CSL), for instance, the sign in Figure 3 is used with the meaning of 'listen to'.

ESCOLTAR.ORELLA 'to listen.ear'

Figure 3. Hear sign in CSL (adapted from Jarque & Pascual, 2015, p. 431)

What is even more interesting is that some of the perception metaphors discussed in this chapter can also be lexicalised into signs (see Zeshan and Palfreyman, this volume, for more examples). For instance,

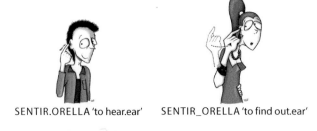

SENTIR.ORELLA 'to hear.ear'   SENTIR_ORELLA 'to find out.ear'

Figure 4a. 'to be told'   **Figure 4b.** 'to be just told'

Figure 4. Perception metaphors in CSL
(adapted from Jarque & Pascual, 2015, pp. 432, 433)

Figure 4a and 4b represent the metaphor BEING TOLD IS HEARING in Catalan Sign Language. The upright index finger points to the ear. If this index moves in a sharp way as in Figure 4b, the sign becomes more complex since there is an additional aspectual value added, 'I just heard', i.e., 'I just found out'.

As in the case of oral metaphorical expressions, the gestural expression of conceptual metaphors also varies from language to language. The gestures in Figure 5 are multimodal expressions for the metaphor SUSPECTING IS SMELLING in two different languages, (European) Spanish and (Southern) Italian. In Figure 5a, the upright index finger has to tap the ala of the nose a couple of times. In Figure 5b, the nose has to be moved side to side with the index and middle fingers.

Figure 5a. 'suspect' in
(European) Spanish

Figure 5b. 'suspect' in Southern Italian
(adapted from LeFevre, 2011, p. 11)

Figure 5. SUSPECTING IS SMELLING gestures

However, we also have to bear in mind that a similar gesture might convey a different metaphor in different languages. For instance, the gesture in Figure 2b where the person cups an ear to indicate they did not hear something conveys a different meaning in French. According to LeFevre (2011, p. 49), this gesture means 'displeasure and to stop speaking altogether' in France. Similarly, the sign in CSL in Figure 6 where the signer points to his nose with the index finger does not mean 'suspect'. This is an evidential in CSL that renders the metaphor SENSING/KNOWING INTUITIVELY IS SMELLING.[5]

PRO.1   OLORAR + AMBIENT [INDEPENDÈNCIA]topic [NO]neg
Lit. 'I smell in the ambience that the independence is not.'
'It seems to me that (The Basque Country) is not going to become independent'

Figure 6. 'sense, know intuitively' in CSL (adapted from Jarque & Pascual, 2015, p. 426)

---

5. This is interesting because it reminds us of an issue discussed in Section 4. The senses can be interpreted in different ways in different cultures. The literature on perception metaphors has taken for granted that smell is related to suspicion, that is, to negative thoughts. However, as the case in CSL, this is not necessarily universally true. In other languages, i.e. Basque, smell is just the source of intuitive knowledge, and it is only when the Object of Perception has negative values that smell could be interpreted as 'suspicion' (see, Ibarretxe-Antuñano, in press).

These multimodal examples are just the tip of the iceberg. They only show how little is known about the lexicalisation of perception metaphors beyond their oral expression across languages and language modalities.

6. Conclusions

In this chapter, I have described my research on perception metaphors from a cognitive linguistics perspective. I have shown that perception metaphors are numerous, motivated, and lexicalised by means of multimodal linguistic expressions across languages. I have also pointed out that it is important to be cautious when dealing with these three findings, especially when trying to carry out typological cross-linguistic semantic comparisons. All languages seem to have some perception metaphors. Some seem to be quite widespread (COGNITION IS PERCEPTION).[6] However, it is paramount not to forget that perceptual metaphors differ with regard to their distribution, their motivation (sensorimotor experience is shared but filtered by each culture), and the linguistic means employed to codify their metaphorical expressions.

There is still a lot of work to be done in this field. More studies using a wide range of methodologies (e.g., parallel corpus, elicitation) are needed in order to investigate the scope and distribution of (general) perception metaphors in different languages. It is crucial, however, for these methodologies to be developed from a semantic typological perspective. It would be a great advance for the field if such a semantic typological tool (or tools) were designed. To date, most studies cannot be compared due to the diverse nature of the data discussed. Such tools would fill this gap and provide researchers with reliable contrastive data, which, in turn, is the only way to validate the lists of perception metaphors that appear in the literature (including Table 1 in this chapter).

Another area for future research is the empirical validation of the embodied nature of these metaphors. Approaches such as the property selection process described in Section 4 are just a first step. Even if all the prototypical properties are actually attested by sound research in the physiology and psychology of the senses, that is, they are not ad-hoc, they are not enough to really demonstrate that we map our senses onto these other conceptual areas. If all the technology (fMRI, EEG, eyetracker, etc.) available nowadays plus all the nonverbal empirical methods already tested (cf. Farias, Garrido & Semin, 2013; Fay & Maner, 2012; Lacey, Stilla & Sathian, 2012; Lee and Schwarz, 2012; Lee, Kim & Schwarz, 2015; Liljenquist,

---

6. Kövecses (this volume) proposes two other general perceptual metaphors, EMOTION IS PERCEPTION and THE GENERAL ATMOSPHERE OF SOMETHING IS PERCEPTION.

Zhong & Galinsky, 2010; Slepian, Weisbuch, Rule & Ambady, 2011, among others) could be used in this field from a cross-linguistic perspective, perception metaphor research would reach another dimension.

As far as the lexicalisation of perception metaphors is concerned, an interesting path to explore is in fact its multimodal expression. Research in gesture and metaphor has already taken off, but cross-linguistic comparisons in the sense described in this chapter (emblems and other types, e.g., metaphorical gestures, McNeill, 1992, 2005) is still scarce.

This chapter has only touched on a handful of possible ways to sniff around perception metaphors. There are many more areas to be explored; areas that will surely satisfy all kinds of tastes. In this regard, I can see a promising future for this type of research – and I'm sure we will hear more about it very soon.

Acknowledgements

This research has been supported by grants FFI2013-45553-C3-1-P and FFI2017-82460-P from the Spanish Ministry of Economy and Competitiveness. I would like to thank Rosario Caballero, Nieves Gascón, Alberto Hijazo-Gascón, Mª Josep Jarque, and Javier Ruiz-Arizmendi for their help in this paper as well as Mark Lynch, Fran Orford, and Ken Wilson for kindly allowing me to use their great cartoons in Figure 1. A big, big thanks goes to the editors not only for their infinite patience and their careful editing but also for organising the Perception Metaphor Workshop in Nijmegen in 2016. Perception has always been a dear topic to me since my doctoral work but this Workshop gave me the chance to realise how much I enjoy researching about the senses, how many people still share my interests in this area, and how much I missed working in this field.

References

Aikhenvald, A. Y., & Storch, A. (2013). Linguistic expression of perception and cognition: A typological glimpse. In A. Y. Aikhenvald, & A. Storch (Eds.), *Perception and cognition in language and culture* (pp. 1–46). Leiden: Brill. https://doi.org/10.1163/9789004210127_002

Bacci, F., & Melcher, D. (Eds.). (2013). *Art and the senses.* Oxford: Oxford University Press.

Bergen, B. (2015). Embodiment. In E. Dąbrowska, & D. Divjak (Eds.), *Mouton handbook of cognitive linguistics* (pp. 10–30). Berlin: Mouton de Gruyter. https://doi.org/10.1515/9783110292022-002

Blake, R., & Sekuler, R. (2005). *Perception.* New York: McGraw-Hill.

Buck, C. D. (1949). *A dictionary of selected synonyms in the principal Indo-European languages.* Chicago: Chicago University Press.

Caballero, R., & Ibarretxe-Antuñano, I. (2014). Ways of perceiving, moving, and thinking: revindicating culture in conceptual metaphor research. *Cognitive Semiotics,* 5(1–2), 268–290. https://doi.org/10.1515/cogsem.2013.5.12.268

Caballero, R., Suárez-Toste, E., & Paradis, C. (in press). *On wine. Sensory perceptions, communication and cultures.* Amsterdam: John Benjamins.

Classen, C. (1997). Foundations for an anthropology of the senses. *International Social Science Journal*, 49(3), 401–412.

Evans, N., & Wilkins, D. (2000). In the mind's ear: The semantic extensions of perception verbs in Australian languages. *Language*, 76(3), 546–592. https://doi.org/10.2307/417135

Farias, A. R., Garrido, M. V., & Semin, G. R. (2013). Converging modalities ground abstract categories: The case of politics. *PLoS ONE*, 8(4), e60971. https://doi.org/10.1371/journal.pone.0060971

Fay, A. J., & Maner, J. K. (2012). Warmth, spatial proximity, and social attachment: The embodied perception of a social metaphor. *Journal of Experimental Social Psychology*, 48(6), 1369–1372. https://doi.org/10.1016/j.jesp.2012.05.017

Gibbs, R. W., Jr. (Ed.). (2008). *The Cambridge handbook of metaphor and thought.* Cambridge: Cambridge University Press. https://doi.org/10.1017/CBO9780511816802

Gisborne, N. (2010). *The event structure of perception verbs.* Oxford: Oxford University Press. https://doi.org/10.1093/acprof:oso/9780199577798.001.0001

Goldstein, E. B. (Ed.). (2005). *Blackwell handbook of sensation and perception.* Oxford: Blackwells.

Goldstein, E. B. (Ed.). (2010). *Encyclopedia of perception.* Thousand Oaks: SAGE.

Grady, J. (1997). Foundations of meaning: Primary metaphors and primary scenes. Unpublished PhD Thesis, University of California Berkeley.

Grady, J. (2007). Metaphor. In D. Geeraerts, & H. Cuyckens (Eds.), *Handbook of cognitive linguistics* (pp. 188–213). Oxford: Oxford University Press.

Howes, D. (Ed.). (1991). *The varieties of sensory experience. A sourcebook in the anthropology of the senses.* Toronto: University of Toronto Press.

Howes, D. (2003). *Sensual relations. Engaging the senses in culture and social theory.* Ann Arbor: The University of Michigan Press. https://doi.org/10.3998/mpub.11852

Howes, D. (Ed.). (2004). *Empire of the senses: The sensual culture reader.* Oxford: Berg.

Hughes, H. C., Fendrich, R., & Streeter, S. E. (2015). The diversity of human experience. In D. Stokes, M. Matthen, & S. Biggs (Eds.), *Perception and its modalities* (pp. 397–326). Oxford: Oxford University Press.

Ibarretxe-Antuñano, I. (1999a). Polysemy and metaphor in perception verbs: A cross-linguistic study. Unpublished PhD Thesis, University of Edinburgh.

Ibarretxe-Antuñano, I. (1999b). Metaphorical mappings in the sense of smell. In R. W., Jr. Gibbs, & G. J. Steen (Eds.), *Metaphor in cognitive linguistics* (pp. 29–45). Amsterdam: John Benjamins. https://doi.org/10.1075/cilt.175.03iba

Ibarretxe-Antuñano, I. (2002). MIND-AS-BODY as a cross-linguistic conceptual metaphor. *Miscelánea. A Journal of English and American Studies*, 25, 93–119.

Ibarretxe-Antuñano, I. (2006). Cross-linguistic polysemy in tactile verbs. In J. Luchenbroers (Eds.), *Cognitive linguistics investigations across languages, fields, and philosophical boundaries* (pp. 235–253). Amsterdam: John Benjamins. https://doi.org/10.1075/hcp.15.16iba

Ibarretxe-Antuñano, I. (2008). Vision metaphors for the intellect: Are they really crosslinguistic? *Atlantis*, 30(1), 15–33.

Ibarretxe-Antuñano, I. (2013a). The power of the senses and the role of culture in metaphor and language. In R. Caballero, & J. Diaz-Vera (Eds.), *Sensuous cognition: Explorations into human sentience -imagination, (e)motion and perception* (pp. 109–133). Berlin: Mouton de Gruyter. https://doi.org/10.1515/9783110300772.109

Ibarretxe-Antuñano, I. (2013b). The relationship between conceptual metaphor and culture. *Intercultural Pragmatics*, 10(2), 315–339. https://doi.org/10.1515/ip-2013-0014

Ibarretxe-Antuñano, I. (In press). The domain of olfaction in Basque. In Ł. Jędrzejowski, & P. Staniewski (Eds.), *Linguistics of olfaction*. Amsterdam: John Benjamins.

Jarque, Mª J., & Pascual, E. (2015). Direct discourse expressing evidential values in Catalan Sign Language. *eHumanista/IVITRA*, 8, 421–445.

Johnson, M. (1987). *The body in the mind. The bodily basis of meaning, reason and imagination*. Chicago: Chicago University Press.

Kendon, A. (2008). Some reflections on the relationship between 'gesture' and 'sign'. *Gesture*, 8(3), 348–366. https://doi.org/10.1075/gest.8.3.05ken

Kövecses, Z. (2002). *Metaphor: A practical introduction*. Oxford: Oxford University Press.

Lacey, S., Stilla, R., & Sathian, K. (2012). Metaphorically feeling: Comprehending textural metaphors activates somatosensory cortex. *Brain and Language*, 120(3), 416–421. https://doi.org/10.1016/j.bandl.2011.12.016

Lakoff, G., & Johnson, M. (1980). *Metaphors we live by*. Chicago: Chicago University Press.

Lee, D. S., Kim, E., & Schwarz, N. (2015). Something smells fishy: Olfactory suspicion cues improve performance on the Moses illusion and Wason rule discovery task. *Journal of Experimental Social Psychology*, 59, 47–50. https://doi.org/10.1016/j.jesp.2015.03.006

Lee, S. W. S., & Schwarz, N. (2012). Bidirectionality, mediation, and moderation of metaphorical effects: The embodiment of social suspicion and fishy smells. *Journal of Personality and Social Psychology*, 103(5), 737–749. https://doi.org/10.1037/a0029708

Lefevre, R. (2011). *Rude hand gestures of the world. A guide to offending without words*. San Francisco: Chronicle Books.

Lehrer, A. (2009). *Wine and conversation*. Oxford: Oxford University Press. https://doi.org/10.1093/acprof:oso/9780195307931.001.0001

Liljenquist, K., Zhong, C.-B., & Galinsky, A. D. (2010). The smell of virtue: Clean scents promote reciprocity and charity. *Psychological Science*, 21(3), 381–383. https://doi.org/10.1177/0956797610361426

Majid, A., & Levinson, S. C. (2011). The senses in language and culture. *Senses and Society*, 6(1), 5–18. https://doi.org/10.2752/174589311X12893982233551

Matthen, M. (2015). *The Oxford handbook of philosophy of perception*. Oxford: Oxford University Press. https://doi.org/10.1093/oxfordhb/9780199600472.001.0001

McNeill, D. (1992). *Hand and mind*. Chicago: University of Chicago Press.

McNeill, D. (2005). *Gesture and thought*. Chicago: University of Chicago Press. https://doi.org/10.7208/chicago/9780226514642.001.0001

Nudds, M. (2015). Is audio-visual perception 'amodal' or 'crossmodal'?. In D. Stokes, M. Matthen, & S. Biggs (Eds.), *Perception and its modalities* (pp. 166–188). Oxford: Oxford University Press.

O'Callaghan, C. (2015). Not all perceptual experience is modality specific. In D. Stokes, M. Matthen, & S. Biggs (Eds.), *Perception and its modalities* (pp. 133–165). Oxford: Oxford University Press.

Pandya, V. (1993). *Above the forest: A study of Andamanese ethnoanemology, cosmology and the power of ritual*. Bombay: Oxford University Press.

Rohrer, T. (2007). Embodiment and experientialism. In D. Geeraerts, & H. Cuyckens (Eds.), *Handbook of cognitive linguistics* (pp. 25–47). Oxford: Oxford University Press.

Rojo, A., & Ibarretxe-Antuñano, I. (Eds.). (2013). *Cognitive linguistics and translation. Advances in some theoretical models and applications*. Berlin: Mouton de Gruyter. https://doi.org/10.1515/9783110302943

Rouby, C., Schaal, B., Dubois, D., Gervais, R., & Holley, A. (2002). *Olfaction, Taste, and Cognition*. Cambridge: Cambridge University Press. https://doi.org/10.1017/CBO9780511546389

Semino, E., & Demjén, Z. (2017). *The Routledge handbook of metaphor and language*. London: Routledge.

Serres, M. (2008). *The five senses. A philosophy of mingled bodies*. London: Continuum.

Slepian, M. L., Weisbuch, M., Rule, N. O., & Ambady, N. (2011). Tough and tender: Embodied categorization of gender. *Psychological Science*, 22(1), 26–28. https://doi.org/10.1177/0956797610390388

Spence, Ch., & Bayne, T. (2015). Is conciousness multisensory?. In D. Stokes, M. Matthen, & S. Biggs (Eds.), *Perception and its modalities* (pp. 95–132). Oxford: Oxford University Press.

Stokes, D., Matthen, M., & Biggs, S. (Eds.). (2015). *Perception and its modalities*. Oxford: Oxford University Press.

Valenzuela, J. (2017). *Meaning in English*. Cambridge: Cambridge University Press. https://doi.org/10.1017/9781316156278

Vanhove, M. (2008). Semantic associations between sensory modalities, prehension and mental perceptions: A crosslinguistic perspective. In M. Vanhove (Ed.), *From polysemy to semantic change: Towards a typology of lexical semantic associations* (pp. 343–370). Amsterdam: John Benjamins. https://doi.org/10.1075/slcs.106.17van

Viberg, A. (2008). Swedish verbs of perception from a typological and contrastive perspective. In M. Á. Gómez-González, J. L.Mackenzie, & E. M. González-Álvarez (Eds.), *Languages and cultures in contrast and comparison* (pp. 123–172). Amsterdam: John Benjamins.

Yu, N. (2008). Metaphor from body and culture. In R. W. Gibbs, Jr. (Ed.), *The Cambridge handbook of metaphor and thought* (pp. 247–261). Cambridge: Cambridge University Press. https://doi.org/10.1017/CBO9780511816802.016

CHAPTER 4

Perception metaphor in English

A bird's-eye view

Wendy Anderson
University of Glasgow

This chapter offers a perspective on perception metaphor based on the evidence of the recorded language history of English. It draws on the analysis carried out by the "Mapping Metaphor with the Historical Thesaurus" project, which in turn exploits lexicographical evidence representing the English language over a period of more than a millennium. The foundation of the project is the principle that metaphor can be discerned in the lexis shared across semantic fields. The chapter gives an overview of metaphors with either a source or a target in each of the five perception categories and uses examples from the relatively neglected senses, Touch, Taste and Smell, to illustrate the richness and long history of perception metaphors in English.

Keywords: metaphor, English, diachronic, perception, digital humanities, semantic change, Historical Thesaurus of English, touch, taste, smell

1. Introduction

> Languages are windows on the senses that we can hardly afford to ignore.
>
> (Majid & Levinson, 2011, p. 7)

The window metaphor used in this statement is conventional, but one that surely retains its vividness and force for speakers. The source concept of a window contributes to the metaphor the notion of visibility, naturally, but importantly also that of framing: a window is not just the glass we see through but also the frame around the glass which directs the line of sight. By analogy, languages do not only allow us insight into the senses, but also offer – or perhaps impose – a particular circumscription.

Different types of language data offer different, complementary, windows on the senses. A corpus approach, for example, offers a particular type of window, based on large quantities of textual evidence. A significant advantage of a corpus study is the ease with which we can look at language in its immediate linguistic co-text, if not so

https://doi.org/10.1075/celcr.19.04and

easily in its wider context of production. An experimental approach, obtaining data direct from speakers in a controlled environment, perhaps makes it more difficult to replicate a natural communicative setting, but allows for a closer focus on particular questions, limiting the "noise" within the data. With an observational approach, as in linguistic anthropology, the authenticity of the linguistic context comes with the territory, but extrapolating from instances of observation may pose a challenge.

The research that underlies this chapter takes a different approach again. It draws on a newly available resource, the "Metaphor Map of English", created by the "Mapping Metaphor with the Historical Thesaurus" project (henceforth Mapping Metaphor),[1] to offer an overview of the senses – and of perception metaphor specifically – based on the recorded history of the English language. The window metaphor still holds. The frame imposed by these data is that of the language system of English, as it is recorded in major lexicographical reference works. This approach does not ignore context and co-text, which come to the fore in a corpus study, but it handles them at several steps removed. Alongside the window metaphor, however, a different vision metaphor is also appropriate: this is the "bird's-eye view" metaphor of the chapter title. This source concept discards the notion of an artificial frame, with the horizon becoming the only external limit to vision. This metaphor is appropriate here because the Mapping Metaphor project opens up a perspective on English with both a broad historical sweep, of around thirteen hundred years, and a broad semantic sweep, indeed the whole of semantic space. From here, we can zoom in on the language of the senses, yet also consider perception metaphors within the context of all of the major metaphorical connections that have been made by speakers across the history of English.

2.   Mapping Metaphor with the Historical Thesaurus

The Mapping Metaphor project's data and methods are unique. The dataset is the entire recorded history of the English language, as represented in the Historical Thesaurus of English (available online, and in print as Kay et al., 2009a), itself based on *A Thesaurus of Old English* (Roberts & Kay, 1995), covering the Old English period up to 1150AD, and the second edition of the *Oxford English Dictionary*, covering the period from 1150AD to the present, and including the Old English words that continued in use after 1150AD. The Historical Thesaurus contains 793,742 word senses, arranged into a complex hierarchy of 225,131 semantic categories.

---

1.   The project website and Metaphor Map resources are available at http://mappingmetaphor. arts.gla.ac.uk/. A collection of studies of semantic domains can be found in Anderson, Bramwell and Hough (2016).

The Historical Thesaurus was begun in the 1960s at the University of Glasgow, before cognitive semantics became dominant; however, the editors commented that "that paradigm [cognitive semantics] has retrospectively proved sympathetic to the problems involved in categorising large quantities of lexical data" (Kay et al., 2009b, p. xix). These data therefore allowed the Mapping Metaphor project to take a broad, diachronic approach to metaphor in the language system – *linguistic* metaphor – although this has its basis in metaphor in the authentic texts that represent the foundation on which the OED lexicographers drew.[2] This textual evidence, ultimately, it might be assumed, also provides evidence of metaphor in the minds of speakers of English over the centuries.

2.1 Methods

Using the dataset of the Historical Thesaurus, the project's aim was to identify all the systematic metaphorical connections over the entire history of English. The starting point was the basic observation that metaphor can be glimpsed in the lexis shared between categories in any semantically-organised reference work, such as a thesaurus. That is, the project exploits the polysemy created by metaphor. For example, the polysemous word forms *rain, tempest, cloudy* and *storm* appear in semantic categories related to Weather (where they are the source of a metaphor) and Emotional suffering (where they are the target), as well as – individually and collectively – in various other places. Thus, in the following citation from the OED, Tennyson draws on a metaphor with its source in the domain of Weather to express the gloominess of King Arthur's mood (the target of the metaphor) before meeting Vivien:

> Vivien…Would fain have wrought upon his cloudy mood.
>
> (1859, Tennyson *Merlin & Vivien* 154 in *Idylls of the King*,
> cited in OED, *cloudy*, adjective, sense 6)

The first step in the project methodology consisted in breaking the Historical Thesaurus down into appropriately sized categories. The Historical Thesaurus has a complex hierarchical categorisation system, with up to twelve nested levels. This depth was not desirable for the Mapping Metaphor analysis, as the methodology required a flatter structure, enabling comparison of the lexical content of categories. Instead, the Mapping Metaphor category structure respects only the top two levels of the Historical Thesaurus system, and then establishes its own third level which

---

2. For more information on the methods of the OED lexicographers, see for example Gilliver (2016) and Mugglestone (2000). See also the prefaces to the second and third editions of the OED, available here: http://public.oed.com/history-of-the-oed/oed-editions/preface-to-the-second-edition/; http://public.oed.com/the-oed-today/preface-to-the-third-edition-of-the-oed/

only partially corresponds to the Historical Thesaurus in order to achieve a greater degree of parity of category size. Level one, therefore, corresponds to the Historical Thesaurus' three primary divisions, The External World, The Mental World and The Social World, reflected in the Mapping Metaphor colour coding as green, blue and red, respectively, and in the category coding system as 1, 2 and 3 as the first part of the code (e.g. in category 2D06 Emotional suffering, used in the example above, the 2 in the code indicates that this category is part of The Mental World). Level two, similarly, corresponds to the Historical Thesaurus' 37 macro-categories; categories at this level have a code incorporating a number and a letter (e.g. 1A The Earth, 2D Emotion and 3M Leisure). Level three of the Mapping Metaphor category structure is the lowest, with a total of 415 roughly basic-level categories, each with a three-part code (a number, a letter, and a two-digit number, e.g. 1A28 Atmosphere and weather, 2D07 Anger and 3M04 Music). Level 3 categories, which do not directly inherit the category structure of the Historical Thesaurus, were the main focus of the analysis. With this set of categories established, the project automatically compared all the lexis in each of the 415 categories with all the lexis in every other category, compiling sets of shared lexis for every pair of categories (see further Section 2.2 below).

The next stage involved manual analysis, to identify where this shared lexis was due to the presence of a metaphorical connection between the pair of categories in question. As part of this analysis, the project team had to find a satisfactory answer to the question of how we knew when what we were seeing in our data was indeed metaphor. This involved constant attention to the nature and boundaries of metaphor. While there has been substantial research recently on the criteria for identifying metaphor, this work has tended to focus on metaphor in discourse (for example, the Metaphor Identification Procedure, MIP, and its refinement MIPVU, see Steen et al., 2010) and does not transfer readily to research based on lexis which has been extracted from its immediate linguistic co-text. Essentially, we were seeking to identify what Deignan (2005a, p. 34) describes as a "non-core use" of a word expressing "a perceived relationship with the core meaning of the word." It will be noted that this definition does not exclude metonymy and while as a general rule we did not include conventional metonymy (e.g. of the INSTITUTION FOR THE PEOPLE WHO WORK IN THE INSTITUTION type, see Deignan, 2005b, p. 74), we did include within our scope connections in which we perceived evidence of a metaphor that was based on an ultimate relationship of contiguity (e.g. *cold* with the sense of 'frightened', instantiating an EFFECT FOR CAUSE metonymy).

Support for metaphorical connections in the project's analysis also came from the typical concrete-abstract directionality of metaphor (although this was not treated as a defining characteristic of metaphor) and from the OED's attestation dates for word senses (that is, the historical priority of senses in the source domain).

While Mapping Metaphor was not a corpus project in the conventional sense of analysing large bodies of texts, the motto of corpus linguistics, that "Language looks rather different when you look at a lot of it at once" (Sinclair, 1991, p. 100), holds equally true for this Digital Humanities approach to metaphor identification. Thus, a further advantage that the project had that is not available to researchers identifying metaphor in text was that our data took the form of *sets* of words shared between categories. There was naturally stronger evidence for a systematic metaphorical connection between a pair of categories if it could be seen to be instantiated in several words rather than in a single instance of use.

2.2   Getting to grips with the data

By way of illustration, this section sets out some examples of the Mapping Metaphor data. Table 1 shows a small sample from the set of words in category 2A09 Understanding, specifically showing those that appear also in category 1I09 Touch. From left to right, the table shows the lexical item itself, its part of speech, the attestation dates from the Historical Thesaurus (drawing on the second edition of the OED, as noted above) and a gloss of the sense. The three right-most columns all correspond to the lexical item in its use in the target category, here 2A09 Understanding. Items are ordered by the date of earliest attested use in the target category.

Table 1. Sample of shared lexis between 1I09 Touch and 2A09 Understanding

Lexical item	POS	Attestation dates	Gloss of sense
gripe	verb	a1340 + 1674–1742	understand
take	verb	1382–	understand
grope	verb	a1400–1642	reach understanding of
feel	noun	c1470–1603 Scots & northern English	understanding, comprehension
take	verb	1513–1882	reach understanding of words or meaning
reach	noun	1542–	understanding
reach	verb	1605–a1822	reach understanding of
touch	noun	1656 + 1872–	understanding
grasp	verb	1680–	understand

It is clear from the lexical evidence contained here that there is a systematic metaphorical connection between Touch and Understanding, with a number of words with core uses in 1I09 Touch being used with extended senses in 2A09 Understanding: *gripe, reach, grope, feel, touch* and *grasp*. The other item here, *take*, is of course a highly polysemous word. It is arguably also metaphorical, but the metaphorical sense would come from its source in a category other than 1I09 Touch (such as N10 Taking).

In other cases, the metaphorical connection was less evident from the data, either because it was instantiated by only one lexical item, or because the set of shared lexis was so large that discerning the metaphor within the surrounding "noise" was difficult. The shared lexis, shown in Table 2, between 1I09 Touch and 2D04 Composure illustrates the first of these scenarios, with only *untouched* providing evidence of a metaphorical connection between these categories. *Soft* here is also metaphorical, but the link is from 1J11 Softness, rather than directly from 1I09 Touch. We can see therefore that metaphor is only one of several reasons for shared lexis between semantic categories in these data: homonymy and forms of polysemy other than that motivated by metaphor are other significant reasons.

Table 2. Sample of shared lexis between 1I09 Touch and 2D04 Composure

Lexical item	POS	Attestation dates	Gloss of sense
take	verb	c1200–	endure patiently
soft	verb	c1400–1533	compose/make calm
take	verb	1470/85–	bear with/tolerate
soft	reflexive verb	c1480	compose oneself
untouched	adjective	1616–	composed/calm

Although the project was working with data numbering in the millions, this stage of the analysis brought more significant challenges than those of scale. We know well from metaphor research that people disagree over what is metaphorical and what is not. Caballero and Ibarretxe-Antuñano have recently expressed this as follows: "metaphoricity may be seen as a matter of degree: not all metaphorical language is regarded as such by all people, underlining the role of context and social convention in metaphor awareness and identification" (2013, p. 274). To the issues of context and social convention, we can add the further difficulties which arise when handling historical language data. While language users may have a good (if not always a conscious) feel for metaphorical usage in the language of their own time, there are more significant limitations when it comes to historical language. Such difficulties are of course to be expected: assuming a prototype approach to language, fuzziness and gradualness are normal (cf. Taylor, 2003, p. 122). Indeed, the Historical Thesaurus editors encountered this in compiling the Thesaurus: "synonym groupings are prototypical in nature, with a clear core of obvious members shading off into the less obvious, and ultimately into subordinate or cognate categories" (Kay et al., 2009b, p. xix). The Mapping Metaphor project's solution to this was to establish a team of coders with a range of expertise in different periods of English, to adopt an inclusive approach to metaphor, and also to build systematic cross-coding and cross-checking into procedures from the outset.

2.3   The Metaphor Map

One result of the Mapping Metaphor project's analysis of the Historical Thesaurus data is the online Metaphor Map, an interactive resource showing all the metaphorical links identified between pairs of categories and allowing users to drill down to see the linguistic evidence at the root of each category connection. In fact, there are two Metaphor Maps, one corresponding to English in the Anglo-Saxon period (until 1150AD) and the other representing English from this date onwards. The decision to keep this separation was motivated by the fact that the data come from two quite different sources, as noted in Section 2, and has the advantage of allowing the much smaller set of Old English data not to be swamped by that from the later period.

Each Metaphor Map contains three additional pieces of information for each metaphorical connection identified in the coding and checking stages. With close reference to the evidence of the Historical Thesaurus and the *Oxford English Dictionary*, the team identified: (a) one or more lexical examples to substantiate each connection; (b) the source and target category in each case (that is, the directionality of the metaphor); and (c) the date of the earliest evidence. The nature of the data did not enable the team to establish when a connection might cease to be "live" for speakers, so we could not identify end-dates for metaphorical connections: we took instead the view, following Kay (2000), among others, that underlying conceptual metaphors can be reawakened by new lexical instantiations or by context.

3.   Perception metaphor

3.1   Overview of perception categories

The major category 1I Physical Sensation (which appears within 1 The External World) in the Metaphor Map contains 15 categories, from 1I01 Physical sensation (containing general concepts of physical sensation, its acuity and dullness) to 1I15 Dirtiness. Within this, categories 1I09 to 1I13 represent the traditional five modes of perception: touch, taste, smell, sight and hearing (the last termed here 'Hearing and noise', in keeping with its semantic range in the Historical Thesaurus). Table 3 shows the number of categories (out of the total of 415) with which each of these five perception categories has a metaphorical connection and the figures for this perception category as both the source and the target of the metaphor.

The three right-most columns in Table 3 include figures for 'Strong' and 'Weak' connections. This distinction is not a precise measure but is simply intended to give a rough indication of the degree of strength of the connection. Connections were labelled as Strong where there was evidence of systematicity, visible, for example, through multiple lexemes instantiating the same conceptual link and metaphorical senses extending over a period of time. Weak connections were those where the evidence was not sufficient to label the connection as Strong: connections instantiated by a single minor lexeme or lexemes restricted to poetic language were typically labelled as Weak.

Table 3. Metaphorical connections involving perception categories in the Metaphor Map

Perception category	Word senses in Historical Thesaurus category	No. of category pairs with a metaphorical connection (Strong, Weak)	As source (Strong, Weak)*	As target (Strong, Weak)*
1I09 Touch	320	103 (34, 69)	99 (33, 66)	4 (1, 3)
1I10 Taste	914	109 (47, 62)	82 (42, 40)	36 (11, 25)
1I11 Smell	910	56 (21, 35)	43 (18, 25)	15 (3, 12)
1I12 Sight	3523	132 (62, 70)	99 (48, 51)	47 (23, 24)
1I13 Hearing and noise	5397	134 (54, 80)	75 (27, 48)	64 (31, 33)

* Bidirectional category links are counted separately as source and target

Table 3 shows that the five perception categories are not equally sized with regard to the number of word senses they contain. 1I13 Hearing and noise is the largest category with 5397 word senses, and also enters into the largest number of metaphorical connections, in line with Vanhove's findings for associations between hearing and mental perceptions (2008, p. 353). This is closely followed by 1I12 Sight. 1I09 Touch is by some distance the smallest category with 320 word senses, yet enters into a greater number of metaphorical connections (103) than the much larger category 1I11 Smell (which has only 56). It is important to note, however, that following the Historical Thesaurus' categorisation system, concepts of sound and noise are included alongside hearing perception in 1I13 Hearing and noise.[3] Conversely, a number of concepts, most notably colour and dimension which are sometimes included in the perception category of sight, are to be found elsewhere in the Historical Thesaurus and therefore also in the Mapping Metaphor categorisation system: in the latter, colour appears in both 1J34 Colour and 1J35 Individual colours, within 1J Matter, and dimension appears as 1L03 Size and spatial extent, within 1L Space. If we were to conflate these categories with 1I12 Sight, clearly its dominance, in terms of size and metaphorical connections, would be far greater

---

3. A full overview of the conceptual range of each category can be found by clicking "show descriptors" for each category in the Browse view of the Metaphor Map.

(see also San Roque et al., 2015, on the dominance of vision verbs in spontaneous conversation).

The tendencies visible here echo those that we might expect based on previous research. The picture provided by these data confirms Cacciari's statement that "the metaphorical use of sensory language is rather unbalanced across modalities" (2008, p. 425). Similarly, we can see some broad similarities with the hierarchy of sense modalities based on the extension of meaning from one sense modality to another proposed by Viberg (1983, p. 136):

> sight > hearing > touch > smell/taste

Viberg's model is not directly comparable with the Mapping Metaphor data, for two reasons: first, his model is based on meaning extension of verbs only, whereas Mapping Metaphor does not treat a change in part of speech to be an obstacle to metaphor, since the latter is a semantic rather than a grammatical connection; second, Viberg's hierarchy applies only to meanings extended from one perception modality to another (see also Strik Lievers & De Felice, this volume), whereas the Mapping Metaphor data shown in Table 3 illustrate the connections between the perception categories and other categories from across the semantic space of English.

The picture is quite different depending on whether we look at each perception category as the source or target of a metaphor. All categories enter into a larger number of metaphorical relationships as the source: only 1I11 Smell is an outlier with a low number of connections whether one looks at the total or only the Strong, systematic connections. As source categories, 1I12 Sight and 1I09 Touch rank highly, and 1I13 Hearing and noise and, especially, 1I11 Smell, rank low. That sight and touch should be of such importance is in line with the Aristotelian hierarchy of senses, which privileged sight as the most highly developed and touch as the primary sense (see for example Cacciari, 2008, p. 428; Synnott, 1991, p. 63; and empirical support by Szwedek, 2000). The data for category 1I11 Smell, while low, nevertheless support Ibarretxe-Antuñano's claim (1999) that this perception category evidences a broader metaphorical scope than has sometimes been recognised (see further Section 3.4). The picture is more mixed for perception categories as the target of a metaphor. 1I13 Hearing and noise and 1I12 Sight, representing the distal senses, and also the largest categories in terms of number of word senses, rank highly. The categories representing the proximal senses, those that require closer proximity to the stimulus – touch, taste and smell – rank low, with 1I09 Touch very low indeed (see Section 3.3 below; on the distinction between distal and proximal senses, see Speed & Majid, 2017).

3.2   A comparison: Overview of emotion categories

Meaningful direct comparisons with other categories are difficult to achieve, as categories are not equally sized, and in fact change their size relative to other categories over time. Nevertheless, a brief look at some categories from the major category 2D Emotion allows for a sense of the importance of metaphor in the perception categories compared with another semantic area in which metaphor has been found to be pervasive. Table 4 shows the metaphorical connections identified for a sample of five emotions: excitement, composure, anger, love and friendship, and fear.

Table 4. Metaphorical connections involving sample emotion categories in the Metaphor Map

Emotion category	Word senses in Historical Thesaurus category	No. of category pairs with a metaphorical connection (Strong, Weak)	As source (Strong, Weak)*	As target (Strong, Weak)*
2D03 Excitement	1061	79 (38, 41)	0 (0, 0)	79 (38, 41)
2D04 Composure	740	35 (13, 22)	1 (0, 1)	34 (13, 21)
2D07 Anger	1958	90 (37, 53)	22 (13, 9)	82 (36, 46)
2D08 Love and friendship	3046	117 (36, 81)	23 (4, 19)	103 (36, 67)
2D16 Fear	1989	59 (23, 36)	10 (2, 8)	52 (22, 30)

* Bidirectional category links are counted separately as source and target

Perhaps most obvious here is that these Emotion categories are much more frequently the target than the source of a metaphor: indeed, there is evidence of 2D03 Excitement *only* as the target (see further Anderson, 2016). This is not surprising: decades of work in conceptual metaphor theory lead us to expect abstract concepts like those associated with emotions to function as the target of a metaphor. Conflating source and target, for all of these emotion categories and most of the perception categories, the number of metaphorical connections per word sense varies within a narrow range (0.02 to 0.07). 1I09 Touch and 1I10 Taste, however, are outliers, with very high rates of metaphor per word sense (0.32 and 0.12 respectively). The focus of attention in the remainder of this chapter is therefore on aspects of metaphor (its survival over time, the relationship between semantic categories and semantic domains, and the directionality of metaphor), illustrated in turn by examples from these two categories and also 1I11 Smell, which has been relatively neglected in previous research on metaphor.

3.3   Touch: Metaphor over time

With 1I09 Touch as the source, the Mapping Metaphor team identified 99 metaphorical connections, that is, a connection with nearly one in four of the semantic categories. Of these, 40 are with other categories in the External World division of the Historical Thesaurus (out of 257), 23 with the Social World (out of 75), and 36 with the Mental World categories (out of 83). The high proportion of connections with the Mental World is to be expected, given the abstract quality of these categories and Sweetser's finding that "The vocabulary of physical perception [...] shows systematic metaphorical connections with the vocabulary of internal self and internal sensations" (1990, p. 45).

Several of these connections can be traced back to the Anglo-Saxon period and appear in the Metaphor Map of Old English as well as the later Metaphor Map of English on which the figures in Table 3 are based. The connection between 1I09 Touch and 2D01 Emotion, for example, can be traced back to Old English through words such as *feel* (from OE *gefelan*). Support for the connection can be found in the Metaphor Map of Old English, in *ophrinan* (with the metaphorical sense 'to touch the heart, mind', from literal sense 'to touch'). Of course, this metaphor is not restricted to the English language: the OED's notes on etymology show *rine* ('to touch') to be cognate with lexemes in several other languages, including Old Icelandic where it had the literal sense 'to touch' and figurative senses including 'to take effect on'.

The continued vitality of this conceptual metaphor is evident from its many more recent lexical instantiations, not only in the Mental World. A weak connection between 1I09 Touch and 1O12 Easiness is illustrated by *back-scratcher* in a sense dated by the OED to 1897:

> *back-scratching* noun[4]
> The performance of mutual services; always with the suggestion of doubt as to the legitimacy of the transactions.
> derivatives *back-scratcher* noun:
> 1897 *Daily News* 9 Jan. 4/7 Does it not rather partake of the ethics of the back-scratcher and the log-roller?
>
> (OED, *back-scratcher* noun in *back-scratching* noun, derivatives)

---

4.   Here and in the OED examples that follow, abbreviations of labels have been expanded (e.g. *n* = noun, *transf.* = transferred). Otherwise, the format of citations and their sources remains as presented in the OED.

More recently still, a weak connection between 1I09 Touch and 3M09 Types of sport is instantiated by *tickle*, for which the relevant OED entry includes the following definition and citation:

> *tickle* verb
> Cricket. Of a batsman: to deflect (a delivery) with a light stroke or glance.
> 1963 *Times* 5 Mar. 4/1 Dowling, who…is probably New Zealand's finest batsman.. today tickled Trueman round the corner.   (OED *tickle* verb 1, sense 6f)

A further weak connection between 1I09 Touch and 3I09 Printing and publishing also relies on *tickle*, in its nominal form:

> *tickler* noun
> A memorandum book, or a series of dated cards on which to enter engagements (U.S.). Also transferred, anything intended to serve as a reminder.
> 1905 E. E. Calkins & R. Holden *Art Mod. Advertising* 351 A tickler is any small piece of printed matter sent out to keep open a prospective sale on the part of the inquirer.   (OED *tickler* noun 1, sense 2j)

There is very little evidence, as Table 3 shows, of 1I09 Touch as the target of a metaphor, less even than 1I10 Taste and 1I11 Smell. The four metaphorical connections that it does show are all with other categories within the External World division of the Historical Thesaurus. By way of illustration, the connection with 1G01 Food and eating is instantiated by the lexical item *nibble* and a recent sense of *knead*:

> *nibble* verb
> *transitive*. To fidget or play with (a thing). *Obsolete rare*. In quotation 1676: specifically to strike repeatedly with the finger (as a technique in playing a stringed instrument).
> 1829 J. Hogg *Shepherd's Cal.* vii The hem of her jerkin, which she was nibbling with her hands.   (OED, *nibble* verb, sense 2b)
>
> *knead* verb
> *transitive* and *intransitive*. To manipulate or paw repetitively with or as with the action of (the claws of) a cat.
> 1954 G. Durrell *Bafut Beagles* iii. 69 The cloud seemed to move,..padding and kneading the mountain crests like a cat on the arm of a gigantic chair.
> 1968 V. Canning *Melting Man* vi. 144 The cat woke me by kneading determinedly on my chest.
> 1968 R. Sawkins *Snow along Border* xii. 102 It began kneading dough, claws exposed.   (OED, *knead* verb, sense 3c)

These are both quite recent figurative senses, as the OED dates indicate. The appearance of the collocate *dough* in the final example of *knead* here ("It began kneading dough") suggests that the metaphor here remains live for this writer. While the project methodology did not enable us to identify systematically the end dates of metaphors, since a good dictionary will give attestation dates but does not give "death dates" for word senses, further work with dictionary citations and corpora may offer a way forward in a future project.

With some further exploration in the OED, it becomes clear that there are other lexical instantiations of the same underlying conceptual metaphor that can be traced further back. *Knead* with a sense related to the perceptual mode of touch appears also in 1C04 Healing and treatment in relation to massage, with a citation from Shakespeare.

> *knead* verb
> To operate on or manipulate by an action similar to that in working dough, etc.
> Said especially in reference to massage.
> 1609 Shakespeare *Troilus & Cressida* ii. iii. 218 I will kneade [1623 knede] him, Ile
> make him supple.   (OED, *knead* verb, sense 3a)

This example highlights that the Historical Thesaurus makes necessarily arbitrary divisions between categories, as any linearly organised thesaurus must. This acts as a reminder that we cannot equate semantic categories with conceptual domains, although they may often give us a rough approximation.

3.4   Smell: Categories and domains

The data for category 1I11 Smell further illustrate the lack of perfect correspondence between the conceptual domains that enter into a relationship as source and target of a conceptual metaphor and the semantic categories that we find in a reference work like a thesaurus. Sweetser (1990, p. 37) found that "The sense of smell has few abstract or mental connotations, although bad smell is used in English to indicate bad character or dislikeable mental characteristics [...] while the active verb *smell* may indicate detection of such characteristics". Kövecses (this volume) finds some of the same conceptual metaphors as Sweetser, and also posits an additional one, THE GENERAL ATMOSPHERE OF SOMETHING IS AN OLFACTORY PERCEPTION, which he illustrates with the linguistic expression 'It had the smell of treason'. Ibarretxe-Antuñano (1999), in response to Sweetser and based on a cross-linguistic study covering English, Spanish and Basque, has argued that the metaphorical scope of smell is not in fact significantly weaker than that of the other senses. She adds to and refines Sweetser's suggestions with metaphorical word senses of suspecting, guessing and investigating. The data from the Metaphor Map provide further support for the claim that the sense of smell has a wider semantic scope than previously thought, although the Mapping Metaphor project and Ibarretxe-Antuñano were working within slightly different parameters. While Ibarretxe-Antuñano notes that some of the semantic extensions of smell are *not* metaphorical as they remain physical not abstract (cf. 'to trail something', 1999, p. 34), Mapping Metaphor nevertheless includes these, as the project team did not make the *a priori* assumption that metaphor should be limited only to concrete-abstract connections, even if these turn out in fact to be the most prototypical.

Considering 1I11 Smell as the source, as Sweetser and Ibarretxe-Antuñano do, Table 3 shows that the Mapping Metaphor team identified 43 metaphorical connections, or a connection with roughly one in ten of the semantic categories. As with 1I09 Touch, the highest proportion are with categories in the Mental World division, illustrating the most prototypical concrete-abstract connections. This includes the conceptual metaphors related to bad character or unappealing mental characteristics identified by Sweetser: for example, links with 2B08 Contempt (*sniff at, stink*), 2C02 Bad (*stinking, stink-pot, stinkard*), 2D09 Hatred and hostility (*stink, stinkingly*), all almost exclusively correlating with bad smells. It also includes metaphorical lexis with senses relating to the detection of such characteristics, guessing, suspecting and investigating: for example, in 2A20 Knowledge and experience (*smell of*), 2A07 Perception and cognition (*savour, scent*) and 2B02 Enquiry and discovery (*nose, sniff*), among others, which correlate with neutral or pleasant smells. Underlying conceptual metaphors therefore spread themselves out over multiple semantic categories, and indeed leak into other parts of the porous Historical Thesaurus categorisation system. BAD SMELL IS BAD CHARACTER can be found, loud and clear, in 3F05 Moral evil (*stinker, stink, smell, smelly*) in the Social World division. SMELLING IS MENTAL DETECTION, with examples like *smell* (defined in the OED as 'that quality by which anything is felt or suspected to be near at hand') is found also in categories in the External World division (1L02 Distance), and there is a very strong connection between 1I11 Smell and 1O10 Endeavour (*smell, outsmell, scent, follow the scent, get scent of, snuffle*) with arguably a very fuzzy boundary between mental detection and the physical detection which is the focus of part of this category.

A large number of more minor metaphors also exploit smell, and some of these have not been commonly identified in other work on smell, highlighting the value of the Metaphor Map as a complementary method of investigating metaphor in English. To pick out just one example, we can see a connection between smell and small size or weak effect. This is illustrated by the connections with 1P31 Moderateness and smallness of quantity (*smack, smell, whiff*) and 1P09 Similarity (*smell* with the sense 'to have a tinge or suggestion of something'). Large size or large effect corresponds to unpleasant rather than neutral smells, as in 1P29 Sufficiency and abundance (*stinkingly*).

1I11 Smell also appears, albeit less pervasively, as the target category of a metaphor. In this role, smell is seen to be conceptualised through lexis from the domains of temperature (*hot, warm, blazing* in 1J03 Weight, heat and cold), strength (*strong* in 1J08 Strength) and shape (*acute* and *pungency* in 1L04 Shape). Indeed, in the case of the last of these, it is the smell senses which now predominate: few speakers today are likely to perceive a metaphorical connection in *acute* or *pungency* (etymologically, 'having sharp points').

Some of the metaphorical links with smell stem from the aroma of particular entities. *Rammy*, for example, instantiates a connection with category 1E17 Ruminants. The OED citations show that the sense has been extended beyond the literal sense 'smelling of a ram':

> *rammy*
> of a smell, taste, etc.: rank, pungent, rammish. Of a person or animal: characterized by such a smell
> *a*1652 R. Brome *City Wit* iv. ii. sig. E6, in *Five New Playes* (1653) Thou Rammy Nastinesse. (OED, *rammy* adjective, sense 1)

Further senses of *rammy* pick up on characteristics of rams other than their pungent smell. The more recent sense 'wild, frisky', identified by the OED as US English, extends from the attribute of liveliness (OED, *rammy* adjective, sense 2) rather than smell.

These examples involving smell illustrate how the Metaphor Map can provide supporting evidence for well-known metaphors as well as enabling a more fine-grained investigation than is possible with intuition-based methods. For the under-explored sense of smell, for example, it allows us to tease out how bad, pleasant, neutral, strong and weak smells have been lexicalised and conceptualised in English.

3.5   Taste: Senses as source and target

For 1I10 Taste, Table 3 shows 109 metaphorical category pairs, that is, a connection with nearly one in four semantic categories, similar to Touch. Roughly two thirds have 1I10 Taste as the source; one third have it as the target. As the figures in Table 3 indicate, a small number of metaphorical connections between categories are bidirectional, that is, particular pairs of categories function as both source and target for each other. Given the distinction we must make between the semantic categories used by Mapping Metaphor and conceptual domains, these do not all correspond to bidirectional conceptual metaphors: nonetheless, many prove interesting in their own right, and I illustrate them here with reference to metaphors involving taste.

Perhaps the most obvious are the so-called synaesthetic metaphors (see for example Cacciari, 2008; Williams, 1976; and Steinbach-Eicke, this volume, for taste-touch mapping in Egyptian; see also Winter, this volume, for a critique of the term 'synaesthetic metaphor'). 1I10 Taste and 1I13 Hearing and noise have a strong metaphorical connection, instantiated by a number of common lexemes: *sweet* (derived from the Old English form *swete*), *sweetness, honeyed/honied, unsweet, dulcified, loud* and *silent*. With 1I10 Taste as the source, as it is for most of these lexemes, the metaphor can be traced back to Old English; with this category as the target (as in *loud* = 'powerful flavour' or *silent* = 'insipid'), there is evidence from the seventeenth century onwards.

However, many of the other bidirectional metaphorical connections are not restricted to perception categories. The category links between 1I10 Taste, on one hand, and both 1A16 Minerals and 3K07 Materials and fuel, on the other, instantiate the same conceptual metaphor, with word senses *metallic, tinny* and *brassy* having their source in the domain of minerals/materials and their target in the perception domain of taste, and word senses *sweet* and *sour* with their source in taste and target in minerals/materials (*sweet* = 'free from corrosive salt'; *sour* = 'not seasoned (of wood)').

The connection between 1I10 Taste and 2D07 Anger is a particularly well evidenced one, showing a stronger connection when 1I10 Taste is the source (*bitter, sour, bitterness, sourness, tartness, acidity, vinegary, acrimony*, the last with the less well known original sense of 'bitter pungency' rather than its more common figurative sense of 'sharpness of tone') than when it is the target (*vehement, angry*, in the transferred sense of 'sharp, acrid in taste', *vehement*). In this category pair, we can also see evidence of the strong evaluative component that Winter (2016) finds for taste (and smell) words.

4. Conclusion

The Metaphor Map offers a bird's-eye view of metaphor as it has entered the language system of English and as it continues to shape the language. The vast dataset of the Historical Thesaurus, as viewed through the Metaphor Map, makes possible more than just an overview, however; it also allows us to zoom in to the level of semantic categories to see how these cross-cut with the semantic and conceptual domains in which conceptual metaphor theory usually deals.

The Metaphor Map allows us a more nuanced picture of the areas of semantic space which have been particularly productive as the source or target of metaphor. The categories that represent the five modes of perception, sight, hearing, touch, taste and smell, are among these, both as target and as source. Indeed, metaphor may be even more productive here than in the highly metaphorical emotion categories. Even for the proximal senses, touch, taste and smell, which have previously been considered to be less metaphorically productive than the distal senses, we can see the broad and long-standing extent of metaphorical connections. ⌐

Many further questions, including some of the most thorny in conceptual metaphor theory, can be addressed using these data. For example, the broad historical sweep of data opens up the possibility of a fresh perspective on the notion of dead metaphor. In relation to the perception metaphors considered here, we can easily explore the evidence of the earliest usage, but further work with dictionary citations or corpora is needed to suggest when – or if – it is appropriate to talk about the death of these metaphors.

Majid and Levinson (2011, p. 7) have commented that: "For both the objective and subjective world, language is a coarse map, but whereas the description of a pyramid can convey the nature of the thing, for subjective 'raw feels' like colour sensations language fails to delineate – I can teach you 'red' only by pointing to it." When we are looking at the language available to speakers at any particular point in time, language is indeed a "coarse map". When we can stitch together the linguistic evidence from many centuries, however, we can begin to create something more closely analogous to a relief map of the territory.

Acknowledgements

"Mapping Metaphor with the Historical Thesaurus" was funded by the UK Arts and Humanities Research Council between 2012 and 2015 and carried out at the University of Glasgow, UK (AHRC grant number: AH/I02266X/1). I would like to thank the Mapping Metaphor team, and especially Carole Hough for her comments on this chapter. Thank you also to the editors, Laura, Carolyn, Lila and Asifa, with whom it has been a great joy to work, and to the anonymous reviewers.

References

Anderson, W. (2016). Waves of excitement, waves of metaphor. In W. Anderson, E. Bramwell, & C. Hough (Eds.), *Mapping English metaphor through time* (pp. 115–136). Oxford: Oxford University Press. https://doi.org/10.1093/acprof:oso/9780198744573.003.0008

Anderson, W., Bramwell, E., & Hough, C. (Eds.) (2016). *Mapping English metaphor through time*. Oxford: Oxford University Press. https://doi.org/10.1093/acprof:oso/9780198744573.001.0001 .

Caballero, R., & Ibarretxe-Antuñano, I. (2013). Ways of perceiving, moving, and thinking: Re-vindicating culture in conceptual metaphor research. In R. Fusaroli, & S. Morgagni (Eds.), *Conceptual metaphor theory: Thirty years after*. Special issue of the *Journal of Cognitive Semiotics*, 5(1–2), 268–290.

Cacciari, C. (2008). Crossing the senses in metaphorical language. In R. W. Gibbs (Ed.), *The Cambridge handbook of metaphor and thought* (pp. 425–443). Cambridge: Cambridge University Press. https://doi.org/10.1017/CBO9780511816802.026

Deignan, A. (2005a). *Metaphor and Corpus Linguistics*. Amsterdam and Philadelphia: John Benjamins. https://doi.org/10.1075/celcr.6

Deignan, A. (2005b). A corpus linguistic perspective on the relationship between metonymy and metaphor. *Style*, 39(1), 72–91.

Gilliver, P. (2016). *The making of the Oxford English Dictionary*. Oxford: Oxford University Press. https://doi.org/10.1093/acprof:oso/9780199283620.001.0001

Historical Thesaurus of English online, <http://historicalthesaurus.arts.gla.ac.uk> (accessed 1 April 2017).

Ibarretxe-Antuñano, I. (1999). Metaphorical mappings in the sense of smell. In R. W. Gibbs, & G. J. Steen (Eds.), *Metaphor in cognitive linguistics* (pp. 29–45). Amsterdam & Philadelphia: John Benjamins. https://doi.org/10.1075/cilt.175.03iba

Kay, C. (2000). Metaphors we lived by: pathways between Old and Modern English. In J. Nelson, & J. Roberts (Eds.), *Essays on Anglo-Saxon and related themes in memory of Lynne Grundy* (pp. 273–285). London: King's College London Medieval Studies.

Kay, C., Roberts, J., Samuels, M., & Wotherspoon, I. (Eds.) (2009a). *Historical Thesaurus of the Oxford English Dictionary*. Oxford: Oxford University Press.

Kay, C., Roberts, J., Samuels, M., & Wotherspoon, I. (2009b). Unlocking the OED: The story of the Historical Thesaurus of the OED. In C. Kay, J. Roberts, M. Samuels, & I. Wotherspoon (Eds.), *Historical Thesaurus of the Oxford English Dictionary* (pp. xiii–xx). Oxford: Oxford University Press.

Majid, A., & Levinson, S. C. (2011). The senses in language and culture. *The Senses and Society*, 6(1), 5–18. https://doi.org/10.2752/174589311X12893982233551

Mapping Metaphor with the *Historical Thesaurus*, <http://mappingmetaphor.arts.gla.ac.uk/> (accessed 31 January 2017).

Mugglestone, L. (Ed.) (2000). *Lexicography and the OED: Pioneers in the untrodden forest*. Oxford: Oxford University Press.

Oxford English Dictionary online (OED), <http://www.oed.com> (accessed 31 January 2017).

Roberts, J. & Kay, C., with Grundy, L. (1995). *A thesaurus of Old English*. Second edition, 2000. Amsterdam: Rodopi.

San Roque, L., Kendrick, K. H., Norcliffe, E., Brown, P., Defina, R., Dingemanse, M., Dirksmeyer, T., Enfield, N. J., Floyd, S., Hammond, J., Rossi, G., Tufvesson, S., van Putten, S., & Majid, A. (2015). Vision verbs dominate in conversation across cultures, but the ranking of non-visual verbs varies. *Cognitive Linguistics*, 26(1), 31–60. https://doi.org/10.1515/cog-2014-0089

Sinclair, J. (1991). *Corpus, concordance, collocation*. Oxford: Oxford University Press.

Speed, L. J., & Majid, A. (2017). Dutch modality exclusivity norms: simulating perceptual modality in space. *Behavior Research Methods*. https://doi.org/10.3758/s13428-017-0852-3

Steen, G. J., Dorst, A. G., Herrmann, J. B., Kaal, A. A., Krennmayr, T., & Pasma, T. (2010). *A method for linguistic metaphor identification. From MIP to MIPVU*. Amsterdam and Philadelphia: John Benjamins. https://doi.org/10.1075/celcr.14

Sweetser, E. (1990). *From etymology to pragmatics: Metaphorical and cultural aspects of semantic structure*. Cambridge: Cambridge University Press. https://doi.org/10.1017/CBO9780511620904

Synnott, A. (1991). Puzzling over the senses: From Plato to Marx. In D. Howes (Ed.), *The varieties of sensory experience: A sourcebook in the anthropology of the senses* (pp. 61–76). Toronto: University of Toronto Press.

Szwedek, A. (2000). The ontology of metaphors: The sense of touch in language formation. *Scripta Periodica*, 4, 193–199.

Taylor, J. R. (2003). *Linguistic categorization.* Third edition. Oxford: Oxford University Press.

Vanhove, M. (2008). Semantic associations between sensory modalities, prehension and mental perceptions: a cross-linguistic perspective. In M. Vanhove (Ed.), *From polysemy to semantic change: Towards a typology of lexical semantic associations* (pp. 341–370). Amsterdam & Philadelphia: John Benjamins. https://doi.org/10.1075/slcs.106.17van

Viberg, Å. (1983). The verbs of perception: A typological study. *Linguistics*, 21, 123–162. https://doi.org/10.1515/ling.1983.21.1.123

Williams, J. M. (1976). Synaesthetic adjectives: A possible law of semantic change. *Language*, 52(2), 461–478. https://doi.org/10.2307/412571

Winter, B. (2016). Taste and smell words form an affectively loaded and emotionally flexible part of the English lexicon. *Language, Cognition and Neuroscience*, 31(8), 975–988. https://doi.org/10.1080/23273798.2016.1193619

CHAPTER 5

Metaphors and perception in the lexicon
A diachronic perspective

Francesca Strik Lievers and Irene De Felice
University of Pisa

Polysemy patterns in the sensory lexicon have been the subject of many studies, mostly synchronically oriented. This paper investigates whether the regularities observed for the intrafield and transfield polysemy of sensory lexemes can also be noted in the semantic changes that the lexemes undergo over time. Based on lexicographic resources, we analyse the sense(s) of Classical Latin sensory adjectives and "follow" them until Contemporary Italian. Our findings indicate that semantic shifts that occurred over time largely conform to the patterns that emerge from synchronic analyses: if some change in meaning occurs, the semantic shift tends to go from a "lower" to a "higher" sensory modality, or from perceptual to cognitive or abstract senses.

Keywords: adjectives, perception, sensory modalities, synaesthesia, metaphor, directionality, Latin, Italian, diachrony

1. Introduction

Sensory lexemes are typically characterised by a high degree of polysemy, which can concern the sole domain of perception (e.g., when the sight-related word *bright* is used to describe a sound) and/or involve non-perceptual domains (e.g., when the sight-related word *bright* is used to describe an idea). Interestingly, such polysemy seems to conform to rather specific patterns. The literature on this topic, and more generally on sensory language, is now vast and includes detailed synchronic analyses of one or more languages (among others, Viberg, 1984, 2001, 2015; Ibarretxe-Antuñano, 1999; Evans & Wilkins, 2000; Vanhove, 2008). The present study explores polysemy patterns in the sensory lexicon from a diachronic perspective, which has not received as much attention so far.

Our aim is to observe which semantic changes sensory lexemes have undergone over a long time span. More specifically, we focus on adjectives. We decided to take Latin as a starting point, and we followed its sensory adjectives down to their Italian

https://doi.org/10.1075/celcr.19.05str

descendants, covering a period of approximately two thousand years. It is worth emphasising that we are interested in changes that concern the established senses[1] (Cruse, 1986, p. 79) of adjectives: we analyse their lexical polysemy, thus excluding creative and occasional meaning extensions, such as those typically found in poetry.

The results of our analysis are presented and discussed in light of the hypotheses advanced in previous studies about the directionality of semantic shifts within and outside the perceptual domain, which we tested in the diachronic dimension.

Semantic shifts *within* the domain of perception are instances of (word-level) synaesthetic metaphor, that is, a type of metaphor featuring a conflict between sensory concepts referring to conceptually separate senses (Strik Lievers, 2017). Since other views on the nature of these shifts have also been proposed (e.g., Barcelona, 2013; Rakova, 2003; Winter, Chapter 6), and a discussion on this topic is not a focus of this paper, we adopt here a more "neutral" terminology, referring to them as *intrafield* (Matisoff, 1978; Evans & Wilkins, 2000) semantic shifts.

It has been suggested in previous work that sensory modalities are hierarchically organised and that intrafield transfers tend to follow specific patterns. Some studies on adjectives propose very fine-grained models of intrafield semantic shifts. For instance, Zhao et al. (2018) on Mandarin Chinese observe a path of transfer from taste to sight, while that from taste to hearing is never attested. On the contrary, Bretones Callejas (2001) on English finds shifts from taste to hearing, but not to sight. Although at this fine-grained level of analysis inter-linguistic differences are often observed, in most languages a general tendency emerges for intrafield sense shifts to go from the "lower" (touch, taste and smell) to the "higher" (sight and hearing) modalities, with touch being the most frequent source and hearing the most frequent target, as in the case of the tactile adjective *rough*, which can also be used to describe sounds. The notion of "hierarchy" of sensory modalities may be subject to criticism, and directionality cannot be taken as a rule (Strik Lievers, 2015; Winter, 2016, Chapter 6). Nevertheless, studies on adjectives present evidence supporting the hypothesis of a low-to-high orientation of semantic transfers (touch > taste / smell > sight / hearing), at least as a strong statistical tendency.

As for metaphorical semantic shifts *outside* the perceptual domain, it has been observed that transfers tend to move from perceptual toward abstract or cognitive senses, as when the visual adjective *brilliant* is used to qualify a person or an idea (Ullmann, 1957 would have considered this case as an instance of "pseudo-synaesthesia"; cf. also Werning et al., 2006; Marotta, 2011). We here adopt the label *transfield* (Matisoff, 1978; Evans & Wilkins, 2000) for this type of transfer. More precisely, according to the classification proposed by O'Meara et al.

---

1. Hereafter, by *senses* we always refer to lexical senses, i.e. the meaning(s) of a word, and not to perceptual senses (i.e. sensory modalities).

(Chapter 1) it is a case of transfield I transfer (vs. transfield II, going from other domains toward the domain of perception). Transfield (I) semantic shifts are discussed in this volume for a variety of spoken languages (e.g., Proos, Chapter 12, on Estonian, Trojszczak, Chapter 11, on English and Polish, Steinbach-Eicke, Chapter 8, on Ancient Egyptian), as well as for sign languages (Zeshan & Palfreyman, Chapter 14; Takashima, Chapter 15). As in the case of intrafield directionality, transfield transfers going in the opposite direction (transfield II) are of course not impossible, nor unattested: they are however less common (see Kövecses, Chapter 16, for smell as both transfield I source domain and transfield II target domain).

Whereas directionality has been widely investigated based on synchronic data (among others, Ullmann, 1957; Rosiello, 1963; Paissa, 1995; Shen & Gil, 2008; Strik Lievers, 2015), studies taking a diachronic perspective are less numerous (in this volume, cf. Anderson, Chapter 4, and Steinbach-Eicke, Chapter 8). However, at least two of them are worth mentioning in relation to the present study.

Williams (1976) observes that intrafield semantic changes undergone by English sensory adjectives over time, starting from their first citations, follow the "low-to-high" directionality in the vast majority of cases (between 83% and 99%). According to Williams (1976, p. 463), "[w]hat we have, then, is the strongest statement about semantic change that has been suggested for English or for any other language." Sweetser (1990) shows that lexemes that in English and other Indo-European languages refer to abstract concepts and cognitive processes often originate from sensory lexemes or roots. For instance: Proto-Indo-European *weid- 'see' > Greek εἶδον '(I) saw', perfect οἶδα '(I) know' (> English idea); English wise, wit; Latin video '(I) see'; Irish fios 'knowledge' (adapted from Sweetser, 1990, p. 33). According to Sweetser, this kind of etymological data can be taken as evidence for a unidirectional "Mind-as-Body Metaphor", with bodily experiences providing the source vocabulary for psychological states (Sweetser, 1990, p. 30; cf. Evans & Wilkins, 2000; Allan, 2008; Vanhove, 2008, and Section 4.3.1 of this chapter for a discussion).

[This study aims to investigate whether the "low-to-high" (touch > taste / smell > hearing / sight) and "sensory-to-abstract/cognitive" directionality proves valid to describe semantic changes in sensory adjectives from Latin to Italian.] In a diachronic dimension, directionality might be intended as predictive both of the development of new senses and of their loss. That is, new (Italian) meanings should arise in sensory domains that are "higher" with respect to the older (Latin) ones, or in previously unattested abstract/cognitive non-sensory domains. Conversely, old (Latin) meanings should be lost (in Italian) in the lower sensory domains (rather than in the higher sensory domains), or in the sensory domain (rather than in the abstract/cognitive domain). While the role of directionality has usually been explored in relation to the acquisition of new meanings, meaning loss has been overlooked. However, we believe that acquisition and loss are two sides of the same coin, and should be investigated together. We will test our hypothesis by providing a detailed description of intrafield and transfield meaning changes in sensory adjectives from Classical Latin to Contemporary Italian.

2.   Our data

First of all, it is important to clearly define which Latin and which Italian our research is based on. For Latin (henceforth Lat.) we chose to focus on Classical Latin (approx. 100 BC – 100 AD), because it is recognised as the standard (and best documented) variety of the language (Cuzzolin & Haverling, 2009). For Italian, we mainly focus on the language of the 20th and 21st centuries (De Mauro, 1972; Migliorini, 1990; Sobrero, 1993; Mengaldo, 1994; D'Achille, 2010), for which we adopt the label Contemporary Italian (henceforth C.It.). In addition to C.It. we also consider the intermediate stage between Lat. and C.It., approximately from the 13th century, when the earliest documents were written, to the end of the 19th century. We are aware that this intermediate phase is far from uniform (see, e.g., Migliorini, 1960; Marazzini, 2002). However, since our focus is on the two poles of the time span under investigation (i.e., Lat. and C.It.), we decided to consider the whole period from the 13th to the 19th century as a unit, and for the purposes of this study we labelled it pre-Contemporary Italian (henceforth preC.It.).

To conduct our research, we needed to build a lexicon of Lat. sensory adjectives. We collected the lexemes mentioned in previous studies on Latin sensory language (Catrein, 2003; De Felice, 2014; Strik Lievers & Sausa, 2016 for olfaction) and also used bilingual dictionaries to translate a list of English and Italian sensory adjectives derived from Strik Lievers (2015) and from lexical computational resources (FrameNet).[2] With this method, we obtained a list of 174 Lat. sensory adjectives.

As a second step, we selected only those adjectives that continued from Lat. until C.It. (e.g., Lat. *amarus* 'bitter' > C.It. *amaro* 'bitter'), whereas we excluded:

1.   Adjectives attested only in Lat. that completely disappeared in preC.It. and C.It. (e.g., *adalgidus* 'chilly, very cold').
2.   Adjectives attested only in Lat. and in preC.It., but not in C.It. (e.g., Lat. *foedus* 'foul (of smell)' > preC.It. *fedo* 'foul', cf. *l'alta valle feda / tremò*, 'the deep and foul abyss / trembled', Dante, *Inf.* XII, v. 40–41; in most C.It. dictionaries *fedo* is still listed, but it is marked as archaic and disused).

---

2.   See Baker et al. (1998). We extracted all perceptual adjectives that belong to FrameNet's sensory-related frames, e.g., Color, Color_qualities, and Chemical-sense_description.

3. Adjectives that survived into C.It. only as Latinisms in poetry (e.g., Lat. *candens* 'shining white, bright' > C.It. *candente* 'shining, resplendent'; e.g., *ghiacciai candenti* 'shining glaciers', Carducci, *Mezzogiorno alpino*, v. 2).

4. Adjectives that continued to exist in C.It. only as domain-specific terms (e.g., Lat. *mellitus* and preC.It. *mellito* 'mixed with honey, honey-sweet' > C.It *mellito* 'mellitus', only referring to diabetes).

5. Sensory adjectives that (already in Lat.) were not modality-specific, such as those expressing a generic positive or negative evaluation (e.g., *suavis* 'pleasant, charming', from *suadeo* 'induce, persuade').

After this selection, the final list of adjectives that we analysed includes 56 Latin lexemes (see Appendix A).[3]

3. Annotation

In order to investigate changes in the lexical polysemy of sensory adjectives over time, we annotated the (sensory or non-sensory) domain(s) to which each adjective refers. There is no full agreement among scholars as to how many sensory domains, and which, should be distinguished in linguistic studies. In accordance with most of the previous literature, we adopted the five so-called Aristotelian categories of touch (which also includes temperature perceptions), taste, smell, hearing, and sight. In addition, we gathered under the label "non-sensory" all uses of adjectives describing a property that does not involve perceptual experience (i.e., abstract and psychological senses, as in *dark secret, sweet love*).

In order to classify all sensory and non-sensory uses of Lat. and preC.It/C.It. adjectives into the above-mentioned six categories, we mainly relied upon lexicographic resources. For Latin we used *Oxford Latin Dictionary*, Forcellini's *Lexicon Totius Latinitatis*, *A Latin Dictionary* by Lewis & Short, and *Dizionario Latino Olivetti*. For C.It., we employed Battaglia's *Grande Dizionario della Lingua Italiana*, *Lo Zingarelli*, *Sabatini-Coletti*, and *Il Vocabolario Treccani*. For preC.It. we used historical dictionaries (*Grande Dizionario della Lingua Italiana*, *Tesoro della Lingua Italiana delle Origini*) and, when needed, we also consulted corpora (*Opera del Vocabolario Italiano* and *Morfologia dell'Italiano in Diacronia*). In all cases, we excluded from our analysis the senses designated in dictionaries as poetic, archaising,

---

3. The list of sensory adjectives actually comprises 55 distinct lemmas, with *frigidus* appearing two times, since it continued into two different Italian adjectives, *frigido* and *freddo* (cf. fn. 10). The list also includes a few participles (such as *ardens, fragrans, modulatus*) that are found as separate entries in dictionaries, and can therefore be also considered as adjectives.

or rare, because we are here interested in established extended meaning, i.e. lexical polysemy (see Section 1). We carried out this classification for all 56 Lat. adjectives, for their C.It. descendants, as well as for the adjectives of the intermediate preC.It. stage, when data were available. This was a relatively easy task, since the dictionaries that we used often explicitly classify lexical senses according to the different sensory modalities; moreover, the relevant sensory modality can also be inferred from the examples provided. Based on our data, the 56 Lat. adjectives can be used in 3.2 different semantic domains on average (mean value for C.It. adjectives: 2.7).

Among the sensory or non-sensory domains that we identified for each adjective, we also individuated the domain to which the primary sense of an adjective points. This was a more difficult task. The notion of "primary sense" itself is difficult to define and may be determined based on many different criteria, such as psychological saliency, frequency of use, or etymology. Psychological saliency cannot be used as a criterion here, because our study involves two varieties of language (Classical Lat. and preC.It.) for which we obviously have no speakers for psycholinguistic tests (see also Steinbach-Eicke, this volume). Moreover, whereas for Lat. and C.It. we have many corpora, for preC.It. fewer resources are available, so that frequency data for the three phases would not be easily comparable. We therefore had to rely on lexicographic resources: we considered the first sense listed in the dictionaries as the primary sense of an adjective. In case of disagreement among our sources, we also took etymology into consideration.

4.   Results

For each adjective, we compared the semantic domains annotated for Lat., preC. It., and C.It., and observed whether some change had occurred over time, focusing first on the primary sense only (Section 4.1), and subsequently on the whole array of senses (both perceptual, Section 4.2, and non-perceptual, Section 4.3) displayed by the adjectives.

4.1   Changes in the primary sense

Figure 1 shows the proportion of adjectives whose primary sense remains in the same sensory modality in Lat., preC.It. and C.It., compared to that of adjectives that undergo some change over time.

Before turning to the discussion of Figure 1, it is necessary to clarify what it means for the primary sense of an adjective to remain in the same sensory modality. It can of course be the case that the primary sense of an adjective, while remaining

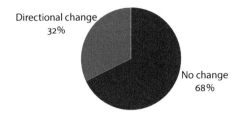

Figure 1. Changes in the primary sense

in the same sensory domain over time, assumes new shades of meaning. In fact, changes in the sensory meanings of adjectives are of two kinds. The first one concerns semantic shifts from one sensory domain to a different one. This is the case for intrafield meaning extensions such as Lat. *acer* 'stinging, pungent', touch > preC. It. and C.It. *acre* 'sour', taste. The second kind of change, which we propose to label *intramodal* meaning shift, concerns semantic changes within the same sensory modality. For instance, both Lat. *lucidus* and C.It. *lucido* refer to a visual property. However, *lucidus* means 'shining, bright, clear' (cf. *lux* 'light', *luceo* 'to shine') referring to things that reflect or emit light (e.g., *lucida saxa* 'shining stones'; *lucida nox* 'shining night'), or to substances/objects that allow light to pass through them (e.g., *lucidus amnis* 'clear river'), while C.It. *lucido* only describes a surface that reflects light (*gemme lucide* 'shining gems', but not **notte* 'night' *lucida*, **fiume* 'river' *lucido*). It is likely that many of our 56 adjectives have undergone similar intramodal semantic shifts over the long time span that we considered.

Although the distinction between intrafield (i.e., within the field of perception) and intramodal (i.e., within a given sensory modality) semantic shifts is worth closer examination in studies on the lexical polysemy of sensory adjectives, we do not address it in this work. Our paper mainly concerns changes in the sensory domains in which an adjective may be used. Therefore, in what follows we only focus on intrafield semantic changes, and by saying that an adjective undergoes "no change" in its primary sense we mean that it undergoes no intrafield change. In fact, as Figure 1 shows, this is what we observe for most of our adjectives (38 out of 56),[4] which show no change in the sensory domain of their primary meaning over time. For instance, the primary meaning of Lat. *tepidus* 'lukewarm' is related to touch (temperature perception); preC.It./C.It. *tiepido* 'lukewarm' still primarily refers to touch, as shown in Table 1.

---

4. *Acidulus, acidus, amarus, ardens, calidus, candidus, clarus, coloratus, dulcis, durus, fervens, f(o)etidus, fragrans, frigidus* (>C.It. *freddo*), *fuscus, gelidus, glacialis, insipidus, lucidus, luminosus, modulatus, mollis, niger, nitidus, obscurus, opacus, pallidus, purpureus, rancidus, roseus, rubicundus, russus, sonorus, splendidus, surdus, tepidus, torridus, viridis.*

Table 1. Lat. *tepidus* and preC.It./C.It. *tiepido*, primary sense 'lukewarm' (touch). Gray shading identifies the primary sense

	Adj.	Touch	Taste	Smell	Sight	Hearing	Non-sensory
Lat.	*tepidus*	✓					✓
preC.It.	*tiepido*	✓					✓
C.It.	*tiepido*	✓			✓		✓

The remaining 18 adjectives[5] display a semantic change in the domain of their primary sense. In all cases of change, the semantic shift goes either from a "lower" to a "higher" sensory domain, or from a sensory meaning to a non-sensory one.

An example of the first kind of shift, i.e., from a "lower" to a "higher" sensory modality, is Lat. *asper* (Table 2), which has a primary sense of 'sharp, stinging', pertaining to the domain of touch (also referring to temperature perception, e.g., *aspera hiems* 'harsh winter'). The adjective maintains this primary meaning in preC. It. (*aspro*). However, in C.It. *aspro* mainly means 'sour' (taste), and it is rarely used to refer to tactile perception (e.g., *superficie aspra* 'sharp surface').

Table 2. Lat. *asper* and preC.It. *aspro*, primary sense 'sharp, stinging' (touch) > C.It. *aspro*, primary sense 'sour' (taste). Gray shading identifies the primary sense

	Adj.	Touch	Taste	Smell	Sight	Hearing	Non-sensory
Lat.	*asper*	✓	✓	✓		✓	✓
preC.It.	*aspro*	✓	✓	✓		✓	✓
C.It.	*aspro*	✓	✓	✓		✓	✓

An example of the second kind of shift, i.e., from a sensory meaning to a non-sensory one (Table 3) is Lat. *consonus*, which had a primary meaning related to hearing ('sounding together, harmonious'). PreC.It./C.It. *consono* no longer has a sensory meaning and only maintains an abstract one ('consistent, consonant with').

Table 3. Lat. *consonus*, primary sense 'sounding together, harmonious' (hearing) > preC. It./C.It. *consono*, primary sense 'consistent, consonant with' (non-sensory). Gray shading identifies the primary sense

	Adj.	Touch	Taste	Smell	Sight	Hearing	Non-sensory
Lat.	*consonus*					✓	✓
preC.It.	*consono*						✓
C.It.	*consono*						✓

---

5. *Acer, acerbus, algidus, argutus, asper, austerus, consonus, fervidus, flagrans, frigidus* (> C.It. *frigido*), *fulgidus, inlustris, insulsus, mitis, mordax, praeclarus, sapidus, umbrosus.*

Changes in the primary sense, going either to a domain located further right on the hierarchy or towards non-sensory domains, support the claims made in previous literature about the directionality of semantic shifts in diachrony (see Section 1). However, changes in the secondary meanings of words may be significant as well. Therefore, in order to better evaluate the validity of the directionality hypothesis, we can now turn to a more fine-grained analysis on the whole array of sensory and non-sensory domains in which each adjective can be used. While in Section 4.1 we only considered one (sensory or non-sensory) domain per adjective, in what follows we deal with a higher number of domains per adjective, because most of the adjectives are polysemous.

As mentioned in Section 1, semantic changes can either occur within the perceptual domain (intrafield changes) or involve non-sensory domains (transfield changes). Obviously, both types of change may occur in the same lexeme, but for the sake of clarity we will consider intrafield and transfield changes separately (Section 4.2 and Section 4.3 respectively).

4.2   Intrafield changes (and persistence)

As shown in Figure 2, many adjectives (46%) are used in C.It. in the same sensory domains in which they were used in Lat. (Section 4.2.1). However, the majority of adjectives (54%) undergo a change, either directional (Section 4.2.2) or non-directional (Section 4.2.3).

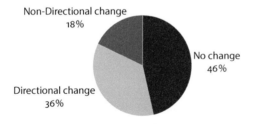

Figure 2. Intrafield changes (and persistence)

4.2.1   *No intrafield changes*
Among the 56 adjectives, 26[6] show no change in their sensory meanings in the transition from Lat. to C.It., as in the case of Lat. *clarus* (Table 4), always referring to sight and hearing.

---

6. *Algidus, asper, clarus, coloratus, fervens, fetidus, fragrans, fulgidus, gelidus, insipidus, lucidus, luminosus, mitis, modulatus, niger, nitidus, pallidus, purpureus, roseus, rubicundus, russus, sapidus, sonorus, splendidus, surdus, umbrosus.*

Table 4. Lat. *clarus* (sight, hearing + non-sensory) > preC.It./C.It. *chiaro* (sight, hearing + non-sensory)

	Adj.	Touch	Taste	Smell	Sight	Hearing	Non-sensory
Lat.	*clarus*				✓	✓	✓
preC.It.	*chiaro*				✓	✓	✓
C.It.	*chiaro*				✓	✓	✓

4.2.2   Directional intrafield changes

For most of the adjectives whose sensory uses change from Lat. to C.It. (20 out of 30 adjectives),[7] the semantic shift follows the "hierarchy" of sensory modalities. That is, either in C.It. they acquire senses that refer to "higher" modalities, with respect to the Latin ones, or they lose senses that refer to "lower" modalities.

The first kind of intrafield change can be exemplified by *calidus* ('hot') and *frigidus* ('cold'). In Latin, these adjectives only had meanings referring to touch (in particular, to temperature perception; see Table 5 and Table 6). However, Italian *caldo* and *freddo* have developed new sensory meanings, in the domain of sight (e.g., *colore caldo/freddo* 'warm/cold colour') and hearing (e.g., *voce calda* 'warm voice').

Table 5. Lat. *calidus* and preC.It. *caldo* (touch + non-sensory) > C.It. *caldo* (touch, sight, hearing + non-sensory)

	Adj.	Touch	Taste	Smell	Sight	Hearing	Non-sensory
Lat.	*calidus*	✓					✓
preC.It.	*caldo*	✓					✓
C.It.	*caldo*	✓			✓	✓	✓

Table 6. Lat. *frigidus* and preC.It. *freddo* (touch + non-sensory) > C.It. *freddo* (touch, sight + non-sensory)

	Adj.	Touch	Taste	Smell	Sight	Hearing	Non-sensory
Lat.	*frigidus*	✓					✓
preC.It.	*freddo*	✓					✓
C.It.	*freddo*	✓			✓		✓

---

7. *Acer, acidulus, ardens, argutus, austerus, calidus, consonus, dulcis, durus, fervidus, flagrans, frigidus* (>preC.It./C.It. *frigido*), *frigidus* (>preC.It./C.It. *freddo*), *glacialis, inlustris, insulsus, mordax, opacus, praeclarus, tiepidus*.

The second kind of change – that is, the loss of senses that are on the left of the hierarchy – can be exemplified by Lat. *acer* (Table 7). This adjective could be used in the domains of touch, taste, smell, sight, and hearing, but in C.It. the tactile sense ('sharp, pungent', also used to refer to a temperature perception) is no longer available.

Table 7. Lat. *acer* (touch, taste, smell, sight, hearing + non-sensory) > preC.It./C.It. *acre* (taste, smell, sight, hearing + non-sensory)

	Adj.	Touch	Taste	Smell	Sight	Hearing	Non-sensory
Lat.	*acer/acris*	✓	✓	✓	✓	✓	✓
preC.It.	*acre*		✓	✓	✓	✓	✓
C.It.	*acre*		✓	✓	✓	✓	✓

Some C.It. adjectives lose *all* perceptual meanings. This is the case, for instance, of Lat. *fervidus* 'very hot', 'passionate' (Table 8): it continues into C.It. *fervido*, which however only maintains the non-sensory meaning of 'passionate'.

Table 8. Lat. *fervidus* (touch + non-sensory) > preC.It. *fervido* (touch + non-sensory) > C.It. *fervido* (non-sensory)

	Adj.	Touch	Taste	Smell	Sight	Hearing	Non-sensory
Lat.	*fervidus*	✓					✓
preC.It.	*fervido*	✓					✓
C.It.	*fervido*						✓

A similar pattern of change is shown (Table 9) by Lat. *argutus* (<PIE *$h_2er\acute{g}$-u- 'white'), which displays a non-sensory meaning of 'sharp, clever', together with sensory meanings related to taste ('pungent'), smell ('keen, pungent'), sight ('sharply defined, bright'), and hearing ('producing sharp or clear sounds'). Most of these uses are still attested in preC.It., but in C.It. only the psychological sense survives (e.g., *frase arguta* 'witty remark').

Table 9. Lat. *argutus* and preC.It. *arguto* (taste, smell, sight, hearing + non-sensory) > C.It. *arguto* (non-sensory)

	Adj.	Touch	Taste	Smell	Sight	Hearing	Non-sensory
Lat.	*argutus*		✓	✓	✓	✓	✓
preC.It.	*arguto*		✓		✓	✓	✓
C.It.	*arguto*						✓

4.2.3   *Non-directional intrafield changes*

As concerns the remaining 10 Lat. adjectives (*acerbus, acidus, amarus, candidus, fuscus, mollis, obscurus, rancidus, torridus, viridis*), not only do the corresponding Italian lexemes not acquire new meanings; they also lose some of the preexisting ones. While the loss of meanings referring to "lower" sensory modalities (see Section 4.2.2) can be interpreted as somehow confirming directionality, for these adjectives the lost senses were not the leftmost ones on the hierarchy. Therefore, these changes shall be considered as non-directional. For instance, Lat. *amarus* (Table 10) could be used for taste ('bitter'), smell ('pungent'), or hearing ('harsh'), whereas PreC.It. and C.It. *amaro* can only refer to taste or smell.

Table 10. Lat. *amarus* (taste, smell, hearing + non-sensory) > preC.It./C.It. *amaro* (taste, smell + non-sensory)

	Adj.	Touch	Taste	Smell	Sight	Hearing	Non-sensory
Lat.	amarus		✓	✓		✓	✓
preC.It.	amaro		✓	✓			✓
C.It.	amaro		✓	✓			✓

It is, however, important to note that in all cases of non-directional change the primary meaning of the Lat. adjective is the primary meaning of the Italian adjective as well. Both Lat. *amarus* and preC.It./C.It. *amaro*, for instance, have taste as the sensory modality of their primary meaning. This means that these 10 adjectives have only lost (some of) their peripheral senses, whereas their primary sense remained unchanged. In this respect, frequency of use probably plays an important role in preserving an adjective's primary meaning: the sense in which speakers most frequently use a lexeme is the less likely to disappear over time.

To summarise so far, according to the data presented in Section 4.1 and Section 4.2, no new meaning that emerged in Italian contradicts the hypothesis of directionality: preC.It. and C.It. adjectives never develop a sense that is not present in Lat. *and* that is to the left in the hierarchy with respect to the Lat. senses. Moreover, the primary meaning of an adjective either remains in the same semantic domain, or shifts toward a higher one. We may now widen the scope of our research and focus on the changes that involve the non-sensory domain.

4.3   Transfield changes (and persistence)

As represented in Figure 3, we grouped sensory adjectives according to whether they show directional (16%) or non-directional (2%) transfield changes, or no transfield changes (82%).

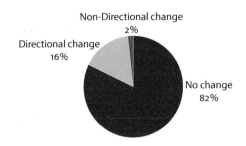

Non-Directional change
2%

Directional change
16%

No change
82%

Figure 3. Transfield changes (and persistence)

4.3.1   *No transfield change*

Most of the Lat. adjectives[8] (40 out of 56) could be also used in non-sensory domains, just as their Italian descendants. This is the case of *dulcis* in Table 11 (and
of *clarus* in Table 4).

Table 11. Lat. *dulcis* (taste, smell, hearing + non-sensory) > preC.It./C.It. *dolce*
(taste, smell, sight, hearing + non-sensory)

	Adj.	Touch	Taste	Smell	Sight	Hearing	Non-sensory
Lat.	*dulcis*		✓	✓		✓	✓
preC.It.	*dolce*	✓	✓	✓	✓	✓	✓
C.It.	*dolce*	✓	✓	✓	✓	✓	✓

Only six adjectives (*acidulus, fragrans, modulatus, purpureus, rubicundus, russus*)
have no abstract/cognitive meaning in Latin, nor do they develop one in Italian.
This indicates that there is a strong tendency to resort to sensory adjectives to express non-sensory meanings, both in Latin and in Italian. This is in line with the
observations made by Allan (2008) on Proto-Indo-European perception-related
roots. According to Allan, Sweetser's hypothesis of a "sensory-to-abstract/cogni-
tive" directionality in semantic change is weakened by the fact that it overlooks a
crucial point: "as far as they can be reconstructed with any certainty at all, most of
these roots seem to have referred to mental processes as well" (Allan, 2008, p. 51).
Therefore, the association between sensory and abstract/cognitive senses in many
(English) lexemes would not be the result of a unidirectional diachronic semantic
shift undergone by (IE) lexemes with a purely sensory meaning, as Sweetser seems to
suggest. Rather, according to Allan (2008, p. 59), such association is likely to reflect

---

8.   *Acer, acerbus, acidus, amarus, argutus, asper, austerus, calidus, candidus, clarus, consonus,
dulcis, durus, fervens, fervidus, fetidus, flagrans, frigidus (> C.It. freddo), frigidus (> C.It. frigido),
fulgidus, fuscus, inlustris, insipidus, insulsus, lucidus, luminosus, mitis, mollis, mordax, niger, nitidus, obscurus, praeclarus, rancidus, sapidus, splendidus, surdus, tepidus, umbrosus, viridis.*

the close connection between sensory and mental processes "in practice", which therefore concerns English and IE, and potentially all languages, in the same way.

Although our data confirm that the link between sensory and abstract/cognitive senses was very strong already in Lat., they also provide some evidence in support of the hypothesis of directionality in diachronic change. As a matter of fact, either Lat. adjectives already had a non-sensory meaning and they kept it until C.It. (Section 4.3.1), or they only had sensory meanings in Lat. and developed a non-sensory meaning in preC.It. or C.It. (Section 4.3.2). It never happens, according to our data, that a Lat. non-sensory meaning disappears, unless it was already very rare and restricted to a specific domain in Lat., as shown in the subsequent sections.

4.3.2   Directional transfield change

There are nine adjectives that have a non-sensory meaning in preC.It. and/or C.It. only (*algidus, ardens, gelidus, glacialis, opacus, pallidus, roseus, sonorus, torridus*). For instance, Lat. *gelidus* 'icy-cold' (Table 12) had a sensory meaning related to touch (temperature perception). A non-sensory use is only attested in poetry (e.g., Ovid. 15. Met. 153. *gelida mors*), and according to our sources it never refers to human beings. In Italian, however, *gelido* is also commonly used with reference to abstract concepts (*accoglienza gelida* 'icy reception') and human beings (*donna gelida* 'cold woman').

Table 12. Lat. *gelidus* (touch) > preC.It./C.It. *gelido* (touch + non-sensory)

	Adj.	Touch	Taste	Smell	Sight	Hearing	Non-sensory
Lat.	gelidus	✓					
preC.It.	gelido	✓					✓
C.It.	gelido	✓					✓

4.3.3   Non-directional transfield change

Among the 56 adjectives considered in this study, only one, *coloratus*, had an abstract meaning in Latin that later disappeared (Table 13). Lat. *coloratus* meant 'coloured' (sight), but also had a non-sensory use, 'specious', which is however lost in C.It.

Table 13. Lat. *coloratus* (sight + non-sensory) > preC.It. *colorato* (sight + non-sensory) > C.It. *colorato* (sight)

	Adj.	Touch	Taste	Smell	Sight	Hearing	Non-sensory
Lat.	coloratus				✓		✓
preC.It.	coloratus				✓		✓
C.It.	coloratus				✓		

This diachronic change might seem to contradict the "sensory-to-abstract/cognitive" directionality (see Section 1). However, *coloratus* in its non-sensory use was a technical term, specific to rhetoric (*colorata oratio* 'specious speech'; the language of rhetoric in Latin often drew from sensory lexicon, see for instance Bradley, 2009). Moreover, it is likely that once classical rhetoric lost the central role it had in ancient society, where it was a crucial tool in politics, the need for using rhetorical terms faded as well. Therefore, to explain the loss of this non-sensory meaning, we probably have to take into account factors such as the complex and close relationship between frequency of use in language and wider changes in the sociocultural context (on this topic, see also San Roque et al., 2015 and references therein). That being the case, we do not believe that *coloratus* can be taken as strong counterexample to the directionality hypothesis.

It is worth noting that counterdirectional shifts in transfield changes (i.e., transfield II changes, according to the classification proposed by O'Meara et al., this volume), going from non-sensory to sensory domains (see Vanhove, 2008, p. 346), are not expected to be found in our data, due to the fact that we analysed the development of Lat. *sensory* adjectives. Our data, therefore, do not include Lat. adjectives with no sensory meaning, even if they eventually developed a sensory meaning in C.It. For instance, C.It. *squisito* means 'delicious', referring to food or odours. However, Lat. *exquisitus* (from *exquiro* 'seek for, search out diligently') did not have a sensory meaning: it only had the abstract meaning of 'carefully sought out, ripely considered, choice, excellent, exquisite' (*A Latin Dictionary*). Thus, Lat. *exquisitus* is not included in our 56 adjectives. This is something we leave for future work: starting from a list – as "complete" a list as possible – of C.It. sensory adjectives and going back in time to look for their Lat. antecedents, be they sensory or not sensory. It is only by evaluating the statistical incidence of cases such as *exquisitus* – that is, shifts from abstract to perceptual senses – that we may understand whether the trend that consistently emerged from our data (i.e., the shift from perceptual to abstract senses) is an artefact of the particular type of data we examined – adjectives that originally had a perceptual meaning – or has a more general validity.

5. Conclusions

As mentioned in the introduction, the hypothesis of directionality has mainly been investigated from a synchronic perspective. In this paper we provided evidence for its validity in diachrony. We explored semantic changes in 56 sensory adjectives from Latin to Italian, considering both intrafield and transfield changes. In the first case, the meaning is expected to shift from a "lower" sensory domain to a "higher" one, whereas in the second case, it is expected to shift from a perceptual sense to an abstract/cognitive one.

As concerns the development of new meanings in preC.It. and C.It., the hypothesis of directionality is fully confirmed by our data and, in our opinion, turns out to have strong predictive value, at least as concerns intrafield changes. If a new meaning arises over time, it is always in a "higher" sensory modality. We also found a clear sensory-to-abstract/cognitive trend, which by itself cannot, however, fully confirm transfield directionality, due to the nature of our data (cf. discussion in 4.3.3). As for intrafield directionality, the fact that it is confirmed by both synchronic and diachronic studies may point to the existence of underlying cognitive and perceptual motivations. Nevertheless, it has to be noted that other factors as well are likely to play a role in determining semantic shifts and are worth further exploration (e.g., frequency of use, and the different distribution of parts of speech in the sensory lexicon; see Strik Lievers, 2015; Winter, 2016; Strik Lievers & Winter, 2018).

Directionality does not seem to be equally predictive as concerns the loss of meanings. We observed that senses may disappear in the transition from Lat. to C.It. not only in the "lower" modalities, as we would expect (cf. *acer*, Table 7), but also in the "higher" modalities / non-sensory domain (cf. *amarus*, Table 10, or *coloratus*, Table 13). Crucially, this seems to only happen for the peripheral (i.e., non-primary) senses, which are usually the less frequently used ones. On the contrary, high frequency of use certainly plays a role in preserving the primary meaning of a Latin adjective from sense shift and from loss. For instance, we discussed the case of *amarus*, that in PreC.It. and C.It. does not refer to smell or sound, as was the case in Latin, but only to taste; it was precisely taste that was the primary and most frequently attested sense of the adjective in Latin as well. Our data, therefore, shed new light on other possible factors, besides directionality, that may drive semantic shifts, not only in the acquisition of new meanings, but also in the loss of older ones.

Although directionality cannot describe all cases of sense loss, considering the whole spectrum of changes undergone by our 56 adjectives, non-directional changes are far fewer in number than directional ones. This is true not only for the semantic shifts that involve the primary meaning, which are *always* directional (Section 4.1), but also for most intrafield changes (36% directional vs. 18% non-directional, see Section 4.2). A similar pattern emerged from the data regarding transfield shifts available so far (16% directional vs. 2% non-directional, see Section 4.3).

To sum up, the main result of our study on the semantic evolution of sensory adjectives from Latin to Italian is that we observed no shifts in the primary meaning, nor did we find development of new senses that were *contrary* to the hierarchy.

Such a neat result may be partly due to the fact that we focused on changes in conventional and fully lexicalised meanings (i.e., lexical polysemy). Synchronic studies that also consider creative uses of sensory adjectives show that counterdirectional sense transfers, in fact, may be found, though most transfers are still directional (e.g., Strik Lievers, 2015 on Italian; De Felice, 2014, 2016 on Latin).

Diachronic research focused on regular patterns of semantic shifts may provide an important contribution in confirming – or otherwise confuting – hypotheses that are usually only investigated in a synchronic dimension. In this regard, Latin and its descendent Romance languages offer a privileged testing ground, because they allow us to follow the evolution of a language along a period of two thousand years and to reconstruct semantic changes over such a long time span.

Acknowledgements

We wish to thank Giovanna Marotta, Romano Lazzeroni, and the editors of this volume for their many constructive comments and helpful suggestions. This paper is the result of the close collaboration of both authors. For the specific concerns of the Italian Academy, Francesca Strik Lievers is responsible for Sections 1, 4.2, 4.3, and Irene De Felice is responsible for Sections 2, 3, 4.1; Section 5 has been written by the two authors.

References

Allan, K. (2008). *Metaphor and metonymy: A diachronic approach.* Oxford: Wiley-Blackwell.

Baker, C. F., Fillmore, C. J., & Lowe, J. B. (1998). The Berkeley FrameNet Project. In *ACL '98 Proceedings of the 36th Annual Meeting of the Association for Computational Linguistics and 17th International Conference on Computational Linguistics,* Vol. 1, 86–90.

Barcelona, A. (2013). Metonymy is not just a lexical phenomenon: on the operation of metonymy in grammar and discourse. In C. Alm-Arvius, N. Johannesson & D. C. Minugh (Eds.), *Selected Papers from the Stockholm 2008 Metaphor Festival* (pp. 13–46). Stockholm: Stockholm University Press.

Bradley, M. (2009). *Colour and meaning in ancient Rome.* Cambridge: Cambridge University Press.

Bretones Callejas, C. (2001). *Synaesthetic metaphors in English.* Technical Reports, TR 01- 008. Berkeley: ICSI.

Catrein, C. (2003). *Vertauschte Sinne. Untersuchungen zur Synästhesie in der römischen Dichtung.* München/Leipzig: K. G. Saur. https://doi.org/10.1515/9783110960969

Cruse, D. A. (1986). *Lexical semantics.* Cambridge: Cambridge University Press.

Cuzzolin, P., & Haverling, G. (2009). Syntax, sociolinguistics, and literary genres. In P. Baldi, & P. Cuzzolin (Eds.), *New perspectives on historical Latin syntax: Syntax of the sentence* (pp. 19–64). Berlin-New York: De Gruyter.

D'Achille, P. (2010). *L'italiano contemporaneo*. Bologna: Il Mulino.

De Felice, I. (2014). La sinestesia linguistica nella poesia latina. *Studi e Saggi Linguistici*, 52(1), 61–107.

De Felice, I. (2016). Per alta silentia: Sinestesie tra i versi. In P. Poccetti (Ed.), *Latinitatis rationes. Descriptive and historical accounts for the Latin language* (pp. 352–368). Berlin-Boston: De Gruyter. https://doi.org/10.1515/9783110431896-024

De Mauro, T. (1972). *Storia linguistica dell'Italia unita*. Bari: Laterza (1st ed. 1963).

Evans, N., & Wilkins, D. (2000). In the mind's ear: The semantic extensions of perception verbs in Australian languages. *Language*, 76, 546–592. https://doi.org/10.2307/417135

Ibarretxe-Antuñano, I. (1999). Polysemy and metaphor in perception verbs: a cross-linguistic study. Doctoral dissertation, University of Edinburgh.

Marazzini, C. (2002). *La lingua italiana: Profilo storico*. Bologna: Il Mulino (1st ed. 1994).

Marotta, G. (2011). Perché i colori chiassosi non fanno chiasso? Vincoli semantici e sintattici sulle associazioni sinestetiche. *Archivio Glottologico Italiano* 96(2), 195–220.

Matisoff, J. A. (1978). *Variational semantics in Tibeto-Burman*. Philadelphia, PA: Institute for the Study of Human Issues.

Mengaldo, P. V. (1994). *Storia della lingua italiana. Il Novecento*. Bologna: Il Mulino.

Migliorini, B. (1960). *Storia della lingua italiana*. Firenze: Sansoni.

Migliorini, B. (1990). *La lingua italiana del Novecento*. Firenze: Le Lettere.

Paissa, P. (1995). *La sinestesia: Storia e analisi del concetto*. Brescia: La Scuola.

Rakova, M. (2003). *The extent of the literal: Metaphor, polysemy and theories of concepts*. London: Palgrave Macmillan. https://doi.org/10.1057/9780230512801

Rosiello, L. (1963). Le sinestesie nell'opera poetica di Montale. *Rendiconti, 7*.

San Roque, L., Kendrick, K. H., Norcliffe, E., Brown, P., Defina, R., Dingemanse, M., Dirksmeyer, T., Enfield, N., Floyd, S., Hammond, J., Rossi, G., Tufvesson, S., van Putten, S., & Majid, A. (2015). Vision verbs dominate in conversation across cultures, but the ranking of non-visual verbs varies. *Cognitive Linguistics*, 26(1), 31–60. https://doi.org/10.1515/cog-2014-0089

Shen, Y., & Gil, D. (2008). Sweet fragrances from Indonesia: A universal principle governing directionality in synaesthetic metaphors. In W. van Peer & J. Auracher (Eds.), *New beginning or the study of literature* (pp. 49–72). Cambridge: Cambridge Scholars Publishing.

Sobrero, A. A. (Ed.). (1993). *Introduzione all'italiano contemporaneo* (2 vols.). Roma/Bari: Laterza.

Strik Lievers, F. (2015). Synaesthesia: A corpus-based study of cross-modal directionality. *Functions of Language*, 22(1), 69–95. https://doi.org/10.1075/fol.22.1.04str

Strik Lievers, F. (2017). Figures and the senses. Towards a definition of synaesthesia. *Review of Cognitive Linguistics*, 15(1), 83–101. https://doi.org/10.1075/rcl.15.1.04str

Strik Lievers, F., & Sausa, E. (2016). Smelling over time: The lexicon of olfaction from Latin to Italian. Paper presented at the 49th Annual Meeting of the Societas Linguistica Europaea, University of Naples Federico II.

Strik Lievers, F., & Winter, B. (2018). Sensory language across lexical categories, *Lingua 204*, 45–61. https://doi.org/10.1016/j.lingua.2017.11.002

Sweetser, E. (1990). *From etymology to pragmatics*. Cambridge: Cambridge University Press. https://doi.org/10.1017/CBO9780511620904

Ullmann, S. (1957). *The principles of semantics*. Glasgow: Jackson.

Vanhove, M. (2008). Semantic associations between sensory modalities, prehension and mental perceptions. In M. Vanhove (Ed.), *From polysemy to semantic change: Towards a typology of lexical semantic associations* (pp. 341–370). Amsterdam/Philadelphia: John Benjamins. https://doi.org/10.1075/slcs.106.17van

Viberg, Å. (1984). The verbs of perception: A typological study. *Linguistics* 21(1), 123–162.

Viberg, Å. (2001). The verbs of perception. In M. Haspelmath, E. König, W. Oesterreicher & W. Raible (Eds.), *Language Typology and Language Universals. An International Handbook* (pp. 1294–1309). Berlin-Boston: De Gruyter.

Viberg, Å. (2015). Sensation, perception and cognition. *Swedish in a typological-contrastive perspective. Functions of Language*, 22(1), 96–131. https://doi 10.1075/fol.22.1.05vib

Werning, M., Fleischhauer, J., & Beseoglu, H. (2006). The cognitive accessibility of synaesthetic metaphors. In R. Sun & N. Miyake (Eds.). *Proceedings of the Twenty eighth Annual Conference of the Cognitive Science Society* (pp. 2365–70). London: Lawrence Erlbaum.

Williams, J. M. (1976). Synaesthetic adjectives: A possible law of semantic change. *Language*, 52, 461–479. https://doi.org/10.2307/412571

Winter, B. (2016). The sensory structure of the English lexicon. Ph.D. thesis, University of California Merced.

Zhao, Q., Huang, C. R., & Long, Y. (2018). Synaesthesia in Chinese: A corpus-based study on gustatory adjectives in Mandarin, *Linguistics*, 56(5), 1167–1194. https://doi.org/10.1515/ling-2018-0019

Dictionaries and corpora

A Latin Dictionary = Lewis, C. T., & Short, C. (Eds.) (1933). *A Latin Dictionary*. Oxford: Clarendon Press (1st ed. 1879).

Dizionario latino Olivetti = Olivetti, E. (Ed.). *Dizionario Latino-Italiano, Italiano-Latino*. Online version: <www.dizionario-latino.com>

Forcellini = Forcellini, A., Furlanetto, I., Corradini, F., & Perin, I. (Eds.) (1940). *Lexicon totius latinitatis*. Patavii: Typis Seminari (1st ed. 1864–1887).

Grande Dizionario della Lingua Italiana (GDLI) = Battaglia, S. (Ed.) (1961–2002). *Grande Dizionario della Lingua Italiana*. Torino: Utet.

Il Vocabolario Treccani = *Il Vocabolario Treccani*= <www.treccani.it/vocabolario>

Lo Zingarelli = Cannella, M., & Lazzarini, B. (Eds.) (2016). *Lo Zingarelli 2017. Vocabolario della lingua italiana*. Bologna: Zanichelli.

Morfologia dell'Italiano in DIAcronia (MIDIA) = <www.corpusmidia.unito.it>

Opera del Vocabolario Italiano database (OVI) = <www.ovi.cnr.it>

Oxford Latin Dictionary = Glare, P. (Ed.) (1968–1982). *Oxford Latin Dictionary*. Oxford: Oxford University Press.

Sabatini-Coletti = Sabatini, F., & Coletti, V. (2008). *Dizionario della lingua italiana*. Milano: Rizzoli Larousse.

Tesoro della Lingua Italiana delle Origini (TLIO) = <tlio.ovi.cnr.it/TLIO>

Appendix A. Latin sensory adjectives

acer/acris,[9] *acerbus, acidulus, acidus, algidus, amarus, ardens, argutus, asper, austerus/auster, calidus, candidus, clarus, coloratus, consonus, dulcis, durus, fervens, fervidus, foetidus/fetidus, flagrans, fragrans, frig(i)dus*,[10] *fulgidus, fuscus, gelidus, glacialis, inlustris, insipidus, insulsus, lucidus, luminosus, mitis, modulatus, mollis, mordax, niger, nitidus, obscurus, opacus, pallidus, praeclarus, purpureus, rancidus, roseus, rubicundus, russus, sapidus, sonorus, splendidus, surdus, tepidus, torridus, umbrosus, viridis.*

---

9. *Acer* and *acris* (as also *austerus/auster* and *foetidus/fetidus*) are considered as variants and thus count as a single lexeme, since they continue in a single C.It. form (*acre, austero, fetido*).

10. Lat. *frigdus* was the syncopated variant of *frigidus*, which is already attested in inscriptions of the Classical period (as also *caldus* for *calidus*). However, we considered the two variants as separated (differently from the variants *acer/acris* or *foetidus/fetidus*; see fn. 9), since they continued into two different Italian forms (*frigido, freddo*).

CHAPTER 6

Synaesthetic metaphors are neither synaesthetic nor metaphorical

Bodo Winter
University of Birmingham

Speakers often use metaphor when talking about the contents of perception. For example, a word such as _sweet_ can be used to talk metaphorically about sensory impressions that are not directly related to taste, as in so-called "synaesthetic metaphors" such as _sweet fragrance_ and _sweet melody_. In this chapter, I present arguments against the synaesthetic and metaphorical nature of such expressions. First, a look at the neuropsychological literature reveals that the phenomenon commonly called "synaesthesia" bears little resemblance to the metaphors investigated by linguists. Moreover, in contrast to synaesthesia as a neuropsychological phenomenon, most "synaesthetic" metaphors involve mappings between highly similar and perceptually integrated sensory modalities, such as taste and smell. Finally, combinations of words that involve dissimilar sensory modalities, such as _sweet melody_, appear to perform largely evaluative functions. Thus, evaluation might be driving the use of these terms, more so than "synaesthetic" perception. I will then compare my analyses to the idea that many metaphors are grounded in primary metaphors and/or metonymies. All in all, this paper suggests that many and perhaps most "synaesthetic metaphors" are neither synaesthetic nor metaphorical. From a broader perspective, the case study of synaesthetic metaphors presented here fleshes out the way language and perception are related and how sensory content is encoded in the lexicon of human languages.

Keywords: synaesthesia, the senses, perceptual metaphors, primary metaphor

1. Introduction

One of the primary functions of language is to communicate perceptual content. Speakers constantly talk to each other about what they see, hear, feel, taste or smell, such as when warning a friend that the leftover chicken in the fridge smells rotten. Not all sensory experience is created equal, and some senses are easier to talk about

https://doi.org/10.1075/celcr.19.06win

than others (Levinson & Majid, 2014). For example, it has been said that odours are particularly difficult to describe (Buck, 1949; Levinson & Majid, 2014). The case of smell is illustrative because the English language has relatively few smell terms, such as *fragrant, aromatic, pungent, rancid* and *stinky*. These terms furthermore appear to be ill-suited for describing the detailed perceptual impressions of actual smells, instead they describe general pleasantness or unpleasantness in the olfactory modality. To make up for this lack of descriptive vocabulary, English speakers often describe smells using taste terms, such as when describing a smell as *sour, coconutty, caramelised, juicy* or *sweet*. Expressions such as *sweet fragrance* are verbal expressions that appear to combine the sense of taste (*sweet*) with the sense of smell (*fragrance*).

When an English speaker says *sweet fragrance*, is the sensory adjective *sweet* used in a metaphorical fashion? Our intuition tells us that the word *sweet* is about taste and the word *fragrance* about smell. If this is true, then *sweet fragrance* marks a mapping between two distinct sensory modalities, namely, from taste to smell (Ullmann, 1959; Shen, 1997; Shen & Gil, 2007; Strik Lievers, 2015). If analysed as involving a "mapping", the *sweet fragrance* would be characterised as metaphorical. Under another analysis, the adjective-noun pair *sweet fragrance* is not a metaphorical expression because olfaction falls under the referential domain of the word *sweet* and is part of its literal meaning (cf. Rakova, 2003; Paradis & Eeg-Olofsson, 2013). This analysis sees the word *sweet* as having both gustatory and olfactory meaning, which would render the expression *sweet fragrance* non-metaphorical. If we see *sweet* as inherently having meanings related to both senses, then no metaphorical meaning extension takes place. This paper deals with these two competing analyses, a metaphor-based one and a literal one. That is, I ask the question: How narrow or broad is the literal meaning of sensory words? Answering this raises deep theoretical questions relating to perception, synaesthesia, lexical semantics and metaphor.

Expressions such as *sweet fragrance* have variously been called "poetic synaesthesia" (Shen, 1997), "linguistic synaesthesia" (Holz, 2007), or "verbal synaesthesia" (Strik Lievers, 2015). These expressions are generally analysed as metaphors, that is, as conceptual mappings between two domains (Lakoff & Johnson, 1980), because they combine two seemingly distinct sensory modalities. For example, the adjective-noun pairs *sharp sound* and *smooth taste* appear to be mappings from touch to audition and from touch to gustation, respectively. In both cases, a touch-related word is used to talk about sensations perceived primarily through another modality. Linguists and non-linguists working on these metaphors have repeatedly made comparisons between these linguistic expressions and synaesthesia as a perceptual and neurological phenomenon (Ramachandran & Hubbard, 2001; Martino & Marks, 2001; Holz, 2007; Strik Lievers, 2017). For example, Martino and Marks (2001) describe the case of a synaesthete who experienced vivid colour sensations when she was in pain; Cytowic (1993) described a synaesthete who experienced vivid shape sensations when tasting food.

In this paper, I will argue that such expressions are neither synaesthetic nor metaphorical. In line with the analyses of sensory words presented in Rakova (2003) and Paradis and Eeg-Olofsson (2013), I will argue that many and perhaps all sensory adjectives have highly multisensory or supramodal meanings that encompass a much broader referential scope than is commonly admitted. And I will argue that in many cases where sensory words are used to describe perceptual sensations, they are used in an evaluative fashion rather than a perceptual one. This is in line with the general view that language is intimately tied to concerns of emotional, affective and evaluative expressions (Wilce, 2009; Hunston, 2011; Majid, 2012; Eeg-Olofsson, 2013). As stated by Wilce (2009, p. 3), "nearly every dimension of every language at least potentially encodes emotion" – and sensory words are no exception. As will be shown below, understanding the emotional dimension of perceptual vocabulary turns out to be key to understanding their involvement in metaphor.

My argument proceeds as follows. After reviewing the literature on synaesthetic metaphors (§ 2), I criticise the use of the label "synaesthesia" to refer to these metaphors based on a short review of the relevant neuropsychological literature (§ 3), and based on empirical evidence which suggests that expressions such as *sweet melody* involve the mapping of evaluative attributes rather than mappings of perceptual content. Then I argue that most cases of synaesthetic metaphors involve highly supramodal sensory adjectives (§ 4). Contra to Shen and Gil (2007), Strik Lievers (2015) and others, cases such as *sweet fragrance* should not be considered synaesthetic metaphors because taste and smell are highly integrated in perception, and a word such as *sweet* is best analysed as literally referring to both gustation and olfaction. I then compare and contrast my analysis with similar analyses that are based on primary metaphors and metonymies (§ 5), arguing that while these approaches capture some aspects of the current proposal rather nicely, they do not fully recognise the underlying continuity of the senses.

2. Background on synaesthetic metaphors

Synaesthetic metaphors are said to be expressions that "transfer one sense to another" (Ullmann, 1945, p. 813), as the following definitions exemplify:

> (…) synaesthesia is the syntactic relation between elements semantically incompatible, denoting sensations from different sensorial spheres.
>
> (Erzsébet, 1974, p. 25)

> An instance of synaesthesia (Greek, 'feeling together') is usually defined as convey-
> ing the perception of, or describing, one sense modality in terms of another (…)
> (Shen, 1997, p. 47)

> (…) a perceptual experience related to one sense is described through lexical means
> typically associated with a different sense (…)   (Strik Lievers, 2015, pp. 69–70)

All of these definitions emphasise that in order to count as an instance of a synaesthetic metaphor, *different* sensory modalities need to be involved. Strik Lievers
(2016, p. 45) makes this explicit by saying that "in synaesthetic expressions, syntactic links between sensory lexemes create connections that generate conflict at
the conceptual level" (see also Strik Lievers, 2017, and Prandi 2012's notion of
conflict). She discusses the example of *yellow voice*, which is seen as creating a conceptual conflict because sounds "do not have a visual manifestation" (Strik Lievers,
2016, p. 45). An adjective-noun pair such as *abrasive touch* would not be treated
as a synaesthetic metaphor precisely because the touch-related adjective *abrasive*
is used in a highly tactile context, i.e., there is no conceptual conflict between the
adjective and the noun.

   Researchers in this literature have proposed a hierarchy of the senses to characterise which sensory modalities are likely sources and which sensory modalities are
likely targets in synaesthetic metaphor (see, e.g., Ullmann, 1945 versus Williams,
1976; see Strik Lievers & De Felice, this volume). All such proposals agree on having
TOUCH, TASTE AND SMELL at the lower end, and VISION AND HEARING at the top,
such as in (1):

(1)   TOUCH > TASTE > SMELL > VISION / HEARING

The hierarchy entails a directionality of metaphorical mappings, from the "lower"
senses to the "higher" ones, i.e., TOUCH TO HEARING mappings should be more
frequent than the reverse, a prediction that is confirmed in a substantial number
of languages, including English, German, Italian, Hebrew, Hungarian and Chinese
(Ullmann, 1945; Erzsébet, 1974; Day, 1996; Shen, 1997; Yu, 2003; Strik Lievers,
2015; see also Anderson, this volume; Strik Lievers & De Felice, this volume).
Participants furthermore rate combinations of sensory words in accord with the
hierarchy as more adequate and sensible than combinations going against the hierarchy (Shen & Gil, 2007; Shen & Aisenmann, 2008; Shen & Gadir, 2009). There
are many methodological concerns regarding research on synaesthetic metaphors
(for detailed discussion, see Winter, 2016b, Chapter 2, 7–8), the most relevant for
the present discussion being that the hierarchy rests on the idea that the senses are
distinct to begin with, i.e., the notion that senses such as taste and smell should
occupy separate rather than overlapping positions on the hierarchy. We will return
to this issue below.

3. Beware of synaesthesia

Should we call expressions such as *smooth taste* and *sweet fragrance* "synaesthetic" metaphors? This is more than just a purely terminological question. Using the term "synaesthesia" suggests a shared mechanism, or some underlying principles that govern both perceptual synaesthesia and linguistic synaesthesia (cf. Deroy & Spence, 2013).

In neuroscience and psychology, "synaesthesia" means something more specific than merely "crossing the senses". People who are characterised as synaesthetes perceive vivid perceptual sensations in one sensory modality reliably triggered by particular stimuli in another modality. For example, a synaesthete might have colour sensations when looking at graphemes (Ramachandran & Hubbard, 2001), or she might have vivid spatial representations of numerals (Galton, 1880a, 1880b). For a long time, research on synaesthesia was met with scepticism because most of the evidence for the phenomenon stemmed from self-report. However, more recent experimental and neuroimaging studies empirically demonstrated the genuine perceptual nature of synaesthesia (Ramachandran & Hubbard, 2001).

Although several definitions for synaesthesia exist (see Simner, 2012 for a discussion), researchers commonly understand synaesthesia to be characterised by automaticity and involuntariness – synaesthetes cannot help but to experience a synaesthetic perception when a trigger is presented. Moreover, synaesthetic experiences are highly persistent within an individual, with the same stimulus-trigger pairings being observed across repeated experimental sessions. It is not entirely clear how many people are adequately classified as synaesthetes, with estimates varying widely and depending on the particular type of synaesthesia, as well as on the assessment criteria used. Using a strict battery of tests, Simner et al. (2006) find that the most common form of synaesthesia (associations between colours and names of the days) has a prevalence of about ~3% among university students.

Synaesthesia needs to be differentiated from the notion of "crossmodal associations" or "crossmodal correspondences" (Marks, 1978; for a recent review see Spence, 2011; see also Deroy & Spence, 2013). For example, five-year old children reliably match the brightness of perceived stimuli to the loudness of a sound (Bond & Stevens, 1969). Moreover, magnitude-related domains that can be expressed in terms of "more" or "less" are often perceptually associated with each other (Marks, 1978; Winter, Marghetis & Matlock, 2015). There are also many studies on the related topic of perceptual integration, such as Shams, Kamitani and Shimojo (2000), who demonstrated that a single light flash can be perceived as two light flashes when presented with two auditory beeps. The literature on perceptual integration and cross-modal correspondences is vast and many different connections between the senses have been reported for both adults and children (Spence, 2011). It is safe to say, then, that while not everybody is a synaesthete, everybody has, to some extent, some form of perceptual integration and some forms of cross-modal correspondence.

Martino and Marks (2001) distinguish between strong and weak forms of synaesthesia, where the existence of weak synaesthesia is understood to characterise the general population. They suggest that a continuum between strong and weak forms of perceptual synaesthesias exist, but even they stress that the two phenomena are not to be equated:

> Over the two centuries since strong synesthesia was first identified in the scientific literature, several heterogeneous phenomena have been labeled as synesthetic. These phenomena range from strong experiences (…), on the one hand, to weaker crossmodal literary expressions, on the other. We believe it is a mistake to label all of these phenomena simply as synesthesia because the underlying mechanisms cannot be identical (…)   (Martino & Marks, 2001, p. 62)

Considering what we know of (strong) synaesthesia as a neurological phenomenon, it is perhaps a misnomer to label expressions such as *smooth taste* "synaesthetic". The same argument has been made for using the term synaesthesia as a cover term for all kinds of cross-modal correspondences (Deroy & Spence, 2013). It is not always clear whether the term "synaesthesia" is used "metaphorically" in linguistics, i.e., the researcher may want to merely make a comparison to perceptual synaesthesia, as a loose analogy. It is clear that *equating* linguistic and perceptual synaesthesia is not appropriate (Martino & Marks, 2001). If the two phenomena were actually rooted in the same underlying system, we would expect much closer connections. Within linguistics, nobody, so far, has empirically demonstrated a link between the usage of these metaphors and the neurological phenomenon of synaesthesia, both in terms of overall frequency of usage (do synaesthetes use synaesthetic metaphors more frequently?) and in terms of the types of mappings involved (are common synaesthesias common synaesthetic metaphors?). There is no empirical evidence showing that synaesthetes actually use synaesthetic metaphors more frequently or in a different way than the general population. And there is no empirical evidence showing links between the specific mappings involved in synaesthesia proper and synaesthetic metaphors. In fact, linguistic and non-linguistic synaesthesia appear to involve quite different mappings. For example, whereas most synaesthetic metaphors discussed in the literature involve touch as a source domain (e.g., *sharp sound, smooth taste, rough smell*), the most common form of synaesthesia according to Simner et al. (2006) is an association between colour and days of the week, something that is not observed in metaphor. Thus, common forms of synaesthesia involve very different mappings from those reported for cross-modal metaphors. The lack of any empirical connection between synaesthesia and "synaesthetic" metaphors (both in terms of usage within individuals and in terms of attested types of mappings) suggests that the two ideas cannot be equated.

Linguists working on perception metaphors are aware that synaesthesia in language and synaesthesia in perception are not exactly the same. It is perhaps no coincidence that many of the researchers who use the term "synaesthesia" in the context of metaphor are keen to stress that their use of the term deviates from perceptual synaesthesia (for discussion, see Strik Lievers, 2017). For example, Ullmann (1945, p. 812) states that "the present paper investigates synaesthesia first and foremost as a linguistic-semantic problem". Strik Lievers (2016, p. 44) clearly states: "In literary and linguistic studies, (…) synaesthesia is a figure associating *linguistic expressions* that refer to different sensory modalities (…)" (italics in original). Holz (2007, p. 193) states that "If we use the term *synesthesia*, we have (…) to distinguish between a neuropsychological and a linguistic phenomenon."

In contrast to this, many linguists have tried to explain regularities of synaesthetic metaphors with respect to some underlying perceptual mechanism, treating linguistic synaesthesia as a linguistic phenomenon whose regularities are rooted in the senses. For example, researchers have long since tried to relate asymmetries in synaesthetic metaphors in language to language-external asymmetries in perception (e.g., Williams, 1976; Shen, 1997; for discussion, see Winter, 2016b). For example, Shen (1997) distinguishes the senses along a scale of "cognitive accessibility", with the "lower" modalities of touch, taste, and to some extent smell, having more direct contact or proximity to a perceptual stimulus. These properties of the corresponding senses are then thought to impose constraints on the use of metaphors, with only mappings from "low" to "high" senses being favoured. Thus, Shen (1997)'s explanation of why certain metaphors are more frequent than others is rooted in language-external perceptual considerations, and it is thus considering "poetic synaesthesia" not just as a purely linguistic phenomenon. As another example of researchers making strong connections between language and perception in the context of these metaphors, consider Holz (2007), who defines what he calls "linguistic synaesthesia" as follows: "We may talk of a *verbal simulation of synesthetic perception* or of a *linguistic creation of cross-modality illusions*" (ibid. 193, italics in original). Just like the term "synaesthesia" is used in perception, this characterisation appears to invoke vivid perceptual representations.

Thus, we have researchers who characterise synaesthetic metaphors, or linguistic synaesthesia, as more of a linguistic phenomenon, as well as researchers who think of it as a linguistic phenomenon that directly relates to extra-linguistic perceptual processes. The term "synaesthesia" is not appropriate for linguistic description because no clear connection between synaesthesia and language has been established yet. And if the term "synaesthesia" were to be used as a mere analogy, it would not be appropriate either, because in perceptual synaesthesia, different kinds of mappings are involved. If "synaesthesia" is used merely as a term to suggest some form of "crossing" between the senses, the term "crossmodality" is theoretically more innocuous and also more generally applicable. There are a myriad of connections between the senses, only some of which can be described as involving synaesthesia (Deroy & Spence, 2013). Using the label "synaesthesia" furthermore easily glosses over more important issues, such as what the precise (cognitive) connection between language and perception is that is evidenced by these expressions. Do these expressions involve actual perceptual imagery or perceptual simulation? Do they stem from underlying perceptual connections or are the sensory connections created through language?

Using "synaesthesia" to talk about expressions such as *smooth taste* conjures up the idea that these expressions actually involve some kind of vivid sensory imagery, the same way that grapheme-colour synaesthetes cannot help but to see colours when they see certain graphemes (Ramachandran & Hubbard, 2001). This understanding of linguistic synaesthesia is exemplified by Holz's description of the phenomenon as "*verbal simulation of synesthetic perception*" (2007, p. 193). While it clearly has been shown in experimental studies (Pecher, Zeelenberg & Barsalou, 2003) and through neuroimaging research (e.g., González, Barros-Loscertales, Pulvermüller, Meseguer, Sanjuán, Belloch, & Ávila, 2006) that processing sensory words involves the activation of perceptual brain areas, it is not clear that expressions involve cross-modal perceptual simulation. In fact, researchers have proposed other plausible connections between source and target concepts in these metaphors. These alternative explanations do not directly have to do with the detailed perceptual qualities of the terms involved rather than with the dimension of evaluation, or emotional meaning more generally.

Rather than *sweet melody* involving mappings of perceptual content (TASTE > SOUND), they could involve mappings of evaluative content. Thus, these sensory terms may be used evaluatively, rather than in a sensory fashion. This proposal has received support from theoretical analyses by various linguists, as well as from several empirical studies (see below). Tsur (2012) discusses the example of *loud perfume* as an instance of a "synaesthetic" expression that – under one analysis – appears to involve the mapping of specific auditory content onto the target domain of smell. However, Tsur (2012) rightly points out that the use of *loud* in this context has a strong evaluative sense, clearly implying that the perfume was annoying, just as when talking about a *loud colour* (Barcelona, 2003). The notion of the perfume being loud in a strictly auditory sense is de-emphasised in this expression; the emphasis is on the negative connotation of *loud*. A similar example can be found in Lehrer (1978), who describes the expression *sour note* as follows: "When sour transfers to sound, it is not because the note sounds as if it would taste sour (…) but rather the transfer of the feature [Displeasing of the Senses]

(...)" (ibid. 121). Barcelona (2003) discusses that the use of *loud* in *loud colour* relates to deviancy; and the use of *sweet* in *sweet music* relates to the experience of pleasure (see also Barcelona, 2008). Shibuya, Nozawa, and Kanamaru (2007) discuss how the comprehension of expressions such as *fragrant music* is based on emotional experiences. Bagli (2016) analyses *sweet* as involving a conceptual metaphor PLEASURE IS SWEET in the works of Shakespeare. Several chapters in this volume outline the emotional qualities of taste (Steinbach-Eicke) or smell (Kövecses; Takashima). More generally, researchers have pointed out that sensory adjectives clearly have evaluative functions on top of their descriptive functions (Lehrer, 2009, p. Chapter 6). In expressions such as *loud perfume, sweet melody* and *sour note* the evaluative function may be highlighted, and modality-specific perceptual content may be de-emphasised at the expense of performing evaluation. From this perspective, the use of *sweet* in *sweet melody* is similar to the colloquial use of *sweet* as an affirmative expression or as a word to describe a spouse, family member or friend (*sweetie*). For example, in response to "*The movie has just come out*", one could respond "*Sweet, let's go to the cinema*". Here too, the perceptual meaning does not appear to be primary.

Direct evidence for the evaluative functions of these expressions being dominant comes from Winter (2016b), who conducted a quantitative corpus analysis of over 140,000 adjective-noun pairs in the Corpus of Contemporary American English (Davies, 2008). This study showed that the more highly valenced a sensory word is, the more likely it is to be used in linguistic contexts outside of its most common sensory modality. For example, whereas *sweet* occurs frequently in expressions such as *sweet melody*, the relatively more neutral word *palatable* does not (?*palatable melody*). Words such as *sweet* are frequently used in appreciation of things, even in contexts that are not gustatory. Thus, Winter (2016b) suggests that precisely those adjective-noun pairs that combine *dissimilar* sensory modalities (i.e., those that would be most likely classified as "synaesthetic") are those pairs that also involve more highly valenced adjectives. In other words, cases commonly classified as "synaesthetic metaphors" appear to have a statistical dispreference for neutral words, suggesting a strong role for an evaluative component in the cross-modal uses of sensory adjectives. The involvement of sensory adjectives in evaluative language makes "synaesthetic metaphors" somewhat less "synaesthetic", since their primary role is not tied to the senses as such, but to the evaluative dimension of these senses.

The findings of Winter (2016b) may explain partly why taste in particular is a common source domain in most hierarchies of the senses: Taste and smell are more strongly emotionally valenced (see Winter, 2016a; Buck, 1949, pp. 1022–1032; Levinson & Majid, 2014), with taste words more likely to have positive meanings than smell words, which are often more negative (see also Kövecses, this volume; Takashima, this volume). The emotional involvement of taste and smell makes them particularly suited for evaluative functions outside the context of their own modalities. This may also partly explain why touch is such a common source domain (see Anderson, this volume; Caballero, this volume). For example, Winter (2016b, Chapter 5) discusses the strong emotional meanings of many touch adjectives, such as *rough* and *smooth*. Many auditory adjectives, on the other hand, do not stand out as particularly emotional, such as *silent* or *whistling* (Winter, 2016a; Winter, 2016b: Chapter 4). Those auditory adjectives that do have strong positive or negative emotional qualities are more likely to be used outside of the context of the auditory modality, such as in the negatively connoted expressions *loud colour, noisy colour* or *shrill colour*.[1]

What has been implicit in the discussion so far is the idea that evaluative and perceptual uses somehow oppose each other. In line with the title of this chapter, "Synaesthetic metaphors are neither synaesthetic nor metaphorical", the suggestion is that expressions which focus on evaluation do not constitute metaphors, at least in the context of cross-modal expressions such as *sweet fragrance*. In the background of this argument is a view of the lexicon where the emotional meaning of a word is part of its lexical representation. There is psycholinguistic evidence that emotional meaning is represented in the mental lexicon (e.g., De Houwer & Randell, 2004). The same way that denotative content determines use (a word is chosen based on whether it fits the referent), expressive content determines use (a word is chosen based on whether it fits the emotional meaning of the message). The corpus evidence presented in Winter (2016b) suggests that if the evaluative content of the adjective is strong, speakers can be more "loose" in their perceptual content. Thus, there is a trade-off between evaluation and (perceptual) denotation, with more emotional expressions affording less perceptual overlap. Crucially, the same way that we would not call the use of *good* in *good deed* versus *good movie* two uses that metaphorically extend the meaning of the word *good*, we do not have to call *sweet* in *sweet fragrance* metaphorical either. In both cases, we are simply dealing with two facets of the same core emotional meaning of positivity.

There is, however, an even more important issue than evaluative uses of sensory adjectives, and this issue relates deeply to how language and perception are related: When researchers use the term "synaesthesia" to talk about perceptual metaphors, they commonly mean mappings between *distinct* sensory modalities, as the Strik

---

1.   If emotional valence is a factor in explaining metaphorical associations, then why are adjectives such as *snarling* or *whimpering* not used as much in synaesthetic metaphors? Winter (2016b, Chapter 8) discusses other reasons for the dispreference of sound and provides evidence that iconicity constrains how these metaphors are used (adjectives that are echoic of sound concepts are used less), as well as their frequency (words such as *loud* and *quiet* that are highly frequent are also used frequently in metaphor).

Lievers' (2016) discussion of "conceptual conflict" between modalities clearly highlights. However, the next sections explore the idea that with many and perhaps most cases commonly subsumed under the category "synaesthetic metaphor", there is in fact no such conflict.

4. Beyond synaesthesia

It clearly is the case that sensory perception is highly multimodal (e.g., Spence & Bayne, 2015), involving all of the senses simultaneously. When it comes to language *about* this multisensoriality, it is commonly assumed that linguistic encoding imposes a different format, as expressed in the following quote by Fainsilber and Ortony (1987, p. 240): "Language partitions the continuity of experience into discrete units comprised of words and phrases having a relatively narrow referential range."

The encoding of perceptual multisensoriality in language is often thought as involving some kind of compression, that is some loss of information, or some profiling of certain aspects of the overall sensorial experience. Rakova (2003) presents an analysis of sensory adjectives having richer, more extensive perceptual meanings (see also Paradis & Eeg-Olofsson, 2013). According to her proposal, sensory adjectives are linked to supramodal concepts that involve multiple modalities, similar to the actual perceptions that are involved in the concepts they describe. A case in point is the sensory adjective *hot,* which dictionaries commonly describe as being literally about heat and metaphorically about food (*hot food,* with the meaning of 'spicy food'). Rakova (2003, Chapter 3) proposes an alternative analysis under which *hot* literally refers to *both* heat and spiciness. She cites neurophysiological research on capsaicin receptors in the mouth (Julius & Basbaum, 2001) which respond to *both* heat and chemical compounds that are characteristic of spicy food. Thus, for human perception, heat and spiciness are *literally* associated with each other by virtue of sharing partially overlapping neurophysiological structures.

My proposal is thus that the use of *hot* in *hot temperature* and *hot food* (as in 'spicy food') is not different from two uses of the colour term *red,* when applied to *red brick* or *red rose.* The two colours denoted by *red brick* and *red rose* fall under the referential scope of *red,* and perceiving both colours involves slightly different but also partially overlapping neural networks. The same way that the colour term encompasses a whole range of light frequencies, all of which receive the same label, the gradable adjective *hot* encompasses a whole range of sensations. In this case, the sensations may be seen as more different than two types of colours, as 'heat' and 'spiciness' are conceptually distinguished by language users, but unaware to the user themselves is the fact that heat-spiciness – just like colour – is processed by a perceptual system that is partially overlapping. This underlying neurological and perceptual integration of heat and spiciness is one explanatory factor behind the frequent use of heat adjectives to denote spicy sensations in a number of the world's languages (Rakova, 2003).

The argument made for *hot* here and in Rakova (2003) carries over to words such as *sweet*, which is a word that similarly denotes a whole range of perceptual experiences, including both taste and smell, which are neurologically and behaviourally integrated. Taste and smell are linguistically associated with each other (Lynott & Connell, 2009; Louwerse & Connell, 2011; Winter, 2016a, 2016b, p. Chapter 7). As noted by Classen (1993, p. 52), "gustatory terms, such as sour, sweet, or pungent, usually double for olfactory terms", with expressions such as *sweet fragrance* having been analysed as "synaesthetic metaphors" by, for example, Shen and Gil (2007). The seemingly "synaesthetic" association between taste and smell words can easily be explained with recourse to taste-smell continuity within the underlying perceptual machinery. The two modalities share partially overlapping brain networks (De Araujo, Rolls, Kringelbach, McGlone, & Phillips, 2003; Delwiche & Heffelfinger, 2005; Rolls, 2008) and in fact, use some of the same macro-physiological structures, with smells being perceived through the so-called retronasal pathway at the back of the mouth (for discussion see Spence, Smith, & Auvray, 2015). The widespread idea that we only smell through the nose is an entirely cultural one. The perceptual construct of flavour is co-determined by taste and smell together (Auvray & Spence, 2008; Spence et al., 2015), i.e., flavour cannot be considered independently of both of these modalities.[2] To the extent that words such as *sweet* and *sour* are literally about flavour, we have to recognise that these words are jointly gustatory and olfactory.

Of course, words do not directly refer to neurological structures. In fact, as argued by Miller and Johnson-Laird (1976) words do not even directly – without intervening conceptual links – refer to low-level perception. But words do refer to concepts that result from perceptual sensations. The lexical concept corresponding to the word form *hot* does not have to be restricted to just a temperature meaning. Concepts about perception can be supramodal, encompassing multiple sensory modalities (see, e.g., Lynott & Connell, 2009). Paradoxically, even though the literature on synaesthetic metaphors deals with cross-domain uses of sensory adjectives, it inherently assumes that sensory adjectives are relatively unimodal, referring only

---

2.   Although taste and smell as perceptual modalities are highly interacting in behavioural terms, and partially overlapping (neurologically and with respect to their sensory organs), the two senses are of course not coextensive. Not all things that can be tasted (such as bitterness) can easily be smelled, for example. Consider, for example, the fact that some people who appreciate the smell of coffee do not like its taste.

to very circumscribed perceptual experiences. Calling *sweet fragrance* a TASTE TO SMELL mapping implicitly assumes the distinctness of the two senses, and it imposes a unimodal analysis on the word *sweet* as being exclusively gustatory; something that is not supported by the neuropsychological evidence.

But what about our intuition that *sweet* is somehow best described as a "taste word"? The categorisation of sensory language into distinct senses may happen at a metalinguistic stage, i.e., when thinking *about* language as opposed to actually using language. The moment that we think *about* the word *hot*, we are compelled by the salience of the temperature dimension to disregard other perceptual dimensions. That is, if we asked a native speaker of English what *hot* means, she would presumably list the temperature meaning first. Another way to think about this is from the perspective of the accessibility of meanings: The temperature meaning of *hot* may be more accessible to native speakers, with the other meaning dimensions not as easily intuited. However, clearly, not all meaning is consciously accessible to speakers and we have to distinguish what a speaker thinks about her own vocabulary from how that vocabulary is actually used. Whereas the usage of words may be more strongly based on how the senses actually behave and how they are intermixed, thought *about* words may be relatively more influenced by cultural belief systems.

Thus, speakers (including linguists) are under the (illusionary) impression that sensory vocabulary is about clearly delimited sensory modalities. In many Western societies, speakers adhere to what is sometimes called the "five senses folk model", otherwise known as the "Aristotelian senses" (Sorabji, 1971). A look towards either cultural anthropology or neuropsychology reveals that this model is a cultural construct. Cultures differ in how they carve up the sensorium, and whether they carve it up into distinct senses at all (see, e.g., Howes, 1991; Goody, 2002; Pink, 2011). And modern sensory science recognises many more than just five senses, including such senses as nociception (pain), kinesthesia, the internal senses, and more (Carlson, 2010; Møller, 2012). Many of these senses do not have direct reflections in the five senses folk model and also no direct reflections in vocabulary (see Pink, 2011: 265). Overall, it is a philosophically thorny issue to individuate and count the senses (Casati et al., 2015), with McBurney (1986, p. 123) saying that the senses "did not evolve to satisfy our desire for tidiness". From this perspective, we have to recognise that calling *hot* a "temperature word", *sweet* a "taste word" and *fragrant* a "smell word" is essentially using the fiction of the five senses folk model to categorise words, to fit them into an existing cultural model. Whereas perception is underlyingly continuous, metalinguistic judgments *about* perception categorise this continuity (cf. Spivey, 2007).

Empirical evidence for the underlying continuity of the senses carrying over to our comprehension of sensory adjectives comes from modality rating studies (Lynott & Connell, 2009). In these studies, native speakers of English rate words according to their sensory modality on a numerical scale (in this case from 0 to 5). Crucially, the task allows participants to assign positive numerical values to multiple sensory modalities, potentially revealing whether they deem a word to be multisensory. In Lynott and Connell (2009), the word *sweet* turns out to have a gustatory strength rating of 4.9 and an olfactory strength rating of 3.9, both relatively high numbers in the context of this study. Hence, speakers shared the intuition that the word *sweet* is both gustatory and olfactory when prompted explicitly to think about the modalities. Lynott and Connell (2009) and Louwerse and Connell (2011) show that the association between taste and smell across sensory words is characteristic of the entire set of 400+ sensory words rated, i.e., taste and smell ratings are correlated with each other.[3] However, if we asked a native speaker what kind of perceptual word a word such as *sweet* is best classified as, she would most likely go with the word's strongest modality, in this case taste, which received the highest rating. Hence, an expression such as *sweet fragrance* is only a mapping between distinct senses if we straitjacket words to belong to one and only one sensory modality. From this perspective, the adjective-noun pairs *sweet fragrance* and *abrasive touch* are not qualitatively different from each other, even though one is described as a synaesthetic metaphor and the other is not.

The argument presented so far has only considered taste-smell and heat-spiciness associations. However, the argument extends beyond these two example cases; for example, to cases where touch language is used to describe sound, as in *sharp sound, rough sound* and *smooth melody*. Tactile properties such as surface roughness can be perceived using audition alone (Lederman, 1979), and auditory stimuli directly affect the perception of surface qualities perceived through touch (Guest, Catmur, Lloyd, & Spence, 2002; Suzuki, Gyoba, & Sakamoto, 2008), showing that the two modalities are perceptually associated. In the so-called parchment-skin illusion, participants report to have dryer hands when the sound of their hands rubbing against each other is amplified in the high-frequency components (Jousmäki & Hari, 1998). Sound perception is furthermore influenced by what is simultaneously being touched (Schürmann, Caetano, Jousmäki, & Hari, 2004), showing that audio-tactile interactions in behaviour are bidirectional. There is also direct neurophysiological evidence for a shared neurological substrate of touch and sound:

---

3.   A concern might be that the argument is circular. It could be that speakers' modality judgments are based entirely on text associations, i.e., speakers think of linguistic use contexts where they could apply *sweet*. In that case, the high olfactory rating of *sweet* may actually be the result of speakers thinking of expressions such as *sweet fragrance*. However, this cannot be the whole story: van Dantzig et al. (2011) collected modality ratings paired with particular concepts, such as *abrasive sandpaper* versus *abrasive lava,* and the resulting average ratings correlate highly with the ratings collected on words in isolation (see Winter 2016b, Chapter 2), which suggests that linguistic context does not play a huge role in this particular case.

single-cell recordings of neurons in the macaque auditory cortex show that some neurons directly respond to both somatosensory and auditory stimuli (Schroeder, Lindsley, Specht, Marcovici, Smiley, & Javitt, 2001). Auditory cortex may also become co-opted to process vibrotactile stimuli in deaf humans (Levänen, Jousmäki, & Hari, 1998). The case of associations between sound and touch appears to be different from the association between taste and smell, which are arguably more coupled, in an almost unavoidable fashion. Yet, the evidence discussed here makes it clear that the auditory system and the touch system are highly interconnected in brain and behaviour. These findings are enough for language users to notice (explicitly or implicitly) the connections between touch and sound. All of this suggests that expressions such as *sharp sound, rough sound* and *smooth melody* do not involve the conceptual conflict between distinct sensory modalities that is often taken to be definitional of "synaesthetic metaphors" (Strik Lievers, 2017).

5. Alternative analyses: Primary metaphors and metonymy

To appropriately understand the scope of the argument presented here, we need to contrast it with existing approaches within cognitive linguistics. The argument presented here bears some superficial resemblance to "primary metaphor theory" (Grady, 1997; Grady, Oakley, & Coulson, 1999), the theory that some metaphors, so-called primary metaphors, derive from repeatedly experiencing particular environmental correlations. For example, psychologically associating darkness with fear and danger throughout our lives is supposed to motivate linguistic expressions such as *these are dark times* (see Winter, 2014).

Many researchers now believe that such primary metaphors involve metonymy, for example, Kövecses (2013) discusses how the primary metaphor SADNESS IS DOWN can be understood as a DOWN FOR SADNESS metonymy. Metonymies commonly refer to within-domain conceptual mappings, as opposed to metaphors, which are cross-domain mappings (for an overview, see Littlemore, 2015). Downward-oriented body postures are associated with sadness in the same embodied scene, and so a speaker can use language about postures to metonymically refer to talk about emotions (Kövecses, 2013). One can easily see how this general line of thinking carries over to the sensory associations discussed above, such as between taste and smell: Since tastes and smells are so highly associated in our environment, we can use one to talk about the other, i.e., one may posit a TASTE FOR SMELL metonymy (rather than a metaphor) to account for expressions such as *sweet fragrance*. Within such an analysis, taste and smell are seen as part of the same conceptual domain.

This analysis of cross-modal uses of sensory words captures some of the essence of the approach outlined in this chapter. However, a metonymical analysis only goes half-way away from metaphor. Consider the case of the colour term *blue*. If we observe light with a wavelength of 470 nanometers, we call this *blue*. If we observe light with a wavelength of 475 nanometers, we call this *blue* as well. In this case, nobody would want to posit a metonymy "470nm-blue FOR 475nm-blue" because our intuition tells us that both instances are literal uses of *blue*. We do not need to posit a "mapping" within the domain of blueness. Colour terms in fact often have large referential scope. Consider the colour of a red brick, which would often be named *orange* outside the contextualised usage of a brick. Here, the colour term *red* encompasses a large range of wavelengths, none of which we would consider "metaphorical" uses in the sense of "involving mapping". If we recognise the underlying continuity of wavelengths and the wide scope of colour terms, we see that the same argument must carry over to other perceptual cases where similarly, a sensory word applies to a whole range of continuous experiences, as with *hot* referring to heat-spiciness and *sweet* referring to taste-smell.

As opposed to a metonymy-based analysis, a primary metaphor analysis is even less appropriate for understanding expressions such as *sweet fragrance*. As argued for by Grady (2005, pp. 1605–1606), of the two domains involved in primary metaphors, the source domain has to be sensory, and the target domain has to be non-sensory. For the metaphors discussed in this chapter, both sources and targets are sensory. Hence, Grady's definition of primary metaphors does not apply. Kövecses (2013, p. 75) talks about the "sufficient conceptual distance" that is necessary for a primary metonymy (e.g., DOWN FOR SADNESS) to result in a primary metaphor (e.g., SADNESS IS DOWN). As discussed above, this conceptual distance is not present in many cases of "synaesthetic metaphors", for example, the concepts of taste and smell are highly interrelated. Hence the concept of primary metaphor – even though superficially related to the present discussion because of the presence of environmental correlations – does not apply to many of the examples discussed here.

From the perspective of this chapter, the problem with any analysis rooted in either primary metaphor or metonymy is that the gustatory meaning and the olfactory meaning of a word such as *sweet* are still seen as distinct, and expressions such as *sweet smell* would be seen as involving a (metaphorical or metonymical) mapping. Of course, the uses of *sweet* in *sweet cake* and in *sweet fragrance* are different from each other; but they can be seen as being related by virtue of engaging the same integrated perceptual system in slightly different ways, and the use of the term in both instances can be seen as literal. Thus, "the extent of the literal", as discussed by Rakova (2003), may be much wider than commonly assumed by cognitive linguists.

Moreover, as stated above, even though more synaesthetic metaphors may be related to experiential contiguities than previously recognised (Marks, 1978, p. Chapter 8; Lehrer, 1978: 119; Shibuya et al., 2007; Sullivan & Jian, 2013), some adjective-noun pairs seem to involve genuinely dissimilar modalities, what Strik Lievers (2016, 2017) would count as "conflictual" mappings. Any metonymy-based or primary-metaphor based account is thus incomplete because these expressions cannot easily be explained by co-occurrence as in primary metaphor or primary metonymy. On this point, it is worth pointing out that precisely the examples that Strik Lievers (2017) discusses as genuine synaesthetic metaphors not easily explainable in terms of experiential contiguities (based on Taylor, 1995, p. 140) are cases such as *loud colour* and *sweet music*, which involve highly evaluative adjectives. In fact, Strik Lievers (2017) discusses Barcelona (2003, 2008)'s account of these expressions as involving evaluation in terms of deviancy or pleasure as a shared denominator (see also Bagli, 2016). Similarly, Shibuya et al. (2007) discuss synaesthetic metaphors as either being based on comprehension through sensory co-occurrence or as based on comprehension through emotional experiences. This suggests that precisely the most typical cases of synaesthetic metaphors, those involving dissimilar modalities, are perhaps more aptly treated as primarily evaluative expressions (Shibuya et al., 2007; Winter, 2016b). The phenomenon of synaesthetic metaphors thus falls apart in two directions: On the one hand, many cases seem to involve experiential contiguities or overlapping domains (although we need not analyse these cases as metonymies, as argued above). On the other hand, those cases that precisely do not involve such contiguities appear to be primarily evaluative.

6.   Conclusions

The present proposal combines two ideas: First, that sensory perception is neurophysiologically and psychologically continuous. Second, that words describing those sensory perceptions *appear to be* categorical (cf. Spivey, 2007). Pink (2011: 266) speaks of "a rather less culturally structured flow of neurological information" that "becomes differentiated into categories that we call the senses". She then says that "we tend to communicate linguistically about our embodied and sensory perception in terms of sensory categories", but warns us that "because one category is never enough to express exactly what we have actually experienced, the illusion of 'separate' senses operating *in relation to* each other is maintained" (ibid. 266, italics in original). These quotes get at the core of the present argument: We only need to talk about senses *relating to each other*, i.e., metaphorical mappings, if we are operating within our culturally imposed system of distinguishing five senses. Once we step outside the boundaries of this system and look at the underlying neurophysiology and studies on multisensory perception and multisensory integration, the continuity of the sensorium becomes apparent. Speakers, as perceptual beings, operate within this sensory continuum and this is, ultimately, what motivates their language use. However, when speakers, including linguists, think *about* the senses, they operate within the five senses folk model and impose categoriality. Only once this happens do we need to talk about metaphorical mappings.

Throughout this chapter, multiple arguments have been presented that suggest that calling expressions such as *sweet melody* or *rough taste* "synaesthetic metaphors" reflects assumptions that are difficult to maintain. These expressions have relatively little connection with synaesthesia as talked about in the neuropsychological literature. Many cases of allegedly "synaesthetic" metaphors actually turn out to involve combinations of sensory modalities that are not only highly associated within our ecology, but that are actually partially the same when looked at from the perspective of neurophysiology and perceptual psychology. Those cases that do seem to involve mappings between relatively dissimilar modalities, such as *sweet melody*, do appear to involve evaluative uses of sensory adjectives rather than concrete perceptual content. Thus, the argument presented here suggests that the notion of "synaesthetic metaphors" is a cultural construct that stems from categorising something that is underlyingly continuous. In short, "synaesthetic metaphors" are neither synaesthetic nor metaphorical.

Acknowledgements

I want to thank Paula Pérez-Sobrino, Francesca Strik Lievers, Andre Coneglian, Marcus Perlman, Clive Winter, the attendees of the MPI Nijmegen Perception Metaphor workshop and Laura J. Speed, Asifa Majid, Carolyn O'Meara and Lila San Roque for very helpful comments and suggestions.

References

Auvray, M., & Spence, C. (2008). The multisensory perception of flavor. *Consciousness and Cognition*, 17(3), 1016–1031. https://doi.org/10.1016/j.concog.2007.06.005

Bagli, M. (2016). "Shaking off so good a wife and so sweet a lady": Shakespeare's use of taste words. *Journal of Literary Semantics*, 45(2), 141–159. https://doi.org/10.1515/jls-2016-0010

Barcelona, A. (2003). On the plausibility of claiming a metonymic motivation for conceptual metaphor. In A. Barcelona (Ed.), *Metaphor and Metonymy at the Crossroads* (pp. 31–58). Berlin & New York: Mouton de Gruyter. https://doi.org/10.1515/9783110894677.31

Barcelona, A. (2008). Metonymy is not just a lexical phenomenon: On the operation of metonymy in grammar and discourse. In C. Alm-Arvius, N., Johannesson & D. C. Minugh (Eds.), *Selected Papers from the Stockholm 2008 Metaphor Festival* (pp. 3–42). Stockholm: Stockholm University Press.

Bond, B., & Stevens, S. S. (1969). Cross-modality matching of brightness to loudness by 5-year-olds. *Perception & Psychophysics*, 6(6), 337–339. https://doi.org/10.3758/BF03212787

Buck, C. D. (1949). *A Dictionary of Selected Synonyms in the Principal Indo-European Languages: A Contribution to the History of Ideas*. Chicago: University of Chicago Press.

Carlson, N. R. (2010). *Physiology of Behavior* (10th Edition). Boston: Allyn & Bacon.

Casati, R., Dokic, J., & Le Corre, F. (2015). Distinguishing the commonsense senses. In D. Stokes, M. Matthen & S. Biggs (Eds.), *Perception and its Modalities* (pp. 462–479). Oxford: Oxford University Press.

Classen, C. (1993). *Worlds of Sense: Exploring the Senses in History and across Cultures*. London: Routledge.

Cytowic, R. E. (1993). *The man who tasted shapes*. New York: Putnam Press.

Day, S. (1996). Synaesthesia and synaesthetic metaphors. *Psyche*, 2(32), 1–16.

Davies, M. (2008) The Corpus of Contemporary American English: 450 million words, 1990–present. Available online at http://corpus.byu.edu/coca/

de Araujo, I. E., Rolls, E. T., Kringelbach, M. L., McGlone, F., & Phillips, N. (2003). Taste olfactory convergence, and the representation of the pleasantness of flavour, in the human brain. *European Journal of Neuroscience*, 18(7), 2059–2068. https://doi.org/10.1046/j.1460-9568.2003.02915.x

De Houwer, J., & Randell, T. (2004). Robust affective priming effects in a conditional pronunciation task: evidence for the semantic representation of evaluative information. *Cognition & Emotion*, 18(2), 251–264. https://doi.org/10.1080/02699930341000022

Delwiche, J. F., & Heffelfinger, A. L. (2005). Cross-modal additivity of taste and smell. *Journal of Sensory Studies*, 20(6), 512–525. https://doi.org/10.1111/j.1745-459X.2005.00047.x

Deroy, O., & Spence, C. (2013). Why we are not all synesthetes (not even weakly so). *Psychonomic Bulletin & Review*, 20(4), 643–664. https://doi.org/10.3758/s13423-013-0387-2

Erzsébet, P. D. (1974). Synaesthesia and poetry. *Poetics*, 3(3), 23–44. https://doi.org/10.1016/0304-422X(74)90021-7

Fainsilber, L., & Ortony, A. (1987). Metaphorical uses of language in the expression of emotions. *Metaphor and Symbol*, 2(4), 239–250. https://doi.org/10.1207/s15327868ms0204_2

Galton, F. (1880a). Visualised numerals. *Nature*, 21(533), 252–256. https://doi.org/10.1038/021252a0

Galton, F. (1880b). Visualised numerals. *Nature*, 22, 494–495. https://doi.org/10.1038/021494e0

Goody, J. (2002). The anthropology of the senses and sensations. *La Ricerca Folklorica*, 45, 17–28. https://doi.org/10.2307/1480153

González, J., Barros-Loscertales, A., Pulvermüller, F., Meseguer, V., Sanjuán, A., Belloch, V., & Ávila, C. (2006). Reading cinnamon activates olfactory brain regions. *Neuroimage*, 32(2), 906–912. https://doi.org/10.1016/j.neuroimage.2006.03.037

Grady, J. (1997). Theories are buildings revisited. *Cognitive Linguistics*, 8(4), 267–290. https://doi.org/10.1515/cogl.1997.8.4.267

Grady, J. (2005). Primary metaphors as inputs to conceptual integration. *Journal of Pragmatics*, 37(10), 1595–1614. https://doi.org/10.1016/j.pragma.2004.03.012

Grady, J., Oakley, T., & Coulson, S. (1999). Blending and metaphor. In R. W. Gibbs & G. Steen (Eds.), *Metaphor in Cognitive Linguistics* (pp. 101–124). Amsterdam: John Benjamin. https://doi.org/10.1075/cilt.175.07gra

Guest, S., Catmur, C., Lloyd, D., & Spence, C. (2002). Audiotactile interactions in roughness perception. *Experimental Brain Research*, 146(2), 161–171. https://doi.org/10.1007/s00221-002-1164-z

Holz, P. (2007). Cognition, olfaction and linguistic creativity: Linguistic synesthesia as a poetic device in cologne advertising. In Plümacher, M., & P. Holz (Eds.), *Speaking of colors and odors* (pp. 185–202). Amsterdam: John Benjamins. https://doi.org/10.1075/celcr.8.11hol

Howes, D. (1991) (Ed.). *The Varieties of Sensory Experience: A Sourcebook in the Anthropology of the Senses*. Toronto: University of Toronto Press.

Hunston, S. (2011). *Corpus approaches to evaluation: Phraseology and evaluative language*. New York: Routledge.

Jousmäki, V., & Hari, R. (1998). Parchment-skin illusion: sound-biased touch. *Current Biology*, 8(6), R190–R191. https://doi.org/10.1016/S0960-9822(98)70120-4

Julius, D., & Basbaum, A. I. (2001). Molecular mechanisms of nociception. *Nature*, 413(6852), 203–210. https://doi.org/10.1038/35093019

Kövecses, Z. (2013). The metaphor–metonymy relationship: Correlation metaphors are based on metonymy. *Metaphor and Symbol*, 28(2), 75–88. https://doi.org/10.1080/10926488.2013.768498

Lakoff, G., & Johnson, M. (1980). *Metaphors we live by*. Chicago: University of Chicago Press.

Lederman, S. J. (1979). Auditory texture perception. *Perception*, 8(1), 93–103. https://doi.org/10.1068/p080093

Lehrer, A. (1978). Structures of the lexicon and transfer of meaning. *Lingua*, 45(2), 95–123. https://doi.org/10.1016/0024-3841(78)90001-3

Lehrer, A. (2009). *Wine & Conversation*. Oxford: Oxford University Press. https://doi.org/10.1093/acprof:oso/9780195307931.001.0001

Levänen, S., Jousmäki, V., & Hari, R. (1998). Vibration-induced auditory-cortex activation in a congenitally deaf adult. *Current Biology*, 8(15), 869–872. https://doi.org/10.1016/S0960-9822(07)00348-X

Levinson, S. C., & Majid, A. (2014). Differential ineffability and the senses. *Mind & Language*, 29(4), 407–427. https://doi.org/10.1111/mila.12057

Littlemore, J. (2015). *Metonymy: Hidden shortcuts in language, thought and communication*. Cambridge: Cambridge University Press. https://doi.org/10.1017/CBO9781107338814

Louwerse, M., & Connell, L. (2011). A taste of words: Linguistic context and perceptual simulation predict the modality of words. *Cognitive Science*, 35(2), 381–398. https://doi.org/10.1111/j.1551-6709.2010.01157.x

Lynott, D., & Connell, L. (2009). Modality exclusivity norms for 423 object properties. *Behavior Research Methods*, 41(2), 558–564. https://doi.org/10.3758/BRM.41.2.558

Majid, A. (2012). Current emotion research in the language sciences. *Emotion Review*, 4(4), 432–443. https://doi.org/10.1177/1754073912445827

Marks, L. E. (1978). *The Unity of the Senses: Interrelations Among the Modalities*. New York: Academic Press. https://doi.org/10.1016/B978-0-12-472960-5.50011-1

Martino, G., & Marks, L. E. (2001). Synesthesia: Strong and weak. *Current Directions in Psychological Science*, 10(2), 61–65. https://doi.org/10.1111/1467-8721.00116

McBurney, D. H. (1986). Taste, smell, and flavor terminology: Taking the confusion out of the fusion. In H. L. Meiselman, & R. S. Rivkin (Eds.), *Clinical Measurement of Taste and Smell* (pp. 117–125). New York: Macmillan.

Miller, G. A., & Johnson-Laird, P. N. (1976). *Language and Perception*. Cambridge: Harvard University Press. https://doi.org/10.4159/harvard.9780674421288

Møller, A. (2012). *Sensory Systems: Anatomy and Physiology* (2nd Edition). Richardson: A. R. Møller Publishing.

Paradis, C., & Eeg-Olofsson, M. (2013). Describing sensory experience: The genre of wine reviews. *Metaphor and Symbol*, 28(1), 22–40. https://doi.org/10.1080/10926488.2013.742838

Pecher, D., Zeelenberg, R., & Barsalou, L. W. (2003). Verifying different-modality properties for concepts produces switching costs. *Psychological Science*, 14(2), 119–124. https://doi.org/10.1111/1467-9280.t01-1-01429

Pink, S. (2011). Multimodality, multisensoriality and ethnographic knowing: social semiotics and the phenomenology of perception. *Qualitative Research*, 11(3), 261–276. https://doi.org/10.1177/1468794111399835

Prandi, M. (2012). A plea for living metaphors: Conflictual metaphors and metaphorical swarms. *Metaphor & Symbol*, 27(2), 148–170. https://doi.org/10.1080/10926488.2012.667690

Rakova, M. (2003). *The Extent of the Literal: Metaphor, Polysemy and Theories of Concepts*. New York: Palgrave Macmillan. https://doi.org/10.1057/9780230512801

Ramachandran, V. S., & Hubbard, E. M. (2001). Synaesthesia – a window into perception, thought and language. *Journal of Consciousness Studies*, 8(12), 3–34.

Rolls, E. (2008). Functions of the orbitofrontal and pregenual cingulate cortex in taste, olfaction, appetite and emotion. *Acta Physiologica Hungarica*, 95(2), 131–164. https://doi.org/10.1556/APhysiol.95.2008.2.1

Schroeder, C. E., Lindsley, R. W., Specht, C., Marcovici, A., Smiley, J. F., & Javitt, D. C. (2001). Somatosensory input to auditory association cortex in the macaque monkey. *Journal of Neurophysiology*, 85(3), 1322–1327. https://doi.org/10.1152/jn.2001.85.3.1322

Schürmann, M., Caetano, G., Jousmäki, V., & Hari, R. (2004). Hands help hearing: facilitatory audiotactile interaction at low sound-intensity levels. *The Journal of the Acoustical Society of America*, 115 (2), 830–832. https://doi.org/10.1121/1.1639909

Shams, L., Kamitani, Y., & Shimojo, S. (2000). Illusions: What you see is what you hear. *Nature*, 408(6814), 788–788. https://doi.org/10.1038/35048669

Shen, Y. (1997). Cognitive constraints on poetic figures. *Cognitive Linguistics*, 8(1), 33–71. https://doi.org/10.1515/cogl.1997.8.1.33

Shen, Y., & Aisenman, R. (2008). Heard melodies are sweet, but those unheard are sweeter: Synaesthetic metaphors and cognition. *Language and Literature*, 17(2), 107–121. https://doi.org/10.1177/0963947007088222

Shen, Y., & Gadir, O. (2009). How to interpret the music of caressing: Target and source assignment in synaesthetic genitive constructions. *Journal of Pragmatics*, 41(2), 357–371. https://doi.org/10.1016/j.pragma.2008.08.002

Shen, Y., & Gil, D. (2007). Sweet fragrances from Indonesia: A universal principle governing directionality in synaesthetic Metaphors. In W. van Peer, & J. Auracher (Eds.), *New Beginnings in Literary Studies* (pp. 49–71). Newcastle: Cambridge Scholars Publishing.

Shibuya, Y., Nozawa, H., & Kanamaru, T. (2007). Understanding synesthetic expressions: Vision and olfaction with the physiological = psychological model. In M. Plümacher, & P. Holz (Eds.), *Speaking of colors and odors* (pp. 203–226). Amsterdam: John Benjamins. https://doi.org/10.1075/celcr.8.12shi

Simner, J. (2012). Defining synaesthesia. *British Journal of Psychology*, 103, 1–15. https://doi.org/10.1348/000712610X528305

Simner, J., Mulvenna, C., Sagiv, N., Tsakanikos, E., Witherby, S. A., Fraser, C., Scott, K., & Ward, J. (2006). Synaesthesia: The prevalence of atypical cross-modal experiences. *Perception*, 35(8), 1024–1033. https://doi.org/10.1068/p5469

Sorabji, R. (1971). Aristotle on demarcating the five senses. *The Philosophical Review*, 80(1), 55–79. https://doi.org/10.2307/2184311

Spence, C. (2011). Crossmodal correspondences: A tutorial review. *Attention, Perception, & Psychophysics*, 73(4), 971–995. https://doi.org/10.3758/s13414-010-0073-7

Spence, C., & Bayne, T. (2015). Is consciousness multisensory? In D. Stokes, M. Matthen & S. Biggs (Eds.), *Perception and its Modalities* (pp. 95–132). Oxford: Oxford University Press.

Spence, C., Smith, B., & Auvray, M. (2015). Confusing tastes and flavours. In D. Stokes, M. Matthen, & S. Biggs (Eds.), *Perception and its Modalities* (pp. 247–274). Oxford: Oxford University Press.

Spivey, M. (2007). *The Continuity of Mind*. Oxford: Oxford University Press.

Strik Lievers, F. (2015). Synaesthesia: A corpus-based study of cross-modal directionality. In R. Caballero, & C. Paradis (Eds.), *Functions of Language, Sensory Perceptions in Language and Cognition* (pp. 69–95). Amsterdam: John Benjamins.

Strik Lievers, F. (2016). Synaesthetic metaphors in translation. *Studi e Saggi Linguistici*, 54(1), 43–70.

Strik Lievers, F. (2017). Figures and the senses. Towards a definition of synaesthesia. *Review of Cognitive Linguistics*, 15(1), 83–101. https://doi.org/10.1075/rcl.15.1.04str

Sullivan, K., & Jiang, W. (2013). When my eyes are on you, do you touch my eyes? A reclassification of metaphors mapping from physical contact to perception. In T. Fuyin Li (Eds.), *Compendium of Cognitive Linguistics Research* Volume 2 (pp. 189–200). Hauppauge, NY: Nova Science Publishers.

Suzuki, Y., Gyoba, J., & Sakamoto, S. (2008). Selective effects of auditory stimuli on tactile roughness perception. *Brain Research*, 1242, 87–94.

Taylor, J. R. (1995). *Linguistic Categorization* (2nd Edition). Oxford: Oxford University Press.

Tsur, R. (2012). *Playing by Ear and the Tip of the Tongue: Precategorical Information in Poetry*. Amsterdam: John Benjamins. https://doi.org/10.1075/lal.14

Ullmann, S. (1945). Romanticism and synaesthesia: A comparative study of sense transfer in Keats and Byron. *Publications of the Modern Language Association of America*, 60, 811–827. https://doi.org/10.2307/459180

Ullmann, S. (1959). *The Principles of Semantics* (2nd Edition). Glasgow: Jackson, Son & Co.

Wilce, J. M. (2009). *Language and Emotion*. Cambridge: Cambridge University Press. https://doi.org/10.1017/CBO9780511626692

Williams, J. (1976). Synaesthetic adjectives: A possible law of semantic change. *Language*, 52, 461–478. https://doi.org/10.2307/412571

Winter, B., Marghetis, T., & Matlock, T. (2015). Of magnitudes and metaphors: Explaining cognitive interactions between space, time, and number. *Cortex*, 64, 209–224. https://doi.org/10.1016/j.cortex.2014.10.015

Winter, B. (2014). Horror movies and the cognitive ecology of primary metaphors. *Metaphor & Symbol*, 29(3), 151–170. https://doi.org/10.1080/10926488.2014.924280

Winter, B. (2016a). Taste and smell words form an affectively loaded part of the English lexicon. *Language, Cognition and Neuroscience*, 31(8), 975–988. https://doi.org/10.1080/23273798.2016.1193619

Winter, B. (2016b). The sensory structure of the English lexicon. Unpublished PhD Thesis, University of California Merced.

Yu, N. (2003). Synesthetic metaphor: A cognitive perspective. *Journal of Literary Semantics*, 32, 19–34.

CHAPTER 7

Sensory experiences, meaning and metaphor
The case of wine

Rosario Caballero
Universidad of Castilla-La Mancha

This chapter provides an overview of metaphorical language used to communicate sensory experiences in the context of wine discourse, particularly in the
tasting note genre where metaphor provides wine critics with the means to
describe what wines feel like in the nose and mouth. Using data from a corpus
of tasting notes written in English (2,053 texts and 100,674 words), it examines
the language used in the description of wines' aromas, flavours and mouthfeel
in order to better understand the contribution of metaphor in the transfer of
the olfactory, gustatory and tactile experiences to readers. The main concern
is to explore expressions that cut across sensory modalities, i.e., instantiate synaesthetic metaphor, and point to the possibility of the synaesthetic motivation
of a good amount of the language presumably informed by metaphors of the
conceptual type.

Keywords: winespeak, metaphor, synaesthesia, tasting note, sensory experience

1. Introduction

As wine has grown in popularity, so has the abundant discussion on the topic, both
inside and outside of wine circles. One of the most debated issues concerns the
language used to describe wine (known as *winespeak*), particularly descriptions
of tasting experiences. Within wine circles, advocates of objective, clear language
clash with people who claim that winespeak must evoke the aesthetic experiences
afforded by wine and, therefore, see subjectivity as unavoidable (Bernstein, 1998;
Gawel & Oberholster, 2001; Gregutt, 2003; Moore, 1999; Nedlinko, 2006; Noble
et al., 1987; Pierre, 1998). The extent of this debate may be summarised in Shapin's
claim that "a cultural history of wine taste belongs to the history of subjectivity and
its relations with notions of objectivity" (Shapin, 2012, p. 52).

A major point of contention is the heavy use of metaphor, regarded as the main
source of subjectivity, and denounced by some wine writers as "disorienting and

https://doi.org/10.1075/celcr.19.07cab

sometimes even unappetizing" (Old, 2013, p. 18) and has given rise to a growing number of books and websites devoted to explaining wine and – directly or indirectly – introducing the most adequate language to discuss it. The problems arise when those same authors decide what is metaphorical – *associative* – and, hence, difficult and what falls into the category of literal, descriptive-only – versus metaphorical and evocative – language. For instance, when explaining the different ways in which wine may be discussed, Old (2013) compares the metaphorical, subjective, and professional-only flavour of the description in (1) to the factual, objective, dispassionate, and user-friendly quality of passage (2):

(1)   This friendly, inky Syrah tastes of stewed boysenberries, with hints of pencil lead and forest floor.

(2)   This Sauternes is full-bodied and sweet, with strong oak flavours and plenty of balancing acidity.

Interestingly, the only metaphorical terms in (1) are "friendly" and "hints", whereas most terms in (2) are either metaphorical ("full-bodied", "strong" and "balancing") or metonymic ("oak") since, for instance, wine is not a three-dimensional, solid thing and, therefore, does not have a body. A different issue is whether a person outside the wine domain would be able to understand any of the terms above when used to describe wine, starting from trying to discern what "stewed boysenberries, with hints of pencil lead and forest floor" taste like.

While I agree that the second passage is easier than the first one, my reasons differ from the ones provided by Old in that I see the adjectives in (2) easier to understand than the taste referents in (1) since "pencil lead" and "forest floor" are not in my taste repertoire.[1] Moreover, being a metaphor scholar I cannot agree with his views of what is metaphorical and what is not, which does not mean that identifying wine metaphors is an easy endeavour. In the first place, as happens in other specific discourses, some metaphorical expressions have become so commonplace that they no longer feel metaphorical, particularly for their users (e.g. "full-bodied" or "strong" above). However, if this were the case, a wine professional should not find the description in (1) metaphorical either.

A second and more substantial difficulty lies in the type of knowledge expressed by the metaphorical language found in the wine domain. As stated in Cognitive Linguistics, our construal of the world relies heavily on imaginative, figurative schemas of diverse sorts (e.g., metaphor, metonymy, simile, etc.) that motivate the language we use to interact with others. Metaphor is one type of figurative schema

---

1.   For a discussion on the cultural and historical evolution of referential vocabulary related to taste, see the discussion in Shapin (2012).

or cognitive operation that consists of transferring (*mapping*) knowledge across two disparate knowledge domains one of which is typically more basic, concrete and easier (the *source*) and, therefore, helps understand the *target* in the metaphor, typically a more difficult or abstract notion or experience (Lakoff & Johnson, 1980, 1999). For instance, when we use the expression *body politic* we – usually, indirectly – liken the more abstract concept of NATION to an organic, living entity's BODY (i.e. the target and source in the metaphor A NATION IS A BODY). This corporeal view is easier to understand and use in communication, and is often further exploited to refer to the highest-ranked individual as its *head* or qualify its problems as *diseases*.

Likewise, wines are conventionally described as having a *body*, a term used to assess their texture or mouthfeel. However, while the term is congruent with other organic language in winespeak (e.g. wines qualified as *healthy*, *broad-shouldered* or *sexy*, as surveyed later in this chapter), describing a wine as *big-bodied* does not necessarily trigger corporeal images of wine, but has to do with the way it feels inside the mouth, its texture. Thus, as defined by prestigious wine critic Robert Parker, body refers to "the weight and fullness of a wine that can be sensed as it crosses the palate. Full-bodied wines tend to have a lot of alcohol, concentration, and glycerine".[2] Some of the alternative terms for this adjective in the many wine glossaries and handbooks available in the market include *deep*, *full* or *plush* which, although also metaphorical, point to non-organic views of wine as a three-dimensional object, a container or a textile. Put differently, while *big-bodied* may be seen as instantiating the conceptual metaphor WINES ARE LIVING ORGANISMS, the term is used for assessing the way wine *feels* inside the mouth – sensory information that is part and parcel of most metaphors in winespeak.

My discussion in this chapter focuses on the metaphorical language used for describing wine, and draws upon several research projects involving scholars from the universities of Castilla-La Mancha (Spain) and Lund (Sweden). As described elsewhere (Caballero & Paradis, 2013, 2015; Caballero & Suárez-Toste, 2008, 2010), we focused on the wine tasting note (hereafter, TN) and built an extensive corpus of texts written by the most authoritative critics in the field and distributed in reputed print and online channels – a corpus that, unless otherwise indicated, is the source of all the examples in this chapter. Combining the procedures followed in Conceptual Metaphor Theory (Lakoff & Johnson, 1980, 1999) and Genre Analysis (Swales, 1990), my colleagues and I described how metaphor meets the needs of wine critics in communicating what wine smells, tastes and feels like for an ever-expanding number of wine aficionados and experts alike.

---

2. www.robertparker.com/resources/glossary-terms

Together with showing the weight of organic, architectural and textile metaphors in winespeak (e.g., the description of wines as *big-bodied*, *buttressed* by tannins and acidity, or *loosely knit*), we also point to the blurred boundaries among various figurative phenomena in wine description. This is because tasting wine involves, on the one hand, making sense of a mélange of VISION, SMELL, TOUCH, and TASTE data (seldom activated one at a time, but experienced in a holistic way) and, on the other, framing this sensory input against knowledge of previous experiences stored in our sensory mental repository, which helps understand the intervention of metonymy and synaesthesia in wine descriptions. For instance, although wines do not actually have fruit, and nor do they smell sweet, they are often described as "full of apple and peach" and having a "sweet nose" by means of the metonymies SUBSTANCE FOR AROMA and PROPERTY FOR FLAVOUR in agreement with metonymy's ability to highlight specific aspects of entities, concepts or experiences (Kövecses, 1999; Panther & Radden, 1999; Paradis, 2004; Radden, 2003; Panther & Thornburg, 2003).

Likewise, visual and aural adjectives are often used to describe wine's aromas and texture, for instance, the qualification of acidity as *bright* or *screeching*. This is not exclusive of winespeak, but can also be observed in everyday language where we use such aural and tactile adjectives as *loud* and *warm* to describe visual properties like colours (for instance, orange and yellow are *warm* colours which, when too bright, can also be *loud*). Both cases illustrate what is known as *synaesthetic metaphor*, a metaphor that maps sensory information across domains, for instance, sound onto sight as in *loud colour* (Day, 1996; Shen, 1997; Tsur, 1992; Yu, 2003), and gets its name after the neurological phenomenon called *synaesthesia* (Ramachandran & Hubbard, 2001). One of the issues in the scarce literature on synaesthetic language is the combination and directionality of cross-modal mappings. The starting point is Ullman's (1945, 1957) proposal of a hierarchy of the sensory modalities (TOUCH-TASTE-SMELL-SOUND-SIGHT), and the *directionality principle* whereby transfers take place from the lower senses (e.g., TOUCH) to the higher ones (e.g., SIGHT), for instance, *warm* or *loud colours*. Thus, while some scholars have refined Ullman's proposal and related it to research on metaphor within the cognitive paradigm (Shen, 1997; Shen & Cohen, 1998; Shen & Eisenman, 2008), others have questioned the lower-to-higher directionality of the transfers (Paradis & Eeg-Olofsson, 2013; Strik Lievers, 2015; Suárez-Toste, 2017).

In this paper, I pick up the thread of these discussions, and explore cross-sensory figurative language as well as the synaesthetic motivation of many of the metaphors typically found in winespeak. Together with providing a good illustration of the weight of the body and the senses in the way we think and talk about the world, synaesthetic language may help challenge the alleged lack of words for communicating sensory experiences, which, in turn, may minimise the differences between expert and non-expert descriptions discussed in the literature (Croijmans & Majid, 2016; Gawel, 1997; Hughson & Boakes, 2001; Lawless, 1984; Levinson & Majid, 2014; Solomon, 1990, 1997). As for metaphor research, the synaesthetic data found in winespeak challenges the easy-onto-difficult quality of general metaphorical mappings and the directionality and hierarchy of lower sense-onto-higher sense mappings in synaesthetic metaphors in particular.

2.   Describing wine through metaphor

The metaphorical language found in TNs draws upon such diverse experiential domains as architecture, music, weaving, or nature, which portray wines in two different ways: as animate LIVING ORGANISMS (animals or human beings) and as inanimate THREE-DIMENSIONAL ARTEFACTS of various sorts (e.g., buildings, textiles). The organic frame focuses on the wine's lineage, development, condition and behaviour whereas the inanimate metaphor covers the wine's structural and textural properties – the former also communicated in anatomical terms within the organic set. Passages (3) and (4) offer a combination of organic and 3D perspectives:

(3)   The blend is similar to that of its siblings [...]. It exhibits a dense purple color, beautiful blueberry, plum, and blackberry aromas, and a tightly-knit style revealing notes of barrique, new saddle leather, and loamy soil. This impressive red requires another 1–2 years of bottle age.

(4)   Dense peach, lime and slate flavors on a light-bodied, harmonious frame. It's all supported by a tensile structure. Long, long finish, with ripe apple and peach.

Together with describing wines' aromas and mouthfeel, TNs set the wine under evaluation in context with similar wines, and estimate its drinking span – two goals often accomplished by anthropomorphic language, as in "siblings" and "age" from Example (3). In turn, wine's keeping potential or drinking window depends on its structure, and this is usually expressed in anatomical ("light-bodied"), textile ("tightly-knit") and architectural terms ("frame", "tensile structure").

Besides allowing reviewers to avoid repetition in wine assessment, the co-occurrence of anatomical, textile and architectural language points to the presence of the primary metaphor ORGANISATION IS PHYSICAL STRUCTURE (Grady, 1997).[3] However, while in everyday contexts physical structure helps us understand abstract organisation (e.g., arguments, relationships and societies described

---

3.   For an overview on metaphor mixing in genre contexts, see Caballero (2006) and Kimmel (2010).

as having a *foundation* or a *fabric*), in the case of wine both source and target are physically grounded concepts. For although "tightly-knit", "light-bodied" and "tensile structure" in (3) and (4) refer to the structural properties of wine, these are inextricably linked to its textural, tactile traits in that discerning wine's structure takes place in the palate stage and, therefore, involves wine's mouthfeel. In this regard, the expressions illustrate a salient trait of figurative lexis in winespeak, namely, its critical role for describing what wines *look, smell, taste* and *feel* like.

In fact, while thinking and talking about wine in anthropomorphic terms is fully compatible with its being a changing, organic substance, the metaphors subsumed by the general frame WINES ARE (INANIMATE) 3D ARTEFACTS are more difficult to explain motivation- or experience-wise. The question is whether adjectives such as *velvety, round* or *low-keyed* actually activate a view of wines as textiles, geometrical bodies or musical pieces or, rather, their use relies on people's general knowledge of what such terms mean in typical situations and their unconscious re-adjustment of those meanings to the wine context (see also the discussion in Paradis & Eeg-Olofsson, 2013; Paradis, 2015). In light of the many terms thus concerned, one way to approach the metaphors in TNs may be to point to both the domains informing them and the sensory information expressed by their lexical instantiations – the exception being physiological and bloodline terms since they are solely concerned with wine's evolution and typology. My take on the relationship between wine metaphors and the senses is shown in Table 1.

Table 1. Metaphors and the sensory modalities involved in tasting notes

Metaphor	Sense
WINES ARE (ANIMATE) ORGANIC BEINGS	
WINES ARE LIVING ORGANISMS	
Physiology: *age, alive, asleep, dead, growth*	N/A
Anatomy: *body, backbone, corpulent, muscular* → → →	TOUCH
Actions: *jump, leap, leave, lurk, move, run, swim, kick* →	SMELL, TASTE, TOUCH
WINES ARE HUMAN BEINGS	
Bloodline: *brother, cousin, sibling*	N/A
Actions: *caress, dance, massage, sing* → → → → → → →	SMELL, TASTE, TOUCH
Gender: *masculine, feminine, virile, voluptuous* → → →	TOUCH
Personality: *assertive, bold, expressive, gentle, shy* → →	SMELL, TASTE, TOUCH
WINES ARE (INANIMATE) 3D ARTEFACTS	
WINES ARE BUILDINGS	
base, buttress, built, fortified, foundation, structure → →	TASTE, TOUCH
WINES ARE TEXTILES	
plush, satin(y), silk(y), velvet(y), loosely knit → → → →	TOUCH
WINES ARE GEOMETRICAL ARTEFACTS	
angular, broad, long, round, short, square → → → → →	TASTE, TOUCH
WINES ARE CONTAINERS	
background, behind, beneath, centre, deep, open → → →	SMELL, TASTE, TOUCH

While the organic frame covers all dimensions of wine (from its evolution as a living entity to its final assessment in human personality terms), parts of this comprehensive scenario are more related to the senses than others – even if, of course, describing and assessing wine necessarily rests upon sensory data. Thus, while the physiology and bloodline dimensions of WINES ARE ORGANIC BEINGS only focus on wine's lifespan and line-up, adjectives such as *muscular, voluptuous* or *gentle* cover the way wine feels in the taster's nose and, above all, mouth and, therefore, help verbalise sensory information.

Drawing attention to the sense modalities – explicitly or implicitly – subsumed by wine metaphors is important because these are primarily used to communicate the organoleptic experiences afforded by wine. A case in point is the recurrent use of motion verbs (the actions in the organic schema shown in Table 1) to express the intensity and/or persistence of wine's flavours and aromas (for a detailed discussion, see Caballero, 2007, in press). Consider the following passages:

(5)   Ripe, luscious fruit bursts from the glass in the pungent nose.

(6)   As big as it is, it's a silky wine that glides across the palate.

Here "burst" is concerned with expressing the intensity of a wine's nose and "glide" describes a pleasant texture of a wine previously qualified as "silky". In this regard, while both verbs may well evoke the image of an animate being performing such actions, strictly speaking the information mapped by the expressions is more concrete and does not necessarily trigger an organic scenario. Thus, the relevant traits from the semantic profile of "burst" are suddenness plus energy, whereas in the case of "glide" the property selected is smoothness – both verbs incorporating some aural information as well, which makes their use even more interesting.

Indeed, as happens with many other products in our everyday life, most metaphors in TNs may be explained as intrinsically concerned with communicating, on the one hand, the PRESENCE of sugar, fruit, alcohol, acidity etc. in wines and, on the other, the INTENSITY and PERSISTENCE with which those elements are perceived. The following example may help illustrate these points:

(7)   Impeccable fruit shines like a beacon. Opens with black-cherry and chocolate aromas, with earth and tobacco notes. In the mouth, the fruit speaks in sweet black-cherry and currant tones, and again, the tobacco accents pop up. Full-bodied, concentrated, tight, and muscular; the full, even tannins portend a fine, long future.

Here a red wine is described in terms of LIGHT ("shines like a beacon"), MOTION ("opens", "pop up"), MUSIC ("notes"), LANGUAGE ("speaks", "accents"), ANATOMY ("full-bodied", "muscular") and THREE-DIMENSIONALITY ("full", "even", "tight"). Of course, the same wine could have been described as follows: the aromas of the wine are clearly perceived ("shine like a beacon") and mostly include black-cherry and chocolate ("notes") which, in the mouth, taste like black-cherry and currant ("tones") and, again, a bit like tobacco ("pop up", "accent"). The wine has a lot of alcohol, glycerine, concentration (is "full-bodied", "muscular") and a lot of ("full") tannins, yet does not feel too astringent (tannins are "even"), and because of the proportions of all these things the wine will last in the bottle a few years (does not reveal all its aromas now, i.e. is "tight").[4]

Put differently, most metaphors in winespeak are concerned with wine's sensory properties, irrespective of the source domains informing them. Among those, the sense of TOUCH seems to matter the most in wine appreciation, to the extent that it is also the target in (purely) synaesthetic metaphors concerned with the aforementioned notion of presence. In the following sections I overview the cross-sensory figurative language used to describe wine in TNs. In order to do so, I have used a small corpus of 6,000 texts (366,226 total words) written in English by the most authoritative critics in the field assessing red and white wines.

3. Sensing wine: Cross-sensory metaphors

A good amount of data from the corpus draw from tactile, visual, hearing and taste experiences. Some expressions typically relate to particular events or entities and, therefore, illustrate some of the metaphors briefly seen earlier (e.g., many tactile terms instantiate the metaphor WINES ARE TEXTILES), but other terms point to a less specific, yet clearly figurative – in the broadest sense of the adjective – and sensory panorama. Figure 1 shows the distribution of sensory data across the sense modalities that function as sources for the expressions.

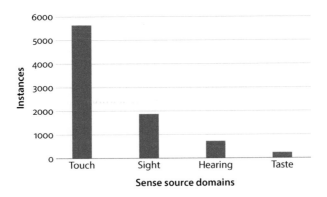

Figure 1. Distribution of language across sense modalities

<hr />

4. Whether this second, more literal and sober description, is more informative and helpful than the former for wine consumers and aficionados is a different issue – and falls outside the scope of the present discussion.

As happens with the senses related to the metaphors shown in Table 1, TOUCH informs the highest proportion of sensory expressions in TNs, followed by SIGHT, HEARING and TASTE. The following descriptions of a white and red wine illustrate the way the expressions thus informed are used in TNs:

(8)   Fresh, bright crisp, expressive nose with notes of apricots and honey.

(9)   This Zinfandel scorches the palate with a double whammy of bright acid and muscular tannins.

These passages also illustrate the tendency of synaesthetic language to cluster at particular sections of TNs, which, in turn, points to the traits that seem to be particularly critical in wine assessment. Concerning the former aspect, many clusters occur at the beginning of TNs, particularly in the first assessment of a wine's smell or nose, as happens in Example (8). As to the second aspect, synaesthetic language is particularly useful to describe such critical traits of wine as alcohol, acidity and tannins, as all three are concerned with texture or mouthfeel. A typical source domain for describing wine's texture is TEMPERATURE, i.e. TOUCH, as shown by the use of "scorch" to qualify the way the combination of acidity and tannins feels to the taster's palate in Example (9).

Table 2 provides a sample of the sensory language found in the corpus, arranged according to its formal and functional dimensions. Regarding this classification, it must be noted that this was done by paying attention to the way language data appeared in their context of use. For instance, adjectives like *creamy* and *oily* typically refer to taste and, therefore, are not cross-modal when qualifying wine's flavours. However, when they co-occur with texture or feel, they are used to describe wine's tactile impression, i.e., are cross-modal and were classified accordingly. Other adjectives, like *crunchy*, are used to express both the texture of food items (e.g., cereal, nuts, etc.) and the sound produced when chewing them, yet the latter is the original sense of the term, and this was also taken into account in the classification.

While wine commentary cannot be understood without synaesthetic language, its main uses appear to be two: on the one hand, synaesthetic metaphors are mostly used for assessing such intrinsic traits of wine as acidity, tannins and alcohol. On the other hand, as shown in Examples (8) and (9), synaesthetic language is recurrently used for expressing and quantifying the notion of PRESENCE – a critical notion in wine assessment in that the greater or lesser amount and ratio of components such as sugar or alcohol determines wine differences even within the same wine paradigm or grape varietal. A prototypical, highly conventionalised case of quantifier is the musical term *note* (a classic in TNs) used to convey the small yet discernible presence of apricots and honey in Examples (3), (7), and (8), and the more innovative *whammy* blending touch and hearing, used for conveying the forceful presence of acidity and tannins in the red wine described in (9). Other terms concerned

Table 2. Form and function of synaesthetic language in TNs

Senses, sources & metaphors	Role/focus in TNs
Touch Unspecific source biting, chewy, coarse, compact, cottony, creamy, dry(ing), dustiness, edge(d), even, grain(ed), grippy, gritty, hard, harsh, heavy, incisive, light, oily, peely, piercing, pointed, prickly, rugged, scratchy, sharp, smooth, soft, solid, sticky, sting TEXTILES cloak (N, V), coat(ing), corduroy, glove, lacy, plush, plushness, satin(y), silk(y), velvet(y) TEMPERATURE burn, cold, cool, fireball, fresh, heat, hot, refresh(ing), scorch(ing), searing, singeing	Assess wine as a whole/mouthfeel <u>Special focus</u>: acidity, tannins, alcohol Quantify presence of elements in wine touch, bite, lick, spik(ed), kiss, whack, hit, pinch, shot, smack, dusting, fillip, lashing, punch, tang, tease, teasing, wallop
Sight Unspecific source clean, definition, delineation, elegant, faded, focus, vivid LIGHT beam, blaze, bright, crystalline, dusky, flare, glow, laser-like, radiant, scintillating, shade, sheen, shimmering, shine, spark COLOURS black, green, monochromatic, pink, sooty, washed out	Assess wine as a whole <u>Special focus</u>: acidity ACIDITY IS LIGHT Quantify presence of elements in wine character(s), trace, streak, tinge(d), flourish, highlight, shading, glimpse, afterglow, sunburst, tint
Hearing Unspecific source crackle, crunchy, echo, jarring, loud, mute(d), resonant, reverberate, ring, screeching, shrill, strident MUSIC crescendo, harmonious, harmony, jazzy, lilt, lilting, low-keyed, offbeat, reprise, sing, song, symphony, tune(d)	Assess acidity ACIDITY IS A (HIGH-PITCHED) SOUND Quantify presence of elements in wine note, hint, accent (N, V), pronounced, tone, undertone, blast, overtones, burst (N), echo (N), undernote
Taste confected, over-sweet, savoury, sweet/-sweet, sweetness, sweetly, tangy	Assess wine's nose, palate

with expressing the greater or lesser amount of things in wine are the aural terms *hint, accent, tone, undertone* or *overtone*, the visual terms *highlight, trace, streak, character*, or *tinge*, the tactile terms *touch, bite,* or *lick*, and the smell noun *whiff* used to quantify flavours. The following passages show the way some such terms occur in the corpus:

(10) Mineral and tinged with beef blood on the nose, then showing solid berry flavors accented by herbal notes on the palate. Develops meaty tones on the finish.

(11) Grapy aromas with teasings of pepper, earth and leather. Intense, lingering finish spiked with mint.

As to the assessment of wine and/or its components, the way acidity is discussed in TNs is highly illustrative of both synaesthetic metaphor proper as well as the synaesthetic motivation of other conventional metaphors in winespeak (for a detailed discussion, see Suárez-Toste, 2013, 2017). The two figurative schemas – explicitly or implicitly – involving acidity may be formulated as ACIDITY IS A SOUND (illustrated in Examples (12) and (13)) and, particularly, ACIDITY IS LIGHT (Examples (14) and (15)):

(12) Sharp lemon-lime acidity rings in the close with light fig overtones.

(13) Juicy flavors of grapefruit, bell pepper and mineral are zesty without being shrill.

(14) This really lights up the palate. Lots of power in this ripe, dense Pinot Gris. The creme brulee, violet and guava flavors are deep and intense, set against an ironlike structure that blazes with minerality on the finish.

(15) It shines bright with focused tropical fruit flavors underlaid with tart citric acids.

Both metaphors are typically used to measure acidity against other constituents of wine such as fruit or alcohol, e.g., the use of "laser-like" in (14) and "focused" in (15). Also, as happens with many other terms in winespeak, sight-related terms (e.g. *vivid, bright, radiant, focused/unfocused*) and sound-related terms (*muted, low-keyed, loud, strident*) help wine critics describe acidity along an intensity cline. For instance, *bright, shine* or *loud* refer to the presence of a certain, and positive, amount of acidity, while the terms *blaze* and *laser* convey large quantity plus intensity, and *flare, beam* and *muted* often combine force and duration. Finally, too much acidity and, therefore, lack of balance are often conveyed by means of aural adjectives such as *strident, shrill* or *screeching* along a metaphor that could be formulated as TOO MUCH ACIDITY IS A HIGH-PITCHED SOUND, as shown in the following TNs:

(16) [T]he flavors are an unbalanced blend of ripe pears and stridently sour lemons.

(17) Juicy flavors of grapefruit, bell pepper and mineral are zesty without being shrill.

Of course, this is not the only metaphor cutting across the senses in winespeak. Other classic examples include ALCOHOL/ACIDITY IS HEAT (alcohol typically measured in terms of heat and acidity in terms of freshness), TANNINS ARE CLOTH, hence, TOUCH (*silky, plush* tannins), COLOURED ENTITIES (*sooty* or *black* tannins) or HAVE A SOUND (*crunchy* tannins). The following passages illustrate some of these metaphors:

(18)   Deep colour with a savoury nose of wet stones and a touch of spice, and a tiny bit of alcoholic heat.

(19)   Every element of this bottle is astounding – super-smooth, velvety plum, cherry and blackcurrant, dark chocolate, tar and briar flavours, dusted with sooty tannins and topped with a never-ending finish.

(20)   The palate is smooth and svelte with good density and ripe, crunchy, well enrobed tannins.

(21)   Light-bodied, with tasty cherry and floral notes, and crunchy acidity on the finish.

The way acidity, tannins or alcohol are described in TNs is highly illustrative of both the potential of figurative language in winespeak, as well as some of the issues derived from exploring it – particularly those concerned with metaphor formulation and classification (Caballero & Suárez-Toste, 2010). Thus, if we set the cross-modal language discussed here against the metaphorical frames informing winespeak, expressions such as *silky tannins* or *boisterous nose* may be explained as part of or, at least, very much related to the textile and organic metaphors informing the way wine is discussed in general (e.g. the use of *boisterous* fits the long-lived personification of wines). In other words, one way to approach such terms is to consider the whole picture and see whether they are compatible with it or not. This decision is particularly easy in those cases where cross-sensory language is concerned with (a) a single property (for instance, the adjective "bright" is always concerned with acidity or its source, e.g., certain fruits, irrespective of the perceiving organ) and (b) properties typical of a single sense domain or experience (e.g., the textile adjectives "velvety" and "silky" or the more syncretic "crunchy" are all concerned with wine's texture).

A different question, however, is whether describing a yoghurt and a facial cream as "velvety" triggers a textile image of such things, i.e., is motivated by a metaphor that could be formulated as YOGHURT/FACIAL CREAM IS CLOTH, even if, in both cases, "velvety" focuses on texture (felt inside the mouth and through the skin, respectively). A similar contention is raised by Paradis & Eeg-Olofsson (2013) and Paradis (2015), who claim that adjectives that span various senses (e.g. "soft", "deep" or "sharp" may qualify colours, smells, tastes and textures) are not metaphorical in the conventional sense of the term since their use does not involve the implicit comparison requisite sanctioning the mapping of information across domains. Rather, such expressions involve a construal of salience and, therefore, result from a process of synaesthetic metonymisation whereby a whole entity stands for the trait being communicated. For instance, qualifying a colour and an aroma as "soft" rests upon – *activates* –the gentle, soothing feeling associated with soft things, that is, originates from our tactile experiences and is used to describe a visual and an olfactory experience. This activation is typical of metonymy in that it does not involve construing colours and aromas as solid, three-dimensional things characterised by softness, but only uses a part of the softness quality to describe a part of another entity or experience. This is also implicit in the classification of cross-modal, synaesthetic data offered in Table 2 where terms like "hard", "sharp", "clean" or "sweet" are not presented as related to a clear metaphorical schema, but appear under the label of the sense modality they typically belong to (see also the discussion by Winter, this volume). More research into their use in contexts other than wine discourse would provide a richer picture of the way people use such language which, in turn, would help refine the issues raised by the specific wine context and briefly discussed here.

4. Concluding remarks

In the present chapter I have provided an overview of some of the figurative language used to assess wines in tasting notes – a type of language often discussed as either too subjective and obscure or indispensable given the difficulties of verbalising sensory perceptions. However, none of these two views is completely true. On the one hand, describing a given wine as *velvety, loud* or *bright* should not necessarily be more challenging than pinpointing its aromas as *mineral* or *Eastern spices* – whatever these smell like. Indeed, winespeak is but a sophisticated version of a good amount of the language we naturally use to describe many of the things in our everyday life – a case in point being what we put in our mouths, from toothpaste to food and, of course, all sorts of beverages. For instance, any person understands what *squeaky clean* means when related to hair, even if they do not analyse the qualification of "squeaky" as combining information from both the senses of hearing and touch, i.e. as referring to the sound made when you pass your fingers along wet, clean strands of hair. Put differently, if we understand expressions such as "squeaky-clean hair", "comfortable moisturising cream", "silky yoghurt" or "tingling fresh toothpaste", making sense of those same qualifiers – figurative in all contexts – when applied to wine should not prove too difficult.

On the other hand, while metaphor does indeed supply wine critics and aficionados with a conceptual and verbal apparatus to discuss wine in general, its form, function and relevance in winespeak remain problematic. For regardless of its critical role, figurative language remains a lesser evil, a compensatory strategy rather than a natural way of doing things (i.e., like any other use of language, automatised through usage). In other words, metaphor in – presumably difficult and highly specific – contexts such as winespeak is still regarded as an anomaly, a trope, rather than a tool that points to the muscular, flexible, adaptive quality of human nature and, therefore, cognition.

Of course, this does not mean that metaphor in winespeak is easy. Far from it. For one thing, as has been suggested throughout the chapter, many so-called conceptual and, above all, synaesthetic metaphors coexist and overlap constantly when talking about wine, to a point where it becomes almost impossible to tell one from the other. For instance, how do we interpret and classify the expression "squeaky-clean aromas", as instantiating a tactile metaphor, a sound metaphor, both? A possible way out is Talmy's (1996, 2000) notion of ception, conflating perception and conception while also including aspects of the processing of sensory stimulation, mental imagery, thinking and affect. Indeed, Talmy's claims that psychological discussion within cognitive research has implicitly or explicitly treated perception as a single category of cognitive phenomena may be reflected in the distinction made in Contemporary Metaphor Theory between conceptual metaphors and other metaphors dealing with more physical knowledge, e.g., image metaphors or synaesthetic metaphors. In this regard, part of the interest of a domain like wine discourse is the fact that it problematises the discreteness or boundaries of notions such as perception and cognition. In short, wine not only proves a stimulating topic of academic research, but the figurative data used to discuss wine experiences may also be used to challenge, among other things, the monosensory specialisation of lexis and claims towards the lack of words to discuss certain topics. Hopefully, the present chapter may be a first step in that direction.

Acknowledgements

The present research is funded by the Spanish Ministerio de Economía and Competitividad MINECO (reference: FFI2013-45553-C3-2-P).

References

Bernstein, L. S. (1998). *The official guide to wine snobbery*. New York: Quill.

Caballero, R. (2006). *Re-viewing space. Figurative language in architects' assessment of built space*. Berlin: Mouton de Gruyter. https://doi.org/10.1515/9783110893892

Caballero, R. (2007). Manner-of-motion verbs in wine description. *Journal of Pragmatics*, 39, 2095–2114. https://doi.org/10.1016/j.pragma.2007.07.005

Caballero, R. (in press). From the glass through the nose and the mouth: Motion in the description of sensory data about wine in English and Spanish. *Terminology*.

Caballero, R., & Suárez-Toste, E. (2008). Translating the senses. Teaching the metaphors in winespeak. In F. Boers, & S. Lindstromberg (Eds.), *Cognitive linguistic approaches to teaching vocabulary and phraseology* (pp. 241–260). Berlin: Mouton de Gruyter.

Caballero, R., & Suárez-Toste, E. (2010). A genre approach to imagery in winespeak. In G. Low, Z. Todd, A. Deignan, & L. Cameron (Eds.), *Researching and applying metaphor in the real world* (pp. 265–287). Amsterdam: John Benjamins. https://doi.org/10.1075/hcp.26.15cab

Caballero, R., & Paradis, C. (2013). Perceptual landscapes from the perspective of cultures and genres. In R. Caballero, & J. Díaz-Vera (Eds.), *Sensuous cognition – Explorations into human sentience – Imagination, (e)motion and perception* (pp. 77–105). Berlin: Mouton de Gruyter. https://doi.org/10.1515/9783110300772.77

Caballero, R., & Paradis, C. (2015). Making sense of sensory perceptions across languages and cultures. In R. Caballero, & C. Paradis (Eds.), *Sensory perceptions in language and cognition* (pp. 1–19). Special issue of *Functions of Language* 22 (1).

Croijmans, I., & Majid, A. (2016). Language does not explain the wine-specific memory advantage of wine experts. In A. Papafragou, D. Grodner, D. Mirman, & J. Trueswell (Eds.), *Proceedings of the 38th annual meeting of the Cognitive science Society* (CogSci 2016) (pp. 141–146). Austin, TX: Cognitive Science Society.

Day, S. (1996). Synaesthesia and synaesthetic metaphors. *Psyche*, 2(32). Online document. http://psyche.cs.monash.edu.au/v2/psyche-2-32-day.html.

Gawel, R. (1997). The use of language by trained and untrained wine tasters. *Journal of Sensory Studies*, 12, 267–284. https://doi.org/10.1111/j.1745-459X.1997.tb00067.x

Gawel, R., & Oberholster, A. (2001). *A mouth-feel wheel: Terminology for communicating the mouth-feel characteristics of red wine*. Adelaide: Department of Horticulture, Viticulture and Oenology, University of Adelaide.

Grady, J. (1997). THEORIES ARE BUILDINGS revisited. *Cognitive Linguistics*, 8(4), 267–290. https://doi.org/10.1515/cogl.1997.8.4.267

Gregutt, P. (2003). Scents and nonsense. *The Seattle Times Pacific Northwest Magazine*. Online document. Date of access: May 12th 2006. http://seattletimes.nwsource.com/pacificnw/2003/0112/taste.html

Hughson, A., & Boakes, R. (2001). Perceptual and cognitive aspects of wine tasting expertise. *Australian Journal of Psychology*, 53, 103–108. https://doi.org/10.1080/00049530108255130

Kimmel, M. (2010). Why we mix metaphors (and mix them well): Discourse coherence, conceptual metaphor, and beyond. *Journal of Pragmatics*, 42, 97–115. https://doi.org/10.1016/j.pragma.2009.05.017

Lakoff, G., & Johnson, M. (1980). *Metaphors we live by*. Chicago: University of Chicago Press.

Lakoff, G., & Johnson, M. (1999). *Philosophy in the flesh: The embodied mind and its challenge to Western thought*. New York: Basic Books.

Lawless, H. (1984). Flavour description of white wine by expert and non-expert wine consumers. *Journal of Food Science*, 49, 120–123. https://doi.org/10.1111/j.1365-2621.1984.tb13686.x

Levinson, S., & Majid, A. (2014). Differential ineffability and the senses. *Mind & Language*, 29, 407–427. https://doi.org/10.1111/mila.12057

Moore, V. (1999). The word on wine: Wine description. *New Statesman*, 3, May.

Nedlinko, A. (2006). Viticulture and winemaking terminology and terminography. *Terminology*, 12(1), 137–164. https://doi.org/10.1075/term.12.1.08ned

Noble, A., Arnold, R., Buechsenstein, J., Leach, J., Schmidt, J., & Stern, P. (1987). Modification of a standardised system of wine aroma terminology. *American Journal of Oenology and Viticulture*, 38(2), 143–146.

Old, M. (2013). *Wine: A tasting course*. London & New York: DK.

Panther, K.-U., & Radden, G. (Eds.). (1999). *Metonymy in language and thought*. Amsterdam: John Benjamins. https://doi.org/10.1075/hcp.4

Panther, K-U., & Thornburg, L. (Eds.). (2003). *Pragmatic inferencing in metonymy*. Amsterdam: John Benjamins. https://doi.org/10.1075/pbns.113

Paradis, C. (2004). Where does metonymy stop? Senses, facets, and active zones. *Metaphor and Symbol*, 19(4), 245–264. https://doi.org/10.1207/s15327868ms1904_1

Paradis, C. (2015). Conceptual spaces at work in sensory cognition: Domains, dimensions and distances. In P. Gärdenfors, & F. Zenker (Eds.), *Applications of geometric knowledge representation* (pp. 33–55). Berlin: Springer Verlag.

Paradis, C., & Eeg-Olofsson, M. (2013). Describing sensory perceptions: The genre of wine reviews. *Metaphor & Symbol*, 28(1), 1–19. https://doi.org/10.1080/10926488.2013.742838

Pierre, B. (1998). War of the words. *Food and Wine Magazine*, May.

Radden, G., & Kövecses, Z. (1999). Towards a theory of metonymy. In K-U. Panther, & G. Radden (Eds.), *Metonymy in language and thought* (pp. 17–59). Amsterdam: John Benjamins. https://doi.org/10.1075/hcp.4.03rad

Ramachandran, V., & Hubbard, E. (2001). Synaesthesia –A window into perception, thought and language. *Journal of Consciousness Studies*, 8(12), 3–34.

Shapin, S. (2012). The tastes of wine: Towards a cultural history. *Rivista di Estetica n.s.*, 51, 49–94. https://doi.org/10.4000/estetica.1395

Shen, Y. (1997). Cognitive constraints on poetic figures. *Cognitive Linguistics*, 8(1), 33–71. https://doi.org/10.1515/cogl.1997.8.1.33

Shen, Y., & Cohen, M. (1998). How come silence is sweet but sweetness is not silent: A cognitive account of directionality in poetic synaesthesia. *Language and Literature*, 7(2), 123–140. https://doi.org/10.1177/096394709800700202

Shen, Y., & Eisenman, R. (2008). 'Heard melodies are sweet, but those unheard are sweeter': Synaesthesia and cognition. *Language and Literature*, 17(2), 101–121.

Solomon, G. (1990). Psychology of novice and expert wine talk. *American Journal of Psychology*, 105, 495–517. https://doi.org/10.2307/1423321

Solomon, G. (1997). Conceptual change and wine expertise. *The Journal of the Learning Sciences*, 6, 41–60. https://doi.org/10.1207/s15327809jls0601_3

Strik Lievers, F. (2015). Synaesthesia: A corpus-based study of cross-modal directionality. *Functions of Language*, 27, 69–95.

Suárez-Toste, E. (2013). One man's cheese is another man's music: Synaesthesia and the bridging of cultural differences in the language of sensory perception. In R. Caballero, & J. E. Díaz-Vera (Eds.), *Sensuous cognition. Explorations into human sentience: Imagination, (e)motion and perception* (pp. 169–191). Berlin: Mouton. https://doi.org/10.1515/9783110300772.169

Suárez-Toste, E. (2017). Babel of the senses: On the roles of metaphor and synesthesia in wine reviews. *Terminology*, 23(1), 89–112.

Swales, J. (1990). *Genre analysis: English in academic and research settings*. Cambridge: Cambridge University Press.

Talmy, L. (1996). Fictive motion in language and "ception". In P. Bloom, M. Peterson, L. Nadel, & M. Garrett (Eds.), *Language and space* (pp. 211–276). Cambridge, MA: MIT Press.

Talmy, L. (2000). *Toward a cognitive semantics. Vol. I, Conceptual Structuring Systems*. Cambridge, MA: MIT Press.

Tsur, R. (1992). *Toward a theory of cognitive poetics*. Amsterdam: Elsevier.

Ullman, S. (1945). Romanticism and synaesthesia: A comparative study of sense transfer in Keats and Byron. *PMLA*, 60(3), 811–827. https://doi.org/10.2307/459180

Ullman, S. (1957). *The principles of semantics*. Oxford: Blackwell.

Yu, N. (2003). Synesthetic metaphor: A cognitive perspective. *Journal of Literary Semantics*, 32, 19–34. https://doi.org/10.1515/jlse.2003.001

CHAPTER 8

Taste metaphors in Hieroglyphic Egyptian

Elisabeth Steinbach-Eicke
Humboldt University of Berlin & Free University Berlin

This paper aims at giving an overview of the multiple meanings of the Ancient Egyptian verb of gustatory perception *tp* 'to taste'. Different mappings from physical onto emotional and mental domains are explained by metaphorical meaning extensions. Data from Ancient Egyptian, as a still under-represented language within studies on perceptual language, is analysed by methods from the fields of Ancient Studies and Cognitive Linguistics.

Keywords: sensory perception, senses, taste, perception verbs, cognition, Ancient Egyptian, Afro-Asiatic, hieroglyphs, Conceptual Metaphor Theory, Property Selection Processes

1. Introduction

The five sensory modalities of sight, hearing, touch, smell, taste and their mental processing are a source of ongoing research interest. Most of the world's languages have lexicalisation patterns for at least the five basic sensory modalities. Usually, linguistic studies on perception verbs restrict themselves to these five modalities (Strik Lievers, 2007, pp. 167–168). Therefore, the present article leaves further controversial debates about the overall number of the senses aside. In recent decades, perception verbs have attracted the attention of several fields of academic research such as anthropology, psychology and linguistics (e.g. Aikhenvald & Storch, 2013; Classen, 1993; Evans & Wilkins, 2000; Howes, 1991; Ibarretxe-Antuñano, 1999, 2002, 2013; Majid & Levinson, 2011; Sweetser, 1990; Vanhove, 2008; Viberg, 1984, 2015). However, studies on the sensory lexicon of ancient languages and research on diachronic meaning change over the centuries are still rare (Anderson, this volume; Strik Lievers & De Felice, this volume; Sweetser, 1990) and for Egyptian under-represented (Steinbach, 2015; Steinbach-Eicke, forthcoming a. and b.). Since the 1990s, approaches from Cognitive Linguistics have also found their way into Egyptology mainly through the works of Orly Goldwasser (1992, 1995, 2002, 2005), and more recently through the outstanding contributions of Rune Nyord (2009,

https://doi.org/10.1075/celcr.19.08ste

2012, 2015). Furthermore, the topic of "metaphor" in general and "metaphorical language" in particular is an important subject of current research within the field of Egyptology (Di Biase-Dyson, 2017).

The challenges of the study of the sensory perception of ancient cultures are numerous. The absence of native speakers combined with the inability to do linguistic field research is the most striking one. The reliance on material culture and/or textual evidence, created by just an elite group of the Egyptian society of whom only one to ten percent were able to read and write (Allen, 2014, p. 661) presents difficulties, too. This often coincides with a lack of coherent ancient sources and thus gaps in continuous meaningful material throughout all time periods. Furthermore, there is no explicit discourse on "senses", "perception" or "knowledge" evident in Ancient Egypt, as can be found for instance in Greek and Roman times in the works of classical authors like Aristotle or Plato. Nevertheless, a study of textual evidence is worthwhile, since texts enable insights into the thinking of an ancient culture (Verbovsek & Backes, 2015, p. 106) and further investigation is needed especially in the study of dead languages like Egyptian.

Against the background of these preliminary remarks, the present paper combines philological traditions from the field of Ancient Studies with more general approaches from Cognitive Linguistics in a case study of the Egyptian verb *tp* 'to taste'. This may open new perspectives for researchers of ancient or dead languages as well as for researchers interested in language comparison and development. Thus, the study fits well into the context of the present interdisciplinary volume on perceptual language. The field of gustatory sensation is worth investigating in more detail since it has often been neglected within perception studies.

Ancient Egyptian is attested by a broad range of various sources of material culture (e.g. temples, tombs, ostraca, papyri, …) as well as different literary genres (e.g. so-called wisdom texts, literary texts, autobiographies, religious spells, administrative texts, …) over a time span of more than three millennia. As we shall see, the high level of iconicity of the Hieroglyphic script (especially classifier usage) gives us some insights into the Egyptians' conception and system of world order. Thus, Egyptian provides us with an extensive and rich textual heritage coming from the ancient world and offers us a stimulating source to test modern theoretical assumptions about the language of perception for dead as well as modern languages.

2.   Particularities of the Ancient Egyptian language and script

Egyptian-Coptic makes up its own branch within the Afro-Asiatic language phylum. Cushitic (esp. Beja), Semitic, Berber and further Chadic show the closest relations to Ancient Egyptian (Allen, 2014, p. 641; Loprieno, 1995, p. 5). Egyptian can be subdivided into several scripts and language stages. The individual language stages can be grouped into Earlier Egyptian (3000 to 1300 BCE including Old and Middle Egyptian) and Later Egyptian (1300 BCE to 1300 CE including Late Egyptian, Demotic and Coptic). Furthermore, different kinds of scripts should be distinguished (see Figures 1 and 2): Hieroglyphs ("print type"), Hieratic (cursive writing of Hieroglyphs), Demotic and Coptic (using the Greek alphabet with seven additional letters coming from Demotic).

Figure 1. The same text of *Papyrus Ebers* in the original cursive writing of Hieratic (right, see Erman, 1917, p. 37) and in the transliterated form of "print type" Hieroglyphs (left), reading direction right-to-left, line for line

Figure 2. The name 'Ptolemy' in Demotic script (reading direction right-to-left, see Brugsch, 1851, p. 10) and in Coptic letters (reading direction left-to-right)

There are three different sign function classes (Kammerzell, 1999) in Hieroglyphic Egyptian: phonograms, logograms and classifiers. Phonograms stand for the phonological repertoire of the language (e.g. German B = /b/; Egyptian ⟋⟍ = /f/, 𓄟 = /m/); logograms show one sign for one word (e.g. German € = 'euro'; Egyptian ☉ = 'sundisk', ⟍⟋ = 'boat') and can have an index stroke as a logogram marker (𓇳 = 'sundisk', 𓊛 = 'boat'); classifiers assign Egyptian lexemes to specific semantic categories (e.g. English © = 'copyright' sign is used with quite different copyright owners). Classifiers only appear in *Written* Egyptian and were not spoken.

The hieroglyph of a sail, written ⌶ or ⌶ꜣ, functions as a logogram for the word *č3w* 'wind'. The same hieroglyph can also function as a classifier of other word-forms, evoking the category 'air; wind', shown in Table 1. The verb 'to sail', for instance, is composed of the root ⟹ *m3ᶜ* and the classifier of the sail ⌶. The noun 'storm' consists of the root ⟍⟍ *čᶜ* and again the classifier of the sail ⌶. In both cases, the classifier assigns the lexemes to the category [WIND].

Table 1. Exemplary word-forms with the 'sail classifier' (Lincke & Kammerzell, 2012, pp. 71–75, 83–85 and Schwarz, 2005, pp. 73–75)

Classifier	Word-forms		Translation
⌶	𓏤𓃀𓏮𓌙	*j3b:tj*	'eastwind'
	𓄿𓌙	*m3ᶜ*	'to sail'
	𓏴𓄿𓌙	*n3w*	'breathe of air'
	𓂝𓌙	*ś:nfj*	'to let somebody breathe'
	𓄿𓌙	*qrr*	'cloud'
	𓈖𓌙	*čᶜ*	'storm'

Thus, word-forms in Hieroglyphic Egyptian consist of a lexeme (or root) and may have one or more classifiers (traditionally called *determinatives*) at the end (Goldwasser, 2002; Goldwasser, 2005; Goldwasser & Grinevald, 2012; Lincke, 2011; Lincke & Kammerzell, 2012, especially pp. 56–67).

A further distinction can be made between lexical classifiers and referent classifiers (Lincke, 2011, pp. 93–107; Lincke & Kammerzell, 2012, pp. 88–98). Lexical classifiers refer to a lexeme in the lexicon, like the classifier of a sitting man 𓀀 in 𓀀 *s.i* 'man' or the classifier of a sitting woman 𓁐 in 𓊃𓈖𓏏𓁐 *śn:t* 'sister'. Referent classifiers are bound to the concrete usage of a word-form in context with connection to a specific referent in the sentence (see Table 2; Lincke, 2011; Lincke & Kammerzell, 2012, pp. 88–98; Werning, 2015, pp. 16–17). For instance, the word for 'child' consists of the root 𓄟 *mś* and is typically written with the lexical classifiers of a child 𓀔 and a sitting man 𓀀. In the *Contendings of Horus and Seth*, a literary text dating from the 12th century BCE (see also Example (4)), the same word is written with the classifiers 𓀔 and 𓅃. The cobra at the forehead of the child as well as the falcon on the standard are signs for gods and kings and give some additional information to the reader of the text. From the co(n)text it is clear, that the child here is the young god Horus who is of royal and divine nature. This information is only visible in the written form.

In this chapter, all examples are given in the transliterated form of Hieroglyphs. The data comes from the time between the third and the first millennium BCE and

Table 2. Lexical and referent classifiers (see also Werning, 2015, p. 17 for the example of 'big one')

	Hieroglyphic writing			Classifier		
Lexical classifier	𓂝𓄿𓏛	ꜥꜣ	'big', 'big one'	𓏛	papyrus scroll	generally used for abstract or immaterial meanings
Referent classifier	𓂝𓄿𓆙	ꜥꜣ	'big', 'big one'	𓆙	snake; worm	usage in text context, refers to a big snake
Lexical classifier	𓄠𓋴𓀔	mś	'child'	𓀔	child	generally used for children
				𓀀	man	generally used for males
Referent classifier	𓄠𓋴𓅔	mś	'child'	𓅔	child with cobra at forehead	usage in context, refers to a royal or divine child
				𓅆	falcon on standard	usage in context, refers to a king or to a divine being (god Horus)

covers Old, Middle and Late Egyptian texts. The *Thesaurus Linguae Aegyptiae* as the largest collection and dictionary of Egyptian texts was especially used as a database. Hieroglyphs have been set with the *JSesh Hieroglyphic editor* (version 6.5.5).

Since the article aims at gaining a coherent picture of the field, there will be no detailed differentiation between literary genres, time periods or speech registers. Nevertheless, the use of figurative language plays an important role in specific genres, such as wisdom texts, where we can find metaphors of *path* (e.g. LIFE IS A JOURNEY), see Di Biase-Dyson (2016).

3.   Methodological background: Conceptual Metaphor Theory and Property Selection Processes

Metaphors are not only bare rhetorical devices (Lakoff & Johnson, 1980/2003, pp. 3–4). In Cognitive Linguistics and more specifically in Conceptual Metaphor Theory, conceptual metaphors are described as mappings between two different conceptual domains, namely a *source domain* and a *target domain* (Kövecses, 2002, p. 4). These mapping processes are understood as being deeply embodied and grounded in the sensorimotor and cultural experience humans have gained through interaction with their environment (Kövecses, 2002, pp. 6, 69–76, 187). Therefore, it is generally assumed that semantic structures mirror conceptual structures and lexical items can portray conceptual categories in a specific manner. With regard to the conceptual metaphors of perception verbs, the source domain of physical perception, consisting of the five sensory modalities, is mapped onto the target domain of emotions and more complex aspects of intellection through motivated and systematic meaning extensions (Kövecses, 2002, pp. 67–68). Lakoff and Johnson (1999, pp. 238–240) formulated a general THINKING IS PERCEIVING metaphor for this phenomenon.

A new framework for the study of perception verbs has been established by Iraide Ibarretxe-Antuñano (1999, 2013, this volume) and concentrates on the inherent physical properties of each of the five sensory modalities. These properties are grounded in the physiological and psychological information generally known about the senses (Ibarretxe-Antuñano, 1999, p. 143 and this volume). Although her method focuses on perception verbs in three modern languages (English, Spanish, Basque), it has proven to be useful for the study of dead languages like Egyptian as well, apart from some minor restrictions. The method assumes that physical properties can be assigned to three groups of participating elements within a perceptual act: the perceiver (or experiencer), the object of perception and the whole perceptual act itself. In addition, every group is set in a specific relation to the other groups through certain properties, which can receive either a positive or negative value. The physical properties of the relation between the perceiver and the object perceived are <contact>, <closeness>, <internal> and <subjectivity> (use of pointed brackets follows Ibarretxe-Antuñano, 1999). The relation of the perceiver and the act of perception is characterised by <detection>, <identification>, <voluntary> and <directness>. Finally, the relation between the object perceived and the act of perception can show <evaluation> and <briefness>. Table 3 shows the properties of taste in comparison to those of vision.

For instance, the first three properties <contact>, <closeness> and <internal> have negative values for vision and positive values for taste. Objects can be seen and perceived from far away whereas the taste of food is only perceived by close contact. Furthermore, to taste food means that it has to enter inside one's mouth while the beauty of a whole landscape can be appreciated from a distance (= external).

Table 3. Physical properties of taste (following the table in Ibarretxe-Antuñano, 2013, p. 118)

Elements	Properties	Vision*	Taste*
perceiver → object of perception	contact	no	yes
	closeness	no	yes
	internal limits	no	yes
	location	yes	
	subjectivity		yes
perceiver → perception	detection	yes	yes
	identification	yes	yes
	voluntary	yes	yes
	directness	yes	yes
	correction-of-hypothesis	yes	
object of perception → perception	effects		
	evaluation	yes	yes
	briefness		yes

* a blank space means that a property is not applicable to a sensory modality

The application of properties allows more accurate statements about what properties are mapped from the source domain onto the target domain in metaphorical meaning extensions and how these mappings include the individual arguments in a sentence. Here, the notion that only parts of the source domain are mapped onto the target domain is of eminent importance and has already been labelled as the "used part of a metaphor" by Lakoff and Johnson (1980/2003, pp. 52–55). Within the next sections, the "used part" of metaphors of taste in Ancient Egyptian will be shown.

4.   The sensory modality of taste in Egyptian

4.1   The verb *tp*

The verb *tp* 'to taste (something)' expresses gustatory sensation and is the only attested verb for the taste domain throughout the whole language history of Egyptian (Erman & Grapow, 1931, pp. 443–444). The verb is still preserved in Coptic as *tôp*, *tôpe* (Westendorf, 1965/1977, p. 240) which is the latest stage of the ancient Egyptian language. The feminine noun *tp:t* 'the taste' coming from the same root as the verb can have similar metaphorical meaning extensions but is not studied in detail within this chapter. Other word classes like sensory adjectives are also omitted here.

The verb does not show any classifiers in its first occurrences in the *Pyramid Texts* of the Old Kingdom (28th–23rd century BCE). Starting in the Middle

Kingdom (22nd–18th century BCE), the verb is mostly classified with ⌐ (tongue of a cow), 𓀁 (man with hand at mouth) and ▬ (book scroll, i.e. for abstraction), either alone or in different combinations with each other. There are a few instances of meaningful classifier change in the data, showing the usage of referent classifiers (see Table 2), for example, in *Papyrus Bremner Rhind,* 27.24 (Faulkner, 1933, p. 65: 𓂀) or in *Papyrus Leiden I 350 recto,* V 15–16 (Zandee, 1948, Pl. V.𓀜). Of special interest is the superordinate classifier of the man with his hand at his mouth, which generally indicates the "'SENSES AND EMOTIONS' category (classified by the icon of 'things which *are put in/come out* from the body-container [through the mouth]'" by Goldwasser (2002, p. 5 and 2005, p. 99). This classifier is used to convey processes of swallowing and eating as well as intellectual activities like speaking and thinking. This assignment to different categories is present within the semantics of the verb in its metaphorical meaning extensions, as will be shown below. The use of classifiers at the end of perception verbs, depicting the respective sense organs for every modality, is seen here as the decisive criterion for attributing lexical items to a particular sensory modality. The classifiers of vision verbs are for example human eyes (𓁹, 𓂀, 𓂩), verbs of hearing have human (𓄔) or bovid (𓄓) ears (Goldwasser, 1995, pp. 68–69), verbs of smell use a human (𓂉) or bovid (𓄛) face in profile (Relats-Montserrat, 2014) and verbs for touch can take hands (𓂝), arms (𓂡, 𓂥) or fingers (�). For *tp* the tongue of a cow (⌐) evokes the domain of gustatory perception.

The semantic potential of the verb is versatile in developing various meanings by intrafield and transfield (Evans & Wilkins, 2000; Matisoff, 1978) mappings. Intrafield mappings mean mappings within the perceptual domain from one sensory modality onto another sensory modality. Transfield mappings mean mappings into physical, emotional or mental domains. Both phenomena are quite common in the world's languages (Aikhenvald & Storch, 2013; Evans & Wilkins, 2000, pp. 553–562). In this article, the focus is on these extended meanings of the verb and their possible motivations.

4.2   Prototypical and physical meanings

The prototypical meaning of the Egyptian perception verb *tp* 'to taste' is clearly bodily based. It is understood as the most central element within the domain of gustatory perception to which all other extended meanings are related in a specific and motivated manner (Nyord, 2012, pp. 143–144; Trim, 2007, pp. 15–21). This aspect of its meaning is illustrated in Example (1), coming from a ritual to invigorate all senses of the deceased king and to renew his ability to speak and breathe.

(1)

h3	Wniś	i:tp-k	tp:t-f
EXLM	Unas	taste.SBJV-2SG.M	taste:F.SG-3SG.M

ḫnt	sḥ-w_nčr-w
in_front_of	hall.M-PL_god.M-PL

'O Unas, you shall *taste* its taste (i.e. a milky product) in front of the halls of the gods.'[1]

In Example (2), the vizier and official Ptahhotep requests his retirement from the king and complains about the burdens of old age and the physical demise of the body.

(2)

ir:ti	nčs-w	ʿnḫ-wi	it-w
eye:F.DU	be_weak.RES-3PL	ear.M-DU	be_deaf.RES-3PL (…)

ṭp:t	nb-t	šmi-ti
taste:F.SG	every-F.SG	go_away.RES-3SG.F

'The eyes cannot see, the ears cannot hear (…) and every *taste* is gone.'

Both, the 'ears' ʿnḫ-wi and the verb 'to be deaf' it-w have bovid ears as classifiers. Even the disability of hearing belongs to the category of [EAR], see Goldwasser (1995, p. 92).

In addition to the meaning 'to taste', the verb tp can also have the physical meanings 'to touch' or 'to feel (physically)' in certain contexts, as shown by many examples in the textual evidence. One such example is given in (3). The god Aten

---

1.   There is no strict convention for the transcription of Hieroglyphic Egyptian into Latin letters. A table of the proximate phonetic values of each of the transcription signs is given in Schenkel (2012, pp. 23–24) as follows: the sign 3 represents /r/ or /ʀ/, i = /ʔ/, ꜥ = /ʕ/, w = /w/, b = /b/, p = /p/, f = /pʼ/ or /f/, m = /m/, n = /n/, r = /r/ or /d/ or /l/, h = /h/, ḥ = /ħ/, ḫ = /γ/, ẖ = /x/, s = /ʼs/, ś = /s/, š = /ʃ/, ḳ = /kʼ/, k = /k/, g = /kʲ/ and /kʷ/ or /kʲʲ/ and /kʼʷ/, t = /t/, č = /tʃ/, ṯ = /tʼ/, ǯ = /tʼʃ/, i = fictitious i-value. Further descriptions can be found in Peust (1999) and Kammerzell (2005). Glossing follows the Leipzig Glossing Rules with a few additional glosses for Ancient Egyptian based upon Di Biase-Dyson, Kammerzell & Werning (2009) and Werning (2016). All glossing abbreviations as well as references to all text examples with an approximate dating are given at the end of this article. Translations of Egyptian texts are my own. The actual meanings of the taste verb are given in italics within the translations. Further detailed examples for the various meanings of tp 'to taste' can be found in Steinbach (2015) and Steinbach-Eicke (forthcoming a.). Shaded hieroglyphs indicate (partial) destruction of the text-bearing artefact.

was especially worshipped during the so-called Amarna-Period (corresponding to the reign of King Akhenaten, 1349–1332 BCE, see Williamson, 2015) as the central god of a monotheistic Egypt state religion, thus abolishing the former polytheism of the country. Aten is the personified and deified disk of the sun that is perceived by humans because the heat of the sunrays could be felt *physically* on the skin.

(3)

irr-k	*tr-w*	*r*	*ś-ḫpr*
do.NMLZ.IPFV-2SG.M	season.M-PL	to	CAUS-become.INF

iri̯:y-k	*nb*	*pr:t*	*r*
do.PTCP.ACT:M.SG-2SG.M	every.M.SG	winter:F.SG	to

ś-ḳb-sn	*ḥḥ*
CAUS-cool.INF-3PL	heat.M.SG

tp-śt	*tw*
taste.SBJV-3PL	2SG.M

'You (= Aten) created the seasons so that everything you made could exist: the winter to cool them and the summer heat so that they may *feel* you.'

Another instance of *tp* being used for physical feeling is shown in Example (4). In the religious understanding of Ancient Egypt, Horus is the son of the gods Osiris and Isis. In the myth, the god Seth has killed his brother Osiris and Horus asks to take up his father's throne and rule over Egypt. This results in a battle over the succession of the throne of Osiris. In the text, the goddess Isis is using a magical weapon to fight against Seth to help Horus win the battle. The weapon is a sharp spear of copper ore. Isis put a magical spell on that spear and thus changed it from an inanimate to an animate being able to move and to perceive like any other living being (personification). In the story, Isis throws this spear into the water where Horus and Seth were but the spear hurts Horus mistakenly instead of Seth.

(4)

ᶜḥᶜ.n	*p3*	*ḥmt*	*ḥr*	*tp*	*m*	*ḥm*
CJVB.ANT	DEF.ART.M.SG	spear.M.SG	at	taste.INF	from	majesty.M.SG

n	*s3-ś*	*ḥr:w*
of	son.M.SG-3SG.F	Horus

'Then, the spear *hit* the majesty of her son Horus.'

These physical meanings listed in (3) and (4) can be understood in terms of another sense modality, namely *touch*. *Tasting* the heat of the sun on one's skin means that the heat is in contact with and *touching* the skin; for a spear to *taste* a target means that it *touches* it, that the target is skewed upon it. Thus, an intrafield mapping is created from the *taste* onto the *touch* domain in Egyptian.

The extended but not abstract meaning of the verb 'to feel (physically) something' still remains in the physical sphere with the emphasis of physical properties shifted. In (4), the semantic weight lies on the properties of <contact> and <closeness>, focusing on the relation between the perceiver and the object perceived. The close contact between Horus as the object of perception and the spear as the perceiver, literally *tasting* the god, is highlighted here.

The meanings 'to taste' and 'to touch' of the verb *tp* are already graspable in Proto-Afroasiatic. Proto-Afroasiatic is a reconstructed language from which all Afro-Asiatic languages, also Egyptian, originate from. The Proto-Afroasiatic root *-dap-* is considered to mean 'to touch, feel, put the fingers on' and is later present in the Egyptian verb *tp* 'to taste, experience' (Ehret, 1995, p. 133, p. 497, root 145; Allan, 2008, p. 71–72). Since there are too few successive and coherent attestations of the verb *tp* from the beginning of textual evidence in the fourth and third millennium BCE onwards, it is difficult to draw conclusions about the exact etymology of the verb.

Based on the above explanations, the following statements can be assumed with almost certainty:

1. The early text examples of the verb in the Old Kingdom (28th–23th century BCE) show typical "taste-co(n)texts", i.e. eating, acquiring food etc.
2. The classifiers of the verb express oral activities and appear from the beginning of the Middle Kingdom (21st–18th century BCE) onwards. Thus, one can suggest, that the verb is clearly considered as being part of the gustatory domain. Nevertheless, the aspect of 'touch' is still inherent in its semantics, based on shared physical characteristics of 'taste' and 'touch', as Popova formulated very appropriately:

> It should not be forgotten that despite its physiological distinctness taste is a kind of touch performed by the tongue. Aristotle classifies touch and taste together, because they are the two senses requiring contact, while the remaining three perceive over a distance. It should also be noted that [...] the majority of words describing gustatory perception, originate as concepts describing touch, even though their contemporary meanings are associated with taste only or, in some instances, have been mapped onto higher domains.   (Popova, 2005, pp. 407–408 [footnote 12])

Both modalities are related in a specific manner as further cross-linguistic evidence from the etymology of the English word *taste* shows: The Latin word *tangere* means *taste* and *touch*. There is still *tactile* in English, *tâter* ('touchable') in French or even *tasten* ('to touch') in German (Sweetser, 1990, p. 36, p. 44; Viberg, 1984, p. 145). Touch and taste share almost all of the physical properties mentioned above – except the property of <internal>, which is negative for touch.

The prototypical and physical meaning extensions of taste cover the following senses: 'to taste something', 'to feel (physically) something' and 'to touch something'. *Taste* can extend its meaning to *touch* and the sensory modality of *touch* itself is able to extend its meaning into the field of *emotions* (EMOTIONAL EFFECT IS PHYSICAL CONTACT, see Lakoff & Johnson, 1980/2003, p. 50; Viberg, 2015, pp. 116–120). This might possibly serve as an explanation for *taste*, as a special kind of *touch*, expanding into *emotional* domains, too.

4.3   Emotional meanings

Emotions can be constructed and lexicalised in various ways in Egyptian. We can grasp some basic emotional concepts by descriptive emotion words (e.g. *mrw:t* 'love', *mśč:yt* 'hate' or *śnč* 'fear') but there is no specific word for a general emotional state, like 'to *feel* something' or 'to *experience* something'. Rather, such emotional states are expressed metaphorically using *tp* 'to taste' in Egyptian. Until now, there are only a few contributions concerned with the topic of emotions or emotional concepts in Ancient Egypt (e.g. Köhler, 2016; Eicke, 2015 and 2017).

Due to the textual sources, it is difficult to draw conclusions about possible earlier and later meanings of the verb or to formulate assumptions about whether one metaphorical meaning could have developed out of another extended meaning. Thus, though it seems plausible that physical ('to feel physically') and emotional ('to feel emotionally') senses of the gustatory verb are quite closely connected, we do not possess any information on their interdependency on a diachronic level.

In the story of Example (5), a wise man called Ipuwer tells the king about the bad and lawless situation in Egypt. In Ipuwer's complaint, the king is asked to put himself in the place of his subjects so that he can sympathise with them and to solve the country's problems.

(5)

ḥ3	tp-k	m	nhi
MODP	taste.SBJV-2SG.M	from	a_little.M

ni	m3r	ir:i
of.M.SG	misery.M	thereof:ADJZ

'O, would that you could *feel* a little of the misery thereof.'

In the next example, the scribe Kheti describes different professions (e.g. barber, gardener, potter, reed worker, weaver etc.) that he thinks are not desirable because of the physically demanding and stressful work they entail. His successor in the office of a functionary is advised to become a respected scribe, belonging to an elite group of the Egyptian society, rather than a bricklayer.

(6)

ǧt-i	n-k	mi	ḳt-w
say.SBJV-1SG	to-2SG.M	like	builder.M-PL

inb-w	mḥr	tp-t<-f>
wall.M-PL	bad.M.SG	taste.REL.IPFV-F-3SG.M

ḥr	wnn-f		m	rw:ti	ni	m3ᶜ:w
OBLV	exist.IPFV-3SG.M		in	outside	of.M.SG	wind:M

'Let me tell you that it is like with the bricklayers: what he *experiences* is bad because he has to be outside in the wind.'

In metaphorical extensions of taste into the domain of emotions, several physical properties are selected to create meanings like 'to feel emotionally (in a wider sense)' or 'to experience'. The relation between the object perceived and the whole perceptual act is emphasised the most. Particularly, the properties of <subjective> and <evaluation> have to be highlighted here. In many examples within the studied corpus, the meanings of *tp* expressing 'to experience' are linked to bad, evil, generally negative or tragic events that the experiencer perceives (e.g. *The Story of the Shipwrecked Sailor* 124 and 179–181, see Blackman, 1972; *The Tale of the Eloquent Peasant* 90–91, see Parkinson, 1991).

Something similar is attested for Indo-European languages where verbs of eating or swallowing also involve expressions of unpleasant emotions or sensations, i.e. in French '*Hier, j'ai été convoquée par le chef. Qu'est-ce que j'ai dégusté!*' (Yesterday, I was summoned by the boss. I didn't half have a rough time!), see Hénault (2008, pp. 297–298). Similar in German: 'Ich musste meinen Ärger runter*schlucken*.' (I had to swallow my anger.').

There is a close connection between the domain of gustatory perception and that of emotions. Apart from descriptive words for specific emotions, general pleasant or unpleasant feelings are expressed by the verb 'to taste', evoking meanings like 'to feel (emotionally) something' or 'to experience something'.

Kövecses (this volume) even proposes an EMOTION IS PERCEPTION metaphor and presumes that there should also be a rank order between conceptual metaphors such as EMOTION IS TOUCH, EMOTION IS TASTE and EMOTION IS SMELL.

Of course, more data is needed to test this assumption, but at least for Ancient Egyptian EMOTION IS TASTE seems to be more common than EMOTION IS SMELL or EMOTION IS TOUCH.

4.4   Cognitive meanings

The are some instances of *tp* 'to taste' creating metaphorical extensions in mental domains. Example (7) is an excerpt from a longer text out of the *Coffin Texts* corpus. The deceased aims at living as a mighty spirit in the realm of the dead. Therefore s/he seeks to identify with different gods or their powerful attributes, especially with the ruler of the netherworld, the god Osiris. To have knowledge about the netherworld, in this case about the *Lord of Buto* (i.e. Osiris or Horus), is therefore important.

(7)

n	*ṯp-i*	*iḫ:t*	*mḥr*
NEG	taste.PFV-1SG	thing:F.SG	bad.M.SG

mi	*nb*	*ꜣbṯ*	*iti:y*
like	lord.M.SG	monthly_festival.M.SG	ruler:M.SG

č:t	*ink*	*ṯp:w*	*r_čr*
eternity:F.SG	1SG	taste.PTCP.ACT:M.SG	all

nb	*P*	*ꜣḫ:n*	*nčr*
lord.M.SG	Buto	excellent:NMLZ.ANT	god.M.SG

nb	*n*	*ṯp:n-i*	*św*
every.M.SG	for	taste:ANT-1SG	3SG.M

'I did not *experience* anything bad, like the lord of the monthly festival, the sovereign of eternity. I am the one who *knows* everything concerning the Lord of Buto. Because I have *experienced* him, every god has become excellent.'

The text shows three transfers from the taste to the mental domain. Thus, it is suggested that knowledge can be consumed like food. The meaning 'to know' is well established for verbs having to do with the acquisition of food, i.e. *to taste*, *to eat* or *to swallow*, in numerous languages and metaphors like IDEAS ARE FOOD or ACQUIRING KNOWLEDGE IS EATING are a wide spread phenomenon (Lakoff & Johnson, 1980/2003, pp. 46–47, pp. 147–148; Lakoff & Johnson, 1999, pp. 241–243; Hénault, 2008, p. 295; Ibarretxe-Antuñano, 1999, pp. 85–86).

In Egyptian, the semantic development of the verb ꜥm 'to swallow' (Erman & Grapow, 1926, pp. 183–184) is another good example of a remarkable diachronic meaning change from the physical to the cognitive domain. Through a step-by-step extension during the second half of the second millennium BCE, the verb shifts its meaning from ꜥm [hieroglyphs] 'to swallow' to ꜥm [hieroglyphs] 'to know'. The verb is even preserved with the meaning 'to know, to understand' in Coptic as *eime* (Westendorf, 1965/1977, p. 49). Furthermore, a significant change in the verb classifier is evident. The verb with the meaning 'to swallow' usually takes the man-with-hand-at-mouth [glyph] classifier, whereas the verb in the sense of 'to know' is later classified with a human eye [glyph], marking intellectual activities. The meaning change as well as the classifier change is not sharply delimited and both meanings still exist next to each other in the texts (Goldwasser, 2005, p. 111; Chantrain, 2014, pp. 45–46).

Similar developments can also be observed in other languages. The Latin *sapere* means 'to taste' and 'to know'. In modern Romance languages like Spanish *saber* means both 'to taste' and 'to know', whereas the French *savoir* is restricted to the meaning 'to know' (Sweetser, 1990, p. 36).

5. Conclusion

In Ancient Egyptian, only one verb is lexicalised in the domain of gustatory perception: ṭp 'to taste (something)'. This polysemous verb has developed multiple meanings into different domains and creates the following perception metaphors:

a. PHYSICAL FEELING/TOUCHING IS TASTING,
b. EMOTIONAL FEELING IS TASTING,
c. EXPERIENCING IS TASTING and
d. KNOWING IS TASTING.

Tracing the various extended meanings of the verb diachronically over the centuries has shown that the semantics of perception verbs is a fluid phenomenon. The meaning of Egyptian *taste* covers aspects of physical, emotional and mental domains. At least for a number of instances, perception metaphors found in Egyptian can be observed in modern languages, too. Egyptology as well as linguistics can thus derive benefit from in-depth studies of perceptual language in Ancient Egyptian which has only just begun. Correlations between Egyptian, as one of the world's oldest recorded languages, and other modern, unrelated languages allow us to prove theories and methods of modern research, to formulate new questions or even claims with respect to possible language universals.

Acknowledgements

I would like to thank the organisers of the *Perception Metaphor Workshop* for giving me the chance to present my topic in front of an expert audience. This contribution represents an insight into my PhD thesis on the syntax and semantics of perception verbs in Earlier Egyptian within the field of Egyptology. Further, I am grateful to the *Ernst-Reuter-Gesellschaft der Freunde, Förderer und Ehemaligen der Freien Universität Berlin e.V.* for the travelling support and Sven Eicke for useful comments on this chapter.

Abbreviations

1, 2, 3	1st, 2nd, 3rd person	IPFV	imperfective
ACT	active	M	masculine
ADJZ	adjectivization	MODP	modifying particle
ANT	anterior	NEG	negation
ART	article	NMLZ	nominalization
CAUS	causative	OBLV	oblative
CJVB	conjunctive verb	PL	plural
DEF	definite	PTCP	participle
DU	dual	REL	relative
EXLM	exclamative	RES	resultative
F	feminine	SBJV	subjunctive
INF	infinitive	SG	singular

List of examples

Ex.	Source	Approx. dating	Reference
(1)	*Pyramid Texts of King Unas*, Spell 34, § 26b.	24th cent. BCE	Allen, 2013, PT 34.
(2)	*The Teaching of Ptahhotep, Papyrus Prisse*, 4.3–5.1.	19th cent. BCE	Žába, 1956, p. 16.
(3)	*Great Hymn to Aten, Tomb of Aja*, 11.	14th cent. BCE	Sandman, 1938, p. 95.
(4)	*The Contendings of Horus and Seth, Papyrus Chester Beatty I*, 9.1.	12th cent. BCE	Gardiner, 1932/1981, p. 48.
(5)	*The Dialogue of Ipuwer with the Lord of All, Papyrus Leiden I 344 recto*, 13.5–6.	12th cent. BCE	Enmarch, 2005, p. 53.
(6)	*The Teaching of Kheti, Papyrus Sallier II*, 6.1–3.	12th cent. BCE	Helck, 1970, pp. 59–60.
(7)	*Coffin Texts*, Spell 316, § 106b, 108e, 108i, source: S2P.	19th cent. BCE	Buck, 1951, 106b & 108e & 108i.

References

Aikhenvald, A. & Storch, A. (Eds.). (2013). *Perception and cognition in language and culture.* Leiden: Brill.

Allan, K. (2008). *Metaphor and metonymy. A diachronic approach.* Oxford: Wiley-Blackwell.

Allen, J. P. (2013). *A new concordance of the Pyramid Texts. Volume II.* Providence, RI: Brown University. Retrieved from https://www.dropbox.com/sh/0xo88uy04urnz0v/o16_ojF8f_ (29 April 2017).

Allen, J. P. (2014). Language, scripts, and literacy. In A. B. Lloyd (Ed.), *A companion to Ancient Egypt* (pp. 641–662). Oxford: Wiley-Blackwell.

Blackman, A. M. (1972). *Middle-Egyptian Stories.* Brussels: Éditions de la Fondation Égyptologique Reine Élisabeth.

Brugsch, H. (1851). *Sammlung demotisch-griechischer Eigennamen ägyptischer Privatleute aus Inschriften und Papyrusrollen.* Berlin: Verlag Rudolph Gaertner.

Buck, A. de. (1951). *The Egyptian Coffin Texts IV. Texts of Spells 268–354.* Chicago, IL: The Oriental Institute of the University of Chicago.

Chantrain, G. (2014). The use of classifiers in the New Kingdom. A global reorganization of the classifiers system? *Lingua Aegyptia*, 22, 39–59.

Classen, C. (1993). *Worlds of sense. Exploring the senses in history and across cultures.* London: Longman.

Di Biase-Dyson, C., Kammerzell, F. & Werning, D. A. (2009). Glossing Ancient Egyptian. Suggestions for adapting the Leipzig Glossing Rules. *Lingua Aegyptia*, 17, 343–366.

Di Biase-Dyson, C. (2016). Wege und Abwege. Zu den Metaphern in der ramessidischen Weisheitsliteratur. *Zeitschrift für ägyptische Sprache und Altertumskunde*, 143(1), 22–33. https://doi.org/10.1515/zaes-2016-0003

Di Biase-Dyson, C. (2017). Metaphor (published 10 April 2017). In J. Stauder-Porchet, A. Stauder & W. Wendrich (Eds.), *UCLA Encyclopedia of Egyptology.* Retrieved from https://escholarship.org/uc/item/4z62d3nn (14 August 2017).

Ehret, C. (1995). *Reconstructing Proto-Afroasiatic (Proto-Afrasian). Vowels, tone, consonants, and vocabulary.* Berkeley & Los Angeles, CA: University of California Press Ltd. & London: University of California Press.

Eicke, S. (2015). Ende mit Schrecken oder Schrecken ohne Ende? Zur Verwendung sprachlicher Ausdrücke für Furcht im Totenbuch. In G. Neunert, H. Simon, A. Verbovsek & K. Gabler (Eds.), *Text: Wissen – Wirkung – Wahrnehmung. Beiträge des vierten Münchner Arbeitskreises Junge Aegyptologie (MAJA 4) 29.11. bis 1.12.2013* (pp. 151–166). Wiesbaden: Harrassowitz.

Eicke, S. (2017). Affecting the gods: Fear in Ancient Egyptian religious texts. In A. Storch (Ed.), *Consensus and dissent. Negotiating emotion in the public space* (pp. 229–246). Amsterdam & Philadelphia, PA: John Benjamins. https://doi.org/10.1075/clu.19.12eic

Enmarch, R. (2005). *The Dialogue of Ipuwer and the Lord of All.* Oxford: Griffith Institute Publications.

Erman, A. (1917). *Die Hieroglyphen.* Leipzig: G. J. Göschensche Verlagsbuchhandlung. https://doi.org/10.1515/9783111584300

Erman, A. & Grapow, H. (1926). *Wörterbuch der Aegyptischen Sprache Band I.* Leipzig: J. C. Hinrichs Verlag.

Erman, A. & Grapow, H. (1931). *Wörterbuch der Aegyptischen Sprache Band V.* Leipzig: J. C. Hinrichs Verlag.

Evans, N. & Wilkins, D. (2000). In the mind's ear: The semantic extensions of perception verbs in Australian languages. *Language,* 76(3), 546–592. https://doi.org/10.2307/417135

Faulkner, R. O. (1933). *The Papyrus Bremner Rhind (British Museum No. 10188).* Brussels: Éditions de la Fondation Égyptologique Reine Élisabeth.

Gardiner, A. H. (1932/1981). *Late-Egyptian Stories.* Brussels: Éditions de la Fondation Égyptologique Reine Élisabeth.

Goldwasser, O. (1992). The Narmer Palette and the "Triumph of Metaphor". *Lingua Aegyptia,* 2, 67–85.

Goldwasser, O. (1995). *From icon to metaphor.* Fribourg: University Press & Göttingen: Vandenhoeck & Ruprecht.

Goldwasser, O. (2002). *Prophets, lovers and giraffes: Wor(l)d classification in Ancient Egypt.* Wiesbaden: Harrassowitz.

Goldwasser, O. (2005). Where is metaphor? Conceptual metaphor and alternative classification in the Hieroglyphic script. *Metaphor and Symbol,* 20(2), 95–113. https://doi.org/10.1207/s15327868ms2002_1

Goldwasser, O. & Grinevald, C. (2012). What are "Determinatives" good for? In E. Grossman, S. Polis & J. Winand (Eds.), *Lexical semantics in Ancient Egyptian* (pp. 17–53). Hamburg: Widmaier.

Helck, W. (1970). *Die Lehre des Dw3-ḫtjj. Teil I.* Wiesbaden: Harrassowitz.

Hénault, C. (2008). Eating beyond certainties. In M. Vanhove (Ed.), *From polysemy to semantic change* (pp. 291–301). Amsterdam & Philadelphia, PA: Brill. https://doi.org/10.1075/slcs.106.14hen

Howes, D. (Ed.). (1991). *The varieties of sensory experience. A sourcebook in the anthropology of the senses.* Toronto: University of Toronto Press.

Ibarretxe-Antuñano, I. (1999). Polysemy and metaphor in perception verbs: A cross-linguistic study. Doctoral dissertation: University of Edinburgh. Retrieved from http://www.unizar.es/linguisticageneral/articulos/Ibarretxe-PhD-Thesis-99.pdf (14 August 2017).

Ibarretxe-Antuñano, I. (2002). MIND-AS-BODY as a cross-linguistic conceptual metaphor. *Miscelánea. A Journal of English and American Studies,* 25, 93–119.

Ibarretxe-Antuñano, I. (2013). The power of the senses and the role of culture in metaphor and language. In R. Caballero & J. E. Díaz-Vera (Eds.), *Sensuous cognition. Explorations into human sentience: Imagination, (e)motion and perception* (pp. 109–133). Berlin & Boston: de Gruyter. https://doi.org/10.1515/9783110300772.109

Kammerzell, F. (1999). Klassifikatoren und Kategorienbildung in der ägyptischen Hieroglyphenschrift. *Spektrum. Informationen aus Forschung und Lehre,* 3, 29–34.

Kammerzell, F. (2005). Old Egyptian and Pre-Old Egyptian. Tracing linguistic diversity in archaic Egypt and the creation of the Egyptian language. In S. Seidlmayer (Ed.), *Texte und Denkmäler des ägyptischen Alten Reiches* (pp. 165–246). Berlin: Achet.

Köhler, I. (2016). *Rage like an Egyptian. Die Möglichkeiten eines kognitiv-semantischen Zugangs zum altägyptischen Wortschatz am Beispiel des Wortfelds [WUT].* Hamburg: Buske Verlag.

Kövecses, Z. (2002). *Metaphor. A practical introduction.* Oxford: Oxford University Press.

Lakoff, G. & Johnson, M. (1980/2003). *Metaphors we live by.* Chicago, IL & London: The University of Chicago Press.

Lakoff, G. & Johnson, M. (1999). *Philosophy in the flesh. The embodied mind and its challenge to western thought.* New York, NY: Basic Books.

Lincke, E.-S. (2011). *Die Prinzipien der Klassifizierung im Altägyptischen.* Wiesbaden: Harrassowitz.

Lincke, E.-S. & Kammerzell, F. (2012). Egyptian classifiers at the interface of lexical semantics and pragmatics. In E. Grossman, S. Polis & J. Winand (Eds.), *Lexical semantics in Ancient Egyptian* (pp. 55–112). Hamburg: Widmaier.

Loprieno, A. (1995). *Ancient Egyptian. A linguistic introduction.* Cambridge: Cambridge University Press. https://doi.org/10.1017/CBO9780511611865

Majid, A. & Levinson, S. C. (Eds.) (2011). The senses in language and culture. *The Senses & Society,* 6(1), 5–18. https://doi.org/10.2752/174589311X12893982233551

Matisoff, J. A. (1978). *Variational semantics in Tibeto-Burman. The "organic" approach to linguistic comparison.* Philadelphia, PA: Institute for the Study of Human Issues.

Nyord, R. (2009). *Breathing flesh. Conceptions of the body in the Ancient Egyptian Coffin Texts.* Copenhagen: Museum Tusculanum Press.

Nyord, R. (2012). Prototype structures and conceptual metaphor. Cognitive approaches to lexical semantics in Ancient Egyptian. In E. Grossman, S. Polis & J. Winand (Eds.), *Lexical semantics in Ancient Egyptian* (pp. 141–174). Hamburg: Widmaier.

Nyord, R. (2015). Cognitive Linguistics (published 31 August 2015). In J. Stauder-Porchet, A. Stauder & W. Wendrich (Eds.), *UCLA Encyclopedia of Egyptology.* Retrieved from https://escholarship.org/uc/item/9tf384bh (14 August 2017).

Parkinson, R. B. (1991). *The Tale of the Eloquent Peasant.* Oxford: Griffith Institute Publications.

Peust, C. (1999). *Egyptian phonology: An introduction to the phonology of a dead language.* Göttingen: Peust & Gutschmidt.

Popova, Y. (2005). Image schemas and verbal synaesthesia. In B. Hampe (Ed.), *From perception to meaning. Image schemas in Cognitive Linguistics* (pp. 395–419). Berlin: de Gruyter. https://doi.org/10.1515/9783110197532.5.395

Relats-Montserrat, F. (2014). Le signe D19, à la recherche des sens d'un déterminatif (I): la forme d'un signe. *Nehet,* 1, 129–167.

Sandman, M. (1938). *Texts from the time of Akhenaten.* Brussels: Éditions de la Fondation Égyptologique Reine Élisabeth.

Schenkel, W. (2012). *Tübinger Einführung in die klassisch-ägyptische Sprache und Schrift.* Tübingen: pagina.

Schwarz, S. (2005). Schiffe und Schiffsteile als Klassifikatoren in der ägyptischen Hieroglyphenschrift. Unpublished Masters thesis, Humboldt-Universität zu Berlin. Retrieved from http://www.sandro-schwarz.com/NaviformeKlassifikatoren.pdf (14 August 2017).

Steinbach, E. (2015). "Ich habe seinen Anblick geschmeckt...". Verben der Wahrnehmung und die semantischen Beziehungen zwischen Perzeption und Kognition. In G. Neunert, H. Simon, A. Verbovsek & K. Gabler (Eds.), *Text: Wissen – Wirkung – Wahrnehmung. Beiträge des vierten Münchner Arbeitskreises Junge Aegyptologie (MAJA 4) 29.11. bis 1.12.2013* (pp. 209–225). Wiesbaden: Harrassowitz.

Steinbach-Eicke, E. (forthcoming a.). Experiencing is tasting. Perception metaphors of taste in Ancient Egyptian. In F. Kammerzell, T. S. Richter & D. A. Werning (Eds.), *Crossroads: Whence and whither? Egyptian-Coptic linguistics in comparative perspectives, 17–20 February 2016.* Hamburg: Widmaier.

Steinbach-Eicke, E. (forthcoming b.). Sensory metaphors in Ancient Egyptian, In D. A. Werning & C. Barth (Eds.). *Metaphors in ancient civilizations.* Berlin: Edition Topoi.

Strik Lievers, F. (2007). Italian perception verbs: a corpus-based study. In A. Sansò (Ed.), *Language resources and linguistic theory* (pp. 167–179). Milan: FrancoAngeli.

Sweetser, E. (1990). *From etymology to pragmatics. Metaphorical and cultural aspects of semantic structure.* Cambridge: Cambridge University Press. https://doi.org/10.1017/CBO9780511620904

Thesaurus Linguae Aegyptiae & Digitalisiertes Zettelarchiv, Berlin-Brandenburgische Akademie der Wissenschaften. Strukturen und Transformationen des Wortschatzes der ägyptischen Sprache. Retrieved from aaew.bbaw.de/tla/ (14 August 2017).

Trim, R. (2007). *Metaphor networks. The comparative evolution of figurative language.* New York, NY: Palgrave Macmillan.

Vanhove, M. (2008). Semantic associations between sensory modalities, prehension and mental perceptions. A cross-linguistic perspective. In M. Vanhove (Ed.), *From polysemy to semantic change* (pp. 341–370). Amsterdam & Philadelphia, PA: John Benjamins. https://doi.org/10.1075/slcs.106.17van

Verbovsek, A. & Backes, B. (2015). Sinne und Sinnlichkeit in den ägyptischen Liebesliedern. In R. Landgráfová & H. Navrátilová (Eds.), *Sex and the Golden Goddess II. World of the Love Songs* (pp. 105–119). Prague: Czech Institute of Egyptology.

Viberg, Å. (1984). The verbs of perception: A typological study. *Linguistics* 21(1), 123–162.

Viberg, Å. (2015). Sensation, perception and cognition. Swedish in a typological-contrastive perspective. *Functions of Language,* 22(1), 96–131. https://doi.org/10.1075/fol.22.1.05vib

Werning, D. A. (2015). *Einführung in die hieroglyphisch-ägyptische Schrift und Sprache. Propädeutikum mit Zeichen- und Vokabellektionen, Übungen und Übungshinweisen.* Berlin: eDoc-Server der Humboldt Universität zu Berlin. Retrieved from http://edoc.hu-berlin.de/oa/books/reNNkyCpqh2c/PDF/21vhwqXNyo6Qc.pdf (14 August 2017).

Werning, D. A. (Ed.). (2016). *Ancient Egyptian: Glossing of common Earlier Egyptian forms* (last modified 24 November 2016). Retrieved from https://wikis.hu-berlin.de/interlinear_glossing/Ancient_Egyptian:Glossing_of_common_Earlier_Egyptian_forms (14 August 2017).

Westendorf, W. (1965/1977). *Koptisches Handwörterbuch.* Heidelberg: Carl Winter Universitätsverlag.

Williamson, J. (2015). Amarna Period. Published 24 June 2015. In W. Grajetzki & W. Wendrich (Eds.), *UCLA Encyclopedia of Egyptology.* Retrieved from https://escholarship.org/uc/item/77s6r0zr (14 August 2017).

Žába, Z. (1956). *Les maximes de Ptahhotep.* Prague: Éditions de l'Academie Tchécoslovatique des Sciences.

Zandee, J. (1948). *De hymnen aan Amon van Papyrus Leiden I 350.* Leiden: Brill.

CHAPTER 9

Why do we understand music as moving?
The metaphorical basis of musical motion revisited

Nina Julich
Leipzig University

Although musical structure is commonly perceived as moving, its motivation remains a debated issue. Conceptual Metaphor Theory approaches assume that musical motion is motivated by conceptual metaphors like TIME IS MOTION and CHANGE IS MOTION. The current study aims to investigate whether these conceptual metaphors successfully describe musical motion. For the analysis, a corpus of 10,000 words taken from the genre of music criticism (academic musicology journals and newspaper concert reviews of classical music) was compiled and exhaustively analysed with respect to metaphorical expressions. The results suggest that whereas many motion expressions for music seem to be motivated by TIME IS MOTION as well as CHANGE IS MOTION, a number of instances may instead present cases of fictive motion.

Keywords: conceptual metaphor, musical motion, fictive motion, time is motion, change is motion, Event Structure Metaphor, music criticism

1. Introduction

It is widely recognised that motion metaphors pervade musical discourse (Adlington, 2003; Aksnes, 2002; Antović, 2014; Bonds, 2010; Brower, 2000; Cox, 1999; Cox, 2016; Guck, 1991; Jandausch, 2012; Johnson & Larson, 2003; Scruton, 1997; Spitzer, 2004; Störel, 1997; Zbikowski, 2002). Motion metaphors are common to the way laymen describe music. They are also part and parcel of the technical language of experts (Adlington, 2003, p. 301; Guck, 1991, p. 2). From a cognitive linguistics perspective, the pervasiveness of motion metaphors in music suggests that motion vocabulary is not merely a linguistic means to refer to music but that the domain of motion in space might be fundamental to how we understand and perceive music. And indeed, music and motion are strongly correlated in our experience: We move our bodies when we dance to music, tap our feet to it, or nod our heads to it. We can also clearly see the movements of a musician and we feel ourselves move when

https://doi.org/10.1075/celcr.19.09jul

we produce music. So, music seems to be conceptualised as motion because it often literally involves motion (cf. Gibbs, 2006, p. 53ff.). The more technical language of musical experts, however, is rather dissociated form this embodied experience of music. Musical experts seek to describe musical structure, which is a relatively abstract activity and requires musico-theoretical expertise. Still, musical experts commonly describe musical structure in terms of an abstract space through which musical elements may be said to be moving. The present study seeks to explore what motivates the use of motion metaphors in expert language by analysing a corpus from the genre of music criticism focussing on Western classical music pieces. As a review genre, music criticism primarily deals with describing musical structure and is thus highly suited for investigating metaphors for musical motion. Based on an inductive analysis of the data, it will be suggested that conventional conceptual metaphors like TIME IS MOTION[1] or CHANGE IS MOTION play an important role for construing music as motion. However, it will also be suggested that many instances of musical motion may rather reflect cases of fictive motion. The present study thus focuses on sensory experience as the target domain ('Transfield II metaphors', see O'Meara et al., this volume) and seeks to find out what motivates the metaphorisation of the perceptual phenomenon of musical motion.

To begin with, let us first consider how elements of musical structure may move. First of all, musical motion fundamentally rests on an understanding of pitch in terms of *high* and *low*. These terms do not literally apply to pitch because, in acoustic terms, pitch is defined by frequency as shown in Figure 1, rendering the terms *high* and *low* metaphorical.[2]

Low pitch   High pitch

Figure 1. High and low pitch frequencies

---

1.   In line with conventions in Conceptual Metaphor Theory research, conceptual metaphors are given in small capitals.

2.   Despite the pervasiveness of conceptualising musical pitch in terms of vertical space, it is not universal. In Liberia, for example, pitches are conceived of as *light* and *heavy*, in Bali they are understood as *small* and *large*, for the Suya, a people of the Amazon basin, pitches are *young* and *old*, and for the Shona of Zimbabwe low pitches are referred to as *crocodiles* and high pitches as *those who follow crocodiles* (cf. Eitan & Timmers, 2010, for a discussion of universal pitch perception see Antović, 2014).

The conception of motion arises when pitches combine to form a melody, which might be said to *move up* or *down* as in the melodic line in Figure 2 where the melody moves downwards from C to E.

Figure 2. Downward melodic motion[3]

The conception of melodic motion is lexicalised and deeply entrenched in musical discourse. In fact, when describing the shape of a melody, we do not have any other means but resorting to spatial language (e.g. a *rising, falling, ascending,* or *descending* melody).

The more music-theoretic notions of harmony and harmonic change are also fundamentally conceptualised in terms of space and motion. In Western classical music, harmonic relations are understood as spatial relations being organised within the circle of fifths, as shown in Figure 3. Keys which are, for example, far away from each other within the circle of fifths are understood as *remote* keys.

Within this abstract space, harmonic changes are understood as movements from one key (e.g. C major) to the next (e.g. G major) (indicated by the arrow in Figure 3).

Apart from these structural aspects (pitch, melody, harmony), music might also be perceived as *moving* the listener emotionally. The current study, however, exclusively focuses on how the structure of music in classical pieces is described and thus the former issue falls out of the scope of this paper. Describing the emotional impact of music may rely on the same conceptual metaphors which have been shown to be a pervasive source for understanding and conceptualising the emotions in general (cf. Kövecses, 2000).

---

3.   The example shows a section of the song Big Swifty Head by Frank Zappa. The whole image is attributed to Sauschwein, 2013, https://commons.wikimedia.org/wiki/File:Big_swifty_head. png. used under Creative Commons Attribution-Share Alike 3.0 Unported License: https://creativecommons.org/licenses/by-sa/3.0. The arrow indicating downward motion was added and is not part of the original image.

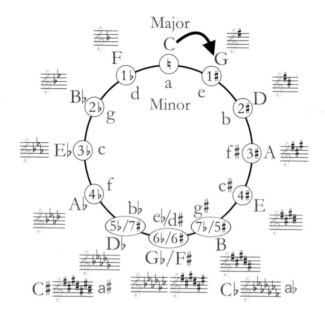

Figure 3. Circle of fifths[4]

This brief overview indicates the pervasiveness of motion metaphors for the conceptualisation of musical structure. It is the aim of this chapter to investigate possible motivations for the understanding and perception of musical structure in terms of motion. The outline of this chapter runs as follows. In section two, different approaches to musical motion – metaphorical, physiological, perceptual – will be discussed and a Conceptual Metaphor Theory approach to musical motion will be introduced focusing on two conventional conceptual metaphors, TIME IS MOTION and CHANGE IS MOTION, which have hitherto been identified as the main motivation for musical motion. This section also introduces the phenomenon of fictive motion which may offer an alternative explanation for the figurative use of motion expressions in music. Section three introduces the music criticism corpus which was compiled for this study and the metaphor identification procedure with which it was subsequently analysed. Results of the analysis are given in section four. The question of whether musical motion might be an instance of fictive motion will be discussed in section five. In section six, the main points will be summarised and areas for further research will be suggested.

---

4.   The image is attributed to Just plain Bill, by derivative work based on Red Roosters: Quintenzirkeldeluxe.png, 2008, https://commons.wikimedia.org/wiki/File:Circle_of_fifths_deluxe.svg used under Creative Commons Attribution-Share 3.0 Unported License: https://creativecommons.org/licenses/by-sa/3.0/. The arrow indicating harmonic change was added and is not part of the original image.

2. Musical motion and Conceptual Metaphor Theory

2.1 The enigma of musical motion

Although we commonly perceive and talk about music as moving, its motivation remains an open question. In a chapter entitled *The Paradox of Tonal Motion*, Zuckerkandl notes that:

> No tone, as long as it sounds, moves from its place. [...] in a melody we have [...] a stringing together of static tones, and, between tone and tone, *no* connection, *no* transition, *no* filling up of intervals, nothing. It is the exact opposite of motion.
> (Zuckerkandl, 1969, p. 83)

Johnson and Larson refer to this as the "enigma" of musical motion (2003, p. 65): Despite our inclination to describe music in terms of motion, there is no inherent motion in the music. For this reason, musical motion is considered to be a metaphorical concept.

Some scholars, however, assume that musical motion is physiologically real. Shove and Repp (1995) suggest a direct physiological link between the perception of music and movement. According to them the most obvious source of musical motion is the human performer and thus "to hear a melody is to hear [...] a musician move relative to the surface of an instrument" (Shove & Repp, 1995, p. 61). Hence, we perceive music as moving because we literally perceive the motion of a human performer when music is produced.

Clarke (2001) dismisses the purely physiological view of musical motion. In contrast to Shove and Repp, he assumes that musical motion is illusory because it does not refer to the real motion of a performer (p. 228). Yet, for Clarke, musical motion is not metaphorical either but still a truly perceptual phenomenon. He suggests that the perception of motion in music is based on the event-detecting nature of our auditory system which allows us to *hear* an entity move without actually seeing it. For example, changes in the acoustic properties of a sound may allow us to deduce that the source of the sound is drawing nearer or moving further away. Thus, motion is perceived upon hearing a change in sound. According to Clarke, it is this principle which underlies our perception of motion in music as well: We hear the pitches of a melody change and thus perceive the melody as moving, the difference being that the motion that we attribute to music is not of real agents but of fictional ones, it is the motion of virtual objects (Clarke, 2001, p. 228).

Clarke's assumption, however, relies on a broad understanding of *sound*. Scruton, for example, clearly differentiates between the "tangible and practical world of *sound*" and the "abstract and incorporeal domain of [musical] *tone*" (in Clarke, 2001, p. 217, my emphasis NJ). For this reason, perceptual features that apply to *sound* do not necessarily have to be applicable to *tone*. For Scruton, thus, the mapping of real sound onto abstract tone still presents a metaphorical transfer.

More recently, scholars have attributed a much more fundamental role to the importance of metaphor in language and cognition giving rise to the Conceptual Theory of Metaphor (Lakoff & Johnson, 1980). From a Conceptual Metaphor Theory perspective, Shove and Repp's physiologically real view as well as Clarke's perceptually real view of musical motion do not necessarily exclude the metaphorical view of musical motion. In fact, both views are in line with Conceptual Metaphor Theory (cf. Johnson & Larson, 2003, p. 77) which posits that conceptual metaphors are experientially grounded in our everyday (perceptual) experience. In the following, the main tenets of Conceptual Metaphor Theory and its applications to musical motion will be introduced.

2.2   A potential answer to the enigma of musical motion: Conceptual Metaphor Theory

In Conceptual Metaphor Theory (henceforth CMT), first introduced by Lakoff and Johnson (1980, further developed in 1999), metaphor is not seen as a rhetorical device but as something that is part of everyday ordinary language. Furthermore, metaphor is not merely a matter of language but a matter of thought. Via a *conceptual* metaphor an (abstract) target domain is *understood* in terms of a (more concrete) source domain. In a conceptual metaphor mapping, semantic relationships that exist in the source domain are carried over to the target domain. Conceptual metaphors are thus assumed to guide reasoning of abstract thought. Conceptual metaphors exist as conceptual links between conceptual domains and thus have to be differentiated from their linguistic surface expressions. For example, the ARGUMENT IS WAR conceptual metaphor, which maps knowledge from the domain of war onto the domain of (verbal) argument, is reflected in a number of related linguistic surface expressions (Examples (1)–(3), taken from the Macmillan Dictionary for Advanced Learners).[5]

(1) *Opponents <u>attacked</u> the government's plan to increase road tax.*

(2) *Hundreds of miners are fighting to <u>defend</u> their jobs.*

(3) *This action <u>destroyed</u> any remaining hope of reaching an agreement.*

Further linguistic evidence for conceptual metaphors comes from the fact that we easily understand novel metaphorical expressions. Understanding a made-up

---

5.   Available at http://www.macmillandictionary.com.

example like (4) presents no problem suggesting that ARGUMENT IS WAR is a stable cross-domain mapping which inheres in long-term memory (cf. Evans, 2010, p. 646).

(4) *In his new paper, he built a carefully constructed defensive <u>wall</u> around his theory.*

As regards their motivation, conceptual metaphors are assumed to be motivated by correlations in experience. In his Primary Metaphor Theory, which presented an important refinement to CMT, Grady (1997) suggests that we associate domains at the conceptual level due to their repeated co-experience in everyday situations (so called "primary scenes"). For example, filling a glass with water causes the level of water to rise, thus correlating quantity with verticality. This gives rise to the primary metaphor MORE IS UP which is instantiated in expressions like *rising unemployment.* Further examples for primary metaphors are AFFECTION IS WARMTH, CHANGE IS MOTION, or TIME IS MOTION. Because primary conceptual metaphors are grounded in everyday experience, that is in the correlation or co-perception of in fact different phenomena, a CMT understanding of musical motion accommodates Shove and Repp's as well as Clarke's assumptions about the physiological as well as perceptual motivations for perceiving music as motion.

Johnson and Larson (2003) discuss possible conceptual metaphor motivations for the perception of musical structure in terms of motion. According to them, musical motion is based on the primary metaphor TIME IS MOTION.[6] In this metaphor, the passage of time is understood as the motion of a temporal event towards an observer (the MOVING TIMES metaphor (5)) or as an observer's motion over a temporal landscape (the MOVING OBSERVER/TIME'S LANDSCAPE metaphor (6)).

(5) *The time has come.*

(6) *We're coming up on Christmas.*

Johnson and Larson (2003, p. 69ff.) show that musical motion exhibits the same pattern: Experiencing a specific musical event within a piece is conceptualised as the motion of this event towards and eventually arriving at the listener's position (the MOVING MUSIC metaphor (7)), or as the motion of the listener towards the musical event (the MOVING OBSERVER / MUSICAL LANDSCAPE metaphor (8)).

---

6. The status of TIME IS MOTION as a primary metaphor is debated. Scholars agree that there is a strong experiential connection between time and space and time and motion, yet some suggest that this gives actually rise to several independently motivated primary time-space metaphors, like DURATION IS LENGTH (Evans, 2013) and (temporal) SEQUENCE IS RELATIVE POSITION ON A PATH (Moore, 2014).

(7)   MOVING MUSIC: *Here comes the recapitulation.*

(8)   MUSICAL LANDSCAPE: *When we get to measure 7*

Besides TIME IS MOTION, another conceptual metaphor that may motivate the perception of music in terms of motion is CHANGE IS MOTION (Jandausch, 2012; Johnson & Larson, 2003; Pérez-Sobrino & Julich, 2014). This conceptual metaphor highlights the common conceptualisation of a change of state in terms of motion from one location to another, as in (9). A corollary of this conceptual mapping is that if change is understood as motion, then states are understood as locations, as in (10), and the cause of a change is understood as forced motion (11). This group of interdependent metaphors is known as the Event Structure Metaphor and it is employed to structure a variety of abstract events (cf. Lakoff & Johnson, 1999).

(9)   CHANGE IS MOTION: *My car has gone from bad to worse lately.*
                                                              (Grady, 1997, p. 286)

(10)   STATES ARE LOCATIONS: *The car is in bad shape.*

(11)   CAUSATION IS FORCED MOTION: *His leadership brought the country out of depression.*   (Lakoff & Johnson, 1999, p. 184)

When the Event Structure Metaphor is applied to music, musical elements are conceptualised as locations (12), and changes in the musical structure are understood as motion (13) (cf. Jandausch, 2012; Pérez-Sobrino & Julich, 2014).

(12)   KEYS, METERS, RHYTHMS ARE LOCATIONS: *The piece is set in A minor.*

(13)   MUSICAL CHANGES ARE CHANGES OF LOCATION: *the harmonic motion from C to A^7*

The conceptual metaphors TIME IS MOTION and CHANGE IS MOTION have been identified as the main motivations for musical motion from a CMT perspective so far. Alternatively, musical motion may also be based on fictive motion. Fictive motion is an instance of figurative language, however, scholars disagree whether it represents a kind of metaphor or whether it is a different process (cf. Kövecses, 2015, p. 25). In fictive motion, a motion event describes an inherently static scene (Matlock, 2004; Talmy, 2000), as in (14)–(16).

(14)   *The road runs along the coast.*

---

7.   Conceptual metaphor labels in Examples (12) and (13) are taken from Jandausch (2012), their linguistic instantiations, however, are taken from the corpus discussed here because Jandausch does not give any examples.

(15) *The fence goes from the plateau to the valley.*

(16) *The tattoo runs along his spine.*

Although these examples describe actual spatial scenes (as opposed to metaphorical scenes), their subjects (*road, fence, tattoo*) are not the agents of the motion event expressed by the verb. Instead, it is the conceptualiser who *mentally scans* or moves along the path associated with the subject noun phrase (Matlock, 2004, p. 225).[8] In this respect, fictive motion differs from literal motion in that no literal motion takes place, yet, it also differs from metaphorical motion because there is no entity that moves metaphorically (cf. Kövecses, 2015, p. 25).[9] To my knowledge, a possible interpretation of musical motion in terms of fictive motion has not been explored so far. The application of fictive motion to musical motion will be further addressed in the discussion in Section 5.

In sum, despite the pervasiveness of perceiving music as moving, the concept of musical motion is by no means straightforward. Several explanations as to its motivation have been proposed. Musical motion might be fictive, metaphorical, perceptually real or even physiologically real. The account of musical motion as being motivated by underlying conceptual metaphors has been assumed to provide the most explanatory power as it also allows for the physiological as well as perceptual grounding of musical motion in tangible and practical everyday experience. In the following section, the explanatory power of the application of CMT to musical motion will be further explored in a corpus of texts from music criticism. Specifically, it will be examined whether TIME IS MOTION and CHANGE IS MOTION successfully explain why we describe musical structure in terms of motion. As a possible alternative, the interpretation of musical motion in terms of fictive motion will also be discussed.

---

8. For this reason Matsumoto (1996) refers to fictive motion as "subjective motion".

9. It is still a debated issue whether fictive motion is metaphorical or not (Caballero, 2007) because fictive motion cases might alternatively be motivated by the conceptual metaphor FORM IS MOTION (Lakoff & Turner, 1989, p. 142–4). Kövecses (2015: 25), however, argues that fictive motion is not metaphorical because it does not exhibit a systematic set of correspondences as for example the conceptual metaphor ARGUMENT IS WAR does (see above). According to him, the construal of a fictive motion event is not based on a metaphorical mapping between a static scene and a more dynamic scene.

3.   Method

Previous applications of CMT to the study of musical motion have largely relied on introspective data. In order to gain more insights into whether the proposed conceptual metaphors successfully describe the phenomenon of musical motion and whether an alternative motivation in terms of fictive motion is feasible, a domain-specific corpus of 10,000 words from the genre of music criticism was compiled and analysed for metaphor. The study is in line with claims put forward by Ibarretxe-Antuñano (this volume) in that it takes into consideration the salience of the source domain of motion for musical structure as opposed to other competing source domains as well as the frequency of motion metaphors for music.

Music criticism is a review genre that involves the analysis of musical scores as well as reviews of public concerts or electronic recordings. For the compilation of the corpus, 37 texts were randomly selected from musicology journals as well as newspaper reviews focusing on Western classical music pieces. The texts were accessed online, downloaded and converted into plain text. From each text, an excerpt of 260 words was sampled, resulting in a music criticism corpus of about 10,000 words. The corpus was analysed in three steps: First, the whole corpus was manually annotated for metaphorically used words. Second, the identified metaphorically used words were annotated for source domain. Third, motion metaphors were further analysed with regard to their possible conceptual metaphor basis. This rather inductive, bottom-up approach was chosen in order to not be restricted by a pre-defined list of motion words but to rather get an overall idea of the use of metaphor in the music criticism corpus. Each of these analytical steps will now be outlined.

In the first step, metaphors were identified applying MIPVU (*Metaphor Identification Procedure Vrije Universiteit (Amsterdam)*, Steen et al., 2010). MIPVU is a metaphor identification procedure for identifying verbal metaphor in discourse.[10] The data gathered from the MIPVU analysis can be taken as a reliable basis for further conceptual analysis (Steen et al., 2010, p. 13). MIPVU requires the analyst to examine the texts on a word-by-word basis in order to find metaphorically used words. The basic unit of analysis is the "lexical unit."[11] In the procedure, metaphor is defined as indirect meaning, arising out of a contrast between the contextual

---

10. MIPVU is a further development of MIP (*Metaphor Identification Procedure*, Pragglejaz Group, 2007, see also Trojszczak, this volume, for an application of MIP to the analysis of corpus concordances). For differences between the two versions see Steen et al. (2010), Chapter 1.

11. In MIPVU, the technical term "lexical unit" is used instead of "word" because lexical units may also include multi-word expressions like "chamber music" which occur as one unit in the dictionary. The present study follows this convention, thus "chamber music" counts as one lexical unit. In this paper the terms "word" and "lexical unit" will be used interchangeably to refer to a lexical unit.

meaning of a lexical unit and its more basic meaning. Hence, if a lexical unit's contextual meaning is different from the lexical unit's more basic meaning and the two meanings can be related by similarity, the unit is marked as metaphorically used (Steen et al., 2010, p. 6). Basic meanings are more concrete and related to bodily action. As suggested by the procedure, basic and contextual meanings were identified by consulting the Macmillan Dictionary for Advanced Learners and the Longman Dictionary of Contemporary English. For the present study, an additional dictionary (On Music Dictionary)[12] was used to identify contextual meanings for technical music vocabulary. Moreover and in line with the procedure, 10% of the music criticism corpus was annotated by a second coder to test for reliability.[13]

Once the corpus was annotated for verbal metaphor, the identified metaphorically used words were annotated for source domain. Source domains were identified based on the basic meaning in the dictionary.

As a third analytical step, the verbal metaphors identified as belonging to the source domain of motion were further analysed with regard to whether they reflect the conceptual metaphors TIME IS MOTION and/or CHANGE IS MOTION as suggested by the literature. This step is highly subjective and difficult to reliably operationalise. For the purpose of this paper the two metaphors are differentiated in the following way. In TIME IS MOTION based instances of musical motion, musical motion is deictic: Music either moves with respect to an ego (the listener), or a moving ego moves over a musical landscape. In CHANGE IS MOTION based instances of musical motion, the motion is not deictic. Rather, a musical element is conceptualised as undergoing a change of state and usually a resultant state is profiled.

4. Results

In this section, results will be given in line with the three steps sketched in the previous section. First, results will be given for the frequency of metaphorically used words in the music criticism corpus. Second, results will be given regarding source domains. Third, potential conceptual metaphor motivations for musical motion will be presented.

---

12. Available at http://dictionary.onmusic.org.

13. As metaphorical meaning is defined as indirect usage in MIPVU, prototypical cases of metaphor are "indirect metaphors", that is words are used in a sense different from their basic meaning (this would also include idioms). The procedure further distinguishes between direct and implicit use of metaphor or cases in which analysts (if there are more than two) do not agree (labeled WIDLII – *when in doubt leave it in*). However, these metaphor types are not relevant to the purpose of the present study and will not be further discussed.

Table 1 reports the frequency of metaphorically used lexical units in the corpus. 10% of the data were annotated by a second coder, resulting in a Kappa value of 0.73 which can be interpreted as marginally reliable (cf. Pragglejaz Group, 2007, p. 21).[14] The somewhat lower Kappa value is largely due to errors in applying the MIPVU procedure. These were resolved in a post-annotation discussion between first and second coder.

Table 1. Metaphor frequency in the music criticism corpus

Total number of lexical units	Non-metaphorically used lexical units	Metaphorically used lexical units
10,146 (100%)	8,011 (79%)	2,135 (21%)

In the corpus, 21% of the total number of lexical units were used metaphorically. In a much larger study applying the same metaphor identification procedure, Steen et al. (2010) identify 18.5% as metaphorically used lexical units for academic discourse, 16.4% for news discourse, 11.7% for fiction and 7.7% for conversation (Steen et al., 2010, based on a sample of 186,688 words from the BNC-Baby).[15] The findings here thus indicate that the use of metaphors is indeed pervasive in music criticism. The pervasiveness of metaphor in music criticism also corroborates the finding by Anderson (this volume) that the domain of hearing frequently functions as the target domain of a metaphorical mapping compared to the other senses.

When it comes to genre, metaphorically used lexical units are more frequent in academic music journals than in newspaper reviews (see Table 2). This difference is highly significant ($\chi2(1) = 36.369, p < .001$). A similar effect regarding the relation between metaphor and genre was observed by Steen et al. (2010, p. 195) which indicates that academic discourse in general exhibits a comparably high number of metaphorically used words. It should be noted however, that metaphorically used words in academic music journals comprise highly technical terms, like *pitch, minor, major, key* or *chromatic* which are probably instances of dead metaphor.

The majority of metaphorically used lexical units relating to music ($N = 1,443$) employs vocabulary from the source domains of motion ($N = 237$, 16%) and space ($N = 215$, 15%). Other less common source domains include physical structure (e.g. *his _architectural_ sense of line*), other senses ('intrafield metaphors', e.g. *the instrument*

---

14. The subtypes of metaphorically used lexical units that MIPVU distinguishes (indirect metaphor, direct metaphor, implicit metaphor, WIDLII (*when in doubt leave it in*)) were collapsed for reliability testing.

15. The BNC-Baby is a 4-million-word sample of the British National Corpus (BNC) containing 1 million words of each register (academic, news, fiction, and conversation).

Table 2. Frequency of metaphorically used lexical units across genre

	Academic music journals	Newspaper reviews
Non-metaphorically used lexical units	3,729 (76%)	4,282 (81%)
Metaphorically used lexical units	1,151 (24%)	984 (19%)
Total	4,880 (100%)	5,266 (100%)

gains a broader _range of colours_), human qualities (e.g. _Bononcini's youthful_ cello pieces) and language (e.g. _an E-minor statement of the opening motif_).

When it comes to their possible conceptual metaphor basis, it was often very difficult to decide whether metaphorically used words can be said to be motivated by TIME IS MOTION or by CHANGE IS MOTION. For this reason, frequency of occurrence for conceptual metaphors will not be given. What the paper reports instead are representative examples of the motion expressions in the corpus that can be interpreted in terms of TIME IS MOTION and CHANGE IS MOTION. Unclear cases which may require an alternative explanation will be discussed below.

Examples (17) and (18) present rather clear cases of TIME IS MOTION based instances of musical motion. In (17), a musical event is conceptualised as moving towards the observer, and upon arriving at the metaphorical location of the observer is experienced. In (18), the sequential order of musical events is conceptualised as motion of musical elements with respect to one another irrespective of the position of the listening ego (see also discussions of non-deictic motion metaphors for time in Evans, 2003, 2013 and Moore, 2014).

(17) _His full conversion to her key of F-sharp minor comes with their homophonic singing in the revenge duet (bars 391–418)_   (COJ10-22.1)[16]

(18) _Colombi sometimes used double-stops on middle strings followed by repeated top-string notes_   (JSCM06Vol12No1)

Examples (19) and (20), on the other hand, present clear cases of CHANGE IS MOTION based instances of musical motion. In (19), the singing styles of declamation and arioso are conceptualised as locations (highlighted by the use of the preposition _between)_, a change in style is conceptualised as motion (highlighted by the motion verb _move)_. Similarly, the sentence in (20) suggests that contrasting styles in a piece – imperative start vs. reverie – conveyed by the famous violinist Nigel Kennedy are conceptualised as locations (highlighted by the use of the preposition _into)_, and the change from one to the other is conceptualised as motion (highlighted by the motion verb _drift)_.

---

16. The index in parentheses indicates the corpus file.

(19) *Monteverdi's recitative style <u>moves freely between</u> declamation and arioso.*

(CT348)

(20) *But from this imperative start, Kennedy immediately <u>drifted into</u> reverie*

(IR1149)

The fact that the sensory experience of music heavily relies on "language that is 'borrowed in' from a different domain" (O'Meara et al., this volume, p. 4) does not necessarily violate the directionality of metaphor from concrete to abstract. As suggested by Kövecses (this volume), if a sensory domain functions as the target, it is usually not the sensory experience per se that is the target of the mapping but a more general aspect ("dimension" in Kövecses, this volume) of it. Here the superordinate notions of change and temporal progression and/or temporal order are the generic-level aspects of musical structure which the conceptual metaphors CHANGE IS MOTION and TIME IS MOTION are meant to highlight.

Apart from these rather clear cases, the music criticism corpus, however, exhibits a number of instances of musical motion which cannot be felicitously explained by TIME IS MOTION or CHANGE IS MOTION (or other conventional metaphors for that matter). Consider (21)–(24):

(21) *The repetition of the opening <u>follows</u> an even more accelerated and complicated [harmonic] <u>course</u>*   (MPR0802)

(22) *Measures 3–4 <u>traverse</u> the same <u>space</u> as measures 1–2*   (MTO11_17.1)

(23) *The little <u>descending</u> chromatic third*   (MTO11_17.1)

(24) *the [melodic] figure again <u>ascends</u> <u>to</u> D*   (BF05spring)

In (21), a section in the music (*the repetition of the opening*) is understood as following a complicated harmonic course. Note that *course* does not primarily refer to the course of time but mainly to the harmonic "path". Unlike in the previous examples, it is not the whole section that metaphorically moves or changes but it is rather the harmonic "shape" of that section which is described by the motion event. The same holds true for the other three examples. In each case the subject of the motion event – *measures 3–4* in (22), the interval of a *little chromatic third* in (23), or *the melodic figure* in (24) – is neither moving through temporal space nor undergoing a change. Rather, the motion expressions function to describe the specific form or "shape" of their subject noun phrases. Thus, they are structurally as well as functionally similar to fictive motion. In the following section, the interpretation of musical motion in terms of fictive motion will be discussed.

5. Musical motion as fictive motion

As described in Section 2, in a fictive motion event, the subject noun phrase denotes a path whose spatial layout is described by the motion event (see Examples (14) to (16) above). The actual agent of motion is the conceptualiser who mentally scans along the path associated with the subject noun phrase.

In order to demonstrate that some cases of musical motion might reflect fictive motion construals instead of having a conceptual metaphor basis in terms of TIME IS MOTION or CHANGE IS MOTION consider Example (21), which is given again in (25):

(25) *The repetition of the opening follows an even more accelerated and complicated [harmonic] course*   (MPR0802)

The motion in (25) is not deictic with respect to the observer, suggesting that this example is not an instance of TIME IS MOTION. However, we have seen that deictic motion is not necessarily a mandatory feature for this metaphor (Example (18)). Yet, unlike (18) where the metaphorically used word *follow* expresses that musical event A follows musical event B, the example in (25) does not reflect the sequence of two musical events. In (25), *an even more accelerated and complicated [harmonic] course* is not followed by *the repetition of the opening*. Rather, (25) describes the "path" of the harmonic progression *in* the repetition of the opening. This is also indicated by the meaning of *accelerated*, which does not refer to an increase in tempo but to an increase in the number of harmonic changes. Moreover, a CHANGE IS MOTION interpretation of (25) is also not felicitous. Despite the fact that the example indirectly highlights the continuous change in harmony, no resultant state-location is profiled. Also, the subject noun phrase *The repetition of the opening* is not the agent of the metaphorical motion. Instead, (25) seems to be more consistent with a fictive motion interpretation because the subject noun phrase specifies the entire musical passage along which the musical motion is fictively construed. To illustrate this, compare the "truly" metaphorical case of musical motion in (26). In this example, the subject noun phrase is a singer who metaphorically moves through densely embellished arias. The manner of motion (*sail through*) metaphorically conveys the ease with which the singer is able to master demanding arias.

(26) *She has the kind of agility that allows her to <u>sail through</u> virtuosic, densely embellished arias*   (NYT12at030212)

Hence, whereas in (26), the vocal competence of the singer is metaphorically conceptualised as unimpeded motion, in (25) no musical entity moves metaphorically, the motion event merely describes the musico-structural properties of the musical passage associated with the subject noun phrase.

For this reason, I will argue here that fictive motion can account for those instances of musical motion which cannot be felicitously explained by TIME IS MOTION or CHANGE IS MOTION. A fictive motion interpretation of cases like (25) is feasible because they are structurally similar to fictive motion. Structurally, in fictive motion, the subject noun phrase denotes a path or linear entity which is predicated of a motion verb thus providing topological information about the subject in a dynamic way. In relation to that consider again Example (22) and (24) given here again in (27) and (28).

(27)   *Measures 3–4 traverse the same space as measures 1–2*   (MTO11_17.1)

(28)   *the [melodic] figure again ascends to D*   (BF05spring)

Similar to fictive motion, in these musical motion cases, the subject denotes a musical "path" or rather passage (underlined in the examples) which is predicated of a motion verb (*traverse, ascend,* respectively) which in turn provides musico-structural information about the subject in a dynamic way. Moreover, fictive motion constructions also include a landmark, which is usually represented as a prepositional phrase (cf. Examples (14) to (16)) or a direct object (e.g. *The road crosses the creak*) and which further specifies the spatial layout of the subject. In line with that, the landmarks in (27) and (28) specify a location in tonal space.

Furthermore, musical motion is also functionally similar to fictive motion. First, fictive motion is a very economical way of describing structure. And this is what the above examples function to do. Examples (25), (27) and (28) are highly economical ways of describing salient properties of the melodic and harmonic structure of a musical piece (cf. Caballero, 2007, p. 2111, in relation to wine tasting notes). Second, fictive motion usually functions to construe a static scene in a dynamic way. Similarly, the musical motion events may function to construe the musical experience more dynamically in order to simulate what attending to the actual musical event feels like. Third, a fictive motion interpretation of musical motion might be further motivated by the fact that music criticism prototypically involves a musicologist scanning the musical score or a particular musical performance in memory in order to describe and evaluate the structure and characteristics of a piece to an audience, who, in turn, are supposed to imagine musical structure when reading the music criticism text.

A fictive motion interpretation of musical motion, however, is not unproblematic. In fictive motion proper a static spatial scene is dynamically construed. Music, however, is neither static nor spatial. So, the musical scenes that are described by a motion event depart from those typically described in fictive motion (cf. Caballero & Ibarretxe-Antuñano 2015, p. 156f.). However, according to Zuckerkandl's *paradox of musical motion* quoted above, music consists of a sequence of static tones. The notion of fictive motion thus would resolve that paradox by fictively construing a sequence of static pitch events as dynamically moving.

A further problematic issue is that the subject noun phrase of a musical motion event may instead be interpreted metonymically. Instead of denoting a path or passage, the subject in (28), *the melodic figure*, might be alternatively interpreted as metonymically standing for its contents, the individual pitches, which may in turn be conceptualised as moving metaphorically. The mapping between constituents of an abstract structure and the contents of a container has been shown to be a common pattern in language and thought (i.e. the Conduit Metaphor, cf. Grady, 1997).

Despite these issues, fictive motion has in fact been applied to other non-spatial domains: Caballero (this volume; 2007) investigates how wine critics describe and evaluate wine in tasting notes. Her findings are strikingly similar to those presented here. The wine tasting notes that she analyses exhibit a high amount of motion verbs which function to render the wine tasting experience more dynamically and which Caballero (2007) interprets as possible cases of fictive motion. In addition to that, Marghetis and Núñez (2013) have shown that also mathematicians heavily rely on a dynamic fictive motion construal of mathematical concepts. For example, mathematicians describe mathematical functions as *increasing, oscillating, crossing* or *approaching a limit* (p. 300). These motional concepts also surface in co-speech gestures during mathematical proof practices suggesting that they actually underlie cognition.

Together with these findings, the data presented here suggest that musical motion may present a case of fictive motion. Thus, instead of being based on a metaphorical transfer between conceptual domains, musical motion may rather rely on the process of mental scanning. However, musical motion deviates from prototypical spatial fictive motion scenes. For that reason, musical motion might be categorised as being situated on a continuum between prototypical cases of fictive motion and prototypical cases of metaphor. This would call for an understanding of both fictive motion and metaphor as radial categories exhibiting degrees of fictiveness and degrees of metaphoricity, respectively (cf. also Caballero & Ibarretxe-Antuñano 2015, p. 156f.).

6. Conclusion

The perception of musical structure as motion is a complex phenomenon that exhibits different types of figurativity. While it is partly based on conventional conceptual metaphors like TIME IS MOTION and CHANGE IS MOTION, musical motion might not exclusively be motivated by these conceptual metaphors. Due to the nature of music criticism, which involves tracing musical structure in the score and simulating musical experience, musical motion might also be the outcome of a fictive motion construal. The findings thus suggest that different cognitive processes may lead to the perception and conception of music in terms of motion. On the one hand, musical motion is motivated by conceptual metaphors. On the other hand, cases of musical motion specifically referring to musical structure rely on the process of mentally scanning along how music progresses within the course of a musical piece.

Although musical motion exhibits striking structural as well as functional similarities with fictive motion events, there are also ways in which the examples from the music criticism corpus depart from what has been prototypically defined as fictive motion: In musical motion, the motion event does not describe a static, spatial scene but rather a musico-temporal dynamic one. Yet, as was shown, the musical motion cases cannot felicitously be explained by the conventional conceptual metaphors TIME IS MOTION and CHANGE IS MOTION either. The findings here thus call for a theory of figurativity that places phenomena like fictive motion and metaphorical motion on a continuum. Such a theory would allow for degrees of fictiveness as well as degrees of metaphoricity (cf. also Anderson, this volume) and would accommodate for intermediate stages like those possibly presented by musical motion.

Further research has to explore whether musical motion can actually be seen as a case of fictive motion, or whether, given the inherently temporal and dynamic nature of music, musical motion is rather fundamentally based on a metaphorical construal of musical space in terms of literal space. Moreover, the relation between fictive motion and metaphorical motion as well as the idea of a continuum of figurativity is still in need of further research.

Acknowledgements

I would like to thank the editors of the volume Laura J. Speed, Carolyn O'Meara, Lila San Roque and Asifa Majid for organising the Perception Metaphor Workshop in Nijmegen and thus providing the time and space for discussion. I would also like to thank the editors for their insightful comments and suggestions on my contribution. Last but not least, I would like to thank the workshop participants for helpful comments on my poster during the poster presentation. This research was funded through a PhD scholarship awarded by Leipzig University, Germany.

References

Adlington, R. (2003). Moving beyond motion: Metaphors for changing sound. *Journal of the Royal Musical Association*, 128(2), 297–318. https://doi.org/10.1093/jrma/128.2.297

Aksnes, H. (2002). Music and its resonating body. *Danish Yearbook for Music Research*, 29, 81–101.

Antović, M. (2014). Metaphor about music or metaphor in music: A contribution to the co-operation of cognitive linguistics and cognitive musicology [Metafora o muzici ili metafora u muzici: jedan prilog za saradnju kognitivne lingvistike i kognitivne muzikologije]. In M. Stanojević (Ed.), *Metaphors We Study: Contemporary Insights into Conceptual Metaphor* [Metafore koje istražujemo: suvremeni uvidi u konceptualnu metaforu] (pp. 233–254). Zagreb, Croatia: Srednja Europa. https://papers.ssrn.com/sol3/papers.cfm?abstract_id=2566258

Bonds, M. E. (2010). The spatial representation of musical form. *Journal of Musicology*, 27(3), 265–303. https://doi.org/10.1525/jm.2010.27.3.265

Brower, C. (2000). A cognitive theory of musical meaning. *Journal of Music Theory*, 44(2), 323–379. https://doi.org/10.2307/3090681

Caballero, R. (2007). Manner-of-motion verbs in wine description. *Journal of Pragmatics*, 39(12), 2095–2114. https://doi.org/10.1016/j.pragma.2007.07.005

Caballero, R. & Ibarretxe-Antuñano, I. (2015). From physical to metaphorical motion: A cross-genre approach. In V. Pirrelli, C. Marzi, M. Ferro (Eds.), *NetwordS 2015. Word knowledge and word usage. Representations and processes in the mental lexicon, Conference Proceedings, Pisa, Italy*, 155–157.

Clarke, E. (2001). Meaning and the specification of motion in music. *Musicae Scientiae*, 5(2), 213–234. https://doi.org/10.1177/102986490100500205

Cox, A. (1999). *The metaphoric logic of musical motion and space*. PhD Dissertation, University of Oregon.

Cox, A. (2016). *Music and embodied cognition. Listening, moving, feeling, and thinking*. Bloomington, In: Indiana University Press. https://doi.org/10.2307/j.ctt2005610s

Eitan, Z. & Timmers, R. (2010). Beethoven's last piano sonata and those who follow crocodiles: Cross-domain mappings of auditory pitch in a musical context. *Cognition*, 114(3), 405–422. https://doi.org/10.1016/j.cognition.2009.10.013

Evans, V. (2003). *The structure of time: Language, meaning, and temporal cognition*. Amsterdam: John Benjamins.

Evans, V. (2010). Figurative language understanding in LCCM Theory. *Cognitive Linguistics*, 21(4), 601–662. https://doi.org/10.1515/cogl.2010.020

Evans, V. (2013). *Language and time. A cognitive linguistics approach*. Cambridge, UK: Cambridge University Press. https://doi.org/10.1017/CBO9781107340626

Gibbs, R. W., Jr. (2006). *Embodiment and cognitive science*. New York: Cambridge University Press.

Grady, J. E. (1997). *Foundations of meaning. Primary metaphors and primary scenes*. PhD Dissertation, University of California, Berkeley.

Guck, M. (1991). Two types of metaphoric transfer. In J. Kassler (Ed.), *Metaphor. A Musical Dimension* (pp. 1–12). Sydney: Currency Press.

Jandausch, A. (2012). Conceptual metaphor theory and the conceptualization of music. *Proceedings of the 5th International Conference of Students of Systematic Musicology, Montreal, Canada*.

Johnson, M., & Larson, S. (2003). Something in the way she moves. Metaphors of musical motion. *Metaphor and Symbol, 18*(2), 63–84. https://doi.org/10.1207/S15327868MS1802_1

Kövecses, Z. (2000). *Metaphor and emotion.* Cambridge, UK: Cambridge University Press.

Kövecses, Z. (2015). *Where metaphors come from: Reconsidering context in metaphor.* Oxford, UK: Oxford University Press. https://doi.org/10.1093/acprof:oso/9780190224868.001.0001

Lakoff, G. & Johnson, M. (1980). *Metaphors we live by.* Chicago: University of Chicago Press.

Lakoff, G. & Johnson, M. (1999). *Philosophy in the flesh: The embodied mind and its challenge to Western thought.* New York, NY: Basic Books.

Lakoff, G. & Turner, M. (1989). *More than cool reason. A field guide to poetic metaphor.* Chicago: University of Chicago Press. https://doi.org/10.7208/chicago/9780226470986.001.0001

Marghetis, T. & Núñez, R. (2013). The motion behind the symbols: A vital role for dynamism in the conceptualization of limits and continuity in expert mathematics. *Topics in Cognitive Science, 5*(2), 299–316. https://doi.org/10.1111/tops.12013

Matlock, T. (2004). The conceptual motivation of fictive motion. In G. Radden & K. U. Panther (Eds.), *Studies in Linguistic Motivation* (pp. 221–247). Berlin: Mouton De Gruyter.

Moore, K. E. (2014). *The spatial language of time. Metaphor, metonymy, and frames of reference.* Amsterdam: John Benjamins. https://doi.org/10.1075/hcp.42

Pérez-Sobrino, P. & Julich, N. (2014). Let's talk music: A corpus-based account of musical motion. *Metaphor and Symbol, 29*(4), 298–315. https://doi.org/10.1080/10926488.2014.948800

Pragglejaz Group (2007). MIP: A method for identifying metaphorically used words in discourse. *Metaphor and Symbol, 22*(1), 1–39. https://doi.org/10.1080/10926480709336752

Scruton, R. (1997). *The aesthetics of music.* Oxford, UK: Oxford University Press.

Shove, P. & Repp, B. H. (1995). Musical motion and performance: Theoretical and empirical perspectives. In J. Rink (Ed.), *The Practice of Performance* (pp. 55–83). Cambridge, UK: Cambridge University Press. https://doi.org/10.1017/CBO9780511552366.004

Spitzer, M. (2004). *Metaphor and musical thought.* Chicago: University of Chicago Press.

Steen, G. J., Dorst, A. G., Herrmann, J. B., Kaal, A. A., Krennmayr, T. & Pasma, T. (2010). *A method for linguistic metaphor identification: From MIP to MIPVU.* Amsterdam: John Benjamins. https://doi.org/10.1075/celcr.14

Störel, T. (1997). *Metaphorik im Fach. Bildfelder in der musikwissenschaftlichen Kommunikation.* Tübingen, Germany: Gunter Narr Verlag.

Talmy, L. (2000). *Toward a cognitive semantics* (Vol. 1). Cambridge, MA: MIT Press.

Zbikowski, L. M. (2002). *Conceptualizing music: Cognitive structure, theory, and analysis.* New York, NY: Oxford University Press. https://doi.org/10.1093/acprof:oso/9780195140231.001.0001

Zuckerkandl, V. (1969). *Sound and symbol. Music and the external world.* Princeton, NJ: Princeton University Press.

CHAPTER 10

Approaching perceptual qualities
The case of HEAVY

Daria Ryzhova[i], Ekaterina Rakhilina[i,ii] and Liliya Kholkina[iii]
[i]National Research University Higher School of Economics /
[ii]V. V. Vinogradov Russian Language Institute of the Russian Academy
of Sciences / [iii]Russian State University for the Humanities

The paper examines the properties of HEAVY as a perceptual concept, based on evidence from 11 languages. We demonstrate that the semantics of this concept is heterogeneous; lexemes of this field can be used in situations of at least three types: Lifting, Shifting and Weighing. These situations are either lexicalised as separate words, or they converge in a single lexeme in various combinations following certain strategies. We also argue that different metaphorical extensions correspond to different situation types; this allows us to use analysis of metaphoric shifts as an additional instrument to establish the semantic structure of direct meanings.

Keywords: lexical typology, frame approach, qualities, heavy, metaphor, perception

1. Perceptual lexicon: The different facets

The perceptual lexicon is often regarded as a key to human cognition: the analysis of lexical domains is believed to shed light on how human beings conceptualise the information they receive via different perceptual channels.

In recent years, several breakthrough psycholinguistic projects have addressed the issue of expressibility of the perceptual human experience (see, for example, Majid & Levinson, 2011; Majid, Senft, & Levinson, 2007; Senft, Majid, & Levinson, 2007). Their approach basically followed Berlin & Kay (1969) in utilising extra-linguistic stimuli (such as the Munsell colour chart) in order to obtain the relevant information about the structure of the corresponding lexical fields. However, the adherents of this paradigm have made substantial progress both in terms of developing the methodology (cf. Kay, Berlin, Maffi, Merrfield, & Cook, 2009), and in the scope of research problems and research material (see Majid, 2015). For instance, the extra-linguistic stimuli have progressed from colour chips to include video clips (Majid, Bowerman, Staden, & Boster, 2007), smell samples (Majid et al., 2007; Majid & Burenhult, 2014), or taste samples (Senft et al., 2007).

https://doi.org/10.1075/celcr.19.10ryz
© 2019 John Benjamins Publishing Company

Nevertheless, certain linguistic domains (such as mental activity, pain, or social relations) cannot be as effectively investigated by means of extra-linguistic methods. Research into such lexical fields benefits from more specific tools that are based on the linguistic behaviour of lexical items, such as co-occurrence patterns of distinct lexemes. It is with such instruments that different types of perception can be described.

The framework we demonstrate in the present paper goes back to the tradition of the Moscow Semantic School (Apresjan, 2000). Similarly to Anna Wierzbicka and Cliff Goddard's approach (Goddard & Wierzbicka, 2007, 2013), our framework relies on in-depth analysis of lexical distribution (see Koptjevskaja, Rakhilina, & Vanhove, 2016). However, while Wierzbicka and Goddard primarily aim at elaborating the universal metalanguage of lexicographic descriptions, our goal is to produce a fine-grained cross-linguistic comparison of lexical systems.

To put it more exactly, for every semantic field, we collect the set of typical contexts for the lexemes that describe it (the contexts correspond to the prototypical situations in the domain). To make a list of typical contexts, we start with the data from our native language (Russian) that is chiefly drawn from the Russian National Corpus, which is well-balanced and large enough for the lexicon analysis, as well as from dictionaries. We analyse the distribution of the lexemes of the field in question, i.e., examine their co-occurrence patterns, and compile a preliminary questionnaire that contains the observed types of contexts. Normally, these are the minimal diagnostic contexts (for adjectives – the nouns that they modify, for verbs – the nouns that fill their argument positions), since in most cases they are sufficient to establish the different meanings of a lexeme, and to define the semantic differences between near-synonyms within one language and the translational equivalents across languages.

To provide a first example, let us consider the Russian adjective *glubokij* 'deep'. Its literal meaning describes water bodies (rivers, lakes, etc.), while its figurative senses modify the names of emotions (e.g. *simpatija* 'sympathy' or *gore* 'grief') or time periods (e.g. *osen'* 'autumn', *noč* 'night', etc.). When combined with a noun denoting an emotion, *glubokij* conveys the meaning 'intensive'; when modifying a name of a time period, *glubokij* indicates that this span of time is about to be over (cf. *late autumn*). Thus, the questionnaire for the field 'deep' would contain at least three groups of contexts: nouns denoting water bodies vs. emotions vs. time periods.

As the next step, we use bilingual dictionaries of several other languages to obtain the translational equivalents; then we turn to text corpora, dictionaries and native speaker surveys to establish their usage patterns. All the usage patterns that have not been attested in Russian are added to the questionnaire. For example, the

English equivalent of the Russian *glubokij* – *deep* – does not commonly combine with the names of time periods. Contrary to its Russian counterpart, it can describe the degree of colour saturation, cf. *deep purple* (cf. the unnaturalness of the combination of the adjective *glubokij* and such colour terms as *krasnyj / purpurnyj / bagrovyj*, which are the typical translations of *purple* into Russian, according to the Russian-English parallel subcorpus of RNC). Following this observation we would extend the preliminary questionnaire by adding the fourth group of contexts – colour terms. In our experience, data from three to five languages is usually sufficient to produce an exhaustive questionnaire, and adding more languages does not yield new context types (except for occasional individual idiosyncratic metaphors).

Typological questionnaires designed along these lines have proved to be an effective tool for cross-linguistic descriptions of various lexical domains, for example, of motion/being in a liquid medium ("aqua-motion") (Lander, Maisak, & Rakhilina, 2012), rotation (Kruglyakova, 2010; Rakhilina, 2010), pain (Reznikova, Rakhilina, & Bonch-Osmolovskaya, 2012), etc. Besides, such questionnaires can also be used to study "colexification" strategies (in terms of François, 2008) – i.e. the principles of clustering different elementary situations within one lexeme. In our terminology, these typical elementary situations characterising and structuring a certain domain are called frames. For example, the domain of "aqua-motion" involves the four frames:

1. Active swimming performed by a human
2. Sailing
3. Passive drifting of an inanimate object
4. Staying on the water surface

It can be easily observed that each of these frames is associated with a specific type of context, most notably, with different types of prototypical subjects: human beings, ships, logs, and floats (or buoys, or leaves), respectively. It is exactly this feature that differentiates the frames from each other.

Metaphor research enjoys special attention within our methodology. We believe that each frame has its own vector of semantic development. To exemplify this point, let us revisit the active swimming situation and restate that it is truly different from the passive drifting, e.g. of a log going with the flow. For example, it is only the situation of active swimming that develops the figurative meaning of overcoming obstacles. The Japanese verb *oyogu* is a good illustration of this pattern: while its direct (non-figurative) meaning describes active swimming performed by a human, *oyogu* can also denote the situation of going through the crowd (see Panina, 2007 for further details). Contrariwise, only passive swimming (the drifting or floating of an inanimate object) shifts to the abstract situation of losing control: cf., for example, the following usage of the German verb *driften* 'drift': *Kosovo driftet auf einen Krieg zu* 'Kosovo moves to war' (Shemanaeva, 2007). Thus, the analysis of metaphorical extensions helps to reveal the organisation of the direct physical domain.

For this reason, we view cross-linguistic study of metaphorical patterns not merely as a self-contained descriptive activity, but also as a tool to reconstruct the initial set of frames in the domain and to verify their relevance. Consequently, examining metaphors is not a supplementary task but rather an indispensable step of the methodology, which makes the description of metaphorical shifts and the ways they match the original meanings an inherent part of each cross-linguistic project. For a more detailed view of our methodology, see Rakhilina and Reznikova (2016). In the present paper, we will apply our approach to the analysis of the semantic domain HEAVY.

The study of this domain is a part of our ongoing typological research on qualitative features (Rakhilina & Reznikova, to appear). We have studied the lexicalisation of HEAVY in six Indo-European languages representing different groups: English, French, Spanish, Russian, Serbian, and Armenian. In addition, to make our sample more representative, we analysed some more distant languages: Arabic, Besleney Kabardian (Circassian, North-West Caucasian), Japanese, Chinese, and also Russian Sign Language.

In complete accordance with our methodological framework, we have developed a typological questionnaire (the list of typical contexts) and populated it with the data obtained from dictionaries and corpora as well as from native speakers. In what follows we shall look at the different situations that can be described by the words from the HEAVY domain, and the semantic grounds that account for the similarities between these situations (Section 2). Then we shall turn to the lexicalisation patterns exhibited by this domain for our language sample (Section 3) and show that the metaphorisation patterns relate directly to the set of original meanings (Section 4).

2.   The case of HEAVY

Defining the semantic class of the lexemes meaning HEAVY is not a trivial task. At first sight, the lexemes of the HEAVY domain do not enter the class of perceptual predicates if only because the quality they denote is not directly related to any of the five perceptual senses – it has nothing to do with taste, smell, sight or hearing. Moreover, although being the closest to the tactile sphere, it doesn't neatly fit this category either. From the psychophysiological point of view, perception of weight involves various mechanisms, including both the receptor responses of the skin and the high-level cognitive processes (see, for example, Lederman & Klatzky, 2009).

The role of tactile sensations in the semantics of HEAVY is self-evident: we perceive the heaviness of an object when we hold it, prototypically in our hands (see also Trojszczak, this volume, where weight is included into the list of tactile properties, along with hardness, solidity, vibrations, and others). However, this is certainly not the only way of dealing with a heavy object. We can carry it on the back, on the shoulder, or even on the head. In each situation, different parts of the human body come into immediate contact with the HEAVY object. However, from the purely linguistic point of view, the correlation between heaviness and the contacting body part has not been firmly corroborated, at least no substantial evidence of it was found in our language sample. No language from our sample was observed to lexically mark the distinctions among the body parts in relation to HEAVY. Instead, each language has one predicate with the general meaning of heaviness to cover all of these situation types. Whenever lexical distinctions were observed in the field of HEAVY, they did not stem from the location of the tactile contact (i.e. the body part that comes into contact), but were due to the type of the frame describing the interaction between the person and the object. We suggest three such types of frames.

1. Prototypically, the quality HEAVY presupposes the following situation (frame): a person lifts an object (Trajector) away from a supportive surface (Landmark), moves it somewhere, and, hence, perceives and estimates its weight. For example, a *heavy bag* is an object that someone lifts or/and carries with difficulty because of its weight.[1]
2. A minor deviation from the prototype of HEAVY occurs in the situation when the entire object (Trajector) does not lose contact with the surface (Landmark). Instead, a part of the object acts as the Trajector; now the Landmark is the object itself along with all its other parts – e.g. stiff bicycle pedals, drawers or buttons. In such situations, it is not the weight of the object that causes the difficulty when the latter is being displaced, but the friction between its parts. However, the idea of hindered movement is still preserved.

    It should be noted that this frame is easy to discriminate when analysing contexts, because it involves objects of a specific kind, that is, parts. Normally functioning parts (bicycle pedals, buttons, or desk drawers) cannot detach themselves from the outside surface and cannot be displaced like bags or suitcases. Whole objects belong to the first frame, while parts are related to the second frame.

---

1. The significance of the difficulty that causes some sort of discomfort may vary, but its presence turns out to be crucial: in most languages of our sample the main lexeme with the meaning 'heavy' is negatively connoted in many of its usages (consider Section 4).

An intermediate position between these two frames is occupied by the objects which, by their nature, allow both conceptualisations: either as a whole that moves in relation to an outside surface, or as a part that moves in relation to the other parts.

Consider a door as an instance of such an object. On the one hand, a door can be perceived as a large-sized weighty object intended to be pulled and pushed by a person (similar to a bag or a trolley with suitcases). On the other hand, a door can be regarded as a component of the door mechanism, and then it resembles bicycle pedals or desk drawers. The first interpretation puts the door in the first frame, while the second interpretation places it into the second frame.[2]

3. The third frame is less trivial. We postulate it on the basis of the comparative analysis of near-synonyms within a language. For example, Russian has two adjectives, *tjažëlyj* and *uvesistyj*, which can be loosely corresponded with the English *heavy* and *weighty*. The first item in each pair is a more frequent word with broader combinability. Contexts in which *uvesistyj/weighty* could not be substituted with *tjažëlyj/heavy* are infrequent, although in some cases *uvesistyj/weighty* appears preferable (e.g. in combination with the words *tom/tome*, or, as suggested by the Russian corpus data, *košelëk* 'wallet', *pačka <deneg>* 'wad <of banknotes>').

The common feature shared by the most frequent contexts of *uvesistyj /weighty* is that the heavy weight of the objects denoted by such nouns is considered an advantage rather than a drawback: a weighty wallet or a wad of notes suggests a considerable amount of money, while a weighty tome implies a large amount of information. The presence of positive connotations in the adjectives *uvesistyj/weighty* is further supported by their most frequent adverbial modifiers. *Uvesistyj* is often modified by the adverb *prijatno* 'pleasantly', and *weighty* – by *satisfyingly* and even *wonderfully*. These adverbs can as well modify *tjažëlyj/heavy*, but only occasionally.

Given these peculiarities of combinability, we propose that one more frame should be distinguished in the semantic field HEAVY, associated with the idea of focusing on weight estimation rather than on displacement of an object (for example, to estimate whether its weight is sufficient for some purpose).

Thus, we end up with the three situation types:

1. *Lifting.* A person displaces a whole object (with difficulty, because of its weight; prototypically, lifting it from a surface)
2. *Shifting.* A person displaces a part of an object in relation to its other parts (with difficulty, because of friction)
3. *Weighing.* A person estimates the weight of an object

---

2. This gives rise to the variations in combinability which are found in English and other languages: cf. *heavy/stiff door*.

Intuitively, these situations are semantically contiguous, yet they are distinctly different: the first and the second categories imply that a person must exert some additional effort and thus experiences certain discomfort while dealing with a "heavy" object; the third describes neutral weighing. The third situation, in its turn, is related to the first one via the idea of the significant weight of the object.

Our data confirm that languages do draw lines between the aforementioned situation types, demonstrating different patterns of their colexification. Additionally, as will be shown in Section 4, the metaphorical extensions of HEAVY depend on the direct meanings and help to establish their frame structure.

3. Typological perspective: Principles of colexification

Different languages conceptualise the three situations constituting the HEAVY domain in various ways. In our sample, we attest the three main strategies:

1. A special linguistic means for each situation;
2. The first and the second situations (Lifting and Shifting) are colexified, while the third one (Weighing) is catered for by a special lexeme or a verbal construction;
3. The first and the third situation types (Lifting and Weighing) are covered by the same lexeme, while the second (Shifting) is denoted by a word from another semantic domain (see Figure 1).

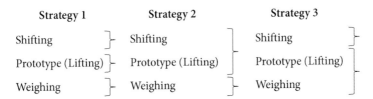

Figure 1. Strategies of colexification in the field HEAVY

3.1 Strategy 1: Differential lexical marking

The first type of lexicalisation strategy is attested in English, French, Spanish, Russian, Armenian and Kabardian: the main adjective meaning HEAVY is used for the most prototypical type of situation (i.e. Lifting). Shifting is described with adjectives from different semantic domains. In most cases, these are HARD, TIGHT or STIFF, cf. English *stiff drawers*, French *bouton dur* 'stiff (lit. 'hard') button' or Russian *tugoj jaščik* 'stiff (lit. 'tight') drawer'. The situation of neutral or positive Weighing uses a verbal construction or a peripheral adjective.

For example, in English, the adjective *heavy* mostly describes Lifting (see the Example (1a)), Shifting is covered with the lexemes *stiff* and *hard* (Example (1b)), while the cognate words *weigh* and *weighty* are special to the Weighing frame ((1c) and (1d)).

(1)   ENGLISH
      Lifting
      a.   *He carried three **heavy** shopping **bags**.*[3]
      Shifting
      b.   *Aside from waxing thread, beeswax can be used to improve the glide of an iron and can even ease **stiff drawers** in old sewing cabinets!*[4]
      Weighing
      c.   *She's written several **weighty tomes** on the subject.*[5]
      d.   *How much does the book **weigh**?*[6]

It is interesting to note that the question from (1d) can also be phrased in an alternative way, with the adjective *heavy* – but only with reference to inanimate objects: *How heavy is the book?* If such a question is addressed to a person, it can be seen as rude or tactless, and in some varieties of English it is used as a euphemism for the meaning 'overweight, fat'; this consideration further corroborates the negative connotations of the adjective *heavy*.

A similar observation can be made in Russian: the Lifting frame is served by the adjective *tjažëlyj* 'heavy' (Example (2a)), Shifting – by *tugoj* 'stiff' (2b), and Weighing – by the verb *vesit'* 'to weigh' and the adjective *uvesistyj* 'weighty' stemming from the noun *ves* 'weight' (see Example (2c)). The question 'How much does it weigh?' in Russian can also be asked with the adjective *tjažëlyj* (*Naskol'ko on tjažëlyj?* 'How heavy is it?'); however, this choice will mean that the speaker holds the presupposition that the weight of the object is above the normal, and gives this fact a negative (to various extents) evaluation. This question must never be asked about people.

---

3.   URL http://www.dailymail.co.uk/tvshowbiz/article-2927040/Robert-Downey-Jr-holds-receipt-mouth-carrying-three-heavy-shopping-bags.html (retrieved 24.04.2017)

4.   URL https://threadtheory.ca/products/tailors-beeswax (retrieved 02.07.2017)

5.   Example from the online Cambridge Dictionary, URL http://dictionary.cambridge.org/dictionary/english/tome

6.   URL http://duranduranboard.proboards.com/thread/36265/music-book-update (retrieved 02.07.2017)

(2)   RUSSIAN
Lifting
a. *On vsegda nosi-l-Ø*   ***tjažël-ye***   ***sumk-i***   (informant)
he   always   carry-PST-3SG.M heavy-ACC.PL bag-ACC.PL
'He's been always carrying **heavy bags**.'

Shifting
b. *Sleva*   *stoja-l-Ø*   *komod*   *s*   ***tug-imi***
on.the.left stand-PST-3SG.M bureau.NOM PREP tight-INS.PL
jaščik-ami   (informant)
drawer-INS.PL
'On the left, there was a bureau with **stiff (lit. 'tight') drawers**.'

Weighing
c. *Našë-l-Ø*   ***uvesist-yj***   ***kamen'***   *i,*
find-PST-3SG.M weighty-ACC.SG stone.ACC.SG and
vernu-vši-s',   *prinja-l-Ø-sja*   *kolotit' im*   *po*
return-GER.PST-REFL take-PST-3SG.M-REFL hit.INF he.INS.SG PREP
kryšk-e   *škatulk-i*
he.INS.SG box-GEN.SG
'(He) found a **weighty stone**, came back and started to hit the lid of the box.'[7]

3.2   Strategy 2: Lifting and Shifting vs. Weighing

Another type of lexicalisation strategy is attested in Japanese and in Russian Sign Language. Here, the Lifting and Shifting situations are described with a single lexical means, and the Weighing situation is handled by a verbal construction or a peripheral adjective.

For instance, in Japanese, the adjective *omoi* handles both of the situations that are associated with resistance and effort (namely Lifting and Shifting, see Examples (3a) and (3b)). The question about the weight of an inanimate object is constructed differently, by means of the abstract noun *omosa* which is formed from the adjective *omoi* 'heavy/stiff'; and an entirely different construction is used when asking about the weight of an animate creature (see (3c)).

7.   URL http://www.bookol.ru/lubovnyie_romani/sovremennyie_lyubovnyie_romanyi/167942/fulltext.htm (retrieved 24.04.2017)

(3)   JAPANESE
Lifting

a. *Ashi ga   warukute **omoi baggu** o   mota-nai*
    foot NOM bad.GER heavy bag   ACC carry-NEG
    '[Her] legs are bad, and [she] does not carry **heavy bags**.'[8]

Shifting

b. *Sakamichi de   jitensha no   **pedaru** ga   **omoi***
    uphill   PREP bicycle GEN pedal   NOM heavy
    'When riding uphill, the **pedals are stiff** (lit. "heavy").'[9]

Weighing

c. *Haru-san, taijū   ga   dore   kurai na   no   ka*
    Haru   body.weight NOM which class ATR NML Q
    'How much does Haru **weigh**? / What is Haru's weight?'[10]

In Russian Sign Language, Shifting and Lifting are served by one sign. Situations belonging to the Weighing frame are described by other means; for example, to describe weighty tomes RSL uses the sign that means 'big', and the question 'What is your weight?' is asked with the sign of 'weighing scale'.

3.3   Strategy 3: Lifting and Weighing vs. Shifting

The third type of lexicalisation is attested in Chinese, Arabic, and Serbian. Here, one and the same adjective is used for Lifting and Weighing, while Shifting is described with an adjective from a different semantic domain. This strategy brings together the situations involving significant weight (irrespective of whether this weight causes difficulty, or is useful for some purpose).

For instance, the situation of Lifting is described in Serbian with the adjective *težak* 'heavy' (4a), and Shifting – by *tvrd* 'hard' (4b). As far as we are aware, Serbian provides no lexeme that would specialise the Weighing frame. The question *Koliko si težak?* 'How much do you weigh?' (lit. 'How heavy are you?', Example (4c)), that makes use of the adjective *težak* 'heavy', is the most neutral form to ask about a person's weight.

---

8. URL http://stylestore.jp/blog/user/T00071/110520148213/ (retrieved 22.04.2017)

9. From the Daijisen Dictionary. Tokyo: Shogakukan. 1997

10. URL http://haru-okkake.blog.so-net.ne.jp/haru-sintyou-taizyu (retrieved 22.04.2017)

(4) SERBIAN

Lifting

a. *Pet   i   po   kilogram-a   je   **tešk-a***
five and half kilogram-GEN.PL be.3SG heavy-F.NOM.SG
torb-a   *prvak-a*
bag-NOM.SG first.grader-GEN.SG
'The first-grader's **heavy bag** is 5.5 kg.'[11]

Shifting

b. *telefon   je   odličan-Ø,   jedin-a*
telephone be.3SG excellent-M.NOM.SG single-F.NOM.SG
*man-a <...>   je   previše **tvrd-o**   **dugm-e***
disadvantage-NOM.SG be.3SG too   hard-N.NOM.SG button-NOM.SG
kamer-e,   koj-e   prilično   otežav-a
camera-GEN.SG that-N.NOM.SG considerably complicate-3SG
slikanj-e
photographing-ACC.SG
'The phone is excellent, the only disadvantage is a too **hard** camera **button**
that complicates photographing.'[12]

Weighing

c. *Koliko   si   **težak-Ø?***
how.much be.2SG heavy-M.NOM.SG
'How much do you weigh?'[13] (lit. 'How **heavy** are you?')

Chinese offers quite a similar picture: the main adjective of the HEAVY field – *zhòng*
'heavy' – originates from the neutral word meaning 'weight' and covers both Lifting
(5a) and Weighing (5c). It is also used in the most neutral version of the question
'How much do you weigh?' The Shifting frame is exclusively handled by the lexeme
jĭn 'stiff, tight' (5b).

---

11. URL http://www.rts.rs/page/stories/ci/story/56/srbija-danas/968386/teska-torba---kriva-ledja.html (retrieved 24.04.2017)

12. URL http://www.mobilnisvet.com/mobilni/2060/Nokia/N86-8MP (retrieved 24.04.2017)

13. URL https://ask.fm/Vule43/answers/20006554587 (retrieved 24.04.2017)

(5)   CHINESE

Lifting

a.   ***Zhuōzi** hěn dà, hěn **zhòng**, tā fèi.le*   *hěn dà de jìnr*
     table   very big very heavy he spend.MOD very big ATR effort
     cái bǎ tā fúqilai
     only BA it carry.from.under.DIR
     'The **table** was very big and very **heavy**, he used great effort to lift it (and only then lifted it).'[14]

Shifting

b.   ***chōuti** tài **jǐn** le,   wǒ de xiǎo nǚ'ér   lā bù kāi.*
     drawer too= stiff = MOD I   ATR small daughter pull not open
     'The **drawer** is too **stiff**, my small daughter can't open it.'   (informant)

Weighing

c.   *Nǐ yǒu duō   **zhòng?***   (informant)
     you have how.much heavy
     'How much do you weigh? (lit. 'How heavy are you?')'

The lexicalisation pattern exhibited by the Arabic language is more obscure, though. The central frame of the HEAVY field, that of Lifting, is covered by the adjective *ṭaqīl*, which is derived from the verb *ṭaqula* 'to be heavy, to have a large weight' (see Example (6a)). The Shifting frame is covered by the adjective *ṣaʿb* 'difficult'. Our study found no lexemes that are specific to the Weighing frame, while *ṭaqīl* 'heavy' readily occurs in the contexts where large weight is not a disadvantage but a merit of the object (see Example (6c)). However, the question about the weight (of a person and an object alike) is built in a different manner, with the help of the noun *wazn* 'weight' or the verb *wazuna* 'to weigh' – this is what differentiates the Arabic system from the Serbian and the Chinese ones.

(6)   ARABIC

Lifting

a.   *taʿib-tu*   *li-'anna-nī kun-tu*   *'a-ḥmilu*
     be.tired-1SG.PRF   PREP-that-I be-1SG.PRF   1SG-carry.IMPF
     al-ḥaqīb-at-a   *aṭ-ṭaqīl-at-a*   *maʿa al-ma'kūl-āt-i*
     DEF-bag-F.SG-ACC DEF-heavy-F.SG-ACC PREP DEF-food-F.PL-GEN
     'I was tired because I carried a **heavy bag** with food in it.'   (informant)

---

14. Center for Chinese Linguistics PKU Corpus (ccl.pku.edu.cn)

Shifting

b. *lā*   *budd-a*   *l-ī*   *’an*   *’a-bdul-a*
NEG avoidance-ACC.SG PREP-I PART 1SG-spend-CONJ

al-ğahd-a   *’an*   *’a-ftaḥ-a*   *hāḏā* *al-bāb-a*
DEF-effort-ACC.SG PART 1SG-open-CONJ this DEF-door-ACC.SG

aṣ-ṣaʿb-a   (informant)
DEF-difficult-ACC.SG

'I have to make an effort to open this **stiff** (lit. 'difficult') door.'

Weighing

c. *yu-mkinu*   *taksīr-u*   *az-zuğāğ-at-i*   *bi-hāḏā*
3M.SG-be.able breaking-NOM DEF-glass-F.SG-GEN PREP-this

al-ḥağar-i   *at̲-t̲aqīl-i*   (informant)
DEF-stone-GEN DEF-heavy-GEN

'This **weighty stone** can break the glass.'

So far, we have demonstrated that languages use different strategies to code the situations of Lifting, Shifting and Weighing. We believe that the fact that the prototypical frame of Lifting in some languages shares its lexeme with the less central frames of Shifting or Weighing proves the integrity of the semantic domain of HEAVY; or, at least, it shows that these three frames are contiguous. This integrity or contiguity can be regarded as an illustration of the overlap and criss-crossing between semantic fields discussed by Majid (2015).

Although our research revealed three lexicalisation strategies within the domain, two additional patterns are potentially possible: [Lifting + Shifting + Weighing] and [Lifting vs. Shifting + Weighing]. The first option, where all the situation types are covered by a single word, is expected to be evidenced in our further research, when we extend our language sample and make it more representative. In principle, existence of such an umbrella lexeme is highly likely, since local combinations of Shifting and Weighing have been reliably attested.

The second option looks unnatural, since displacement of an object's part has nothing in common with the process of weighing. These situations are not contiguous; they share the same domain only by virtue of their connectedness with the core situation, displacement of a whole object (i.e. Lifting). Thus, we anticipate that this strategy will be not represented in natural languages.

To sum up, we have shown that the scope of the semantics of directly used HEAVY terms differs from language to language. The same holds for metaphoric meanings that will be addressed in the next section – they vary across languages. The most important consequence for us lies in the fact that these metaphorical extensions vary depending on the combination of situations that are covered by the lexeme HEAVY in its direct meaning.

4. Metaphorical extensions

4.1   Perceptual metaphor

We receive information from the outer world via the five channels – sight, hearing, touch, smell and taste – and therefore physical objects are perceived in correspondence with these five aspects. Words of physical qualities in their direct meanings usually profile the object characteristics as defined by one of the five senses, cf.:

1. 'blue', 'round' – colour or shape of the objects, visual processing,
2. 'loud', 'quiet' – sound, auditory processing,
3. 'soft', 'smooth' – touch, tactile processing,
4. 'stinking', 'fragrant' – odours, olfactory processing,
5. 'sweet', 'bitter' – flavor, gustatory processing.

As is well established (cf. Williams, 1976; Viberg, 1984; Sweetser, 1991; Vanhove, 2008, and many others), regular polysemy can arise as a result of the change of perceptual channel in the process of semantic extension. Importantly, such semantic changes can take place both synchronically and diachronically, see Strik Lievers and De Felice (this volume) and Anderson (this volume).

Many adjectives denoting taste can describe the corresponding smell, cf. *sweet tea* vs. *sweet smell*, *slatki sok* vs. *slatki miris* (Serbian: 'sweet juice' vs. 'sweet smell'), *kislaja jagoda* vs. *kislyj zapax* (Russian: 'sour berry' vs. 'sour smell'), etc.[15]

Another common type of regular polysemy is the change of perceptual channel from haptic to visual. For example, the sharpness of a *sharp spear* would be prototypically perceived through touch, while a *sharp* (lit. 'pointed') *nose* is primarily perceived via the visual channel. The same shift is attested in Serbian (*oštri nož* 'sharp knife' vs. *oštri lakat* 'sharp elbow'), Russian (*tupaja igla* 'blunt needle' vs. *tupoj podborodok* 'square (lit. 'blunt') chin'), and many other languages. See also a similar example in Strik Lievers & De Felice (this volume): the Italian adjectives *caldo* 'warm' and *freddo* 'cold' which in Latin belonged exclusively to the sphere of tactile temperature terms, in Italian can also describe visual stimuli, cf. *colore caldo/ freddo* 'warm/cold colour' (see also Koptjevskaja-Tamm (2015) for a more detailed discussion of typologically relevant metaphorical extensions of temperature terms).

Furthermore, languages abound with instances of the change of perceptual modality from haptic to auditory. For example, normally one has to touch an object

---

15. These two types of usages are so closely bonded that some researches argue they represent different instantiations of one and the same meaning, cf. the following citation from Winter (this volume): "…taste and smell are highly integrated in perception, and a word such as *sweet* is best analysed as literally referring to both gustation and olfaction".

to ascertain whether it is soft or not (*soft chair*), but *soft voice* describes something we hear. Cf. also Russian *mjagkoe sidenie* vs. *mjagkij golos* ('soft seat' vs. 'soft (i.e., quiet and peaceful) voice'), French *main dure* vs. *son dur* ('hard hand' vs. 'hard (i.e., non-palatalised) sound'). Similarly, the Italian adjective *caldo* 'warm' can denote the property of a sound (*voce calda* 'warm voice'), according to Strik Lievers & De Felice (this volume).

Examples of this kind are widely attested, and they are not restricted to adjectival lexicon (cf. also Viberg, 1984; Brown, 2011, among others). They can be regarded as metaphorical shifts, but of a very specific nature, the one that is peculiar to perceptual lexicon. Thus, words like *clever*, denoting a mental quality, do not develop any cross-modal extensions. Instead, these quality words display more ordinary semantic shifts directed from the Source domain of human beings into the Target domain of inanimate objects, cf. (7):

(7) *clever woman → clever program*

When the change affects the channel of perception, the taxonomic class (of the item perceived) behaves differently: it remains either concrete (*sharp knife – sharp nose*) or abstract (*loud sound – loud colour*), without crossing the taxonomic borders. Due to this, the core mechanism of metaphor, as it is construed in the classic research, since Lakoff and Johnson (1980), seems not to be at work here. The change of perceptional channel is viewed as an exceedingly marginal type of metaphor (if any at all), called "cross-modal" in Levinson and Majid (2014). "Cross-modal" semantic shifts are likely to be an inherent feature of the perceptional domain as a whole.

The quality HEAVY seems to follow the linguistic behaviour typical of perceptual lexicon. In the first place, HEAVY is very close to a haptic concept; as a consequence, it can switch the channel to the visual one (*heavy bag -> heavy clouds*) and the auditory one (*heavy bag -> heavy sound*),[16] similarly to prototypical tactile adjectives like *soft*, *smooth* or *sharp* (see the examples above).[17]

---

16. Lit. 'loud and sonorous, usually in a low pitch'. Consider the following example: *What happens to the ear when we hear heavy sounds? The ear drum and the nerves may be damaged and ultimately hearing loss can occur.* [https://www.lybrate.com/question/643413994/what-happen-to-ear-when-we-hear-heavy-sound643413994] Usages of this kind are quite rare in the languages of our sample. However, from the psychophysiological perspective, some sounds (namely, back/open vowels) tend to correlate with felt heaviness, see Walker & Parameswaran (2018) for further details.

17. Note that the shift of perceptual channel, or cross-modal metaphor, that is found in the quality HEAVY (among the others) is distinctly different from the phenomenon observed in the words of the *strong* or *rich* kind. These lexemes can also be applied to a large variety of percepts, cf. *strong/rich taste/sound*. But, firstly, these words are not perceptual in their origin: *strong* is a specific feature of a living creature ('the one that possesses considerable physical power'), while *rich* is a quite exclusive human quality ('the one that owns large amounts of money or other material

However, the opportunities for semantic shifts that are available to the lexemes of the HEAVY field are not solely confined to cross-modal metaphors. They can also produce the "canonical" metaphors involving the change of the taxonomic class of the object that bears the quality of 'heavy', and, consequently, a more dramatic change in the meaning of the word *heavy*. The directions of such semantic development that are observed among the lexemes of this field are numerous and diverse. However, they exhibit a distinct pattern across languages, and therefore they can be systematised, shedding light on the frame structure of direct meanings. Such metaphoric shifts will be discussed in the following section.

4.2   "Canonical" metaphors

The languages of our sample indicate two major directions for metaphorical extension of words with the meaning of HEAVY. Extensions in the first direction carry a negative evaluation of some situation, while extensions in the second direction are neutral or can be positively connoted. A variety of individual metaphors is found within each type of extension.

Manifestations of the 'negative' metaphor are highly diverse. Thus, for example, a period of time can be HEAVY (see Example (8)): it is "loaded" with events, and in the end of it a person can feel tired. A HEAVY phrase in the French Example (9) is overfilled with ideas and underlying meanings; it takes extra effort to comprehend it. A person whose temper is HEAVY (10) is difficult to communicate with. This list can be continued; in different languages, HEAVY can refer to a film that evokes intense negative emotions, or to a long-standing disease that is difficult to bear; to difficulty in breathing, to a challenging math problem that is difficult to solve, or to money that is difficult to earn.

(8)   ENGLISH
  *Let's go to bed. We've got a **heavy day** tomorrow.*[18]

(9)   FRENCH
  J' ai   reformulé   une **phrase trop lourd-e-Ø.**
  I   have.1SG.PRS reformulate.PTCP INDF phrase too   heavy-F-SG
  'I have reformulated an **overloaded** (lit. 'heavy') **phrase**.'[19]

---

values'). Their usage in the sense of 'intensive'/'saturated' is metaphoric in itself. Secondly, the non-figurative meanings of *strong* and *rich* possess broad combinability that extends far beyond modifying percepts: cf. *strong/rich emotions, impression,* etc.

18.   From the online Longman Dictionary of Contemporary English (http://www.ldoceonline. com/dictionary/heavy-schedule-timetable-day-etc)

19.   URL https://fr.wikipedia.org/wiki/Discussion:Individualisme (retrieved 24.04.2017)

(10) ARMENIAN

Canr *bnavorut'y-a-n*   *patčaṙ-ov* *ašxatakic'-ner-ə* *nra* *het*
heavy character-DAT-DEF reason-INS colleague-PL-DEF him with

č'ē-in   *šp'v-um*   (informant)
not-be.PST.3PL talk-PTCP.PRS

'Because of his **heavy temper** his colleagues refused to deal with him.'

On the other hand, heaviness may be associated with the idea of significance and thus it may evoke positively connoted meanings. For instance, the Chinese lexeme *zhòng* 'heavy' can be used in the sense of 'important, significant' (about persons or events, see Example (11)). A similar meaning is expressed by the Arabic *ṭaqīl* 'heavy' (12). The English *weighty* (13) can describe an important argument, a piece of reasoning, or other sorts of inputs in an act of speech (as if they are tipping the scale in favour a decision).

(11) CHINESE

Zhǎngdà yǐhòu *cái* *fāxiàn*, *xiǎoshíhòu kàn* *de* *hěn* ***zhòng de***
grow.up after only find.out childhood watch EV very heavy ATR

shì, *zhēn de* *méi*   *shénme.*   (informant)
thing real ATR not.have something

'Only after I grew up, I realised that the matters that seemed very **important** (lit. 'heavy') to me when I was a kid, are really nothing.'

(12) ARABIC

'aṣbaḥ-a   *zayd-un*   *wazīr-an*   *wa-'al'āna* *huwa*
become-PRF.3M.SG Zeid-NOM.SG minister-ACC.SG CONJ-now he

šaḫṣ-un   ***ṭaqīl-un***   (informant)
person-NOM.SG heavy-NOM.SG

'Zeid became minister: he is a very **big** (lit. 'heavy') person now.'

(13) ENGLISH

*The terrible death of the young female solider provided a **weighty argument** against women fighting on the front line.*   (informant)

The semantic foundation of the "negative" metaphor of HEAVY is absolutely clear. We have attested it in every language from our sample, which is unsurprising considering that it goes back to the prototypical situation of the field (Lifting, or Lifting and Shifting). This metaphor inherits from the primary meaning the idea of some effort that causes discomfort and thus receives negative evaluation (see Examples (14) and (15)). Winter (this volume) also argues that evaluative attributes in metaphorical meanings go back to the direct, perceptual usages of the corresponding words. Example (16) below also supports this idea: the prepositional adverbial phrase *with ease* marks an unexpected behaviour of the woman, while *with difficulty* emphasises the intensity of the discomfort.

(14)   *Children lose interest in coming to school with the stress of carrying heavy bags.*[20]

(15)   *Carrying around pounds of possessions in a heavy bag can lead to disabling back pain.*[21]

(16)   *She lifted the heavy bag with ease / with difficulty.*[22]

The "positive" metaphor correlates with the third frame (Weighing), and namely with the idea of having significant weight that may prove useful for some purposes. In this case, the weight does not cause any uncomfortable sensation, being instead a property of an object, critical to its functioning. This metaphor can either be developed by the words that are specified on the Weighing frame (cf. the English *weighty*, Example (1c)), or by lexemes combining Weighing and Lifting (according to the third strategy of colexification of the direct meanings, see Section 3); cf. the examples from Arabic, English and Chinese above. The presence of the positive metaphor offers additional corroborative evidence in favour of distinguishing Weighing as an individual frame.

To summarise, figurative meanings correlate with the direct meanings; consequently, the analysis of Target domains can be instrumental in revealing the principles according to which Source domains are organised. Of course, a sample of 11 languages is not sufficient enough to form overarching typological generalisations, but the major tendency is evident; we believe that data from new languages will fit into this roughly outlined paradigm. To be more explicit, in the new languages we expect lexemes from the HEAVY field to converge in the direct meanings (Lifting, Shifting and Weighing) in accordance with the rules presented in this research; i.e. either each individual frame will be described by words that are specific to it; or Lifting will be combined with either Shifting or Weighing (but never will Shifting combine with Weighing); or, lastly, all the three types of situations will deploy to jointly describe all of them. Furthermore, the "negative" metaphor can be developed by any word denoting the situation of Lifting, while the "positive" metaphor is possible only in the words that cater for the Weighing frame.

---

20. [http://www.thehealthsite.com/parenting/childrens-health-parenting/the-ill-effects-of-carrying-heavy-schoolbags/], retrieved 25.06.2017

21. [http://www.everydayhealth.com/back-pain/is-your-bag-hurting-your-back.aspx], retrieved 25.06.2017

22. We thank the Editors of the volume for this valuable example.

5. Conclusion

We have demonstrated that the perception of such a habitual physical quality as HEAVY in a natural language produces the reflection that is far from trivial. Although the closest to it are tactile sensations, this sense involves high-level cognitive processes along with receptor responses of the skin. Furthermore, the analysis of lexemes with the meaning of HEAVY can be complicated by the utterly subjective perception of weight: an object that is perceived as heavy by one person will be felt as being lightweight by another individual.

We suggest a possible way for overcoming these complications; our method is based on the analysis of contexts in which lexemes of the HEAVY field occur. Primarily, we examine nouns that denote the objects possessing this quality. We have used a similar method to study various groups of vocabulary. Thus, we have applied it to the predicates of pain (Reznikova et al., 2012), and pain sensation is just as subjective as perception of heaviness.[23]

Analysing the combinability of words with the meaning of HEAVY reveals that they are used in the three types of situations. These situation types can be labelled as Lifting (e.g. lifting and carrying a heavy bag), Shifting (when certain parts of an object move in relation to the other parts, e.g. pressing a stiff button), and Weighing (neutral assessment of an object's weight). Differences among them go beyond mere tactile sensations: all these situations imply heaviness as a result of the natural interaction of a special kind between a person and a property-bearing object. These situations can either be lexicalised as separate words or, contrariwise, they can be combined within a single lexical means according to certain strategies.

Our experience shows that the inventory of such situations and the major strategies of their lexicalisation can be established by an in-depth analysis of 10–12 languages (see also Haspelmath's remark on the general understanding of grammatical systems, in Haspelmath, 2003). But of course, even if we continue to significantly extend the language sample, we can never be quite confident that a new language will not introduce new lexical oppositions into the already established system. The presented inventory of primary meanings (or frames, in our terminology) in any case requires some additional verification. For a diagnostic test, we use the analysis of metaphoric shifts in the lexemes under consideration.

A crucial capability of the proposed methodology is that it can examine figurative meanings alongside direct meanings, because a semantic shift nearly always entails changes in the combinability. Words of the HEAVY field exhibit two

---

23. A kindred approach was successfully used by Maria Koptjevskaja-Tamm (2015) to study temperature terms.

dramatically different types of shifts (intrafield vs. transfield shifts, in terminology of Matisoff, 1978; Evans & Wilkins, 2000; see also O'Meara et al., this volume and Strik Lievers & De Felice, this volume). On the one hand, being a perceptual feature, HEAVY develops so-called "cross-modal", or intrafield, metaphors where the shift of perceptual channel occurs without changing the taxonomic class of the feature. In this regard, HEAVY behaves as an ordinary haptic feature, allowing the change of the perceptual channel from the haptic to the visual and the auditory (cf. *heavy clouds/sounds*).

Metaphors of another – "canonical", or transfield – type translate physical sensations to more abstract ones, like emotional or mental, and are strongly associated with their semantic sources. The target meanings inherit the initial evaluation and the other semantic features from complex perceptive situations; therefore, analysis of metaphors of this type can be instrumental in revealing the semantic structure of the field. Thus, in our case, the frames Lifting and Shifting generate shifts with negative connotations, while Weighing is a source for neutral or positive metaphors. This opposition facilitates drawing the line between Lifting and Weighing within the direct usages of the HEAVY lexemes.

Thus, we proposed a method for a linguistic description of lexical typology and tested it on the perceptual field HEAVY. The next step to be undertaken is to verify our findings by extending and diversifying the language sample; we intend to add both major languages with rich written traditions (Persian, Korean, other European languages) and unwritten minority languages, such as Shughni (Iranian), Chukchi (Chukotko-Kamchatkan), or the North Caucasian languages.

Acknowledgements

The authors thank the Editors of this volume, Laura J. Speed, Carolyn O'Meara, Lila San Roque, and Asifa Majid, for their detailed and insightful comments and express their deepest gratitude to Maria Kyuseva, Anastasia Vyrenkova, Yulia Badryzlova, and all the informants and experts without whom this research would not have been possible: Kristine Bagdasaryan, Viktoria Kruglyakova, Anna Panina, Andrey Rizhenko, Alexander Letuchiy and Sofia Lakhuti. This research is supported by the Russian Foundation for Basic Research, grant 17-06-00184 A.

Abbreviations

2	second person	INS	instrumental
3	third person	M	masculinum
ACC	accusative	MOD	modal particle
ATR	attributive particle	NEG	negation
BA	fronted object marker	NML	nominaliser
CONJ	conjunction	NOM	nominative
DAT	dative	PL	plural
DEF	definite	PREP	preposition
DIR	directional morpheme	PRF	perfect
EV	marker of evaluation	PRS	present
F	feminine	PST	past
GEN	genitive	PTCP	participle
GER	gerund	Q	question marker
INDF	indefinite	REFL	reflexive
INF	infinitive	SG	singular

References

Apresjan, J. D. (2000). *Systematic lexicography*. Translated from Russian by K. Windle. Oxford: Oxford University Press.

Berlin, B. & Kay, P. (1969). *Basic colour terms: their universality and evolution*. Berkeley, CA: University of California Press.

Brown, P. (2011). Colour me bitter: Crossmodal compounding in Tzeltal perception words. *The Senses & Society*, 6(1), 106–116. https://doi.org/10.2752/174589311X12893982233957

Evans, N., & Wilkins, D. (2000). In the mind's ear: The semantic extensions of perception verbs in Australian languages. *Language*, 76, 546–592.

François, A. (2008). Semantic maps and the typology of colexification: Intertwining polysemous networks across languages. In: Vanhove, M. (ed.) *From Polysemy to Semantic change: Towards a Typology of Lexical Semantic Associations*. Studies in Language Companion Series, 106, 163–216. https://doi.org/10.1075/slcs.106.09fra

Goddard, C., & Wierzbicka, A. (2007). NSM analyses of the semantics of physical qualities: sweet, hot, hard, heavy, rough, sharp in crosslinguistic perspective. *Studies in Language. International Journal sponsored by the Foundation "Foundations of Language"*, 31 (4) 765–800.

Goddard, C., & Wierzbicka, A. (2013). *Words and meanings: Lexical semantics across domains, languages, and cultures*. OUP Oxford. https://doi.org/10.1093/acprof:oso/9780199668434.001.0001

Haspelmath, M. (2003). The geometry of grammatical meaning: semantic maps and crosslinguistic comparison. In: Tomasello, M., (ed.). *The new psychology of language*, vol.2. Mahwah, NJ, 211–242.

Kay, P., Berlin, B., Maffi, L., Merrifield, W. R., & Cook, R. (2009). *World Colour Survey*. Stanford: CSLI (http://www1.icsi.berkeley.edu/wcs/)

Koptjevskaja-Tamm, M. (Ed.). (2015). *The linguistics of temperature* (Vol. 107). John Benjamins Publishing Company. https://doi.org/10.1075/tsl.107

Koptjevskaja-Tamm, M., Rakhilina, E., and Vanhove, M. (2016). The semantics of lexical typology. In: Riemer, Nick (ed.). *The Routledge Handbook of Semantics*, 434–454.

Kruglyakova, V. A. (2010). Semantika glagolov vraščenija v tipologičeskoj perspektive [Semantics of rotation verbs in a typological perspective]. Ph.D. thesis, Russian State University for Humanities.

Lakoff, G., & Johnson, M. (1980). The metaphorical structure of the human conceptual system. *Cognitive science*, 4(2), 195–208. https://doi.org/10.1207/s15516709cog0402_4

Lander, Yu., Maisak, T., & Rakhilina, E. (2012). Verbs of aquamotion: semantic domains and lexical systems, in: *Motion Encoding in Language and Space*, 67–83. https://doi.org/10.1093/acprof:oso/9780199661213.003.0004

Lederman, S. J., & Klatzky, R. L. (2009). Haptic perception: A tutorial. *Attention, Perception, & Psychophysics*, 71(7), 1439–1459. https://doi.org/10.3758/APP.71.7.1439

Levinson, S. C., & Majid, A. (2014). Differential ineffability and the senses. *Mind & Language*, 29(4), 407–427. https://doi.org/10.1111/mila.12057

Majid, A. (2015). Comparing lexicons cross-linguistically. In *The Oxford handbook of the word*, 364–379. Oxford University Press.

Majid, A., Bowerman, M., Staden, M. V., & Boster, J. S. (2007). The semantic categories of cutting and breaking events: A crosslinguistic perspective. *Cognitive Linguistics*, 18(2), 133–152. https://doi.org/10.1515/COG.2007.005

Majid, A. & Burenhult, N. (2014). Odors are expressible in language, as long as you speak the right language. In *Cognition* 130(2), 266–270. https://doi.org/10.1016/j.cognition.2013.11.004

Majid, A., & Levinson, S. C. (2011). The senses in language and culture. *The Senses & Society*, 6(1), 5–18. https://doi.org/10.2752/174589311X12893982233551

Majid, A., Senft, G., & Levinson, S. C. (2007). The language of olfaction. *Field Manual Volume*, 10, 36–41.

Matisoff, J. A. (1978). *Variational semantics in Tibeto-Burman*. Philadelphia, PA: Institute for the Study of Human Issues.

Panina, A. 2007. Vyraženie peremeščenija i naxoždenija v vode v japonskom jazyke. [The expression of motion and being in water in Japanese.] // T. Maisak, E. Rakhilina (eds.). *Glagoly dviženija v vode: Leksičeskaja tipologija.* [Aqua-motion verbs: a study in lexical typology.] Moscow: Indrik.

Rakhilina, E. (2010). Verbs of rotation in Russian and Polish//V. Hasko, R. Perelmutter (eds.). *New Approaches to Slavic Verbs of Motion*, 115. 291–314. https://doi.org/10.1075/slcs.115.17rak

Rakhilina, E., & Reznikova, T. (2016). 4. A Frame-based methodology for lexical typology. *The Lexical Typology of Semantic Shifts*, 58, 95–130.

Rakhilina, E., & Reznikova, T. (Eds.) *The Typology of Physical Qualities*. Benjamins, to appear.

Reznikova, T., Rakhilina, E., & Bonch-Osmolovskaya, A. (2012). Towards a typology of pain predicates. In: *Linguistics*, 50(3), 421–465. https://doi.org/10.1515/ling-2012-0015

Senft, G., Majid, A., & Levinson, S. C. (2007). The language of taste. *Field Manual*, 1, 42–5.

Shemanaeva, O. 2007. Vyraženie peremeščenija v vode v nemeckom jazyke. [The expression of aqua-motion in German.] // T. Maisak, E. Rakhilina (eds.). *Glagoly dviženija v vode: Leksičeskaja tipologija.* [Aqua-motion verbs: a study in lexical typology.] Moscow: Indrik.

Sweetser, E. (1991). *From etymology to pragmatics: Metaphorical and cultural aspects of semantic structure.* Vol. 54. Cambridge University Press.

Vanhove, M. (2008). Semantic associations between sensory modalities, prehension and mental perceptions. In M. Vanhove (Ed.), *From polysemy to semantic change: Towards a typology of lexical semantic associations* (pp. 341–370). Amsterdam/Philadelphia: John Benjamins. https://doi.org/10.1075/slcs.106.17van

Viberg, Å. (1984). The verbs of perception: A typological study. In B. Butterworth, B Comrie & Ö. Dahl (eds.), *Explanations for Language Universals*, 123–162. https://doi.org/10.1515/9783110868555.123

Walker, P., & Parameswaran, C. R. (2018). Cross-sensory correspondences in language: Vowel sounds can symbolize the felt heaviness of objects. *Journal of Experimental Psychology: Learning, Memory, and Cognition.* Advance online publication. https://doi.org/10.1037/xlm0000583

Williams, J. M. (1976). Synaesthetic adjectives: A possible law of semantic change. *Language,* 52, 461–479. https://doi.org/10.2307/412571

CHAPTER 11

Grounding mental metaphors in touch
A corpus-based study of English and Polish

Marcin Trojszczak
State University of Applied Sciences in Konin & University of Lodz

This study aims to describe how experiences of tactile properties of physical objects give rise to metaphorical conceptualisations of mind and thought in English and Polish based on linguistic data from the British National Corpus and the National Corpus of Polish. This issue is approached from the perspective of corpus-based cognitive linguistics by combining the Theory of Objectification framework and the methodological tools of corpus linguistics. By analysing a wide range of tactile properties ascribed to the selected mental phenomena in light of the Theory of Objectification, the study aims to demonstrate how active, exploratory, tactile experiences of physical objects' qualities ground our talk about impalpable cognitive phenomena.

Keywords: Theory of Objectification, English, Polish, corpus-based linguistics, conceptualisation, touch, mind, thought, conceptual metaphor, metaphor

1. Introduction

What is the experiential basis of metaphorical linguistic expressions related to abstract entities such as time, society, emotions, or thoughts? This question has been asked and answered time and again by numerous researchers within cognitive linguistics (see, for instance, Lakoff & Johnson, 1980, Sweetser, 1990; Jäkel, 1995; Johansson Falck & Gibbs, 2012). Despite various approaches, it is generally agreed that metaphorical linguistic expressions present in various languages are grounded in some type of embodied and physical experience that involves culturally-mediated interactions with the physical world and other human beings (see Lakoff & Johnson, 1999; Pecher & Zwaan, 2005; Kövecses, 2010, 2015).

The role of sensory modalities in the creation of metaphorical conceptualisations is inextricably linked to discussions of how figurative language is grounded and enabled by our physical bodies and experiences. It encompasses a plethora of questions such as which senses are involved and to what extent they contribute

https://doi.org/10.1075/celcr.19.11tro

to culture-specific metaphors, how they interact with each other, which sensory properties are used in metaphorical conceptualisations and, last but not least, how to explain in a principled way the transfer of information from various senses to metaphorical linguistic expressions. These questions are important for all sensory modalities. However, they are especially important in the case of touch – a modality which due to its heterogeneous nature and its seemingly secondary and background character has received less attention than audition and vision (see, for instance, the discussions of the seeming nobility of sight in Merleau-Ponty, 1945; Jonas, 1954), although it has phenomenological primacy over other senses and is so crucial to our existence that, as put by Ratcliffe (2013, p. 132), "one would not have a world at all without touch".

The present study aims to investigate some of these questions in relation to the sense of touch, i.e. (1) which tactile properties of physical objects perceived by means of active, exploratory, and manual touch are used in metaphorical conceptualisations of mind and thought in English and Polish, and (2) what are the underlying conceptual processes that enable us to ascribe properties of palpable objects to impalpable mental entities. The first question will be answered by a detailed analysis of metaphorical linguistic expressions related to the concepts of mind and thought found in two reference corpora: the British National Corpus and the National Corpus of Polish. The second will be addressed drawing upon the Theory of Objectification (Szwedek, 2011, 2014, see Section 3).

2. Touch

In humans, the senses can be seen as modes of accessing information about the world and the differences between them correspond to differences in how information is picked up and used (Matthen, 2015). In this context, touch is seen as arguably the most complex and heterogeneous sensory modality (Macpherson, 2011a; Classen, 2012; Fulkerson, 2014a). Its special nature is best seen when analysed from the perspective of philosophical approaches to individuating the senses, i.e. The Proximal Stimulus Criterion, The Sense-Organ Criterion, The Representational Criterion, and The Phenomenal Character Criterion (Macpherson, 2011b).

The Proximal Stimulus Criterion is an approach that individuates senses based on what directly affects the sensory organ of the sense. In the case of touch, proximal stimuli include mechanical pressure and temperature (Macpherson, 2011b, p. 28). In contrast, vision can be characterised by the proximal stimulus of electromagnetic waves of between 380 and 750 nanometres (Macpherson, 2011b, p. 26). The Sense-Organ Criterion individuates senses by the sensory organs used when perceiving. Unlike vision or audition, sensory organs of touch include a wide range of heterogeneous physiological receptors in the skin such as cutaneous and motion receptors (see Hertenstein, 2011, for a comprehensive discussion). Cutaneous receptors include mechanoreceptors for pressure, weight, and stretching, as well as thermoreceptors, chemoreceptors, pain receptors, and possibly receptors for gentle stroking (see Matthen, 2015, for more details). In turn, motion receptors include receptors localised in the muscles and joints which are crucial in *proprioception* (sense of the body's position) and *kinaesthesia* (sense of awareness of the movement of our body) (Proske & Gandevia, 2012). These distinct underlying physiological systems give rise to a larger range of object properties (phenomenal qualities) than in the case of other sensory modalities (Fulkerson, 2014b; de Vignemont & Massin, 2015).

This leads us to another approach to individuating the senses, i.e. The Representational Criterion, which aims to distinguish them by objects and properties represented by the experiences in a given sensory modality. In the case of touch, this includes both *proper sensibles* (properties detected by only one sense) such as pressure, temperature, and pain, and *common sensibles* (properties that can be detected also by other senses).[1] The list of all tactile properties includes, among others, hardness, solidity, impenetrability, texture, movement at the surface of our body, weight, mass, humidity, contact, vibrations, ticklishness, and wetness (de Vignemont & Massin, 2015, p. 295).

The Phenomenal Character Criterion refers to specific aspects of sensory experiences which are not present in other senses. In the case of touch, this is, for instance, *bipolarity of touch*, i.e. the fact that every instance of tactile perception presents us with both our body and an external object (de Vignemont & Massin, 2015). In other words, touch is the only sense that allows us to be the perceiver and the perceived at the same time (Merleau-Ponty, 1945; Ratcliffe, 2013). This is closely linked to another specific characteristic of touch, i.e. the distinction between *active touch* and *passive touch*. The first is an active, manual exploration of objects (from mere feeling their surface through more detailed manual investigations to moving and changing the shape of the objects) that allows us to perceive their properties in an intentional and purposeful manner (see Hatwell, Streri & Gentaz, 2003; Radman, 2013 and Foolen, 2017 for reviews of a key role of hands in this process). The latter is the perception of the condition of one's own body that does not involve goal-oriented actions (Matthen, 2015). Another phenomenological peculiarity of touch is visible in the phenomenon of *background touch*, i.e. a sense of being in (inhabiting) some medium, e.g., air, water, which is already a tactile experience (akin to passive touch but more diffuse) and which serves as the experiential context for more localised and purposeful palpable experiences (Ratcliffe, 2013, p. 142–144).

---

1. Sensibles are those features or aspects of reality that can be perceived by the senses. A proper sensible of vision is colour, and of audition is sound.

In this respect, background touch could be seen as the basic condition for our experience of the world which is related to another crucial characteristic of touch, namely its *phenomenological primacy* (objectivity of touch). Phenomenological primacy refers to the fact that touch enables us to experience physical effort and resistance, which is based on the experience of counteracting forces coming from our body and from the external world. In this way, unlike other senses, it provides us with the strongest and the most clear-cut phenomenological experience of the physical world as independent from us (de Vignemont & Massin, 2015).

3.   Theory of Objectification

The intuition about the special role of touch in human experience is shared by the Theory of Objectification (Szwedek, 2011, 2014; see also Jelec, 2014; Trojszczak 2016, 2017a, 2017b). This approach to metaphor has been developed within the context of Cognitive Linguistics which is a theoretical perspective that views language as a symbolic system for categorising human experience. In this account, language is ultimately embodied, situated, and influenced by other non-linguistic processes (Croft & Cruse, 2004; Evans, 2012). As in Conceptual Metaphor Theory (Lakoff & Johnson, 1980, 1999), the Theory of Objectification defines metaphor as a conceptual process in which one conceptual domain (more abstract) is understood in terms of another conceptual domain (more concrete).

However, it argues (Szwedek, 2011) that the original framework (Lakoff & Johnson, 1980) does not handle in a satisfactory way the two most fundamental theoretical issues related to the notion of conceptual metaphor: (1) how to tell which entities involved in metaphorical mappings are abstract and which are concrete; and (2) what the experiential basis of conceptual metaphors is. As for the first issue, the search for the criterion of concreteness starts from the definition of the prototypical PHYSICAL OBJECT image schema. According to Szwedek (2011, p. 357), it can be characterised by the following features: (1) the object can be both a natural and man-made thing; (2) the object is not necessarily something that can be held in one hand; (3) animate beings are objects; and (4) touch is a fundamental way of sensing objects – more fundamental than vision.[2]

The last point is critical to this framework as Szwedek (2011, p. 360) proposes "the experience of density (physicality) through touch to be the only, simple, and clear criterion of distinction between material and phenomenological worlds". In

---

2.   Szwedek (2011, p. 356) claims that all other image schemas, e.g. path, link, force, are aspects of objects, or relations between them, and thus they are dependent on the PHYSICAL OBJECT image schema.

this way, he provides a clear answer to the first fundamental question: concrete objects have density which is palpable, and abstract objects are bereft of this feature. In effect, density (firmness, mass) is seen as the most fundamental property of physical objects which serves as the basis for identifying their other physical characteristics such as size, weight, shape, and surface, and for proper definition of conceptual metaphors (Szwedek, 2011, p. 358).

In order to support his claims, Szwedek (2000, 2011) provides a range of arguments for the primacy of touch which complement the discussion about the special nature of this sense presented in the previous section. They include the fact that touch is the only sense that gives us access to a three-dimensional image of physical reality, including such properties as containment and boundedness (Szwedek, 2000). Moreover, it is special in that it is "the only whole-body sense, it is the only physical contact sense, and in that the touching organs – hands and mouth – have the biggest neuronal representation in the brain" (Szwedek, 2011, p. 358). Another argument for the primacy of touch is that it is the earliest sense to be developed in pregnancy. It starts developing at the 8th week concurrently with the development of the neural system. This is the reason why the sense of touch is programmed at the deepest level of the neural system and plays a critical role for foetal and newborn development (Szwedek, 2000, 2011).

The primacy of touch is also supported by numerous linguistic facts. Szwedek (2000) gives a wide range of examples from various languages showing that touch is used to describe more abstract activities, e.g. English *behold*, 'to catch sight of', *perceive* (Lat. *cipio* 'seize'), or German *fassen* 'to touch' and 'to understand'. This process is also reflected in non-Indo-European languages, e.g. in Hungarian, *ért* 'to understand' comes from the Old Turkish *er* 'to touch, to reach', in Japanese, *toraeru* has two meanings 'to catch' and 'to understand' (see also Sweetser, 1990).

The above-mentioned data indicate that touch could be seen as a privileged means of experiencing the physical world. According to the Theory of Objectification, seeing the sense of touch in this way enables us to answer the second fundamental issue related to conceptual metaphor by stating that the "ultimate experiential basis is our experience of physical objects, the only entities directly accessible to our senses" (Szwedek, 2011, p. 350). In this account, the experience of density through active and passive touching of various physical objects gives rise to the development of the PHYSICAL OBJECT image schema which is then used as an intermediary conceptual tool for creating various metaphorical conceptualisations of impalpable abstract entities, e.g. thoughts, love, time. In other words, our tactile interactions with material objects provide us with knowledge of their various properties which can be later activated and employed when we attempt to talk about immaterial abstractions. This process is called *objectification* (*concrete-to-abstract metaphorisation*)[3] and can be defined as identifying, conceptualising, and verbalising abstract entities in terms of "the only world that had been known to our ancestors, the world of physical objects" (Szwedek, 2011, p. 344).

As claimed by Szwedek (2011), objectification involves the creation of new, abstract entities. It is important to note that this claim is a controversial, theoretical assumption which, to the best of my knowledge, so far has not been verified empirically. The reservations concerning this issue are closely linked to arguments used in the Invariance Hypothesis debate within Conceptual Metaphor Theory (see Murphy, 1996 for arguments against such claims). This study does not address this aspect of the Theory of Objectification and sees this process only as a conceptual mechanism in which non-touchable entities are conceptualised in terms of touchable entities making at the same time no claims as to whether abstract concepts exist or have any structure before they are conceptualised in terms of touchable objects.

4. Tactile properties and conceptualisations of mental phenomena

According to the Theory of Objectification (Szwedek, 2011, 2014), speaking about abstract mental entities is possible only because we conceive of them in the image and after the likeness of various objects that we experience through touch by metaphorically ascribing their physical properties to abstract mental concepts. In this way, tactile properties could be seen as building blocks that provide us with the basic means of talking about mind and thought. By analysing a wide range of corpus data, the following study aims to demonstrate which tactile properties experienced through active, exploratory, manual touch are used in the process of objectification of these mental concepts in English and Polish. In so doing, it attempts to show corresponding ways in which users of two different languages (Clackson, 2007) metaphorically refer to this aspect of their inner lives.

Mind and thought are par excellence examples of abstract entities which have been studied by numerous scholars. Ground-breaking research by Reddy (1979), Lakoff and Johnson (1980, 1999), Classen (1993), Jäkel (1995), Barnden (1997), Croft (2009), and Szwedek (2011, 2014) revealed their various metaphorical conceptualisations including, among others, MIND IS A CONTAINER, MIND IS A BODY, IDEAS ARE (PHYSICAL, SOLID) OBJECTS, and IDEAS ARE FOOD.

However, despite their illuminating character, the research on metaphorical conceptualisations of mental phenomena have so far shied away from a systematic

---

3. Another important type of objectification is called *abstract-to-abstract metaphorisation*, e.g. LOVE IS A JOURNEY and ARGUMENT IS WAR (for details see Szwedek, 2014).

analysis of the role of tactile properties[4] in the creation of metaphorical mappings. This study attempts to push forth research in this area by presenting a wide range of corpus-attested examples of tactile properties of physical objects which are used to talk about the analysed mental phenomena.

5. Methodological framework

This study aims to investigate which tactile properties are used to conceptualise the abstract mental concepts of mind and thought from the perspective of *corpus-based cognitive linguistics* (Heylen, Tummers & Geeraerts, 2008; Lewandowska-Tomaszczyk, 2012; Fabiszak & Konat, 2013; Waliński, 2014). This perspective combines a theoretical framework of cognitive linguistics (Croft & Cruse, 2004; Janda, 2015), in particular the above-described Theory of Objectification, with a corpus linguistic methodology, in particular a *corpus-illustrated approach* (Tummers, Heylen & Geeraerts, 2005). Corpus Linguistics is "the study of language data on a large scale that involves computer-aided analysis of extensive collections of spoken and written texts" (McEnery & Hardie, 2012, p. 1). In turn, corpus-illustrated linguistics is a methodological approach within corpus linguistics in which corpora (large collections of texts) are used as data sets for the selection of examples. Here, corpus data serves to test a pre-existing theory and is used to supplement and complement introspective data with a more systematic, comprehensive, and representative set of real language expressions (for details, see Tummers, Heylen & Geeraerts, 2005).

The use of corpus linguistic data has long been advocated by numerous scholars (see, for instance, Gibbs, 1999; Deignan, 2005). It is argued (Semino, Heywood & Short, 2004; Fabiszak & Konat, 2013) that grounding research on metaphor in language-in-use enables us to deal with the overreliance on decontextualised and self-elicited examples of metaphorical linguistic expressions. Moreover, corpus data allows us to make a more accurate definition of conceptual mappings and to assess their systematicity and frequency (Deignan & Cameron, 2013; Fabiszak & Konat, 2013). Using this type of data also shows that networks of metaphorical senses are not free forming as partly suggested by early research in conceptual metaphor (Deignan, 2005, 2008), but are subject to a number of linguistic (grammatical) constraints (Stefanowitsch, 2006a). If we add to that the fact that corpus data "can reveal many linguistic details that could be passed over in the examination of single texts, and might not be observed at all when data are elicited rather than gathered from

---

4. Other sensory properties are also understudied. See, however, Anderson (this volume) for a discussion of a systematic metaphorical connection between touching and understanding.

language in use" (Deignan, 2008, p. 293), then we are left with a methodological approach which enables us to achieve higher inter-subjectivity and verifiability of research (Stefanowitsch, 2006a; Fabiszak & Konat, 2013).

In order to ground the investigation of tactile properties and experiences used in metaphorical conceptualisations of mind and thought in real and representative language data, the study makes use of two large and widely-acclaimed reference corpora: The British National Corpus and The National Corpus of Polish (Xiao, 2008). The first (later called the BNC) is among the most popular reference corpora for English which includes 100 million words of spoken and written British English covering a wide range of genres, registers, and subject fields (Aston & Burnard, 1998; see www.natcorp.ox.ac.uk for more information). The latter (later called the NCP) is a collection of 240 million words developed on the basis of the procedures used in the compilation of the BNC (Przepiórkowski, Bańko, Górski & Lewandowska-Tomaszczyk, 2012; see www.nkjp.pl for more information).

The language data from these two reference corpora was extracted by means of the HASK browser developed by Piotr Pęzik (2013, 2014) at the University of Łódź. This advanced search engine enables the user to extract verb-noun, adjective-noun, and noun-noun word combinations together with statistical information and KWIC (key word in context) concordances, i.e. the fragments of the original texts in which a given collocation or a key word can be viewed in a broader left and right context.

This tool was used to collect language data featuring adjective-noun and verb-noun collocations of the target domain lexemes, i.e. *mind* and *thought* for English and *umysł* and *myśl* for Polish. In this way, the extracting procedure followed a search for target domain vocabulary (see Stefanowitsch, 2006a, for a review of other possible methods), which focuses on lexemes that are related directly to target domain concepts. Although this approach gives access only to metaphorical expressions that include a given lexeme, it is argued that the results can be seen as representative of the analysed conceptual mapping (see Stefanowitsch, 2006b).

The data collection procedure for both languages included: (1) typing in the selected lexemes into the HASK browser; (2) studying the returned verb-noun and adjective-noun collocations of the selected lexemes and their KWIC concordances in order to tease out literal word combinations (at this stage slightly modified Metaphor Identification Procedure (Pragglejaz, 2007) was used),[5] repetitions,

---

5.   This procedure includes reading a longer or shorter piece of discourse (in this case, a given KWIC concordance) to get a general understanding, determining the lexical units, and establishing their contextual meanings. The next step is about determining whether the unit has a more basic contemporary (or past – my modification, M. T.) meaning in other contexts, i.e. more concrete, related to bodily actions, historically older, or more precise. In cases where the lexical unit has other meanings, the decision is made "whether the contextual meaning contrasts with

word combinations that do not refer to the analysed concepts, word combinations referring to non-active and non-exploratory tactile experiences,[6] non-tactile[7] and non-physical properties, activities, and experiences, as well as word combinations that are etymologically non-transparent or share a linguistic pattern by coincidence; (3) compiling the list of collocations and KWIC concordances related to tactile properties perceived through active, manual exploration used to describe the concepts of mind and thought.

In the search of adjectives and verbs referring to these tactile properties three sources of semantic information are used: (1) their dictionary meanings from the Oxford English Dictionary (2009) and the PWN Dictionary of Polish (2015); (2) their etymology;[8] (3) other collocates extracted from the BNC and the NCP by means of the HASK browser.

6. Results

The objective of this study is to investigate various kinds of tactile properties experienced by means of active, manual exploration which are ascribed to abstract mental concepts. The first subsection looks at the concept of mind and the second subsection focuses on the concept of thought. Collocates of tactile properties (relevant word combinations) presented in both subsections include all adjectives referring to physical qualities of static, inanimate objects which could be experienced by means

---

the basic meaning but can be understood in comparison with it" (Pragglejaz Group, 2007, p. 3). If the answer is in the affirmative, then the lexical unit can be marked as metaphorical. For details see Pragglejaz Group (2007).

6. This includes various types of self-propelled and induced motion ascribed to abstract mental entities as well as properties related to animacy and embodiment which can be experienced through touch, as in examples such as *thought pops in*, *to get mind around something*, *to poison mind*, *wytężać umysł* 'to exert mind', *myśl kłuje* 'thought pricks'.

7. Properties that can be experienced exclusively by other senses include, for instance, smell, taste, colour.

8. In the following analysis both synchronic (dictionary meanings) and diachronic (etymology) data are used. They are used in order to arrive at the most complete image of underlying metaphorical objectifications, which are understood as conceptual mechanisms operating in evolutionary, diachronic, and synchronic timescales (Szwedek, 2011). This, in turn, means that 'dead metaphors' could be included in the study. However, assessing which of them are present in the minds of contemporary speakers and which are non-transparent for them is a matter of experimental research, and, therefore, beyond the scope of methodological tools used in this study. See Sweetser (1990), Trim (2011), and Diaz-Vera (2015) for etymological studies and discussions about diachronic dimension of metaphor study.

of active touch, e.g. shape, weight, as well as verbs related to these features, e.g. *to form mind* (to change its shape) and to manual manipulations of static, inanimate objects, e.g. *to put a thought aside*. This criterion excludes adjectives and verbs referring to static properties experienced only by other senses, e.g. *bright mind* (colour), *bitter thoughts* (taste) as well as collocations referring to self-propelled motion and self-initiated actions in which mind or thought are agents.

The lists of tactile qualities used to metaphorically describe mind and thought include: (1) qualities experienced solely by means of touch, i.e. temperature, density, weight (based on the Sense-Organ criterion); and (2) qualities experienced both by vision and touch, e.g. size, shape, liquidity, containment.[9] The fact that there exist tactile/visual qualities is a consequence of the multisensory character of human perception (Bayne & Spence, 2015). However, according to the Theory of Objectification, these properties can be included here as tactile properties because touch is a more basic (ontogenetically, phenomenologically) means of experiencing them, e.g. shape in vision is always presented at a distance and in touch it can be inspected more precisely as it is perceived at the surface of our body.

6.1   Mind

Typing in the English lexical item *mind* returned 398 matching combinations (adjective-noun, verb-noun). In turn, typing in the Polish lexeme *umysł* returned 815 matching combinations (adjective-noun, verb-noun). After teasing out word combinations irrelevant for the purposes of the study, 76 metaphorical linguistic expressions related to tactile properties experienced through active, manual, exploratory touch (34 for English, 42 for Polish) were selected.

These 76 metaphorical linguistic expressions indicate various corresponding tactile qualities of physical objects which are used in the conceptualisation of mind in two analysed languages. They include:

6.1.1   *Size (physical dimensions)*
Active, tactile, and manual explorations enable us to assess how big a given physical object is. In addition, they allow us to experience its dimensions such as breadth and width. This tactile, physical property is indicated by the following metaphorical linguistic expressions referring to the concept of mind: (1) *narrow mind*, (2)

---

9.   Gustatory qualities, which could be used to conceptualise mental entities, e.g. *sweet memories*, and the special character of the sense of taste, which has a close affinity with the sense of touch, are not addressed in this study. However, it is important to note that the sense of taste could also stand in for touch and experience in general. This phenomenon could be explained either by treating taste as a special case of touch or by viewing this in terms of synesthesia.

ograniczony umysł 'limited mind', (3) *szeroki umysł* 'broad mind', (4) *rozległy umysł* 'vast mind', (5) *great mind*, (6) *wielki umysł* 'big mind', (7) *little mind*, (8) *tiny mind*, (9) *small mind*, (10) *mały umysł* 'small mind', and (11) *maleńki umysł* 'tiny mind'.

6.1.2   Shape

Active touch also enables us to experience a specific external contour or form of a given piece of matter by feeling its surface. This tactile property as a feature of mind is exemplified by expressions such as (12) *warped mind*, (13) *twisted mind*, (14) *pokrętny umysł* 'twisted mind', (15) *prosty umysł* 'straight mind', and (16) *rozwinięty umysł* 'unfolded/unrolled mind'. This tactile property is also indicated by the expressions referring to a specific type of shape or to the mind's capacity to undergo a change in shape such as:

a.   having edges: (17) *sharp mind*, (18) *razor-sharp mind*, (19) *incisive mind*, (20) *tępy umysł* 'blunt mind', and (21) *to dull the mind*.
b.   changeable shape: (22) *flexible mind*, (23) *giętki umysł* 'flexible mind', (24) *to broaden the mind*, (25) *to develop the mind*,[10] (26) *to expand the mind*, (27) *to form the mind*, (28) *formować umysł* 'to form the mind', (29) *kształtować umysł* 'to shape the mind', or (30) *to break the mind*.

6.1.3   Containment

The sense of touch enables us to experience whether a given physical object has a specific type of shape that is characteristic for receptacles designed for storing other objects. Physical objects, which are containers, are characterised by various physical properties which can be experienced through active, manual touch and exploration. They include, for instance, having clear physical boundaries, being open or closed, as well as having internal depth. This general characteristic is indicated by a range of metaphorical linguistic expressions such as (31) *open mind*, (32) *closed mind*, (33) *zamknięty umysł* 'closed mind', (34) *otwarty umysł* 'open mind', (35) *płytki umysł* 'shallow mind', (36) *głęboki umysł* 'deep mind', (37) *ciasny umysł* 'cramped mind', and (38) *pusty umysł* 'empty mind'.

The property of containment refers not only to physical characteristics ascribed to the concept of mind but also, by extension, to various processes and activities that can metaphorically take place in the mind. They include:

a.   getting inside the physical container-mind: (39) *wprowadzać coś do umysłu* 'to introduce something to the mind', (40) *coś trafia do umysłu* 'something gets inside the mind', (41) *wejść do umysłu* 'to enter the mind', (42) *to enter to*

---

10.   The original etymological sense of *to develop* was 'to unfold, to unroll, to unfurl' (OED, 2009).

the mind, (43) *to come to mind*, (44) *to bring something to mind*, (45) *wnikać w umysł* 'to penetrate the mind', (46) *wdzierać się do umysłu* 'to burst into the mind', (47) *to penetrate the mind*, (48) *to flood the mind*, (49) *to invade the mind*, (50) *opanować umysł* 'to get control over the mind', (51) *zawładnąć umysłem* 'to conquer the mind', and (52) *to probe the mind*.

b.   being inside the physical container: (53) *the mind is filled with something*, (54) *wypełniać umysł* 'to fill the mind', (55) *przepełniać umysł* 'to overfill the mind', (56) *something occupies the mind*, (57) *the mind contains*, (58) *nosić coś w umyśle* 'to carry something in the mind', (59) *istnieć w umyśle* 'to exist in the mind', (60) *tkwić w umyśle* 'to be stuck in the mind', (61) *ukryć coś w umyśle* 'to hide something in the mind', (62) *zaprzątać umysł* 'to occupy the mind', (63) *zaśmiecać czymś umysł* 'the mind is littered with something', (64) *something crowds the mind*, (65) *something throngs the mind*,[11] and (66) *to explore the mind*.

c.   controlling access to the physical container: (67) *to open the mind*, (68) *otworzyć umysł* 'to open the mind', (69) *to shut the mind to something*, and (70) *to close the mind to something*.

d.   removing something from the physical container: (71) *to empty the mind* and (72) *oczyścić umysł* 'to rid the mind of something'.

6.1.4   *Liquidity*

The mind is also objectified in terms of a special type of a physical object, i.e. liquid. Liquids are material substances that differ from solids in that they do not have a determinate shape. Particles that make up liquids move freely over each other and take the shape of the physical container in which they are currently stored. A liquid, e.g. water, oil, or alcohol, can be experienced through active tactile exploration, which enables us to directly feel its density, its movements, as well as to feel the presence of other physical objects in it.

The language data from the BNC and the NCP demonstrate that mind is objectified as a turbid liquid. In other words, it is conceptualised as a thick and opaque substance with suspended matter inside. This aspect of liquidity is exemplified by the expressions such as (73) *mącić umysł* 'to muddle the mind', (74) *niezmącony umysł* 'un-muddled mind', (75) *troubled mind*,[12] and (76) *muddled mind*.

---

11.   The English lexeme *to throng* means 'to fill or occupy (a place, etc.) with a large number of things' (OED, 2009).

12.   The English lexeme *troubled* means 'stirred up so as to diffuse the sediment, made thick or muddy, turbid' (OED, 2009).

6.2   Thought

The HASK browser returned 587 matching combinations (adjective-noun, verb-noun) for the English lexeme *thought* and 2421 matching combinations (adjective-noun, verb-noun) for the Polish lexeme *myśl*. After teasing out word combinations irrelevant for the purposes of the study, 70 metaphorical linguistic expressions related to tactile properties experienced through active, exploratory, and manual touch (30 for English, 40 for Polish) were selected.

These 70 metaphorical linguistic expressions refer to various aspects of physical objects which indicates that the conceptualisation of thought in the two analysed languages reflects the multi-aspectual, active, manual experience of tactile objects. As revealed by the corpus data, thought conceived of as a physical object is characterised by the following tactile properties:

6.2.1   *Density (firmness)*

The property of having a close consistency of solid and compact structure is the basic characteristic of physical objects. It is not only connected to their relative mass but also to the fact that material objects do not yield to external pressure or impact. For Szwedek (2011, 2014), this property is the ultimate experiential basis for distinguishing between material and immaterial objects. This quality is experienced through touch which gives us direct access to the physical object's resistance to external pressure. This could be done by means of active, exploratory touch (preferably by means of hands and arms). This property is indicated by expressions such as (77) *coherent thought*, (78) *spójna myśl* 'coherent thought', (79) *hard thought*, (80) *twarda myśl* 'hard thought', as well as their opposites which indicate a lack of density such as (81) *luźna myśl* 'loose thought' and (82) *disjointed thoughts*.[13]

6.2.2   *Weight*

Material objects are characterised by their relative heaviness. The weight (mass) is the amount of resistance offered by a given physical object to external forces trying to raise it. The direct way of experiencing weight is through the sense of touch. Humans evaluate the weight of material objects on the basis of the amount of pressure they exert on their skin, muscles, and bodies (see Ryzhova, Rakhilina, & Kholkina, this volume, for the analysis of HEAVY as a perceptive concept).

The data from the BNC and the NCP demonstrate that this basic quality of physical objects which can be experienced through active handling of a given piece

---

13. The Polish *luźny* like the English *loose* means 'not bound together, not tied up or secured, whose elements are not tightly bound'; The English *disjointed* means 'consisting of separated or ill-connected parts' (OED, 2009).

of matter is present in various metaphorical expressions of thought. They include (83) *depressing thought* and (84) *depresyjne myśli* 'depressing thoughts',[14] (85) *nieznośna myśl* 'unbearable thought', (86) *to bear a thought*, (87) *znieść myśl* 'to bear a thought', (88) *to ponder a thought*,[15] and (89) *rozważać myśl* 'to weigh a thought'.

6.2.3   Temperature
The sense of touch allows for directly experiencing the temperature of a physical object including inorganic entities such as stone or sand, as well as animate beings, which produce heat as an outcome of their life functions. The temperature refers to the state of a physical object or body with regard to sensible coldness or warmth. It is one of the basic qualities of material objects which can be experienced by feeling their surfaces. This tactile property is conceptualised both in English and Polish in expressions such as (90) *zimna myśl* 'cold thought', (91) *chilling thought*, (92) *myśl mrozi* 'thought freezes', (93) *warm thought*, (94) *ciepłe myśli* 'warm thoughts', and (95) *najgorętsza myśl* 'hottest thought'.

6.2.4   Size (physical dimensions)
This property refers to specific aspects of size such as width, range, height, and general magnitude, all of which can be experienced through active, careful, and manual exploration. In English and Polish, this tactile property is indicated by the expressions such as (96) *big thought*, (97) *wielka myśl* 'big thought', (98) *little thought*, (99) *mała myśl* 'small thought', and (100) *drobna myśl* 'tiny thought'.

6.2.5   Shape
Physical objects possess various external forms and contours which can be identified and compared by means of active touch. They can also undergo changes which can be experienced in a similar way. English and Polish speakers profile this property in manifold metaphorical linguistic expressions related to thought such as (101) *half-formed thought*, (102) *urwana myśl* 'broken thought', (103) *zawiła myśl* 'intricate thought', (104) *zgrabna myśl* 'slender thought', (105) *prosta myśl* 'straight thought', (106) *to shape thought*, (107) *to develop thoughts*, and (108) *rozwijać myśl* 'to unfold/unroll thought'.

---

14. Both English and Polish adjectives stem from the Latin *depressare* 'to press down' (OED, 2009).

15. The English *ponder* stems from the Latin *ponderare* 'to weigh' (OED, 2009).

6.2.6   *Containment*

This physical property is a defining characteristic of receptacles for keeping other objects. Such objects are distinguished by their clear boundaries, which can be explored by means of active, manual touch. Moreover, active touch enables us to verify the contents of the container and its inner structure. This tactile property is exemplified by metaphorical linguistic expressions such as (109) *thought contains*, (110) *myśl zawiera* 'thought contains', (111) *napełniać myśli* 'to fill thoughts', (112) *idle thought*,[16] (113) *deep thought*, (114) *profound thought*,[17] (115) *głębsza myśl* 'deeper thought'.

6.2.7   *Liquidity*

Thought is also conceptualised in terms of liquidity. This quality is experienced by means of active touch, which enables us to verify the liquid's density, temperature, as well as its movements at the surface of our skin. This property is exemplified by the expressions such as (116) *zatopić się w myślach* 'to submerge oneself in thoughts', (117) *troubled thoughts*, (118) *mętna myśl* 'turbid thought', (119) *mącić myśli* 'to muddle thoughts'.

6.2.8   *Manipulability*

As independent pieces of matter, physical objects are also distinguished by their manipulability, i.e. the capability of being moved by manual or other means. This property can be experienced through active touch which is an intentional and purposeful manual exploration that is not limited to feeling the surface of physical objects but involves also actions such as putting or throwing away, catching, putting in order, or gathering into one place or group. The language data from the BNC and the NCP show a wide range of such tactile manipulations used to talk about the concept of thought. They include:

a.   Establishing a physical distance: (120) *to put a thought aside*, (121) *odłożyć myśl* 'to put a thought away', (122) *odpychać myśl* 'to push a thought away', (123) *odsunąć myśl* 'to shove a thought away', (124) *to cast thoughts*, (125) *to reject a thought*,[18] (126) *odrzucić myśl* 'to throw a thought away', (127) *to dismiss thoughts*, and (128) *porzucić myśl* 'to ditch a thought'.

---

16. The original etymological sense of *idle* is 'empty' (OED, 2009).

17. The English *profound* stems from the Latin *profundus* 'deep (as a physical or material quality)' (OED, 2009).

18. The English *reject* stems from the Latin *rejacere* 'to throw away' (OED, 2009).

b. Establishing and maintaining physical contact: (129) *podsunąć myśl* 'to draw up a thought', (130) *uchwycić myśli* 'to catch thoughts', (131) *to pin thoughts down*, (132) *uczepić się myśli* 'to cling to a thought', (133) *trzymać się myśli* 'to hold on to a thought', (134) *to entertain a thought*,[19] and (135) *nosić się z myślą* 'to carry a thought'.

c. Grouping together: (136) *to collect thoughts*, (137) *to gather thoughts*, (138) *to pull thoughts together*, (139) *zebrać myśli* 'to collect thoughts', and (140) *pozbierać myśli* 'to gather thoughts'.

d. Putting in a specific order: Physical objects do not have to be merely assembled in one place as in the case of grouping together. They can also be arranged, so that they form a whole with mutually connected and dependent parts. This type of active, tactile manipulation which gives rise to a definite and orderly structure is also used to talk about operations on thoughts as indicated by the expressions (141) *to order thoughts*, (142) *to marshal thoughts*, (143) *poukładać myśli* 'to arrange thoughts', and (144) *uporządkować myśli* 'to put thoughts in order'.

e. Sharing: Another type of active, manual manipulation that is metaphorically ascribed to thoughts is sharing, which in its most concrete sense refers to the action of dividing some piece of matter into portions and giving them out (OED, 2009). This is manifested in the expressions such as (149) *to share thoughts* and (150) *dzielić się myślami* 'to share thoughts'.

7. Results summary

How is it possible, as shown in the two previous sections, that both in English and Polish we can use such a wide array of linguistic expressions indicating that we conceptualise our minds and thoughts as if they had various tactile properties? It is argued that the presence of expressions such as *narrow mind*, *prosty umysł* 'straight mind', *ciepłe myśli* 'warm thoughts', or *to collect thoughts* can be derived from tactile experiences based on active, exploratory, and manual touch which is the most direct and intentional means of identifying a physical objects' qualities. Feeling their surface as well as careful, manual explorations, including manipulations such as catching or putting in one place, are seen as a perceptual basis that grounds the linguistic representations at hand. It is these rich, diverse, and repeated tactile experiences which enable language speakers to identify basic properties of physical objects, e.g. their temperature, shape, density or liquidity. Later these properties, as

---

19. The English *entertain* stems from the Latin *intertenere* 'to hold among' (OED, 2009)

the inventory of metaphorical linguistic expressions attests, are mapped onto the concepts of mind and thought.[20] They can be found either in the form of a direct reference to the property of a mental entity, e.g. *ciasny umysł* 'cramped mind' (the adjective-noun collocation indicating a shape of a container), or in the form of an indirect reference, e.g. *to bear a thought, to reject a thought* (verb-noun collocations indicating weight and manipulability). Overall, both types of examples can be interpreted as evidence for the transfer of different kinds of perceptual, tactile information related to physical objects to mental entities which are conceptualised as if they were equally palpable objects with the same or nearly the same amount of tactile qualities. In other words, they can be viewed as evidence for the process of objectification.

8. Conclusions and further research

This work set out to address which tactile properties of physical objects perceived through active, exploratory, and manual touch are used in metaphorical conceptualisations of mind and thought in English and Polish and what the underlying conceptual processes that enable us to ascribe properties of palpable objects to impalpable mental entities are.

As for the first question, language data collected from the BNC and the NCP show that mind and thought are described by means of a vast array of physical properties that can be experienced by touch. In the case of mind, these tactile properties include size (physical dimensions), shape (and its specifications such as having edges and undergoing changes), containment (and activities by extension related to this property), and liquidity. In turn, thought is metaphorically described as having density (firmness), weight, temperature, size (physical dimensions), shape, containment, liquidity, and manipulability. The last property is related to various tactile manipulations of physical objects such as holding, throwing away, grouping, and catching.

These results could be interpreted as both confirming and complementing previous research. On the one hand, the analysed tactile properties such as containment, having edges, firmness (density), weight, and manipulability could be seen as indicative of conceptual metaphors such as MIND IS AN ENTITY, MIND IS A CONTAINER, MIND IS A TOOL, IDEAS ARE SOLID OBJECTS, IDEAS ARE LOCATIONS, THINKING IS WEIGHING, and IDEAS ARE MANIPULABLE OBJECTS (Lakoff & Johnson, 1980, 1999; Jäkel, 1995; Barnden, 1997, Fortescue, 2001). On the other hand, the

---

20. The question of various meanings which are conveyed by tactile properties ascribed to mind and thought is in itself a worthwhile enterprise but beyond the scope of this chapter.

analysis of corpus data shows that the range of tactile properties ascribed to mind and thought is far richer than previously envisaged. This includes properties such as size (physical dimensions), shape, and liquid state (for mind and thought), and temperature (for thought).

As far as the second question is concerned, the fact that corresponding tactile properties have been found in two different languages and cultural milieus (see Clackson, 2007) suggests that these metaphorical linguistic expressions could be motivated by shared embodied experiences (Lakoff & Johnson, 1999; Kövecses, 2005). In keeping with the Theory of Objectification (Szwedek, 2011), it is argued that the analysed expressions such as *incisive mind* or *ciepłe myśli* 'warm thoughts' are created on the basis of tactile interactions with physical objects.[21] In this account, these are manual handling and active exploration of physical objects with various tactile properties such as size, shape, and temperature that provide us with the necessary perceptual information used when we think and speak about abstract mental entities. Perceptual information about tactile properties picked up whilst interacting with various physical objects feeds into the PHYSICAL OBJECT schema, which serves as a model for identifying material objects and for conceptualising immaterial, abstract entities. This second process, which is key to understanding the analysed metaphorical linguistic expressions, is called *objectification* (*concrete-to-abstract metaphorisation*). In this case, this process ascribes the set of the most basic and salient tactile properties of prototypical physical objects to concepts of mind and thought. The analysed metaphorical linguistic expressions demonstrate its end results, where we can see the completed transfer of tactile properties onto impalpable, mental entities.

By shedding light on this phenomenon, the Theory of Objectification not only enables us to account for the analysed linguistic data in a comprehensive way but it also provides us with a principled way in which we can explain the path from tactile perception to figurative language. Its focus on the basic role of touch and information picked up by this sensory modality in the creation of metaphorical linguistic expressions allow us to see a clear connection between perception and metaphorical conceptualisation. From this standpoint, the findings presented in this study could be seen as the point of departure for further research on the relationship between metaphor and other facets of tactile experience, e.g. passive touch, proprioception, kinaesthesia, as well as other sensory modalities. It is argued that this ambitious "from perception to metaphor" enterprise has every chance of bringing us closer to understanding metaphor and embodiment of meaning.

---

21. Apart from everyday interactions with physical objects this also includes tactile interactions in ontogenetic and phylogenetic timescales.

References

Aston, G. & Burnard, L. (1998). *The BNC Handbook: Exploring the British National Corpus with SARA*. Edinburgh: Edinburgh University Press.

Barnden, J. A. (1997). Consciousness and common-sense metaphors of mind. In S. O'Nuallain et al. (Eds.), *Two Sciences of Mind: Readings in Cognitive Science and Consciousness* (pp. 311–341). Amsterdam: John Benjamins. https://doi.org/10.1075/aicr.9.20bar

Bayne, T. & Spence, C. (2015). Multisensory Perception. In M. Matthen (Ed.), *The Oxford Handbook of Philosophy of Perception* (pp. 603–620). Oxford: Oxford University Press.

Clackson, J. (2007). *Indo-European Linguistics*. Cambridge: Cambridge University Press. https://doi.org/10.1017/CBO9780511808616

Classen, C. (1993). *Worlds of Sense: Exploring the Senses in History and Across Cultures*. London and New York: Routledge.

Classen, C. (2012). *The Deepest Sense: A Cultural History of Touch*. Champaign, IL: University of Illinois Press.

Croft, W. & Cruse, D. A. (2004). *Cognitive Linguistics*. Cambridge: Cambridge University Press. https://doi.org/10.1017/CBO9780511803864

Croft, W. (2009). Connecting frames and constructions: a case study of "eat" and "feed". *Constructions and Frames*, 1(1), 7–28. https://doi.org/10.1075/cf.1.1.02cro

De Vignemont, F. & Massin, O. (2015). Touch. In M. Matthen (Ed.), *The Oxford Handbook of Philosophy of Perception* (pp. 294–313). Oxford: Oxford University Press.

Deignan, A. (2005). *Metaphor and Corpus Linguistics*. Amsterdam: John Benjamins. https://doi.org/10.1075/celcr.6

Deignan, A. (2008). Corpus linguistics and metaphor. In R. W. Gibbs (Ed.), *The Cambridge Handbook of Metaphor and Thought* (pp. 280–294). Cambridge: Cambridge University Press. https://doi.org/10.1017/CBO9780511816802.018

Deignan, A. & Cameron, L. (2013). A re-examination of UNDERSTANDING IS SEEING. *Journal of Cognitive Semiotics*, 5(1–2), 220–243.

Diaz-Vera, J. (Ed.). (2015). *Metaphor and Metonymy Across Time and Cultures*. Berlin: De Gruyter Mouton. https://doi.org/10.1515/9783110335453

Evans, V. (2012). Cognitive linguistics. *Wiley Interdisciplinary Reviews: Cognitive Science*, 3(2), 129–141.

Fabiszak, M. & Konat, B. (2013). Zastosowanie korpusów językowych w językoznawstwie kognitywnym [The use of language corpora in cognitive linguistics]. In P. Stalmaszczyk (Ed.), *Metodologie językoznawstwa: Ewolucja języka, Ewolucja teorii językoznawczych* (pp. 131–142). Łódź: Wydawnictwo Uniwersytetu Łódzkiego.

Foolen, A. (2017). The hand in figurative thought and language. In Athanasiadou, A. (Ed.), *Studies in Figurative Thought and Language* (pp. 179–198). Amsterdam: John Benjamins. https://doi.org/10.1075/hcp.56.07foo

Fortescue, M. (2001). Thoughts about thought. *Cognitive Linguistics*, 12(1), 15–39. https://doi.org/10.1515/cogl.12.1.15

Fulkerson, M. (2014a). *The First Sense: A Philosophical Study of Human Touch*. Cambridge, MA: MIT Press. https://doi.org/10.7551/mitpress/9780262019965.001.0001

Fulkerson, M. (2014b). What Counts As Touch? In D. Stokes, M. Matthen, & S. Biggs (Ed.) *Perception and Its Modalities* (pp. 191–204). New York: Oxford University Press. https://doi.org/10.1093/acprof:oso/9780199832798.003.0008

Gibbs, R. W. (1999). Taking metaphor out of our heads and putting it into the cultural world. In R. W. Gibbs & G. J. Steen (Eds.), *Metaphor in Cognitive Linguistics* (pp. 146–166). Amsterdam: John Benjamins. https://doi.org/10.1075/cilt.175.09gib

Hatwell, Y., Streri, A. & Gentaz, E. (Eds.). (2003). *Touching for Knowing: Cognitive Pychology of Haptic Manual Perception*. Amsterdam: John Benjamins. https://doi.org/10.1075/aicr.53

Hertenstein, M. J. (Ed.). (2011). *The Handbook of Touch: Neuroscience, Behavioral, and Health Perspectives*. New York: Springer.

Heylen, K., Tummers, J. & Geeraerts, D. (2008). Methodological issues in corpus-based cognitive linguistics. In G. Kristiansen & R. Dirven (Eds.) *Cognitive Sociolinguistics: Language Variation, Cultural Models, Social Systems* (pp. 91–128). Berlin and New York: de Gruyter Mouton. https://doi.org/10.1515/9783110199154.2.91

Janda, L. A. (2015). Cognitive Linguistics in the Year 2015. *Cognitive Semantics*, 3(1), 131–154. https://doi.org/10.1163/23526416-00101005

Jäkel, O. (1995). The metaphorical conception of mind: "Mental activity is manipulation". In Taylor, J. R. & MacLaury, R. E. (Eds.), *Language and the Cognitive Construal of the World* (pp. 197–229). Berlin: de Gruyter Mouton. https://doi.org/10.1515/9783110809305.197

Jelec, A. (2014). *Are Abstract Concepts Like Dinosaur Feathers?*. Poznań: Wydawnictwo Naukowe UAM.

Johansson Falck, M., & Gibbs, R. W. (2012). Embodied motivations for metaphorical meanings. *Cognitive Linguistics*, 23(2), 251–272. https://doi.org/10.1515/cog-2012-0008

Jonas, H. (1954). The nobility of sight. *Philosophy and Phenomenological Research*, 14, 507–519.

Kövecses, Z. (2005). *Metaphor in Culture: Universality and Variation*. Cambridge: Cambridge University Press. https://doi.org/10.1017/CBO9780511614408

Kövecses, Z. (2010). *Metaphor: A Practical Introduction* (2nd Ed.). New York: Oxford University Press.

Kövecses, Z. (2015). *Where Metaphors Come From*. Oxford: Oxford University Press. https://doi.org/10.1093/acprof:oso/9780190224868.001.0001

Lakoff, G. & Johnson, M. (1980). *Metaphors We Live By*. Chicago: University of Chicago Press.

Lakoff, G. & Johnson, M. (1999). *Philosophy in the Flesh: The Embodied Mind and Its Challenge to Western Thought*. New York: Basic Books.

Lewandowska-Tomaszczyk, B. (2012). Cognitive corpus studies: A new qualitative & quantitative agenda for contrasting languages. MFU Connexion. A Journal of Humanities and Social Sciences, 29–63.

Macpherson, F. (Ed.). (2011a). *The Senses: Classic and Contemporary Philosophical Perspectives*. Oxford: Oxford University Press.

Macpherson, F. (2011b). Individuating the Senses. In F. Macpherson (Ed.), *The Senses: Classic and Contemporary Philosophical Perspectives* (pp. 3–43). Oxford: Oxford University Press.

Matthen, M. (2015). The Individuation of the Senses. In M. Matthen (Ed.), *The Oxford Handbook of Philosophy of Perception* (pp. 567–586). Oxford: Oxford University Press.

McEnery, T. & Hardie, A. (2012). *Corpus Linguistics: Method, Theory and Practice*. Cambridge: Cambridge University Press.

Merleau-Ponty, M. (1945). *Phénoménologie de la perception*. Paris: Gallimard.

Murphy, G. L. (1996). On metaphoric representation, *Cognition*, 60, 173–204. https://doi.org/10.1016/0010-0277(96)00711-1

Oxford English Dictionary. (2009). Oxford: Oxford University Press.

Pecher, D. & Zwaan, R. A. (2005). *Grounding Cognition: The Role of Perception and Action in Memory, Language, and Thinking.* Cambridge: Cambridge University Press. https://doi.org/10.1017/CBO9780511499968

Pęzik, P. (2013). Paradygmat Dystrybucyjny w Badaniach Frazeologicznych. Powtarzalność, Reprodukcja i Idiomatyzacja [Distributional Paradigm in Phraseological Research. Repetitivity, Reproduction, and Idiomatization]. In P. Stalmaszczyk (Ed.), *Metodologie Językoznawstwa: Ewolucja Języka, Ewolucja Teorii Językoznawczych* (pp. 143–160). Łódź: Wydawnictwo Uniwersytetu Łódzkiego.

Pęzik, P. (2014). Graph-Based Analysis of Collocational Profiles. In V. Jesenšek & P. Grzybek (Eds.), *Phraseologie Im Wörterbuch und Korpus/Phraseology in Dictionaries and Corpora* (pp. 227–243). Maribor/Bielsko-Biała/Budapest/Kansas/Praha: Filozofska Fakulteta.

Pragglejaz Group. (2007). MIP: A method for identifying metaphorically used words in discourse. *Metaphor and Symbol*, 22(1), 1–39. https://doi.org/10.1080/10926480709336752

Proske, U. & Gandevia, S. C. (2012). The Proprioceptive Senses: Their Roles in Signaling Body Shape, Body Position and Movement, and Muscle Force. *Physiological Reviews*, 92, 1651–1697. https://doi.org/10.1152/physrev.00048.2011

Przepiórkowski, A., Bańko, M., Górski, R. L. & Lewandowska-Tomaszczyk, B. (Eds). (2012). *Narodowy Korpus Języka Polskiego.* Warszawa: PWN.

Radman, Z. (Ed.). (2013). *The Hand, an Organ of the Mind.* Cambridge, MA.: The MIT Press.

Ratcliffe, M. (2013). Touch and the Sense of Reality. In Radman, Z. (Ed.), *The Hand, an Organ of the Mind* (pp. 131–157). Cambridge, MA.: The MIT Press.

Semino, E. & Heywood, J. & Short, M. (2004). Methodological problems in the analysis of metaphors in a corpus conversations about cancer. *Journal of Pragmatics*, 36, 1271–1294. https://doi.org/10.1016/j.pragma.2003.10.013

Stefanowitsch, A. (2006a). Corpus-based Approaches to Metaphor and Metonymy. In A. Stefanowitsch & T. S. Gries (Eds.), *Corpus-based Approaches to Metaphor and Metonymy* (pp. 1–17). Berlin and New York: Mouton de Gruyter.

Stefanowitsch, A. (2006b). Words and their metaphors: A corpus-based approach. In A. Stefanowitsch & T. S. Gries (Eds.), *Corpus-based Approaches to Metaphor and Metonymy* (pp. 63–105). Berlin and New York: de Gruyter Mouton.

Szwedek, A. (2000). Senses, perception and metaphors (of Object and Objectification). In S. Puppel & K. Dziubalska-Kołaczyk (Eds.), *Multibus vocibus de lingua* (pp. 143–153). Poznań: Wydział Neofilologii UAM.

Szwedek, A. (2011). The ultimate source domain. *Review of Cognitive Linguistics*, 9(2), 341–366. https://doi.org/10.1075/rcl.9.2.01szw

Szwedek, A. (2014). The nature of domains and the relationships between them in metaphorization. *Review of Cognitive Linguistics*, 12(2), 342–374. https://doi.org/10.1075/rcl.12.2.04szw

Sweetser, E. (1990). *From etymology to pragmatics: Metaphorical and cultural aspects of semantic structure.* Cambridge: Cambridge University Press. https://doi.org/10.1017/CBO9780511620904

Trim, R. (2011). *Metaphor and the historical evolution of conceptual mapping.* London: Palgrave Macmillan. https://doi.org/10.1057/9780230337053

Trojszczak, M. (2016). Selected aspects of conceptualization of 'insight' in English and Polish. In I. Czwenar, D. Gonigroszek & A. Stanecka (Eds.), *Foreign Languages and Cultures: Contemporary Contexts* (pp. 57–68). NWP: Piotrków Trybunalski.

Trojszczak, M. (2017a). Problem solving in English and Polish – a cognitive study of selected metaphorical conceptualizations. In P. Pęzik & J. T. Waliński (Eds.), *Language, Corpora, and Cognition* (pp. 201–220). Frankfurt am Main: Peter Lang.

Trojszczak, M. (2017b). On "paying attention": The objectification of attention in English and Polish. In W. Wachowski, Z. Kövecses & M. Borodo (Eds.), *Zooming In: Micro-Scale Perspectives on Cognition, Translation and Cross-Cultural Communication* (pp. 81–100). Frankfurt am Main: Peter Lang.

Tummers, J., Heylen, K. & Geeraerts, D. (2005). Usage-based approaches in Cognitive Linguistics: A technical state of the art. *Corpus Linguistics and Linguistic Theory*, 1(2), 225–261. https://doi.org/10.1515/cllt.2005.1.2.225

Waliński, J. T. (2014). *Complementarity of Space and Time in Distance Representations: A Corpus-based Study* (2nd Ed.). Łódź: Wydawnictwo Uniwersytetu Łódzkiego. https://doi.org/10.18778/7969-441-9

Xiao, R. (2008). Well-known and influential corpora. In A. Lüdeling & M. Kytö (Eds.), *Corpus linguistics: An International Handbook* (pp. 383–457). Berlin: de Gruyter Mouton.

CHAPTER 12

Polysemy of the Estonian perception verb *nägema* 'to see'

Mariann Proos
University of Tartu

This paper focuses on the polysemy of the Estonian perception verb *nägema* 'to see'. The aim of the paper is to analyse polysemy using two different methods; and to show how and why the results of the two methods differ. The methods used are a sorting task and a behavioural profile analysis. Hierarchical cluster analysis is used to show which senses of *nägema* are more similar to each other based on each method, and why. The results show that the main differences stem from the fact that important elements of meaning for the language user are not necessarily objectively annotatable in the corpus. It is argued, however, that both experimental as well as corpus-based methods are valuable tools for polysemy research.

Keywords: Estonian, perception verbs, polysemy, sorting task, behavioural profile

1. Introduction

The theory of embodied language states that our language is motivated by our physical bodies and the kind of physical world that surrounds us (Gibbs, Jr, 2006). How we experience the world, i.e. how we sense it, how we manipulate things, how we communicate with each other and our surroundings all have a role in how we express ourselves with the linguistic tools at our disposal. These patterns of experiencing are re-occurring and are the basis for most of our concepts (Gibbs, Jr, 2006; Lakoff, 1987; Talmy, 2000).

This means that the way we talk about abstract experiences is directly influenced by the way we experience the physical world. Our senses like seeing, hearing, and touching are the most important tools for this task. The experience of using our senses and the nature of them greatly influence our understanding of other concepts. For example, the nature of our sense of sight allows us to follow the path of a moving object. We can also single out an object that is stationary. When it starts to move, we can follow its trajectory. Furthermore, we can comprehend whether it is a

https://doi.org/10.1075/celcr.19.12pro

straight route or if the path has any obstacles, and the point where the object stops. This basic pattern of movement is one of the patterns that we (at least in Western cultures) use to conceptualise life. We see life as a continuous path along which we are moving. We start to move when we are born, important events are understood as obstacles that we need to overcome, and our movement stops when we reach the end of our life. But which notions are conceptualised with the linguistic means that we use to denote that physical sensation of experiencing itself?

To be able to communicate about the process of experiencing, we use specific linguistic elements, one of which is perception verbs. However, these verbs are also used to express non-physical experiences. This phenomenon of one linguistic unit being used to express different, but related concepts, is traditionally called polysemy; or semasiological variation by some authors (e.g. Geeraerts (2006) or Glynn (2014)). This study focuses on our visual perception, specifically on the verb *nägema* 'to see' in Estonian and its polysemy.

Cognitive semantics handles polysemy as a linguistic category whose members are connected to each other. This is a kind of "polycentric structure" (Taylor, 1995) where the members of the category need to bear some similarity to the prototype(s). This similarity is the result of such meaning extension processes like metaphor and metonymy, which in turn are motivated by our bodily experiences (Gibbs, Jr, 2006; Langacker, 2008). Thus, different senses of a lexical item form a kind of a network, albeit one that has no discrete units, and where the connections between these units are not unidirectional.

As stated earlier, there are underlying patterns to how we conceptualise the world around us and how we talk about it. These patterns are what make some of the senses in the polysemy network more similar to each other, i.e. senses with the same underlying patterns form groups in the meaning network. What cognitive semantics is particularly interested in is discovering what these patterns are, which senses group together more tightly, and what motivates this kind of a structure. The hope is that this will give us a possible peek into how the structure functions in the mind of the language user, because a description and understanding of the mind of the language user is ultimately the goal of cognitive semantics. In this study, I will show what kind of underlying patterns shape polysemous senses of *nägema* 'to see' in Estonian and the role these patterns play.

Estonian is a Finno-Ugric language with approximately one million native speakers. It is an agglutinative language with a lot of fusional traits (Erelt, 2003, p. 7). Verbs expressing vision have largely the same logic as Indo-European languages: there is an opposition between simple perception, and intentional perception (*nägema* vs *vaatama*, 'see' vs. 'look'), and a number of verbs specifying the duration or manner of the perceptual act, such as *jälgima* 'to observe', *piiluma* 'to peek', *jõllitama* 'to stare'.

In the context of the languages of Europe, Estonian holds an interesting position. Historically, Estonian has been mainly influenced by German, and to a lesser extent by Russian and Finnish. Estonian has a large number of German and Low-German loanwords, followed by a considerable number of Russian loanwords. Lately, English foreign words have been making their way into the vocabulary. The grammar, however, has remained Finno-Ugric in nature. Compared to Finnish, Estonian bares less similarities to the traditional Proto-Finno-Ugric. For example, while Finnish exhibits the traditional Finno-Ugric conjugable negation (e.g. *minä en ole, sinä et ole, hän ei ole*) Estonian has the same negative form in every person (*mina/sina/tema/meie/teie/nemad ei ole* 'I am/you are/(s)he is/we are/you are/they are not).

The Finno-Ugric heritage and widespread contact with German and other languages places Estonian in a unique position. Especially interesting is to what extent and in which layers of the language Estonian has stayed true to its origin and in which ways it has been influenced by other languages; and where the semantic extensions fit into all of this.

The perception verb *nägema* and its different senses have received little attention in studies of Estonian. While the verb and its variations have been mentioned in previous work (e.g. Born, 1995; Labi, 2006; Sepper, 2006), until recently (Proos, 2016), no extensive research has been done. However, relevant studies have been made on many other languages. Within the list of studies that approach perception verbs and their polysemy from a cross-linguistic perspective are works by Evans & Wilkins (2000), Ibarretxe-Antunano (1999, 2008), San Roque et al. (2015), Vanhove (2008), and Viberg (1983). In addition, different methods and sources have been used to study perception verbs, as exemplified by Divjak (2015), Gisborne (2010), Jansegers, Vanderschueren & Enghels (2015), Johnson & Lenci (2011), and Whitt (2010). Focusing on the verb 'to see' are works by Alm-Arvius (1993) for English, Sjöström (1999) for Swedish and Usoniene (2001) for Lithuanian. This far from exhaustive list shows that 'to see' and perception verbs in general have been, and continue to be an exciting topic.

My aim is to fill the gap in the current research about the polysemy of the Estonian verb *nägema*. In order to provide an in-depth overview, I used experimental as well as corpus-based methods. More specifically, I focus on which elements in the sense network connect more tightly. This, in turn, offers an insight into how the polysemy of *nägema* is organised in the mind of the language user, following the theory of embodied language and categorical nature of polysemy discussed earlier.

The chosen experiment was a free sorting task, where the participants had to sort the different senses of *nägema* into groups. For the corpus-based study, I used behavioural profile analysis, which allows for an overview of how the senses are used in a large set of sentences. The aim of the present paper is to give an overview of the results of the two methods, and to show how and why the results differed. First, the design of the sorting task and its results are introduced. The behavioural profile method and the respective results are then discussed. The discussion focuses on the comparison of the results as well as the methods themselves.

2.   Sorting task

2.1   Method and participants

Experimental methods have been applied to various research topics in cognitive semantics. It is often the case that the questions that cognitive semanticists are most interested in cannot be sufficiently answered by introspection (Croft, 1998) or by corpus data (Gilquin & Gries, 2009). In addition, experiments are used to complement and/or validate corpus-based research, as exemplified in Dąbrowska (2008), Divjak (2008), and Klavan (2012).

In order to answer the question of how language users perceive the polysemy of *nägema*, a sorting task was conducted. It is generally presumed that when presented with a task of sorting stimuli into groups on the basis of a specific condition, the participants base their decisions on mental representations, thus mirroring distinctions made in the process of language acquisition (Sandra & Rice, 1995, p. 107).

The aim of the sorting task was to find out which senses of *nägema* language users perceive as being more similar to each other, and thus get an insight into the organisation of the senses in the language user's mind. Following similar tasks in polysemy research, conducted by Beitel, Gibbs, Jr, & Sanders (2001) and Gibbs, Jr & Matlock (2001), image schemas (Johnson, 1987) are used to characterise the organisation of the senses.

As discussed in the introduction, the similarities between different senses of a lexical unit are based on the underlying patterns that motivate them. One tool for describing these patterns is an image schema, which Johnson (1987) describes as a reoccurring pattern in our perception and movement, creating coherence in our experiences. In the analysis of the results of the sorting task, image schemas are used to describe the emerged structure to show that there is, indeed, a structural similarity to the senses that were sorted together in the task. However, no claims are made as to the psychological reality of these image schemas. In the present work, image schemas are used purely as descriptive tools.

The aforementioned studies show that image schemas can be a useful tool to describe the structure of polysemy. In these studies, the participants themselves were also introduced to image schemas, and they were instructed to use the schemas in various parts of the experiments. The participants managed this mostly without problems, which shows how beneficial this instrument can be for studying semantics.

Thirteen senses of *nägema* were used in the sorting task, and one sentence for each sense. The list of senses follows (with minor adjustments) the one in the Explanatory Dictionary of Estonian (Langemets et al., 2009). The adjustments consisted of splitting some sub-senses to independent senses, to give the broadest possible range of senses; in addition, one sense from the dictionary was not included in the list of experimental items, as it was marked as being outdated.[1] The sentences were extracted from the Corpus of Written Estonian. The senses and sentences can be seen in Table 1.

Table 1. Senses of *nägema*, exemplified by sorting task sentences

N1	'physical perception'	*Kas näe-d seda viilkatuse-ga hoone-t?* Q see-2SG that.PART gable.roof-COM building-PART 'Do *you see* that building with a gable roof?'
N2	'not shareable visual perception'	*Kui karu unenägu-si-d näe-ks, või-ks ta neid* if bear dream-PL-PART see-COND can-COND he this.PL.PART *terve talve nauti-da.* whole winter.GEN enjoy-INF1 'If a bear *could see* dreams, it could enjoy them all winter.'
N3	'meet'	*Ma pea-n jooks-ma kahjuks, näe-me kunagi!* I must-1SG run-INF2 unfortunately see-1PL sometime 'Unfortunately, I have to run, *see you* (lit. 'we see') sometime!'
N4	'understand'	*Aga nüüd ma näe-n, et muretsemine on mõttetu.* but now I see-1SG that worrying is pointless 'But now *I see* that worrying is pointless.'
N5	'understand / have a presentiment'	*Missuguse-i-d ohte te siin näe-te?* what.kind-PL-PART danger.PL.PART you.2PL here see-2PL 'What kind of dangers do *you see* here?'
N6	'experience'	*Vaese-d inimese-d saa-vad ikka päevi näh-a* poor-PL human-PL get-3PL PRTC day.PL.PART see-INF1 'Poor people often go through difficult times.'
N7	'experience (inanimate agent)'	*Maja ol-i näi-nud parema-i-d ja halvema-i-d* house be-PST.3SG see-APP better-PL-PART and worse-PL-PART *aegu ning üleela-nud mitmesuguse-i-d* time.PART.PL and live.through-APP various.kind-PL-PART *asuka-i-d.* inhabitant-PL-PART 'The house *had seen* better and worse times, and survived all kinds of inhabitants.'

(continued)

---

1. This kind of note is added to senses in the dictionary that are no longer used productively, but have been found e.g. in old fiction texts.

Table 1. (*continued*)

N8	'state something'	*Ja näe-te, mu-l oli õigus!* and see-2PL I-ADE be-PST.3SG right 'And *you see*, I was right!'
N9	'wish/hope'	*Kuidas te näe-ks-ite Venemaa lähitulevikku?* how you.2PL see-COND-2PL Russia.GEN near.future.PART 'How would you describe the near future of Russia?'
N10	'know in the future'	*Ei tea, mis edasi saa-b, ela-me-näe-me.* no know what further get-3SG live-1PL-see-1PL 'I don't know how things are going to turn out, *we'll see.*'
N11	'watch'	*Ta ol-i ju toda tükki enne mitme-l* he be-PST.3SG PRTC that.PART piece.PART before many-ADE *korra-l näi-nud.* time-ADE see-APP 'He *had seen* the play many times before.'
N12	'notice/glimpse'	*Raamatu-i-d ol-i-n näi-nud Tamuri riiuli-s.* book-PL-PART be-PST-1SG see-APP Tamur.GEN shelf-INE '*I had seen* the books in Tamur's shelf.'
N13	'make a judgement'	*Vaata-d otsa ja näe-d, see mees on intellektuaal.* look-2SG ADV and see-2SG this man is intellectual 'You look at him and *you see* that this man is an intellectual.'

The task was conducted in person, i.e. the participants sat behind a table and sorted the sentences, which were printed on slips of paper. Altogether 20 participants with an average age of 24 years (age range 20–50 years) completed the sorting task. There were 11 women and 9 men amongst the participants. The participants were instructed to sort the sentences into groups according to the meaning of *nägema*. No further instructions were given (i.e. participants were free to choose the number of groups and the number of sentences in each group). The final result was then photographed and later coded.

After the task, the participants were asked to explain their sorting decisions. The comments were collected via a casual, non-obligatory conversation, and were written down by the experimenter. The aim of this was firstly to give the participants a chance to add a comment to their decisions, if they felt they wanted to, and secondly, to get an insight to what the participants were focusing on when sorting the sentences.

The results of the sorting task were converted into a co-occurrence table, which showed how many times each sense was sorted together with each of the other senses. This co-occurrence table was then analysed with hierarchical cluster analysis (HCA) using the package cluster (Maechler et al., 2016) (e.g. Divjak & Fieller (2014) offers a thorough overview of HCA and its applications in cognitive linguistics).[2] The structure that emerged is analysed making use of image schemas as well as the participants' comments. Image schemas are used to describe the emerged structure to show that there is, indeed, a structural similarity to the senses that were sorted together in the task.

2.2   Results of the sorting task

The results of the sorting task were analysed using HCA; the Canberra distance measure and complete linkage method were used. Figure 1 shows the results as a dendrogram, which is to be understood the following way: initially, the algorithm starts out with taking all the elements as separate clusters. Elements are then linked on the basis of similarities. The 'sooner' the elements are linked, the more similar they are. As all elements are initially unlinked, the process is depicted from the bottom up. The horizontal axis is not important in interpreting the dendrogram, i.e. it makes no difference if the clusters are formed on the right or on the left side.

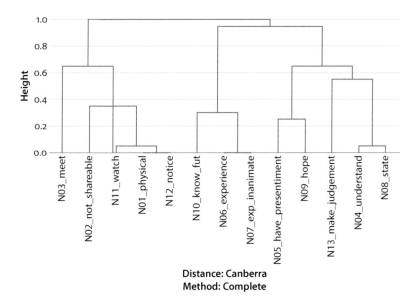

Figure 1. Senses of *nägema* on the basis of a sorting task, analysed with HCA

---

2.   The program R (R Core Team, 2016) was used for all of the statistical analysis.

Taking into account the comments of the language users, and the fact that a successful dendrogram should be logically interpretable, it is proposed that the dendrogram contains the following 5 clusters:

1. *nägema* as a physical activity
   - N1 – 'physical perception'
   - N12 – 'notice/glimpse'
   - N11 – 'watch'
   - N2 – 'not shareable visual perception'
2. *nägema* as meeting someone
   - N3 – 'meet'
3. *nägema* as understanding something/someone
   - N4 – 'understand'
   - N8 – 'state something'
   - N13 – 'make a judgement'
4. *nägema* as having a presentiment
   - N5 – 'understand / have a presentiment'
   - N9 – 'wish/hope'
5. *nägema* as experiencing something
   - N6 – 'experience'
   - N7 – 'experience something (inanimate agent)'
   - N10 – 'know in the future'

Each cluster will be analysed in the following sub-sections, making use of image schemas and participants' comments.

2.2.1   nägema *as a physical activity*

This cluster contains senses that express the physical experience of seeing, all characterised by the PATH image schema (Johnson, 1987, p. 28). The schema works as follows: the sight travels along a trajectory, beginning from point A (the subject of seeing), and ending at point B (the object of seeing).

As can be seen from Figure 1, the senses N1 'physical perception' and N12 'notice/glimpse' were sorted together in every individual task. Not far apart is the sense N11 'watch' which is also situated quite low on the dendrogram, suggesting it is similar to senses N1 and N12. These senses are all dependent on the physical act of visual perception, but are differentiated by the intensity and duration of the act.

At first glance, sense N2 'not sharable visual perception' might seem like an atypical member of the cluster. It is also situated higher on the dendrogram compared to the other senses of the cluster. Two out of the 20 participants formed a cluster only containing this sense, which further affected the outcome of the HCA. A physical experience does exist when seeing dreams, visions, hallucinations etc., albeit one not sharable with other people. According to the participants' comments, the deciding factor for some was the notion of "something being in front of their eyes", which can be interpreted as an element of physicality in the perception.

2.2.2 nägema *as meeting someone*

'*Nägema* as meeting someone' is the only cluster containing only one sense. The dendrogram shows it as being on the highest position out of all the other senses. This is the result of sense N3 'meet' being sorted as a group on its own by 5 out of 20 participants (25%): no other sense was grouped separately from other senses so consistently. This increases the distance of dissimilarities, and makes the sense stand out from the others. When asked to describe the clusters and give a reason for their decisions, the participants who sorted 'meet someone' as a separate group clearly made a distinction between this meaning and the others, stating mostly without hesitation that "this is *meeting someone*". This suggests that although *nägema* in this sense is productive (i.e. there are no limits for the morphological variation), it is still a fixed expression.

As the notion of contact turned out to be the deciding factor in the group, the image schema CONTACT describes the structure motivating the group. The schema can also be interpreted as two PATH schemas, directed towards each other, with the critical element being the point of contact between the two schemas.

2.2.3 nägema *as understanding and* nägema *as having a presentiment*

The two clusters containing senses N4 'understand', N8 'state something', N13 'make a judgement'; and N5 'understand / have a presentiment' and N9 'wish/hope', can be summed up with the SEEING IS UNDERSTANDING metaphor (Lakoff & Johnson, 1980, p. 48). This metaphor is based on the similarities between the field of intelligence/understanding and seeing. Both share the characteristics of being objective and sharable (i.e. two people looking at something from the same point will generally see the same thing and share the visual experience, hence also the expression 'see it from my point of view'). Seeing is objective as we generally trust our sight to give us the most direct evidence from the world (Sweetser, 1990, p. 39).[3] Similarly, knowing something is based on facts, not opinions – facts are controllable and sharable, which makes them objective.

The PATH image schema with its constituents transferred to an abstract domain is also of use here. Transferring the schema allows us to understand the beginning and ending points as states (Johnson, 1987, p. 114). In the case of understanding,

---

3. However, Sweetser (1990) only focuses on Indo-European languages. E.g. Evans & Wilkins (2000) have shown that in many Australian languages, the sense of hearing, not seeing, is associated with understanding and knowing.

the trajectory expresses 'gaining knowledge', the starting point being the state of 'not understanding', the ending point 'understanding'. As this kind of transferred schema can be used to characterise all the members in the group, their underlying structure is the same and they are thus perceived as being similar or more tightly connected in the language user's mind.

2.2.4 nägema *as experiencing*

This cluster contains three senses: N6 'experience', N7 'experience (inanimate agent)', and N10 'know in the future'. The senses in the cluster follow the opposite logic to those in the 'understanding' cluster. Instead of the meaning extension being based on the objective characteristics of seeing, the senses in this group focus on the subjectivity of the perceptual act. Thus 'seeing' extends to mean generally 'experiencing', and senses relating to this transformation are grouped together.

Out of the 20 participants, seven grouped all of these senses together and called the group 'experiencing'. In addition, four others formed the same group, but did not explain their decisions with 'experiencing'. Explanations included "the aspect of time" and "these are fixed expressions". The concept of experiencing can be described using the FORCE image schema (Johnson, 1987, p. 43).

This schema shares important parts with the PATH schema. It includes the source of the force, the goal of the force, i.e. the object that is being manipulated, and a trajectory. Additionally, force has a dimension of intensity and a cause-effect relationship. Transferring the schema onto the domain of experiencing, we understand the thing that is experienced as the source of the force, and the experiencer becomes the goal of the force, thus "reversing" the PATH schema. The dimension of intensity is expressed with various possible adjectives and adverbs that describe the experience as in (1).

(1) *Tule-b   näha   pisut/palju vaeva*
     come-3SG see.INF1 little/lot   trouble.PART
     'You have to go to a little bit of / a lot of trouble.'

Using the same kind of devices with the other senses will result in quantifying, rather than intensifying the experience as in (2), separating these senses and their underlying schema from the others.

(2) *Ole-n   teda   palju näi-nud*
     be-PRS.1SG he.PART lot   see-APP
     'I have seen him a lot'

3. Behavioural profile analysis

3.1 Overview of the methods and material

Behavioural profile analysis (Divjak & Gries, 2006) is a method for analysing how a language item is used in natural language sentences. The method is based on the idea that information about frequency and co-occurrences reflects functional information. It can thus be used to describe the possible organisation of a language unit in the language user's mind. In the context of the study of (near-)synonymy and polysemy this method can be used to look at which elements of language are more similar to each other (Gries & Divjak, 2009, p. 61). For polysemy, this element of language is the word in its different meanings. The more similar the behavioural profile of a specific sense is to that of another, the more similar the senses are. For example, if two senses appear mostly in sentences where the agent of the action is animate, then these are more similar to each other than a sense which is only used in sentences with an inanimate agent. It is a combination of a multitude of these kinds of characteristics that makes up the behavioural profile (BP) of a sense.

The method makes use of several semantic and morphosyntactic characteristics (called ID-tags), the number and nature of which are left up to the researcher. All of the sentences are annotated for each ID-tag (e.g. if one of the ID-tags is "mood", then all of the sentences would be annotated either as indicative, conditional, imperative, quotative or N/A). This results in a co-occurrence table, which is then converted into a relative frequency table. These frequency tables constitute the behavioural profile; what follows, is the analysis of the profile with various methods, the most common being HCA (Gries & Divjak, 2009, p. 61).

For this study, 700 sentences from the Balanced Corpus of Estonian were analysed, including only texts from fiction and journalism. Scientific texts were excluded as these traditionally offer less semantic variation. The corpus consists of altogether 15 million words (equal parts fiction, non-fiction, and scientific) and represents texts from the early 1990s until the late 2000s. The corpus is freely accessible via a user interface or download. Eighty-nine semantic (e.g. sense, animateness of source/goal of *seeing*) and morphosyntactic ID-tags (e.g. case, number, person) were used.

Twelve instead of 13 meanings were taken into account: the sense N12 'notice/glimpse' was eventually not included. It became clear that the characteristic *aspect* should be included as a variable, as this seemed to be an important part of the meaning N12. However, there is no grammatical aspect in Estonian, aspect is expressed sometimes with lexical means, sometimes with contextual means. As including aspect would have been a highly subjective and token-based process, it was opted to not include it. This, however, would also have meant that the assignment of the sense itself would be completely intuition-based. Also considering the fact that this sense was not separated by the language users from the sense 'physical perception' in the sorting task conducted beforehand, it was decided to leave the sense 'notice/glimpse' out of the corpus study.

In order to validate the clustering, two techniques were used. The Silhouette plot technique (the R package cluster (Maechler et al., 2016) was used) shows how well each member fits in the cluster it was assigned to. Repeating the analysis with a different number of clusters shows which solution is best (i.e. which solution shows clusters with best-fitting members) (Divjak & Fieller, 2014, p. 432). To further ensure a proper interpretation, bootstrapping was used. Bootstrapping assigns p-values to all of the clusters by imitating the present data a set number of times, and running the analysis on these new data. The R package pvclust (Suzuki & Shimodaira, 2015) was used for bootstrapping. This makes it possible to assess the validity of the present clustering solution (Robinson, 2014, p. 99).

3.2   Results of the BP analysis

Similarly to the results of the sorting task, the results of the corpus-based BP analysis were analysed by applying HCA using the R package cluster (Maechler et al., 2016). The resulting dendrogram can be seen in Figure 2. The Euclidean distance measure and Ward's amalgamation method were used.[4]

Taking into account the results of the validation techniques described in Section 3.1 (Silhouette plot and bootstrapping), Figure 2 is interpreted as containing the following 4 clusters:

1. *nägema* with a concrete bounded goal
    – N2 – 'not shareable visual perception'
    – N1 – 'physical perception'
    – N3 – 'meet'
2. *nägema* with an abstract bounded goal
    – N6 – 'experience'
    – N5 – 'understand / have a presentiment'
    – N9 – 'wish/hope'
    – N11 – 'watch'
3. construction-specific senses
    – N10 – 'know in the future'
    – N8 – 'state something'

---

4. Although the Canberra measure has been used to analyse behavioural profiles, the validation techniques showed a much better result when the Euclidean measure was used. Ward's method is recommended by Divjak (2010).

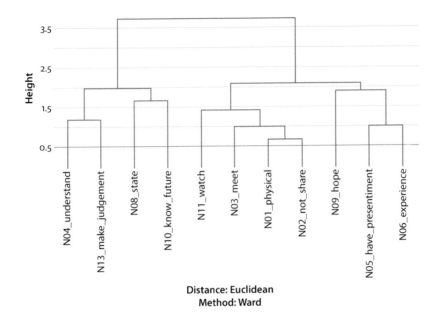

Figure 2. Senses of *nägema* on the basis of the BP analysis, analysed with HCA

4.   *nägema* with an un-bounded goal
   –   N13 – 'make a judgement'
   –   N4 – 'understand'

In the following analysis, the first and second on the one hand, and third and fourth clusters on the other hand are analysed together, taking the division into two larger branches as a basis. As such, one branch contains senses that prefer bounded entities, the other one senses that prefer un-bounded entities, as their objects. Notice that the sense N7 'experience (inanimate agent)' does not appear on the dendrogram – this is because this sense was not found in the corpus sample. This result is further addressed in the discussion section.

3.2.1   *Senses preferring a bounded entity as their object*
The first cluster contains senses which prefer a physical, bounded entity as the goal of perceiving. The distance between senses N1 'physical perception' and N2 'not sharable visual perception' is minimal. Looking at the behavioural profile of both senses reveals that there is, in fact, very little difference between them. Both are used in morphologically varied contexts and the semantic characteristics, e.g. animateness of the source/goal, type of goal, are mostly the same. Most of the differences come from marking the 'place of seeing' and the use of impersonalising devices. Some examples from the corpus can help illustrate these points. For example, the adverbial *unes* 'in a dream' is used to mark the place of seeing in (3). This is

necessary, as the rest of the characteristics show high similarity with N1 'physical perception' in (4). Impersonalising devices are not used with N2 'not sharable physical perception', as the sense expresses an experience that is not shareable. This also means that it is not possible to hide the agent of seeing. N3 'meet' and N11 'watch' also follow similar trends as N1.

(3) *"Ma nägi-n   sind   täna ööse-l   unes,"   ütles*
    I   see.PST-1SG you.PART today night-ADE dream-INE say.PST.3SG
    ta.   – N2
    (s)he
    '"I *saw* you *in a dream* last night," (s)he said.'

(4) *Nüüd nägi   Aidann üsna selgelt Pilar-i   nägu.*   – N1
    now see.PST.3SG Aidann quite clearly Pilar-GEN face.PART
    'Now Aidann *saw* Pilar's face quite clearly.'

Similar to the first cluster, the second cluster also groups senses that take a bounded entity as the goal of perceiving. However, the entity is an abstract one. Though the profiles of N6 'experience' and N5 'understand/have a presentiment' are similar to each other, there are important differences. One of the crucial characteristics here is the type of goal. Sense N6 sets a limitation to the possible objects in the sentences. In other words – combined with a limited set of expressions (e.g. *vaev* 'pain, trouble', *paremad päevad* 'better days'), *nägema* gets the sense of 'experiencing', while other expressions (e.g. *mõte* 'thought, point', *isiksus* 'personality', *seos* 'connection') favour the interpretation of 'understanding something'.

Sense N9 'wish/hope' is also a part of this cluster, but is an atypical member. As can be seen from Figure 2, this sense diverges from the larger group – it is positioned quite high on the y-axis, which means it is not very similar to the other members. It is difficult to say whether it should or should not belong here, mostly because the sense was the most infrequent one compared to the others. Or rather – the sense is grouped this way because of the limited number of contexts to study.

3.2.2   *Senses preferring an un-bounded entity as their object*

Clusters three and four both contain senses that prefer an un-bounded object of perceiving. This object is some kind of a state or event. The third cluster contains construction-specific senses N8 'state something' and N10 'know in the future', i.e. senses that only get their meaning in certain constructions. For example, out of the 13 possible ID-tags relating to morphological form (e.g. person, number, infinitives), N8 occurs with 5, and N10 with 4 ID-tags. In comparison, senses N1 'physical perception' and N5 'understand / have a presentiment' occurred in all of the possible morphological forms. Also, senses N8 'state something' and N10 'know in the future' did not occur with any adverbials in the sample, further confirming their specificity.

Senses N4 'understand' and N13 'make a judgement' make up the second cluster in this bigger branch. While N4 indeed takes only states or events as its objects, as in (5), it is not that straightforward with N13 (6). N13 can occur with all types of goals – abstract, physical, bounded, and un-bounded. Taking a deeper look at the sense, one can say that this is a sense that in its nature lies between the physical and abstract domains or rather combines the two.

(5) *Varem ma pole   näi-nud, et   paratamatus tõesti*
     before I   NEG.be see-APP that inevitability really
     olema-s   on.
     be.INF2-INE be.3SG
     '*I have not seen* before that inevitability really exists.'

(6) *Nende   rõõm ol-i   enamasti näha   nende   silm-i-st.*
     they.GEN joy be-PST.3SG mostly see.INF they.GEN eye-PL-ELA
     'Their joy could mostly *be seen* from their eyes'.

The true object of seeing in (6) is a physical entity, but the object of seeing that is expressed, is something abstract, resulting in being able to see "joy in someone's eyes".

4. Discussion

4.1 Comparison of the results

Because HCA was applied to the results of both the behavioural profile analysis and the sorting task, it is possible to compare the results on equal grounds. The most noticeable difference is that the sorting task grouped the senses into two larger branches according to the dimension of physical-abstract. This division did not occur in the BP analysis. Instead, the senses split into two groups based on the nature of the goal of perception (bounded vs. un-bounded entities).

The division into abstract and physical senses seems more intuitive, especially when a language user is asked to make a distinction on the basis of the meaning of the verb in sentences. Three of the 20 task participants decided to use only this distinction and accordingly formed only two groups. The BP analysis, however, does not inherently take one kind of characteristic as being more important than others, but instead gives equal weight to all of the characteristics.

The importance of the language user's intuition can be seen, for example, from the position of sense N2 'not sharable visual perception'. In the sorting task it belonged to the 'physical activity' cluster, but was not close to the other members. This suggests it was a rather atypical member. In the BP analysis, however, N1 'physical perception' and N2 'not sharable visual perception' were deemed as the two most similar senses. Although the language user mentally distinguishes (in most cases) dreams or visions from the physical world, it is not expressed explicitly in the language. There are only a limited number of textual linguistic clues as to what kind of event is described (real or not). Most of the clues are more contextual, drawing from our experience of the world and encyclopaedic knowledge. Thus, the main components of seeing (the source, the goal, the action of seeing) often do not differ from "real" seeing, which results in similar corpus-profiles for the two senses.

When N2 'not sharable physical perception' was sorted as a group on its own, the fact that the sense "feels different" was a good enough reason to not sort it together with the other physical senses. When it was sorted into the same group as the other physical senses, the decision was often accompanied by a justification. The participants stated that the sense is an atypical member, but still "kind of similar" to the others. This kind of base for distinction also comes into play with sense N3 'meet'. As stated before, it was sorted separately more often than any other sense, although this kind of a separation was not evident in the BP analysis.

Construction-specific senses N10 'know in the future' and N8 'state something' made up a separate cluster based on their BPs, but were sorted into different groups by the language users in the sorting task. It is reasonable to interpret that the senses do not share underlying similarities in meaning and this is why they were grouped separately by language users. This was shown with the use of image schemas. A different underlying schema was shown for N8 'state something' and N10 'know in the future', which suggests different patterns of conceptualisation. Thus, even though these two senses share what seems to be a differentiating factor at first glance, i.e. differences or similarities in form and its variation, this is not necessarily a measure of similarity for the language user.

One of the major differences between the two sets of results is that the BP analysis does not include sense N7 'experience (inanimate agent)'. N7 was always sorted together with N6 'experience' in the sorting task, suggesting that language users do not differentiate between the two. However, unlike N12 'notice, glimpse', N7 'experience (inanimate agent)' was originally included in the BP analysis, because the method is well-suited to show differences between the two senses, should there be any (i.e. with the help of semantic characteristics such as type of source/goal). However, sense N7 did not occur in the corpus sample at all. Because the sample does not fully represent the population, it would be misleading to make any conclusions about N7. Thus, the results cannot be compared regarding sense N7.

The cluster of 'physical senses' exhibits the highest degree of similarity across the two methods. Although there are a number of differences between the structures of the cluster on each dendrogram, it remains the most similar compared to the other clusters. Other similarities can be found between the two analyses, e.g. senses N4 'understand' and N13 'make a judgement' belonging to the same cluster, but no other groups exhibit a high degree of similarity. This suggests that the other senses are more ambiguous, and their difference depends more on subjective factors like intuition.

4.2 Comparison of the methods

The BP analysis and the sorting task can be seen as complementary methods, as corpus-based and experimental methods, in general (see also Carlson & Hill (2007) and Gilquin & Gries (2009)). In this chapter, a few points of comparison between the two chosen methods are discussed. The main difference is that important elements of meaning for the language user are not necessarily objectively annotatable in the corpus sample. When annotating corpus data, one, of course, aims to include as many variables as needed to get as close as possible to how the language user might make their decisions. However, the fact remains that the language user might make the ultimate decision on the basis of something that cannot be predicted (n)or objectively tagged, in which case the results cannot be reproduced with corpus-based methods.

Other points of comparison mainly fall back on the general differences between experimental and corpus-based methods. While experimental methods allow the researcher to access the source of language, i.e. the language user, relatively directly, the amount of data a human can process or produce is always limited. The corpus offers an amount of data that would be extremely difficult to use in an experiment. However, as was shown with the case of sense N7 'experience (inanimate agent)', it is possible the relevant data cannot be found in the sample, whereas designing an experiment allows for control over the manipulable variables.

The amount of data that is available for processing in the BP analysis in most cases minimises the possibility of conclusions being made upon highly divergent data. As the task participants based their decisions only on one sentence, the weight of that one sentence is disproportionally large. A corpus sample offers much more variation, which, in itself, is a more natural state of language.

As such, the corpus data represents the most natural data, and the data collected experimentally, the most un-natural data. However, an experiment allows the researcher to focus on a particular phenomenon and manipulate variables to fit their needs. This design minimises the amount of noise in the data, while corpus data tends to be very noisy. For example, it was no trouble for the language users to base their groupings on the meaning of the verb. However, assigning semantic characteristics to corpus data proved to be the most difficult part of the BP analysis due to the small amount of possible formal semantic characteristics and highly varying data.

BP analysis also offers the possibility to address the question of a prototypical sense of *nägema*. According to Gries (2006), a prototypical sense should be the most entrenched in the language user's mind out of all the senses. It should be productive, and, thus, exhibit a large degree of variability. Taking these requirements into consideration, the sense N1 'physical perception' can be understood as the prototypical sense. Usage-based linguistics believes that there is a correlation between entrenchment and frequency of use (Langacker, 1987). The sense N1 'physical perception' makes up 54% of the sample, making it by far the most frequent sense. This would strongly suggest that N1 is also the most entrenched sense. Variability can be seen from co-occurrence with the annotated variables. Namely, the more variables the sense occurs with, the more variation it exhibits. Out of the 89 ID-tags, N1 did not occur with only 5 ID-tags, making it the most variable sense. Although it has been questioned whether it is reasonable to equate entrenchment with frequency so lightly (e.g. Schmid (2010)), in the framework of this study, there is likely no reason to doubt that 'physical perception' can be understood as the prototypical sense.

It was discussed in the introduction that Estonian has a unique profile amongst European languages. Because of long-lasting contact with Indo-European languages it might be reasonable to presume that typical metaphors and meaning extensions also follow the example of at least German. However, Estonian is a Finno-Ugric language and it is also plausible that this heritage, different from that of Indo-European languages, plays a role in how the speakers of a language conceptualise abstract notions. The analyses showed that there is a group of polysemous senses of *nägema* that are used to express experiencing abstract concepts like *vaev* 'trouble, pain', *rõõm* 'joy', or *nälg* 'hunger'. These are clearly different from concepts like *probleem* 'problem', *mõte* 'meaning, point', last of which belong to the field of intelligence.

This phenomenon is, however, characteristic of other languages as well. In his typological study of perception verbs, Viberg (1983) shows this kind of a meaning extension also to be true in Swahili. Finnish also exhibits this kind of extension, e.g. *nähdä vaivaa* 'to see trouble/pain' or *nähdä nälkää* 'to go hungry'. The present study makes no claims as to the reason why this kind of sense is not found in Indo-European languages.

5.   Conclusion

This paper aimed to first give an overview of the nature of polysemy of *nägema* 'to see' in Estonian, and second, to compare two methods used to complete the first aim. Generally, the metaphorical extensions from a physical sense of seeing to abstract senses of seeing in Estonian are similar to those in English (as represented by Alm-Arvius (1993) and Sweetser (1990)). However, there is a group of senses that seem to defy the logic of seeing being tied to the field of knowledge, intelligence, and objectivity. It is not uncommon in Estonian to use *nägema* to mean 'experience', referring to states of mind and feelings. The motivation behind this kind of a meaning extension and its generalisability is something to consider in future research.

The paper also showed how two methods – a sorting task and a behavioural profile analysis depict a different sense network for the Estonian perception verb *nägema* 'to see'. Senses of *nägema* relating to physical perception showed the highest degree of similarity across methods in their grouping. The division of other senses, however, is not so straightforward, depending more on the method used. One of the more distinct differences is the overall division of senses – both methods rendered a structure, where the senses group into two larger units. However, the sorting task showed a structure that follows the contrast of physical vs. abstract senses, while the behavioural profile divided the senses according to the nature of the goal of seeing (bounded vs. un-bounded).

The differences in the results can be traced back to the fundamental differences of experimental and corpus-based methods. For example, the decision-making process of a language user cannot easily be translated into observable characteristics. The research shows that language users base their decisions on intuition, which, in itself, is not a novel concept. However, the two methods can be seen as complementary. Applying both methods helps to get closer to the extent that intuition is involved in sense categorisation, and how much of the categorisation is explainable through observable context characteristics.

Acknowledgements

This study was supported by the Estonian Research Council (PUT1358 The Making and Breaking of Models: Experimentally Validating Classification Models in Linguistics).

Abbreviations

1, 2, 3	person	INF2	infinitive 2
ADE	adessive	NEG	negation
ADV	adverb	PART	partitive
APP	active past participle	PL	plural
COM	comitative	PRS	present
COND	conditional	PRTC	particle
ELA	elative	PST	past
GEN	genitive	Q	question particle
INE	inessive	SG	singular
INF1	infinitive 1		

Corpus

BCE = Balanced Corpus of Estonian.
Retrieved from http://www.cl.ut.ee/korpused/grammatikakorpus/

References

Alm-Arvius, C. (1993). *The English verb see: A study in multiple meaning*. Göteborg: Acta Universitas Gothoburgensis.

Beitel, D. A., Gibbs, Jr, R. W., & Sanders, P. (2001). The embodied approach to the polysemy of the spatial preposition *on*. In H. Cuyckens & B. Zawada (Eds.), Polysemy in cognitive linguistics: Selected papers from the fifth International Cognitive Linguistics Conference. (pp. 241–260). Amsterdam/Philadelphia: John Benjamins Publishing Company.

Born, T. (1995). Eesti keele tajuverbid. Tähendusallikad ja tähendusmuutused [Estonian perception verbs. Meaning sources and meaning changes]. (Diploma thesis). Tartu: Tartu Ülikool.

Carlson, L. A., & Hill, P. L. (2007). Experimental methods for studying language and space. In M. Gonzalez-Marques, I. Mittelberg, S. Coulson, & M. J. Spivey (Eds.), *Methods in cognitive linguistics* (Vol. 18, pp. 250–276). Amsterdam/Philadelphia: John Benjamins Publishing Company. https://doi.org/10.1075/hcp.18.18car

Croft, W. (1998). Linguistic evidence and mental representations. *Cognitive Linguistics*, 9(2), 151–173. https://doi.org/10.1515/cogl.1998.9.2.151

Dąbrowska, E. (2008). Questions with long-distance dependencies: A usage-based perspective. *Cognitive Linguistics*, 19(3), 391–425. https://doi.org/10.1515/COGL.2008.015

Divjak, D. (2008). On (in)frequency and (un)acceptability. In B. Lewandowska-Tomaszczyk (Ed.), *Corpus linguistics, computer rools, and applications – State of the art* (Vol. 17, pp. 213–233). Frankfurt am Main: Peter Lang.

Divjak, D. (2010). *Structuring the lexicon : A clustered model for near-synonymy*. Berlin/New York: Walter de Gruyter GmbH&Co. KG. https://doi.org/10.1515/9783110220599

Divjak, D. (2015). Exploring the grammar of perception. A case study using data from Russian. *Functions of Language*, 22(1), 44–68. https://doi.org/10.1075/fol.22.1.03div

Divjak, D., & Fieller, N. (2014). Cluster analysis. Finding structure in linguistic data. In D. Glynn & J. A. Robinson (Eds.), *Corpus Methods for Semantics. Quantitative studies in polysemy and synonymy* (pp. 405–441). Amsterdam/Philadelphia: John Benjamins Publishing Company. https://doi.org/10.1075/hcp.43.16div

Divjak, D., & Gries, S. T. (2006). Ways of trying in Russian: Clustering behavioural profiles. *Corpus Linguistics and Linguistic Theory*, 2–1, 23–60.

Erelt, M. (Ed.). (2003). *Estonian language* (Vol. 1). Tallinn: Estonian Academy Publishers.

Evans, N., & Wilkins, D. (2000). In the mind's ear: The semantic extensions of perception verbs in Australian languages. *Language*, 76(3), 546–592. https://doi.org/10.2307/417135

Geeraerts, D. (2006). *Words and other wonders. Papers on lexical and semantic topics*. Berlin/New York: Mouton de Gruyter. https://doi.org/10.1515/9783110219128

Gibbs, Jr, R. W. (2006). *Embodiment and cognitive science*. Cambridge: Cambridge University Press.

Gibbs, Jr, R. W., & Matlock, T. (2001). Psycholinguistic perspectives on polysemy. In H. Cuyckens & B. Zawada (Eds.), Polysemy in cognitive linguistics: Selected papers from the fifth International Cognitive Linguistics Conference (pp. 213–239). Amsterdam/Philadelphia: John Benjamins Publishing Company.

Gilquin, G., & Gries, S. T. (2009). Corpora and experimental methods: A state-of-the-art review. *Corpus Linguistics and Linguistic Theory*, 5(1), 1–26. https://doi.org/10.1515/CLLT.2009.001

Gisborne, N. (2010). *The event structure of perception verbs*. Oxford: Oxford University Press. https://doi.org/10.1093/acprof:oso/9780199577798.001.0001

Glynn, D. (2014). Polysemy and synonymy. Corpus method and cognitive theory. In D. Glynn & J. A. Robinson (Eds.), *Corpus methods for Semantics. Quantitative studies in polysemy and synonymy* (pp. 7–38). Amsterdam/Philadelphia: John Benjamins Publishing Company. https://doi.org/10.1075/hcp.43.01gly

Gries, S. T. (2006). Corpus-based methods and cognitive semantics: The many meanings of *to run*. In S. T. Gries & A. Stefanowitsch (Eds.), *Corpora in cognitive linguistics: Corpus-based approaches to syntax and lexis* (pp. 57–99). Berlin/New York: Mouton de Gruyter. https://doi.org/10.1515/9783110197709.57

Gries, S. T., & Divjak, D. (2009). Behavioral profiles: A corpus-based approach to cognitive semantic analysis. In V. Evans & S. Pourcel (Eds.), *New Directions in Cognitive Linguistics* (pp. 57–77). Amsterdam/Philadelphia: John Benjamins Publishing Company. https://doi.org/10.1075/hcp.24.07gri

Ibarretxe-Antunano, B. I. (1999). Polysemy and metaphor in perception verbs: A crosslinguistic study (PhD thesis). University of Edinburgh.

Ibarretxe-Antunano, I. (2008). Vision metaphors for the intellect: Are they really crosslinguistic? *Atlantis. Journal of the Association of Anglo-American Studies*, 30(1), 15–33.

Jansegers, M., Vanderschueren, C., & Enghels, R. (2015). The polysemy of the Spanish verb *sentir*: A behavioral profile analysis. *Cognitive Linguistics*, 26(3), 381–421. https://doi.org/10.1515/cog-2014-0055

Johnson, M. (1987). *The body in the mind. The bodily basis of meaning, imagination, and reason*. Chicago: The University of Chicago Press.

Johnson, M., & Lenci, A. (2011). Verbs of visual perception in Italian FrameNet. *Constructions & Frames*, 3(1), 9–45. https://doi.org/10.1075/cf.3.1.01joh

Klavan, J. (2012). Evidence in linguistics: Corpus-linguistic and experimental methods for studying grammatical synonymy (PhD thesis). University of Tartu, Tartu.

Labi, K. (2006). *Eesti regilaulude verbisemantika* [Verb semantics of Estonian runic songs]. Dissertationes Philologiae Estonicae Universitatis Tartuensis 18. Tartu: Tartu Ülikool.

Lakoff, G. (1987). *Women, fire, and dangerous things: What categories reveal about the mind*. Chicago and London: The University of Chicago Press. https://doi.org/10.7208/chicago/9780226471013.001.0001

Lakoff, G., & Johnson, M. (1980). *Metaphors we live by*. Chicago and London: The University of Chicago Press.

Langacker, R. W. (1987). *Foundations of cognitive grammar. Volume 1. Theoretical prequisites*. Stanford, California: Stanford University Press.

Langacker, R. W. (2008). *Cognitive grammar. A basic introduction*. Oxford: Oxford University Press. https://doi.org/10.1093/acprof:oso/9780195331967.001.0001

Langemets, M., Tiits, M., Valdre, T., Veskis, L., Viks, Ü., & Voll, P. (Eds.). (2009). *Eesti keele seletav sõnaraamat* [Explanatory Dictionary of Estonian]. Tallinn.

Maechler, M., Rousseeuw, P., Struyf, A., Hubert, M., & Hornik, K. (2016). *cluster: Cluster Analysis Basics and Extensions. R package version 2.0.5.*

Proos, M. (2016). Mida ütleb korpus tähenduse kohta? Käitumisprofiili analüüsi ja klasteranalüüsi meetod eesti keele tajuverbi *nägema* tähenduse uurimisel [What can the corpus say about meaning? Applying behavioural profile analysis and cluster analysis to the study of the Estonian perception verb 'see']. (MA thesis). Tartu: Tartu Ülikool.

R Core Team. (2016). *R: A language and environment for statistical computing*. Vienna, Austria: R Foundation for Statistical Computing. Retrieved from https://www.R-project.org/

Robinson, J. A. (2014). Quantifying polysemy in cognitive sociolinguistics. In D. Glynn & J. A. Robinson (Eds.), *Corpus methods for semantics. Quantitative studies in polysemy and synonymy* (pp. 87–115). Amsterdam: John Benjamins Publishing Company. https://doi.org/10.1075/hcp.43.04rob

San Roque, L., Kendrick, K. H., Norcliffe, E., Brown, P., Defina, R., Dingemanse, M., Dirksmeyer, T., Enfield, N. J., Floyd, S., Hammond, J., Rossi, G., Tufvesson, S., van Putten, S., & Majid, A. (2015). Vision verbs dominate in conversation across cultures, but the ranking of non-visual verbs varies. *Cognitive Linguistics, 26*(1), 31. https://doi.org/10.1515/cog-2014-0089

Sandra, D., & Rice, S. (1995). Network analyses of prepositional meaning: Mirroring whose mind – the linguist's or the language user's? *Cognitive Linguistics, 6*(1), 89–130. https://doi.org/10.1515/cogl.1995.6.1.89

Schmid, H.-J. (2010). Does frequency in text instatiate entrenchment in the cognitive system? In D. Glynn & K. Fischer (Eds.), *Quantitative methods in cognitive semantics: Corpus-driven approaches* (pp. 101–137). Berlin/New York: Mouton de Gruyter. https://doi.org/10.1515/9783110226423.101

Sepper, M.-M. (2006). Indirektaal eesti 19. sajandi lõpu ja 20. sajandi aja- ja ilukirjanduskeeles [Indirect speech in Estonian newspaper and fiction texts of the end of the 19th century and the beginning of 20th century]. (MA thesis). Tallinn: Tallinna Ülikool.

Sjöström, S. (1999). From vision to cognition. A study of metaphor and polysemy in Swedish. In J. Allwood & P. Gärdenfors (Eds.), *Cognitive Semantics. Meaning and Cognition* (pp. 67–85). Amsterdam/Philadelphia: John Benjamins Publishing Company. https://doi.org/10.1075/pbns.55.05sjo

Suzuki, R., & Shimodaira, H. (2015). *pvclust: Hierarchical Clustering with P-Values via Multiscale Bootstrap Resampling. R package version 2.0-0.*

Sweetser, E. E. (1990). *From etymology to pragmatics. Metaphorical and cultural aspects of semantic structure*. Cambridge: Cambridge University Press. https://doi.org/10.1017/CBO9780511620904

Talmy, L. (2000). *Toward a cognitive semantics. Volume I: Concept structuring systems*. Cambridge: The MIT Press.

Taylor, J. R. (1995). *Linguistic categorization. Prototypes in linguistic theory*. New York: Oxford University Press.

Usoniene, A. (2001). On direct/indirect perception with verbs of seeing and seeming in English and Lithuanian. *Lund University, Dept. of Linguistics. Working Papers, 48*, 163–182.

Vanhove, M. (2008). Semantic associations between sensory modalities, prehension and mental perceptions. A crosslinguistic perspective. In M. Vanhove (Ed.), *From polysemy to semantic change. Towards a typology of lexical semantic associations* (pp. 341–370). Amsterdam/Philadelphia: John Benjamins Publishing Company. https://doi.org/10.1075/slcs.106.17van

Viberg, Å. (1983). The verbs of perception: A typological study. *Linguistics, 21*, 123–162. https://doi.org/10.1515/ling.1983.21.1.123

Whitt, R. J. (2010). Evidentiality, polysemy, and the verbs of perception in English and German. In G. Diewald & E. Smirnova (Eds.), *Linguistic Realization of Evidentiality in European Languages* (pp. 249–278). Berlin/New York: Walter de Gruyter GmbH&Co. KG.

CHAPTER 13

Evidential vindication in next turn

Using the retrospective "see?" in conversation

Kobin H. Kendrick
University of York

Perception verbs are frequent in conversation across diverse languages and cultures. This chapter presents a case study of a recurrent but previously undocumented use of the perception verb *see* in everyday English conversation. Using conversation analysis, the chapter explicates the use of "See?" – the verb *see* produced with rising intonation as a possibly complete turn-constructional unit – as claim of evidential vindication. With "See?" a speaker claims a just prior turn, action, or event as support for a previous assertive action. The analysis demonstrates that the practice exploits two distinct forms of sequence organisation, adjacency pairs and retro-sequences, and reflects on the fit between the perception verb *see* and the action it implements within this practice.

Keywords: conversation analysis, sequence organisation, retro-sequences, social action, perception verbs, perceptual metaphor, evidence, disputes, English

1. The phenomenon

In conversation, assertive actions, such as claims and statements of fact or opinion, whether valid or not, can be met with opposition from other participants. To manage this opposition and defend the validity of these actions, participants can and commonly do appeal to evidence, grounding the assertion in the objective reality of the perceptible world (cf. Pomerantz, 1984, 1989). In a dispute, in which two parties display commitments to contradictory versions of reality (Pollner, 1987), appeals to observable evidence can lead to a resolution. Consider, for example, the dispute between two participants in Extract (1) as they play a special anniversary edition of the board game Monopoly.

https://doi.org/10.1075/celcr.19.13ken
© 2019 John Benjamins Publishing Company

Extract 1. [Monopoly Boys]

```
 1  Luke:     Ventnor isn't called Ventnor, in the [other
 2  Rick:                                           [You:
 3            ca:n't bui:ld on it. <Yeah it is. It's called
 4            Ventnor.=
 5  Luke:     =No, it's not.
 6  Rick:     It's always called [Ventnor.
 7  Luke:                        [It's not. It's not.
 8  Rick: ->  D'you want me t'go get the original one.
 9            (0.2)
10  Rick: ->  from underneath my bed, I'll show you it's
11        ->  called Ventnor.
12            (0.7)
13  Luke:     Oh I'm thinking of fucking Nate's ga:me.
14  Rick:     Oh.
15  Luke:     Okay.
```

After Luke's piece lands on Ventnor Avenue, he states as a matter of fact that Ventnor is not called Ventnor in what would presumably be a reference to the standard edition of the game, in contrast to the anniversary edition (line 1). In the sequence that follows, Rick employs three practices to challenge the validity of Luke's assertion:

1. he produces an assertion that inverts the polarity of Luke's ("Ventnor isn't called…" becomes "It is" and "It's called…"; lines 3–4);
2. he expands the generality of the counter-assertion through the addition of "always" (line 6; cf. Pomerantz, 1986);
3. and, finally, he appeals to evidence (lines 8–11).

A distinction should be made between the first two practices, which challenge the assertion through reformulations of its original format, and the last practice, which appeals to an external source that would potentially support Rick's challenge and reveal Luke's assertion to be invalid. First, the practices appear to be ordered. It is only after Rick's counter-assertions fail twice that he appeals to evidence for support. Second, whereas Rick's counter-assertions are tacitly grounded in his own knowledge or beliefs (or claims thereto), the evidence he appeals to is grounded in a shared material world that both participants can perceive and evaluate. Rick's offer to retrieve and present this evidence serves to bring the dispute sequence to a close.

Evidence that speaks to the validity of an assertive action can be offered up and introduced into the interaction, as in Extract (1), or it can arise in the interaction itself. Consider, for instance, the evidence that Stacy finds to support her assessment in Extract (2), which comes from an interaction between three sorority sisters as they talk and make food.

Extract 2. [Sorority Breakfast]

```
1 Stacy:     ((spreads peanut butter on a rice krispie treat))
2 Tara:      Eww. What are you doing.=
3 Stacy:     =That's so: go:od,
4 Tara:      It's so gross,
5 Tricia: -> Oh that's so good? [Try it.]
6 Stacy:  ->                    [OH. SEE?] ((points to Tri.))
7 Tricia:    Ye::ah.
```

To support the validity of her assessment, in the face of opposition from Tara, Stacy produces "OH. SEE?" to notice and mobilise attention to Tricia's prior assessment, treating it as evidence for her own. Stacy does not claim that such evidence exists or offer to retrieve it; she merely (and literally) points to evidence that can be found in the local setting. We return to the analysis of this extract in subsequent sections.

2. The present study

This chapter analyses the use of "See?" – the verb *see* produced with rising intonation as a possibly complete turn-constructional unit (Sacks, Schegloff, & Jefferson, 1974) – as a practice that implements the action of *evidential vindication*, that is, a claim that a just prior turn, action, or event constitutes evidence for a previous assertive action, which the recipient should therefore accept as valid.[1] The study uses conversation analysis (CA), a method for the study of linguistic and embodied conduct in naturally occurring interaction (Hoey & Kendrick, 2017; Sidnell & Stivers, 2013). It draws on a collection of 27 instances of "See?" identified opportunistically over the course of several years in 27 different audio and video recordings of informal conversation, including many commonly used in CA research (e.g., *Auto Discussion, Debbie and Shelley, Fraternity Guys, Game Night, Newport Beach, Sorority Breakfast, Virginia*) and others available to me. All data extracts are transcribed according to standard CA conventions (Hepburn & Bolden, 2017).

CA understands language as a resource for the formation of recognisable social actions (Levinson, 2013; Schegloff, 1996). Such actions, CA research has shown, do not occur in isolation but rather cohere to form orderly sequences, defined as courses of action implemented through talk (Schegloff, 2007). From a CA perspective, social actions – and the forms of talk and other conduct that comprise

---

1. Throughout this chapter the term evidential is used straightforwardly as the adjectival form of evidence and should not be confused with a grammatical evidential, which refers to a form that indicates the source of information in a language in which evidentiality is a grammatical category (Aikhenvald, 2006). English does not encode evidentiailty in this way.

them – cannot properly be understood without reference to the sequential environments in which they naturally occur because their recognisability depends not only on their form but also on their position within a sequence (see Levinson, 2013). The importance of a sequential analysis of talk and action is underscored by the analysis of "See?" as a claim of evidential vindication. The analysis demonstrates that "See?" exploits two distinct types of sequence organisation. In broad terms, "See?" operates both prospectively, making relevant a response that deals in some way with its claim of vindication (e.g., Tricia's agreement), and retrospectively, treating the immediately prior turn or action as evidence for some earlier assertive action. In technical terms, to be defined in the next section, "See?" launches two distinct types of sequence: an adjacency pair sequence and a retro-sequence.

The analysis also demonstrates how speakers in conversation use perception verbs such as *see* as resources for social action. With few exceptions (San Roque et al., 2018; Sidnell, 2007; Vázquez Carranza, 2014, 2015), research on perception verbs has generally focused on their lexical semantics and their tendency to have both perceptual and non-perceptual semantic associations (see, e.g., Aikhenvald & Storch, 2013; Evans & Wilkins, 2000; Ibarretxe-Antuñano, this volume; Lakoff & Johnson, 1980; Sweetser, 1990; Viberg, 1983). The verb *see* is often cited as a prime example of perceptual metaphor because it can refer not only to visual perception – considered its source domain – but also to, for example, cognition or intellection – understood as possible target domains (see, e.g., Sweetser, 1990; see also Proos, this volume). Evans and Wilkins (2000) have argued that such extensions of meaning arise in bridging contexts where both the original and novel interpretations are simultaneoulsy available (see also San Roque and Schieffelin, this volume). Despite this, the authors considered only single utterances in isolation, mostly drawn from recorded narratives, and provided only general glosses of the relevant bridging contexts. Previous research on perception verbs has thus not yet fully recognised that speakers use them as resources for social action and that the relevant contexts in which such actions naturally occur are coherent sequences of action in conversation.

This chapter presents a case study of one perception verb in English – *see* – as it is used by speakers in a specific linguistic practice – "See?" – to accomplish a recognisable social action – a claim of evidential vindication. Although the main objective of the analysis is to explicate the sequential organisation of this practice, for which the concept of perceptual metaphor is not necessary, the data nonetheless reveal that "See?" occurs in environments with and without plausible visual percepts and thus provide an empirical demonstration of perceptual metaphor in action, as it were.

The chapter is organised into four sections. After I introduce the concept of a retro-sequence and argue that "See?" operates as a retro-sequence initiator, I then examine the actions and events that comprise the retro-sequence: the assertive action which "See?" retrospectively targets and the immediately prior turn, action, or events that "See?" claims as evidence. In the final section I reflect on the sequential organisation of "See?" and the fit between the practice and the action it implements.

3. "See?" as a retro-sequence initiator

The most basic and ubiquitous form of action-sequencing in conversation is the adjacency pair (Schegloff, 2007). Such sequences have a prospective organisation: the first action in the sequence, the first pair-part, projects the relevance of a second, the second pair-part. In an adjacency pair, the absence of a second pair-part is a meaningful and accountable event in the interaction (e.g., not responding to a request is understood as projecting a refusal). Not all sequences of action are organised as adjacency pairs, however. In contrast to the prospective orientation of adjacency pairs, retro-sequences have a retrospective orientation. Although no systematic study of the organisation of retro-sequences yet exists, Schegloff (2007, p. 217–219) defines and exemplifies the features of their organisation in reference to a ubiquitous exemplar: other-initiated repair. Because Schegloff's analysis of other-initiated repair is the clearest and most explicit discussion of retro-sequences in the literature, it will be useful to summarise it here.

According to Schegloff (2007), a repair initiator, such as "Met whom?" in Extract (3) below, operates both prospectively and retrospectively.

Extract 3. [SBL 2,1,8] (Schegloff, 2007, p. 217)
```
1 Bet:  Was last night the first time you met Missiz Kelly?
2       (1.0)
3 Mar:  Met whom?
4 Bet:  Missiz Kelly
5 Mar:  Yes.
```

As Schegloff observes, an analysis of other-initiated repair sequences such as that in Extract (3) must make reference to three components: a trouble source ("Missiz Kelly"; line 1), a repair initiator ("Met whom?"), and a repair solution ("Missiz Kelly"; line 4). The repair initiator retrospectively treats some feature of the prior talk as problematic (i.e., as a trouble source) and prospectively makes relevant a candidate trouble solution as a response. Crucially, the trouble source (or more precisely what comes to be treated as the trouble source) does not itself make remediation relevant as a next action. Indeed, the trouble source does not exist as such until the repair initiator invokes its problematicity. In contrast to the trouble source, the repair initiator ("Met whom?") is designed as an initiating action for which a response is accountably due.

Schegloff uses the term retro-sequence to describe sequences that are "*launched from their second position*" (2007, p. 217; emphasis in original). Thus a repair sequence can be said to begin with a repair initiator, which is itself the second component (and therefore in the second position) of the sequence. But it is also the first component of the adjacency pair that serves to prompt the repair solution. The 'firstness' and 'secondness' of the repair initiator belong to two distinct types of sequence organisation, which as Schegloff's analysis of other-initiated repair demonstrates, can operate concurrently. A turn or action that launches a retro-sequence, such as a repair initiator, can be referred to as a retro-sequence initiator.

According to Schegloff, the most generic type of retro-sequence initiator is a noticing:

> Doing a noticing makes relevant some feature(s) of the setting, including the prior talk, which may not have been previously taken as relevant. It works by mobilizing attention on the features which it formulates or registers, but treats them as its source, while projecting the relevance of some further action in response to the act of noticing.   (Schegloff, 2007, p. 219)

In the case of other-initiated repair, the repair initiator constitutes a specific type of noticing that treats some feature(s) of the prior talk as problematic and projects the relevance of a repair solution in response.

Like other-initiated repair, "See?" also operates as a retro-sequence initiator that mobilises attention on features of the local setting, namely an evidential relationship between what has just occurred and a previously contested action, thereby projecting the relevance of a response. In this way, "See?" launches both a retrospective sequence and a prospective sequence concurrently. The retro-sequence that "See?" initiates differs, however, from that of other-initiated repair in one crucial respect: "See?" targets not just the prior turn but a relationship between the prior turn and some previous action. "See?" retroactively *positions* these two objects into a sequential relationship. Insofar as "See?" occurs as the third component of the retro-sequence, it may be said to be launched from a *third* position.

The sequential organisation of "See?" is depicted in Figure 1. Throughout the analysis I refer to the prior turn, action, or event that "See?" locates as evidence as the *prior* and the previous assertive action which the prior supports as the *provable*.

Note that while "See?" invariably occurs in the next turn after the prior, the prior need not, and typically does not, immediately follow the provable. I return to the question of the sequential organisation of the practice in the discussion.

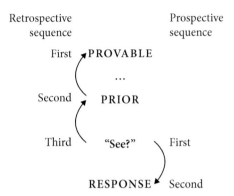

Figure 1. The sequential organisation of "See?"

The next two sections examine five instances of "See?" representative of the diversity of the collection. The analysis makes two passes through the set of cases in order to capture the prospective organisation of the sequences in which they occur rather than the retrospective organisation of the sequences they engender. The first pass considers the provables, the action that the speakers of "See?" subsequently find evidence to support, and the second pass considers the prior and its relationship to the provable, specifically, how it can be seen as evidence.

4.   Provables: Actions that can be evidenced

The prior turn, action, or event which "See?" targets typically relates to an earlier turn, action, or event in the interaction. As a method of analysis, one can locate an instance of "See?" and work one's way back through the prior events of the interaction until one identifies the related item. I term this item the 'provable' to characterise its proclivity to take (or necessitate) evidence. The analysis in this section reveals that, in the sequential positions in which they occur, provables consist of three general, not mutually exclusive types of actions: claims in the service of disagreement, statements about recurrent or invariable events, and 'predictives', each of which will be explained in detail below. As a claim of vindication, "See?" retroactively invokes the provability of these actions, just as a repair initiator invokes the (until that moment unrecognised) problematicity of some prior segment of talk.

Across the collection of cases, what come to be treated as provables exhibit a recurrent shape. In particular, such turns typically include extreme (or generalised) formulations and constitute claims, assertions, or statements of fact. Consider, for example, the five provables below, each of which subsequently becomes the target of "See?" and will be analysed in detail in this section.

```
a. Stacy:     That's so: go:od
b. Tex:       No I didn't.
c. Virginia:  always have to pay for gas,
d. Jennifer:  Every time you take over a country you get cards.
e. Adult:     Be careful of your ha:nd too please.
```

Across these five items, a number of generalisations can be made. The provables in (a) through (d) each exhibit a 'strong' or unmitigated formulation through terms that formulate the claim or assertion as extreme in one respect or another (Edwards, 2000; Pomerantz, 1986). "Always" in (c) and "every time" in (d) formulate the speakers' claims as recurrent and invariable; and the use of "so:" and marked prosody in (a) serve to 'upgrade' the assessment. The turn in (b), though lacking an extreme formulation, constitutes an unmitigated challenge to a prior speaker in the sequential position in which it occurs (i.e., after a statement about something the speaker did; see Extract (5)). The final item in the list (e) is unlike the others in that it is not an assertion and does not include an extreme formulation, but as the analysis below reveals, it too exhibits similarities to the other items in this list. The extreme and unmitigated formulations of these turns reveal ongoing commitments on the part of their speakers to the positions and courses of action to which the turns belong. The subsequent use of "See?" as a claim of evidential vindication is thus a resource for the maintenance and defence of these commitments.

One recurrent home for provables is disputes and disagreements between participants. The provable "that's so: go:od" in Extract (4) (repeated from Extract (2)), for instance, occurs after Tara has just called into question Stacy's decision to put peanut butter on a rice krispie treat (a snack food made from cereal and marshmallows).

Extract 4. [Sorority Breakfast]
```
1 Stacy:     ((spreads peanut butter on a rice krispie treat))
2 Tara:      Eww. What are you doing.=
3 Stacy: -> =That's so: go:od,
```

In response, Stacy designs her turn not only as a positive assessment of the food item, but also as a disagreement. The use of "so:" and marked prosody on "go:od" both formulate the assessment as contrastive and work to oppose the negative stance conveyed by Tara's prior turn.

Similarly, the provable "No I didn't" occurs in the midst of a dispute between two housemates, one of whom has refused to tell a story about a past romantic encounter.

Extract 5. [Fraternity Guys]
```
1 Steve:    Tex.
2 Tex:      Steve.
3 Steve:    Why won't you tell this sto:ry.
4 Tex:      There is no sto(h)ry [to t- You were here that night.
5 Steve:                        [Obviously you came ba:ck and
6           told 'em you almost got on her.
7 Tex:   -> [No I didn't.
```

Here the provable comes in response to Steve's attribution of a past action to Tex. The unmitigated formulation of Tex's response is designed as an unequivocal challenge to this (apparently false) attribution.

The provable "<u>a</u>lways have to <u>p</u>ay for gas", which occurs in a dispute between Virginia and her mother over whether Virginia should get a raise in her allowance, formulates a recurrent and invariable account for the raise.

Extract 6. [Virginia]
```
1 Vir:    See: Mo::m (0.2) it's like this, when
2         you're my age .hh you need alota extra money
3         because you need to do things <I mean (.)
4    ->   ((swallow)) always have to pay for gas, you
5         know when Sherry an' Wen drive me around an'
6         everything.
```

Virginia, who is fourteen-years old, launches the turn in which the provable is embedded as an explanation to her mother about the monetary needs of teenagers. The turn-initial "see"-preface projects that her turn will implement a type of informing (see Kendrick, 2006) and her use of the second person pronoun "you" serves to formulate the explanation as generic and thus applicable to a class of persons, not Virginia alone. The provable itself (line 4) provides a specific case for why Virginia (or a teenager generally) would need "a lot of extra money". With "<u>a</u>lways" Virginia formulates the specific case as recurrent and invariable – as a rule – and thereby increases its suitability as an account for a raise in allowance.

The provability that "See?" orients to is highly relevant and invokeable in disputes. However, provables also occur in sequences with little evidence for misalignment between the participants. The provable "every time you take over a country you get cards", for instance, comes as an answer to a question, as one participant teaches another the rules of a computer game.

Extract 7. [SBC024]
```
1 Dan:    When do you get-- h- when do you get
2         cards though. [I don't understand that].
3 Jen: ->               [Every time you take] over
4    ->   a country you get cards.
```

Unlike the previous cases, the provable here does not reveal any indication of mis-alignment between the participants. Jen's answer is an explanation of a rule, and the invariability that she builds into the design of her explanation with "every time" serves to formulate the universality of that rule within the game.

A claim that is formulated as a recurrent or invariable rule is also as a conse-quence predictive. If an event "always" takes place or does so "every time", then it can be expected to happen again. A provable need not be an explanation of a rule in order to be predictive, however. Consider the warning in Extract (8), which comes as two young children play a game in which one repeatedly tips over a large plastic box to cover a toy the other has placed on a table. Prior to this extract, Shane has quickly removed the toy just before Tom is able to cover it with the box.

Extract 8. [ICS SK T1]
```
1 Tom:     Shane you're teasing me.
2          (2.0)
3 Adult: -> Be careful of your ha:nd too please.
```

The provable here is a warning that anticipates a possible problematic outcome in the course of action that the two children are engaged in. Within the context of the game, the warning can be heard to anticipate that one of the children's hands could get hurt as the plastic box tips over onto the table. The provable is not formulated as a claim about a recurrent or invariable state of affairs, but like such claims, it is also predictive.

Provables and the interactional projects in which they occur serve as the back-drop against which the turns, actions, or events to which "See?" responds become noticeable as evidence. I now turn to an analysis of the relationship between these turns, actions, and events – which I term priors – and the provable which they are taken to support.

5.   The relationship between the prior and the provable

In this section I continue the analysis of the five cases from the previous section to examine the relations that hold between the prior turn or action which "See?" targets and the provable for which the prior is treated as evidence. At issue here is how the prior can come to be seen as evidence and hence can serve as a resource for a claim of vindication. In order to formulate a claim of evidential vindication, the speaker of "See?" must first notice in the prior a relation to his or her own previous assertive action, such that the prior may be taken to support, prove, corroborate, etc. the validity of the provable and, in turn, the larger course of action or position to which the provable belongs. The analyses in this section explicate a number of such evidential relations.

5.1   An independent assertion corroborates the provable

As discussed above, many of the turns or actions that "See?" retrospectively targets
and treats as provables occur in disputes or disagreements between two participants. In dispute sequences such as these, a participant may find evidence for his or
her position in the talk or actions of a third party. Consider again the disagreement
between Stacy and Tara in Extract (4), given here in expanded form as Extract (9).

Extract 9. [Sorority Breakfast]

```
1 Stacy:      ((spreads peanut butter on a rice krispie treat))
2 Tara:       Eww. What are you doing.=
3 Stacy: ->   =That's so: go:od,
4 Tara:       It's so gross,
5 Tricia: ->  Oh that's so good? [Try it.]
6 Stacy:                         [OH. SEE?] ((points to Tri.))
7 Tricia:     Ye::ah.
```

As noted above, after Tara calls into question Stacy's decision to put peanut butter
on a rice krispie treat, Stacy produces a positive assessment of the food item that
disagrees with the implicit negative assessment conveyed by Tara's prior turn.
The two then reach a potential stalemate after Tara produces a second assessment
that disagrees with Stacy's (line 4). At this point, Tricia, who has yet to weigh in
on the matter, produces a positive assessment that repeats Stacy's but includes an
"oh"-preface, which Heritage (2002, p. 201) argues serves as "a declaration of epistemic independence" on the part of the speaker. In other words, Tricia builds her
assessment not only to align with Stacy's but also to claim independent knowledge
of the referent and thus independent rights to assess it (cf. Heritage & Raymond,
2005).[2] In response to Tricia's independent assessment, Stacy formulates its no-
ticeability with "oh", and with "See?" retrospectively treats the assessment as evidence in support of her own previous assessment, thereby claiming evidential
vindication.

What is likely at issue for these participants – for Stacy in particular – is not
merely the tastiness or likability of an item of food, but rather more importantly a
commitment to a course of action. Tara treats Stacy's behaviour – spreading peanut
butter on a rice krispie treat in preparation to eat it – as non-normative and thus in
need of explanation (accountable). Stacy's positive assessment is thus a resource for
the defence of a course of action that she is actively engaged in. By using Tricia's prior
talk as evidence, Stacy displays an ongoing commitment to that course of action.

---

2.   Tricia's claim of epistemic independence may also serve to challenge Tara's negative assessment. In the next component of her turn, Tricia directs Tara to "try it", thus proposing that Tara
has not tried the combination before and therefore lacks adequate grounds on which to produce
an assessment.

Unlike the previous case, in which the prior is a near-verbatim repeat of the provable, the prior in Extract (10) below (an expanded version of Extract (5)) is an alternative formulation by a third party of the 'same' action as the provable. Prior to this extract, Tex has refused to tell a story about a past romantic encounter to Steve. Here Steve makes another attempt to elicit the story from Tex.

Extract 10. [Fraternity Guys]

```
1   Steve:    Tex.
2   Tex:      Steve.
3   Steve:    Why won't you tell this sto:ry.
4   Tex:      There is no sto(h)ry [to t- You were here that night.
5   Steve:                         [Obviously you came ba:ck and
6             told 'em you almost got on her.
7   Tex:   -> [No: I didn't.
8   Steve:    [(   ) proud of it then. So [tell me now.
9   Tex:                                  [Were you here that
10            night.
11            (0.3)
12  Tex:      When I went hottubbing?
13            (.)
14  Steve:    Right.
15            (0.2)
16  Jake:  -> Rick said that you almost got on her.
17            (0.5)
18  Tex:      See, that's not Tex:.
```

At issue in this sequence is whether Tex will tell the story of what happened between him and an unnamed woman. One tack that Steve takes to elicit the telling is to report that Tex has told the story in the past (lines 5–6). If the story were tellable before, then presumably it should be tellable now. In so doing, Steve formulates what he can surmise about the events, based on his limited knowledge (Pomerantz, 1980), namely that Tex told people that he had "almost got[ten] on" the woman. In response, Tex produces an unmitigated denial: "No I didn't" (line 7).

The turn which "See?" targets (line 16) is an alternative formulation of Steve's report. It attributes the telling not to Tex, as Steve's had done, but rather to someone else. Jake designs his formulation to stand in noticeable contrast with Steve's, placing additional stress on the contrasting item "Rick". The attribution of the report to someone else not only refutes Steve's initial attribution of it to Tex (lines 5–6) but also corroborates Tex's denial (line 7). In other words, Tex uses Jake's prior turn as evidence to support his previous assertive action.

In Extracts (9) and (10), then, the priors which "See?" targets are both independent productions by third parties of the 'same' claims or assertions as the provables – that is, the priors are corroborations.

5.2 An event instantiates the provable

"See?" may also be used to mobilise attention to an evidential relation between an event in the local setting and a previous assertion of that event's occurrence (or recurrence). In such cases, "See?" treats the prior as a concrete, observable instance of the event formulated in the provable. The prior event which "See?" targets in Extract (11) (expanded from Extract 7), for example, can be understood as an observable occurrence of a recurrent event that Jen formulates in her explanation to Dan at lines 3–4.

Extract 11. [SBC024, audio only]

```
1 Dan:    When do you get- h- when do you get
2         ca:rds though. [I don't understand that].
3 Jen: ->                [Every time you take] over
4      -> a country you get cards.
5         (7.0)
6 Dan:    Ruh-roh. ((playful "uh-oh"))
7         (0.2)
8 Jen:    Attack with the twenty-two.
9         (1.6)
10 Jen:   Press twenty-two, (0.8) attack.
11        (0.6)
12 Dan:   °Wow°.
13 Jen:   °Look at that°.
14        (1.1)
15 Dan:   hhh
16     -> (7.7)
17 Jen:   OOOHHH, see look, you just got all of his cards.
18        (0.9)
19 Jen:   Press okay.
```

In this game – a computer version of the classic board game Risk – opponents battle to occupy territories on a map of the world. As Jen explains, one receives cards (which may then be used to enhance one's position in the game) after each successful battle in which one takes over an opponent's territory. After she explains this rule to Dan, she instructs him on how to mount an attack (lines 8–10), which he then apparently wins (line 17). Upon this win, the rule that Jen had previously explained to Dan would apply (within the pause at line 16). Jen responds to this event in the game first with a prosodically marked variant of "oh" that here serves not only to formulate the event as noticeable but also display her own affective reaction to the prize that Dan – who is also one of *her* opponents in the game – has just received. With "See?" Jen then treats the event as evidence that instantiates the rule that she had previously stated and, in so doing, continues the larger course of action to which that explanation belongs, namely teaching Dan how to play the game.

The formulation of a recurrent event, such as Jen's rule in Extract (11), allows a subsequent occurrence of that event to be taken up as evidence in support of the rule. Such formulations of recurrent events may thus be understood to predict or anticipate future occurrences of the event. Although assertions that include recurrent temporal references such as "every time" or "always" (cf. Extract (13) below) anticipate a subsequent occurrence, so too do other actions, such as the warning in Extract (8), given here in expanded form as Extract (12). As noted previously, the two children here are engaged in a game in which one tips over a large plastic box to cover a toy. The adult caregiver warns one of the children to watch out for his hand.

Extract 12. [ICS SK T1]

```
1 Tom:      Shane you're teasing me.
2           (2.0)
3 Adult: -> Be careful of your ha:nd too please.
4        -> (0.3)((box slips and falls flat on the table))
5 Adult:    Oop. See?
```

The event which "See?" targets is an implicit or tacit basis for warning. The adult's warning anticipates a problematic outcome in the projected trajectory of a course of action, namely that the child may hurt his hand as he tips the plastic box onto the table. Although the child's hand does not get hurt, the adult uses "See?" in reaction to the event to claim it retroactively as an instantiation of the problematic event that his warning had anticipated.

As a caregiver for young children, both the adult's warning and his subsequent claim of vindication can be understood as instructive, formulating and anticipating events that the children may not themselves notice or may not notice as instances of events of a particular type (e.g., potentially harmful behaviours). The use of "See?" in Extract (11) is similarly instructive, adducing evidence for a prior assertion as a resource to continue the speaker's instructions on the rules of the game. In both cases, then, the claim of evidential vindication that "See?" makes is done not in the service of a dispute (as was observed for Extracts 9 and 10) but as a means to notice and formulate mutually observable features of the local setting for recipients who may not notice or appreciate their import.

5.3   A prior turn supports the provable

In the context of a dispute between two participants, a third party may produce an assertive action that independently corroborates one or another position. As discussed above, "See?" may then be used in response to the third party's contribution to claim it as evidence in support of the speaker's previous assertive action. Such evidence does not always come from third parties, however. A participant in a dispute may produce a turn at talk that undermines his or her own previous assertion. Consider again the dispute between Virginia and her mother in Extract (6), repeated here as Extract (13) with an additional segment that occurs approximately five minutes after Virginia produces the turn that later becomes the provable.

Extract 13. [Virginia]

```
1   Vir:       See: Mo::m (0.2) it's like this, when
2              you're my age .hh you need alota extra money
3              because you need to do things <I mean (.)
4       ->     ((swallow)) always have to pay for gas, you
5              know when Sherry an' Wen drive me around an'
6              everything.
7              (0.5)
8   Wes:       °You need any i:ce?°
9   Mom:       I th[ink you must be keeping ga:s] in=
10  Bet:           [(                           )]
11  Mom:       =everybody's ca:rs these days.
12  Vir:       ↑No I do:n't
13  Mom:       .hh Well e- THAT IS SOMPIN ELSE that you are
14             co::nstantly coming an' asking me for two dollas
15             .hh every time I turn aroun for ga:s, an you don'
16             e:ven have a CA::R.
17             ((five minutes ommitted))
18  Vir:       MOM after dinner can um (.) .hh Beth an' I go
19             over ma- um (0.7) si- um (0.8) go just riding
20             around for a little whi:le?
21             (3.4)
22  Mom:  ->   Put ga:s in the ca:r.
23             (0.3)
24  Vir:       (n)SEE:?
25  Mom:       O:H [you're ri:ght  ] you're ri:ght.
26  Vir:           [uhh heh heh heh]
27  Vir:       mm hm hm hm hm hm hh. ( ) I mean that's not
28             even (puttin) gas in the car (with) all I was
29             gettin is five dollars a wee:k.
```

In response to Virginia's explanation of the monetary needs of teenagers and her ongoing bid for a raise, the mother challenges Virginia's claim. First, she picks up on Virginia's reference to her friends, Sherry and Wen (line 5), and expands the scope of the reference to "everybody" (line 11). This exaggerated formulation encompasses not only Virginia's friends but also countless others for whom such a payment would be inappropriate. Second, the mother treats Virginia's need for gas money itself as inappropriate by asserting that Virginia does not in fact own a car (lines 13–16). The dispute sequence continues beyond what can be seen in Extract (13), but the topic soon shifts to matters unrelated to Virginia or her allowance. Then, approximately five minutes later, Virginia asks to borrow the family car (lines 18–20). The mother responds to the request with a form of conditional granting: Virginia can borrow the car if she agrees to buy gas (line 22). At this point

Virginia could simply accept the condition (e.g., with "okay") and potentially bring her request sequence to a close. Instead, Virginia replies to her mother's condition with "See?", claiming it as evidence for her previous assertion that she "always has to pay for gas" (line 4).

The mother's prior turn is presumably noticeable to Virginia as a contradiction. Virginia's provable formulates the conditions of life as a teenager, one of which is that one "<u>a</u>lways has to <u>p</u>ay for ga<u>s</u>" (line 4). The mother challenges the validity of such a condition as part of her ongoing opposition to Virginia's bid for a raise in her allowance. In subsequently placing a condition on Virginia's request for the car – "Put ga:s in the ca:r" (line 22) – the mother provides Virginia with an observable instance of the condition that she previously claimed to exist. Moreover, the mother's condition undermines her own previous arguments. The mother challenged both the type of people that Virginia buys gas for and the assumption that Virginia would need money for gas when she does not herself own a car. But Virginia's request is presumably for use of the family's car, which, since Virginia is only 14-years-old, would be driven by her older sister, Beth. The mother directs Virginia to put gas in a car she does not own for the benefit of an immediate family member, thus undermining her previous claim that Virginia is "keeping ga:s in everybody's <u>ca</u>:rs these days" (lines 9–11). Virginia apparently notices her mother's contradiction and uses "See?" not only to call attention to it but also to use it as leverage against her mother by claiming it as evidence that supports her previous assertion and, in turn, her ongoing bid for a raise in her allowance. In response, the mother concedes to Virginia's claim with "O:H you're ri:ght you're ri:ght" (line 25).

To summarise, "See?" has been observed to target actions that 'redo' the claim or assertion in the provable on independent grounds (Extracts 9 and 10); to events in the local setting that instantiate either a statement of a recurrent event (Extract 11) or have otherwise been anticipated by a 'predictive' action (such as the warning in Extract 12); and to actions that both serve to instantiate the claim in the provable and to undermine or contradict opposition to that claim (Extract 13). What the speaker of "See?" notices in each of these priors is a mutually observable action or event that may be taken as the basis or grounds for the action previously implemented in the provable.

6.   Discussion

This chapter has examined a common yet previously undocumented linguistic practice: using "See?" in next turn to claim evidential vindication. The analysis has demonstrated that "See?" retroactively establishes a sequential relationship between an immediately prior action or event in the conversation (the prior) and a previous assertive action (the provable). With "See?" the speaker claims that the prior has an evidential relation to the provable: it corroborates, instantiates, or otherwise lends support to the previous assertive action. "See?" thus commonly (but not invariably) occurs in disputes, that is, sequences in which parties formulate and display commitments to contradictory versions of reality (see Pollner, 1987). As an appeal to evidence, "See?" grounds the previous assertive action in the objective reality of the material world, which can be seen to include the world of talk as well as action, and thereby proposes a resolution to the dispute (albeit one that affirms the speaker's version of reality). The practice demonstrates one way in which speakers use perception – and perceptual language – as a resource for action in interaction. Such actions make visible, and hence available to analysis, an association between the seemingly disparate domains of visual perception and justification, in other words, metaphor. In this section I reflect on the sequential organisation of "See?" and the fit between the practice and the action it implements.

6.1 The sequential organisation of "See?"

In an adjacency pair, the relevance of the second pair-part is conditional on the production of the first. The conditional relevance established by a first pair-part is such that the absence of a second is a 'noticeable' or 'official' event in the conversation (Schegloff, 2007). Although "See?" occurs in a specifiable sequential environment, the 'relevance' of its production is different in kind than the conditional relevance of an adjacency pair. To be sure, the environment in which "See?" occurs provides fertile ground for the claim of evidential vindication, but this environment does not create a normative obligation for its production, nor has its speaker necessarily been selected to take the next turn (Sacks et al., 1974). The prior and the provable only come to form a coherent sequence of action once the claim of evidential vindication retroactively positions them into one. The retrospective sequence that "See?" initiates thus begins from its third position. At the same time, "See?" initiates a prospective sequence in which the recipient may respond to the claim of evidential vindication (e.g., with concession, as Virginia's mother does in Extract (13)).

Retrospective sequences are common in conversation, despite the dearth of research on them. In addition to other-initiations of repair, Schegloff (2007) also mentions, but does not examine, 'noticings' and some forms of laughter as cases of retro-sequences (see also Schegloff, 2005). To this list one can add offers of assistance occasioned by troubles (Curl, 2006; Kendrick & Drew, 2016), as well as the claims of evidential vindication examined here. Retro-sequences enable speakers to use a just prior turn, action, or event as a basis for a next action, even if the prior had not made such a next action, or indeed any next action, relevant. Retro-sequence initiators retroactively invoke some feature of the prior – its problematicity, laughability, provability, etc. – and treat *it* as the basis for the initiation of the sequence. Thus the prior can relevantly become something other than what it accountably was when it first occured. A reference to a person can become a source of trouble (Extract 3) just as the conditional granting of a request (Extract 13) or the falling of a box (in Extract 12) can become a source of evidence. Retrospective sequences, though less studied, may well prove to be just as basic and ubiquitous as the prospective sequences that have been the focus of research on sequence organisation to date.

6.2   The fit between the practice and the action

Thus far the analysis of "See?" has centred on the action it implements and the sequences of action it engenders. But what is it about this linguistic form – the verb *see* produced with rising intonation – that suits its use as a claim of evidential vindication? In other words, to borrow a question from Schegloff (1996), what is the fit between the practice and the action? The answer to this question has three parts.

The first is that vision is the dominant sensory modality, providing the most reliable and veridical source of sensory experience. Evidence for the primacy of vision is abundant (see Stokes & Biggs [2014] for a view from psychology). In terms of language, the differential ineffability of the senses suggests that visual experience is more linguistically codable than the other senses (Levinson & Majid, 2014). Languages with grammatical evidentials frequently contrast direct visual observation with indirect evidence such as inference or hearsay (Aikhenvald, 2006). And the sheer frequency with which speakers across cultures use perception verbs in conversation attests to the dominance of vision (San Roque et al., 2015). Vision has also been argued to be the most objective of the senses (e.g., Sweetser, 1990) and a primary source of evidence (Wierzbicka, 2010). While two people who taste the same food may have different experiences (e.g., Extract 9), those who see the same object before them should not, lest the basic assumption of the reciprocity of perspectives be called into question (Schutz, 1962) and an account be generated to repair the breach of intersubjectivity (e.g., that one participant is colour blind or joking). A shared visual experience in co-present interaction (e.g., the event observed on the computer screen in Extract 12) thus provides a source of virtually incontrovertible evidence. To dispute it would tear at the very fabric of reality. "See?" exploits and reinforces the primacy and objectivity of visual experience, claiming that what has just occurred is directly perceptible and that the evidence for the previous assertion is obvious, objective, and hence indisputable.

The second part of the answer is that the verb *see* does not necessarily refer to visual perception. What *see* refers to depends on its use in conversation. To give but two examples, in a report of an event (e.g., "on the way home we saw the most goshawful wreck" [Sacks, 1992, p. 536]), *see* can be said to refer to the speaker's visual perception, but in a receipt of an answer to a question (e.g., "oh I see"), it cannot. With the former the speaker makes an accountable claim as to having had an experience of visual perception. With the latter no such claim is made, yet the speaker will be accountable for having heard and understood the answer. The cases of "See?" presented in this chapter involve not only possible visual percepts (e.g., the box falling on the table in Extract 12), which can be seen in a literal sense, but also audible ones (e.g., the assessment in Extract 9). Thus if one is to attribute a meaning to *see* in this practice, the verb would refer not to vision as such but rather to intellection or apperception (i.e., mental perception). This use of *see* thus provides evidence of an association between perception and cognition (Evans & Wilkins, 2000; Sweetser, 1990; see also Ibarretxe-Antuñano, this volume). Moreover, the observation that "See?" can have both visual and non-visual percepts suggests that the action of evidential vindication and the complex sequence of actions in which it occurs together constitute a possible bridging context (Evans & Wilkins, 2000). What is at stake for the participants is whether the recipient notices or perceives what has just occurred, regardless of the sensory modality used to do so, and apprehends its relevance for the previous assertion.

The third and final part of the answer concerns neither vison nor *see* but the prosodic production of the practice, namely its rising intonation. There is a persistent and pernicious myth, even among some linguists, that rising intonation is indicative of questionhood and that questions most frequently occur with rising intonation; this is not the case. The most common intonation contour for questions in English is in fact falling (Geluykens, 1988; see also Couper-Kuhlen, 2012), and rising intonation occurs not only in questions, but also non-final turn-constructional units, try-marked utterances, and solicitations of attention (Heritage, 2013). Indeed, the most frequent use of rising intonation is to indicate the incompleteness of a turn, not questionhood (Geluykens, 1988, p. 483). The rising intonation of "See?" does not express the speaker's doubt over whether the recipient can perceive or apprehend what has just occurred. It does not, in Heritage's (2013) terms, encode a K- epistemic stance. That the recipient can "see" the evidence asserted is not called into question. Instead, the rising intonation of "See?" constructs the action as an *appeal* to the recipient – to perceive what has just occurred for its relevance to the previous assertion – and solicits a response that, in one way or another, addresses the claim of evidential vindication.

In sum, then, the practice – *see* produced with rising intonation as a possibly complete turn-constructional unit – fits the action of evidential vindication because it constitutes an appeal to the recipient to perceive and apprehend what has just occurred in the interaction as objective and indisputable evidence. This prompts the recipient to search for what the prior turn, action, or event can be seen to corroborate, instantiate, or otherwise support, a search which retroactively locates the provable.

Acknowledgements

I would like to thank Gene Lerner for his advice and guidance while I was a master's student and for his substantive contributions to this work; Manny Schegloff, Jack Sidnell, and Sandy Thompson for helpful comments on an earlier draft; and Carolyn O'Meara, Lia San Roque, and Laura J. Speed for their detailed feedback and thoughtful advice. I would also like to thank Asifa Majid for inviting me to contribute to this volume.

References

Aikhenvald, A. Y. (2006). *Evidentiality*. Oxford: Oxford University Press.

Aikhenvald, A. Y., & Storch, A. (2013). Linguistic expression of perception and cognition: A typological glimpse. In A. Y. Aikhenvald, & A. Storch (Eds.), *Perception and cognition in language and culture* (pp. 1–46). Leiden: Brill. https://doi.org/10.1163/9789004210127_002

Couper-Kuhlen, E. (2012). Some truths and untruths about final intonation in conversational questions. In J. P. de Ruiter (Ed.), *Questions: Formal, functional and interactional perspectives* (pp. 123–145). Cambridge: Cambridge University Press. https://doi.org/10.1017/CBO9781139045414.009

Curl, T. S. (2006). Offers of assistance: Constraints on syntactic design. *Journal of Pragmatics*, 38(8), 1257–1280. https://doi.org/10.1016/j.pragma.2005.09.004

Edwards, D. (2000). Extreme case formulations: Softeners, investment, and doing nonliteral. *Research on Language and Social Interaction*, 33(4), 347–373. https://doi.org/10.1207/S15327973RLSI3304_01

Evans, N., & Wilkins, D. (2000). In the mind's ear: The semantic extensions of perception verbs in Australian languages. *Language* 76(3): 546–592. https://doi.org/10.2307/417135

Geluykens, R. (1988). On the myth of rising intonation in polar questions. *Journal of Pragmatics*, 12(4), 467–485. https://doi.org/10.1016/0378-2166(88)90006-9

Hepburn, A., & Bolden, G. B. (2017). *Transcribing for social research*. London: SAGE Publications Ltd. https://doi.org/10.4135/9781473920460

Heritage, J. (2002). Oh-prefaced responses to assessments: A method of modifying agreement/ disagreement. In C. E Ford, B. A. Fox, & S. A Thompson (Eds.), *The language of turn and sequence* (pp. 1–28). Oxford: Oxford University Press.

Heritage, J. (2013). Action formation and its epistemic (and other) backgrounds. *Discourse Studies*, 15(5), 551–578. https://doi.org/10.1177/1461445613501449

Heritage, J., & Raymond, G. (2005). The terms of agreement: Indexing epistemic authority and subordination in talk-in-interaction. *Social Psychology Quarterly*, 15–38. https://doi.org/10.1177/019027250506800103

Hoey, E. M., & Kendrick, K. H. (2017). Conversation analysis. In P. Hagoort & A. M. B. De Groot (Eds.), *Research Methods in Psycholinguistics and the Neurobiology of Language*. Chichester: Wiley-Blackwell.

Kendrick, K. H. (2006). Linguistic Form and Social Action: The Use of "See" in Conversational Interaction (Master's thesis). University of California, Santa Barbara, Department of Linguistics.

Kendrick, K. H., & Drew, P. (2016). Recruitment: Offers, requests, and the organization of assistance in interaction. *Research on Language and Social Interaction*, 49(1), 1–19. https://doi.org/10.1080/08351813.2016.1126436

Lakoff, G., & Johnson, M. (1980). *Metaphors we live by*. Chicago: Chicago University Press.

Levinson, S. C. (2013). Action formation and ascription. In J. Sidnell & T. Stivers (Eds.), *The handbook of conversation analysis* (pp. 101–130). Malden: Blackwell Publishing Ltd.

Levinson, S. C., & Majid, A. (2014). Differential ineffability and the senses. *Mind & Language*, 29(4), 407–427. https://doi.org/10.1111/mila.12057

Pollner, M. (1987). *Mundane reason: Reality in everyday life and sociological discourse*. Cambridge: Cambridge University Press

Pomerantz, A. (1980). Telling my side: "Limited access" as a "fishing" device. *Sociological Inquiry*, 50(3), 186–198. https://doi.org/10.1111/j.1475-682X.1980.tb00020.x

Pomerantz, A. (1984). Giving a source or basis: the practice in conversation of telling "how I know". *Journal of Pragmatics*, 8, 607–625. https://doi.org/10.1016/0378-2166(84)90002-X

Pomerantz, A. (1986). Extreme case formulations: A way of legitimizing claims. *Human studies*, 9(2), 219–229. https://doi.org/10.1007/BF00148128

Pomerantz, A. (1989). Giving evidence as a conversational practice. In D. T. Helm, W. T. Anderson, A. J. Meehan & A. W. Rawls (Eds.), *The interactional order: New directions in the study of social order* (pp. 103–115). New York, NY: Irvington Publishers.

Sacks, H., Schegloff, E. A., & Jefferson, G. (1974). A simplest systematics for the organization of turn-taking for conversation. *Language*, 50(4), 696–735. https://doi.org/10.1353/lan.1974.0010

Sacks, H. (1992). *Lectures on conversation*. (G. Jefferson, Ed.) (Vol. 1). Cambridge: Blackwell Publishers.

San Roque, L., Kendrick, K. H., Norcliffe, E., Brown, P., Defina, R., Dingemanse, M., Dirksmeyer, T., Enfield, N. J., Floyd, S., Hammond, J., Rossi, G., Tufvesson, S., Van Putten, S., & Majid, A. (2015). Vision verbs dominate in conversation across cultures, but the ranking of non-visual verbs varies. *Cognitive Linguistics*, 26(1), 31–60. https://doi.org/10.1515/cog-2014-0089

San Roque, L., Kendrick, K. H., Norcliffe, E., & Majid, A. (2018). Universal meaning extensions of perception verbs are grounded in interaction. *Cognitive Linguistics*, 29(3), 371–406. https://doi.org/10.1515/cog-2017-0034

Schegloff, E. A. (1996). Confirming allusions: Toward an empirical account of action. *American Journal of Sociology*, 102(1), 161–216. https://doi.org/10.1086/230911

Schegloff, E. A. (2005). On complainability. *Social Problems*, 52(4), 449–476. https://doi.org/10.1525/sp.2005.52.4.449

Schegloff, E. A. (2007). *Sequence organization in interaction: A primer in conversation analysis*. Cambridge/New York: Cambridge University Press. https://doi.org/10.1017/CBO9780511791208

Schutz, A. (1962). Common-sense and scientific interpretation of human action. In M. Natanson (Ed.), *Collected Papers I* (pp. 3–47). Springer Netherlands. https://doi.org/10.1007/978-94-010-2851-6_1

Sidnell, J., & Stivers, T. (Eds.). (2013). *The handbook of conversation analysis*. Malden: Blackwell Publishing Ltd.

Sidnell, J. (2007). 'Look'-prefaced turns in first and second position: launching, interceding and redirecting action. *Discourse Studies*, 9(3), 387–408. https://doi.org/10.1177/1461445607076204

Stokes, D., & Biggs, S. (2014). The dominance of the visual. In D. Stokes, M. Matthen, & S. Biggs (Eds.), *Perception and its modalities*. Oxford Scholarship Online.
https://doi.org/10.1093/acprof:oso/9780199832798.003.0015

Sweetser, E. (1990). *From etymology to pragmatics: Metaphorical and cultural aspects of semantic structure*. Cambridge: Cambridge University Press.
https://doi.org/10.1017/CBO9780511620904

Vázquez Carranza, A. (2014). Sequential markers in Mexican Spanish talk: A conversation-analytic study (Ph.D. thesis). University of Essex.

Vázquez Carranza, A. (2015). Análisis de oye como marcador secuencial y de acción en la conversación. *Estudios de Lingüística Aplicada*, 61, 73–103.

Viberg, Å. (1983). The verbs of perception: A typological study. *Linguistics*, 21, 123–162.
https://doi.org/10.1515/ling.1983.21.1.123

Wierzbicka, Anna. (2010). *Experience, evidence, and sense: The hidden cultural legacy of English*. Oxford: Oxford University Press. https://doi.org/10.1093/acprof:oso/9780195368000.001.0001

CHAPTER 14

Sensory perception metaphors in sign languages

Ulrike Zeshan and Nick Palfreyman
University of Central Lancashire

In this chapter, we explore perceptual metaphors across a convenience sample of data from 24 sign languages. To do this, the chapter uses the framework of Sign Language Typology, the systematic comparative study of grammatical/ semantic domains across sign languages (Zeshan & Palfreyman, 2017). Sign languages differ from spoken languages due to iconic mapping, that is, the tendency for signs of perception to be articulated at or near the sense organs. This is the basis for two types of signs: those with double-stage metaphors have literal and metaphorical lexical meanings, while those with single-stage metaphors lack literal lexical meanings of perception and instead rely on sublexical iconicity. We cover cross-linguistic patterns of metaphorical extensions of meaning in these signs, and the grammaticalisation of a class of prefixes that are associated with sensory perception.

Keywords: sign languages, Sign Language Typology, sublexical iconicity, sense prefixes, grammaticalisation, re-metaphorisation

1. Introduction

The aim of this chapter is to compile and analyse information from sign languages on metaphors that have sensory perception as their source domain. This is of interest for two reasons. Firstly, the discussions in this chapter are situated in the framework of Sign Language Typology. In Sign Language Typology, a grammatical, functional or semantic domain is compared across a diverse range of sign languages (Zeshan & Palfreyman, 2017), and over the past decade there have been several major studies, focusing on clause types (interrogative and negatives, Zeshan, 2006), possession and existence (Zeshan & Perniss, 2008), and the semantic fields of colour, kinship and quantification (Zeshan & Sagara, 2016). The initial observations made in this chapter constitute a first step towards more extensive typological studies on perception metaphors across sign languages.

https://doi.org/10.1075/celcr.19.14zes

Secondly, sensory perception itself is of intrinsic interest for the purpose of comparison between signed and spoken language modalities. As sign languages, in most cases, have emerged within communities of deaf people,[1] they are based on language users whose sense perception is radically different from users of spoken languages. This raises some intriguing questions. For instance, how do deaf sign language users talk about visual and auditory perception, and how are relevant expressions recruited for metaphors? Are metaphors based on aural perception excluded from sign languages, and conversely – given how deaf people are often referred to as visual people – is there a preference for visual perception as the source of metaphors in sign languages? Moreover, what is the role of iconically motivated sign-meaning correspondence – the fact that many signs "look like what they mean" – that is so pervasive across sign languages?

We address such issues in this chapter, and begin with how signers talk about literal sensory perception (Section 2), before moving to a summary of perceptual metaphors in sign languages (Section 3). We then examine the properties of metaphors across sign languages that draw upon sensory perception (Section 4). By incorporating evidence from a variety of sign languages around the world, it is our hope that this chapter will stimulate more in-depth research in the future.

2. Talking about sensory perception in sign languages

Before embarking on a discussion of perceptual metaphors in sign languages, it is useful to consider some basic facts about how signs are structured, and the way in which sensory perception is expressed in sign languages.

At the word level, signs in sign languages consist of so-called "parameters", that is, the sublexical formational elements that are equivalent to phonemes in spoken languages. However, unlike spoken languages, parameters are largely simultaneous with each other rather than sequential (cf. Brentari, 1998; Wilbur, 2000; Sandler et al., 2011). The main parameters recognised in sign language linguistics are the handshape, place of articulation (PoA), movement, and hand orientation; sometimes, it is necessary to consider an additional parameter, namely non-manual aspects of signs such as eyebrow movement, eye gaze, and mouth patterns.

---

1.   A sub-type of sign languages have arisen from mixed communities of deaf and hearing people, where the community – typically a small-scale rural community – has long-standing hereditary deafness resulting in an unusually high proportion of deaf people (see Zeshan & De Vos, 2012, for an overview). These communities have sometimes been referred to as "shared signing communities" (Kisch, 2008), and their sign languages are co-created and co-used by deaf and hearing people together.

The example in Figure 1 shows a sign meaning 'to see' in many different sign languages. The sign has a handshape with two extended fingers, a hand orientation with the palm facing the signer and the finger tips pointing upwards, a straight movement away from the signer, a PoA in front of the signer's body at head height, and no specific non-manual formational features.

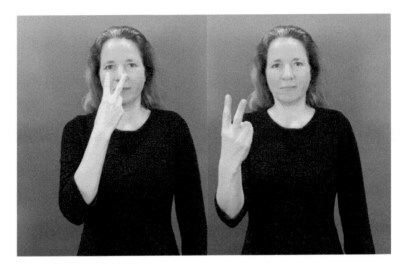

Figure 1. The sign SEE[2]

At the same time, this sign illustrates another general principle that operates across sign languages. In sign languages, the semantics of sensory perception is visible in the form of the sign in an overwhelming number of cases. We call this the Transparency Principle of Sensory Perception in sign languages. In the case of perception signs, this principle means that the PoA of a perception sign is linked to its meaning. The mapping is as follows (see Table 1).

Signs can involve contact with the body part (e.g., touching the tongue), or a proximal and/or distal movement (e.g., towards or away from the ear). The only meaning where there is more variation across sign languages is with signs for 'feeling' (in the haptic sense). It is common for signs with this meaning to be articulated on the chest, but other places of articulation are possible, such as the arm in

---

2. Customarily, the manual forms of sign languages are represented by glosses, in capital letters, that correspond to the meaning of the sign. Researchers now routinely use 'ID-glosses' for a given sign language, whereby each form is assigned a unique gloss (Johnston 2008). In this article, we discuss many sign languages, and sometimes refer to forms that have a similar meaning in different sign languages; our glosses reflect only forms and meanings, and should not be understood as ID-glosses.

Table 1. The meaning and place of articulation for signs

Meaning of the sign	Place of articulation (PoA)
seeing	eye(s) or near the eye(s)
hearing	ear(s) or near the ear(s)
smelling	nose or near the nose
tasting	tongue, lips, or near the mouth
feeling	torso or upper limb(s)

Turkish Sign Language. A double meaning of both haptic perception and emotion, as in English 'feel', is common across sign languages. Signs for sensory perception often have a handshape with an extended index finger (or two extended fingers in the case of 'seeing' to represent the two eyes), but other handshapes are possible.

Signs for sensory perception are distinct from signs for sense organs, the latter typically being indicated by (index finger) pointing, touching, or holding, which is also used for indicating other body parts that are not sense organs. Although iconically motivated, perception signs abstract away from the biological basis of human perception. For instance, although biologically visual perception is caused by light entering the eyes, the common sign in Figure 1 has a movement away from the eyes. Takashima (this volume) argues for Japanese Sign Language that this indicates an active reaching for visual information rather than passive visual experiencing. In Kata Kolok, a rural sign language from Bali, to talk about a hearing person the hand is placed next to the ear and the fingers flicked open with the fingertips pointing away from the ear. By contrast, in Indian Sign Language, a similar sign with the same meaning has the fingertips pointing towards the ear. However, it is not necessary or possible to interpret each formational aspect of a sign individually, and besides the PoA, other parameters in perception signs may well be arbitrary.

The iconic basis for many sensory perception signs involves metonymy, in that a sense organ is conventionally recognised as the 'seat' of a particular sensory phenomenon, and can stand symbolically for that sensory modality. This interpretation is strengthened by the observation that the same kind of metonymy also applies to other semantic "families" of signs, for example signs of cognition (with the head/temple as the 'seat' of cognition), or signs that are related to time concepts, with the wrist as the place of articulation (Zeshan, 2003).

The fact that sensory perception signs "look like what they mean" makes sign languages radically different from spoken languages in this domain, and this aspect will be important for the discussion in Section 4.

3. Data on perceptual metaphors in sign languages

To date, no systematic surveys have been undertaken on perceptual metaphors in sign languages. Therefore, this chapter relies on a collection of several types of information. Firstly, informal interviews have been conducted with several native signers who have high levels of metalinguistic understanding – often deaf professional linguists or advanced students of linguistics. We have an extensive network of deaf colleagues from around the world, and we used convenience sampling to generate data. Our interviewees are deaf users of Chinese Sign Language (ZGS), Indian Sign Language (ISL), Indonesian Sign Language (BISINDO), South Korean Sign Language (SKSL), Turkish Sign Language (TİD) and British Sign Language (BSL).

It is worth providing some background about these languages. While they are not known to be related, the very notion of "sign language families" is problematic because it is not clear what constitutes a "genetic relationship" between sign languages (Palfreyman, Sagara & Zeshan, 2015). As a rule, little is known about the origins of these sign languages, as all of them emerged prior to the 1960s in a time when their linguistic nature was overlooked by, for example, philologists. Only relatively recently has it been possible to capture sign languages using technology, and even for the best documented sign languages, such as ASL (American Sign Language), comparatively few recordings are available.

There is evidence to suggest that what is now known as BSL (British Sign Language) may have been a conventional language as early as the second half of the seventeenth century (Cormier, 2007), which might suggest a time-depth for BSL of something like 350 years. On the other hand, BISINDO (Indonesian Sign Language) has a likely time-depth of just over 60 years (Palfreyman, 2017). It is likely that signed languages are considerably younger than spoken ones, and the implications of this are not well understood. However, language change for sign languages has been documented at the phonological level (Frishberg, 1975), and in grammaticalisation processes (Pfau & Steinbach, 2011), while synchronic variation also occurs (Schembri & Johnston, 2012).

Returning to the interviews, we explained the notion of perceptual metaphors, and gave examples known to us from other sign languages. Informants were then prompted to come up with examples from their own native sign language. We discussed these examples to make sure the meanings were clear, and that they were genuine instances of perceptual metaphors. We then made notes on each example. The interviews took place on a one-to-one basis, except for informants from South Korea and China, who were interviewed together. Some of the interviews were held in person, while others were conducted via Skype.

A second source of data was from signs publicly available on the website www. spreadthesign.com, which originated from an EU-funded project, and therefore mainly incorporates European sign languages. However, some non-European sign languages are also included, for example, from Brazil, Japan, and India. This site is organised on the basis of word-to-sign matches, and therefore it is mainly a word list. The site is searchable on the basis of written words that can be typed into the search window. The search output is in the form of clickable tabs of the target countries' flags, and videos of the signs open from the tabs.

It should be noted that this site was not constructed for the purposes of research, and therefore has some limitations. For instance, complexities of meaning may not be represented. This is particularly important given that this chapter deals with subtle semantic distinctions. Because of these issues, signs taken from this website have been used cautiously and only to provide additional evidence for phenomena already identified elsewhere, in order to get a better idea of their distribution across sign languages. Moreover, arguments where subtle semantics would be important are not based on signs taken from this website.

Finally, some published data have also contributed to this chapter. As mentioned in the introduction, publications in this area are rather limited, but where available and important for the arguments being made, we have relied on such sources. In particular, this applies to the data from Israeli Sign Language, discussed in Section 4.2. Dictionaries and wordlists on sign languages, though available for a substantial number of languages, have not been consulted because of time constraints. However, we did rely on our own respective personal knowledge of BSL, BISINDO, ISL (Indian Sign Language), TİD (Turkish Sign Language), and International Sign. For reference, a list of all sign languages mentioned in this article, with associated acronyms, is presented in Table 2.

Table 2. Sign language acronyms

ASL	American Sign Language	LIBRAS	Brazilian Sign Language
BISINDO	Indonesian Sign Language	LIS	Italian Sign Language
BSL	British Sign Language	LSE	Spanish Sign Language
CzSL	Czech Republic Sign Language	LSF	French Sign Language
DGS	German Sign Language	LSL	Latvian Sign Language
ESL	Estonian Sign Language	NS	Japanese Sign Language
GSL	Greek Sign Language	ÖGS	Austrian Sign Language
IS	International Sign	PJM	Polish Sign Language
ISL	Indian Sign Language	SKSL	South Korean Sign Language
IsraelSL	Israeli Sign Language	STS	Swedish Sign Language
ÍTM	Icelandic Sign Language	TİD	Turkish Sign Language
LGP	Portuguese Sign Language	ZGS	Chinese Sign Language

In line with the exploratory nature of this research, the scope of our search domain was kept quite broad and, therefore, examples discussed in this chapter go well beyond simple perception verbs. Rather, the domain of perception is considered more comprehensively, and data include metaphorical mappings from a wide range of concepts related to sensory perception. Identifying examples was partly guided by consultants' intuitions and partly facilitated by the Transparency Principle, in that it was often helpful to try and think of other signs using the targeted PoAs.

4.   Properties of sensory perception metaphors in sign languages

In this section, the properties of signs that are used in perceptual metaphors are considered in two parts. In Section 4.1 we examine two kinds of perceptual metaphor that occur across sign languages. We then turn to the formational properties of some signs in this domain in Section 4.2. As the latter Section is framed in terms of grammaticalisation theory, it also includes semantic aspects along with discussion of phonological and morphological properties.

4.1   The semantics of sensory perception metaphors in sign languages

Signs that express metaphors derived from sensory perception can be grouped into two types, depending on the kind of semantic shift involved. The two types of semantic shift are referred to as "single-stage metaphor" and "double-stage metaphor" here, and discussed in reverse order below. Neither of them occurs in spoken languages in quite the same way.

(i)   Double-stage metaphors

Double-stage sensory perception metaphors are partially similar to the type of metaphorical semantic shift familiar from spoken languages. That is, one and the same sign has both a literal meaning and a metaphorical meaning, and both meanings coexist in the current state of the language. Metaphorical mappings such as those between hearing and obeying, seeing and understanding, etc., are found across spoken languages (Sweetser, 1990), and similar examples from sign languages are shown in Figures 2–6. However, spoken languages do not involve any sublexical iconicity, whereas in sign languages the semantics involves an initial sublexical level of iconicity (the PoA), and then an additional semantic shift from lexical to metaphorical meaning (hence the term "double-stage metaphor").

Figure 2. BLIND / NOT-WANT-TO-KNOW-ABOUT (ZGS, SKSL)

The sign in Figure 2 is identical in the sign languages ZGS (northern China) and SKSL.[3] The sign means both 'blind' in the literal sense, and 'not want to know about (something)' in the metaphorical sense. The metaphorical sense is based on the association between seeing and knowing that is well-documented across spoken languages (e.g., Lakoff & Johnson, 2003). However, there is an added, volitional sense – that is, if someone who is not blind actively puts one's hand over one's eyes, it signals that one does not want to see what is there, and by metaphorical extension means that one does not want to know about something. While the form of the sign is the same for both literal and metaphorical meanings, this volitional element is clearly in evidence when the sign refers to someone who is *not* blind, and who therefore does not 'want' to see/know.

Figure 3 shows a sign from Indian Sign Language that means both 'a wink/ winking at someone' or 'a secret understanding/tip' (for both meanings, the finger tips touch each other briefly, as in a pinching motion). Here the metaphorical meaning is based on the fact that, in the surrounding gestural culture, winking at someone often means that one has a secret understanding with them. Interestingly, in its metaphorical meaning, the sign is formationally fixed and cannot be modified. By contrast, in its literal meaning, the sign can be modified if the signer wants to express the exact way in which the wink was executed. For example, there could be an additional head movement or body posture, and the duration of the wink could be shorter or longer. When used in a metaphorical sense, these details are not relevant as the meaning abstracts away from the physical eye movement, and

---

3.   Sign language varieties in China have a major split between northern and southern varieties (Fischer & Gong, 2010). The Korean consultant is from South Korea. It is not known how different the sign language varieties in North Korea are from those in the South.

Figure 3. WINK / SECRET-UNDERSTANDING (ISL)

therefore such modifications cannot be added to the sign. However, it is still possible and common to have the formationally identical sign expressing both meanings.

The sign in Figure 4 is from Turkish Sign Language, and there is a subtle difference in form that distinguishes between the literal and the metaphorical meanings. With a straight outward movement, the sign means 'look' but it is also used in the sense of 'let's see about that', in which case the hand movement is shorter and repeated, as if tapping the cheek just below the eye. This sign is used to express uncertainty about what may happen and implies being non-committal about an upcoming decision or action. For example, when discussing whether and how to put forward an official proposal, a person using this sign may express that they are

Figure 4. LOOK (with straight movement) and LET'S-SEE-ABOUT-THAT (with repeated tap) (TİD)

unable to decide now and have to 'wait and see' how the situation develops first, and what additional information becomes available. When used in this sense, this sign is often accompanied with a Turkish mouthing *bakalım*, which also means 'let us see'. In its literal sense, the sign may have no mouthing, or may have the mouthing *bak*, which is the verb stem as well as the singular imperative of the Turkish verb 'to look'. A formally similar sign occurs in British Sign Language, with the meaning 'let's wait and see'.

In BISINDO, the sign EYE-BROKEN (Figure 5) has the literal meaning of 'broken eye', for example as a result of being hit, but is used metaphorically to explain or excuse lack of visual attention. For example, one might use this sign if one drives over a pothole in the road on one's motorbike, because one is careless and not looking at the road. Another appropriate context for the sign would be turning up for an engagement at the wrong time because one misread the invitation. The sign comprises a point to the eye followed by a sign meaning broken (the latter sign, BROKEN, is usually articulated with two hands, but in this case one hand is dropped, and the PoA of the sign is moved closer to the eye, to facilitate assimilation with the indexical sign).

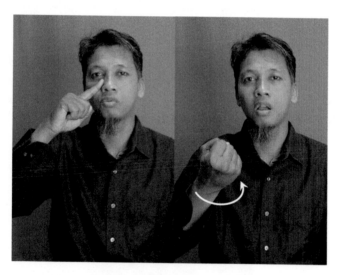

Figure 5. BROKEN-EYE / CARELESS (BISINDO)

Perhaps unsurprisingly, sensory perception metaphors that have to do with 'seeing' are particularly common across sign languages (see Section 4.3 for a discussion of this point). However, many other types of sensory perception metaphors can also be found. The sign in Figure 6a, also from Turkish Sign Language, means 'pepper' and is based on the idea of pepper being something that tastes spicy. If the sign is articulated more vigorously, with a larger movement and an additional tongue wiggle, as in Figure 6b, this means 'to talk angrily'. This is an interesting case because

Figure 6a. PEPPER (TİD)

Figure 6b. TALK-ANGRILY (TİD)

the semantic logic proceeds in three steps, that is, from 'spicy taste' to 'pepper' to 'talking angrily'.

(ii) Single-stage metaphors

Single-stage perception metaphors found in sign languages are unlike perception metaphors in spoken languages. To illustrate the difference between the two types, let us consider the signs in ISL and BISINDO that mean 'not want to know about (something)', in exactly the same way as the Chinese and Korean signs mentioned above, and that uses the same form as in Figure 2. The difference between ISL and BISINDO on the one hand, and CSL and SKSL on the other, is that in ISL and BISINDO this sign has only one sense, and does not mean 'blind'. In fact, there are different and formationally unrelated signs for 'blind' in ISL (Figure 7a) and BISINDO (Figure 7b).

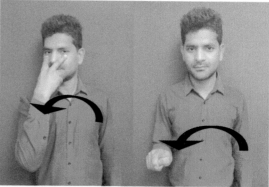

Figure 7a. NOT-WANT-TO-KNOW and BLIND (ISL)

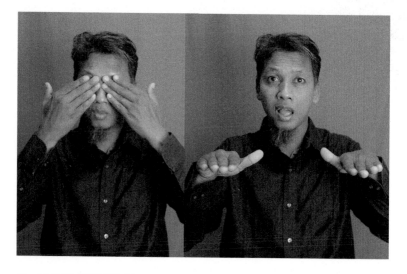

Figure 7b. BLIND (BISINDO)

The Indian and Indonesian signs glossed NOT-WANT-TO-KNOW involve a perceptual metaphor of the type SEEING IS KNOWING but their lexical semantics do not include any literal meaning of sense perception at all. In other words, the metaphor is based on the PoA mapping that associates the signs with visual perception, but the only lexical meaning is in the domain of cognition. The lexical meaning of sense perception from which a metaphorical extension would normally be derived is absent in this type of sign. The following examples (discussed in relation to Figures 8–11) all have these same properties.

The sign in Figure 8 from Indonesian Sign Language also includes a volitional element but in this case the sign involves pretending to take the ear off and throwing it away. This sign would be used, for example, if someone is gossiping, and one wishes to indicate that one does not want to know the gossip. Although this sign is used by deaf signers, who perceive gossip that is relayed gesturally rather than audibly, it draws upon the notion of "deactivating" the ear, rather than the eyes.

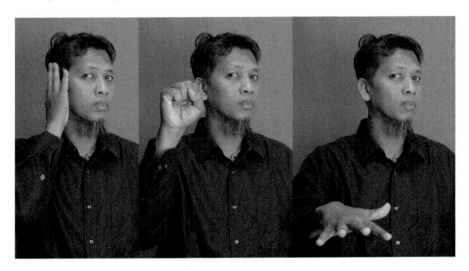

Figure 8. NOT-WANT-TO-KNOW-ABOUT (BISINDO)

A similar motivation is behind the signs meaning 'news/information' in ISL, CSL and Polish Sign Language (PJM) which all involve a listening gesture with the hand cupped behind the ear (Figure 9 is from ISL).

Figure 9. NEWS (ISL)

The two-handed South Korean sign NO-INFORMATION (Figure 10) has an up-and-down hand wave next to both ears.

In Brazilian Sign Language (LIBRAS), GREEDY (Figure 11) is related to 'making big eyes' for something. 'Big eyes' or 'eyes opening up widely' is also often associated with SURPRISE across sign languages. However, these signs do not literally mean "to open the eyes widely" but are used in the metaphorical sense only.

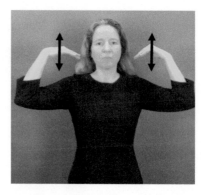

Figure 10. NO-INFORMATION (SKSL)

Figure 11. GREEDY (LIBRAS)

It is remarkable that we find signs with meanings that have to do with taking in information, and which are based on the auditory sense. Since deaf people do not actually take in information by hearing, this is initially somewhat surprising, and one might argue that the expected conceptual metaphor for information-related meanings in sign languages should be based on the visual sense. In fact, this does happen, for example with signs for '(visual) learning' or '(visual) information intake' that are directed towards the eyes. Despite the fact that signers perceive visually rather than aurally, a metaphorical extension from hearing to knowing, as in Figures 9 and 10, is also regularly attested across sign languages. Moreover, other metaphorical extensions are also based on spoken communication, as we shall see below.

The reason these signs have their semantic motivation in a perceptual metaphor even though they do not have any literal meaning of sense perception has to do with the Transparency Principle mentioned in Section 2. The sense perception is evoked by the fact that the PoA of the signs is located at the sense organs. The PoA is itself a sublexical component in each of these signs. The fact that sublexical components can have meaning due to their iconicity, without having morphemic status, is characteristic of sign languages in general, as discussed in more detail in Zeshan (2003). Equivalents in spoken languages are sound symbolic components of words such as *spl* in *splash, splatter* etc., where a sound in a word mimics the sound of the referent.

While this is relatively rare in spoken languages, it is pervasive in sign languages and has led some sign language linguists to posit that the phoneme-morpheme distinction does not hold for sign languages (e.g., Cuxac, 2000, 2004). However, Zeshan (2003) argues that it is appropriate to maintain the phoneme-morpheme distinction for sign languages, but to allow for meaningful sublexical units in signs which are due to their visual iconicity. The same principle is at work in the examples in Figures 8–11.

Importantly, this implies that whether or not a single-sense sign involves metaphorical transfer can be a matter of interpretation, as it depends on whether one feels that sense perception is invoked by virtue of the PoA or not. For example, the BSL sign SEEM is articulated from the nose, with a flat hand with fingertips pointing upwards moving away from the face. It is a matter of interpretation whether this is regarded as a metaphorical extension from smell to intuition, or whether one regards the PoA as an arbitrary sublexical component of the sign.

The differences between the two types of signs discussed in this section are schematically represented in Figure 12. Both types involve meaningful sublexical components based on the iconic mapping between the PoA and the associated sense of perception. In the first type, the initial step is from sublexical iconicity (SLI) to a sign whose initial lexical semantics (LS1) falls within the source domain semantics of sensory perception in the actual, literal sense. The second step is the transfer from the source domain to the secondary lexical semantics (LS2) of the target domain, which involves metaphorical mappings such as from seeing to knowing, hearing to knowing, smelling to intuition. The label SLI → LS1 → LS2 reflects the fact that two separate lexical semantics are involved. By contrast, in the second type, the conceptual transfer proceeds directly from sublexical iconicity to the target domain semantics. There is no lexical meaning of sensory perception involved at all, which is why we use the label SLI → LS2, reflecting the fact the literal lexical meaning (LS1) is absent.

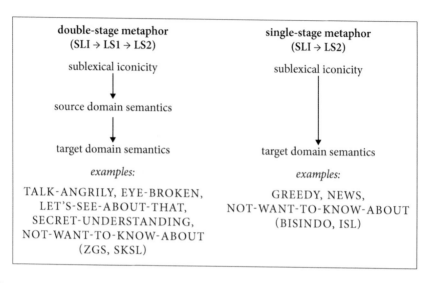

Figure 12. Schematic difference between two types of signs based on sensory perception metaphors

4.2   Grammaticalisation of sense prefixes

In this section, we turn to morphologically complex signs in sensory perception metaphors. The detailed evidence discussed here comes from Israeli Sign Language (IsraelSL), where the phenomenon of so-called "sense prefixes" has been discussed in several publications (Aronoff, Meir, Padden & Sandler, 2005; Aronoff, Meir & Sandler, 2005). As we shall see, similar forms also occur in other sign languages, although the distribution of these forms is not yet known.

Figure 13 illustrates what is meant by a sense prefix. The prefix consists of a short contact on or near one of the sense organs with an extended index finger. In the example, this involves the "eye" prefix, followed by the sign SHARP. In combination, the sign EYE+SHARP means 'to discern visually'. The initial index finger form is a prefix because it only occurs in combination with the following sign as the stem, to which it is attached. In the case of EYE+SHARP, this does not involve a perception metaphor but retains the literal meaning of visual perception.

When looking at additional signs in IsraelSL that have the same characteristics, it becomes clear that there is an organised group of signs with sense prefixes which have been affected by processes of grammaticalisation. Grammaticalisation theory (e.g., Hopper & Traugott, 1993; Heine & Kuteva, 2002) systematically accounts for processes by which grammatical markers develop, and the most typical instances trace the development of bound affixes. These processes can be found in many unrelated languages, often operating in similar ways (see Heine & Kuteva,

Figure 13. EYE+SHARP "to discern visually" in IsraelSL
(based on Aronoff, Meir, & Sandler, 2005)

2002), and therefore one can identify grammaticalisation pathways that are valid cross-linguistically (e.g., Heine, 1997, on the domain of possession).

In the case of IsraelSL sense prefixes, we can identify the same sub-processes in the development of affixation that have been found across many spoken languages, and indeed signed languages (cf., Steinbach & Pfau, 2007; Pfau & Steinbach, 2011). One of these sub-processes affects the combinatorial meaning of the constituents in a grammaticalised morphologically complex form. To illustrate this, Figure 14 shows several other members of the family of signs with sense prefixes in IsraelSL. The arrows between signs indicate semantic shifts away from the literal sensory perception meaning.[4]

As mentioned above, the first sign EYE+SHARP shows no transfer away from the source domain yet. The sign NOSE+SUSPECT meaning 'to suspect intuitively', involves the familiar metaphorical transfer from the source domain of smelling to the target domain of intuition, which was discussed in Section 4.1. The literal meaning of 'smell' is no longer present in this sign.

A different semantic shift is seen in the next sign, EYE+CATCH meaning 'to catch red-handed'. Originally, this sign would have meant catching someone on the basis of visual evidence. However, judging from the translation, it appears that the meaning has generalised and now involves catching someone on the basis of any source of information, not only visual evidence. Semantically, this patterns with the shift from *experiencing via a specific sense* to *experiencing in general* discussed in Section 4.3.

---

4. The pictures of signs and their glosses and translations are based on Aronoff, Meir & Sandler (2005) but their arrangement in the figure and the labelled arrows are our own.

Transfer, as in the case of NOSE+SUSPECT, and generalisation, as in EYE+ CATCH, are two different ways in which the meaning of signs can shift away from the original semantics of sense perception.

Finally, the sign MOUTH+[BASE] meaning 'cunning' is a complete semantic abstraction, and therefore even further removed from the original lexical meaning. Not only is the meaning unrelated to the PoA, whether in terms of speaking, tasting, or any other action or property of the mouth, but the second sign also has no meaning on its own. It only occurs in combination with sense prefixes, which is why it is glossed [BASE], as its meaning independent of this particular combination cannot be established.

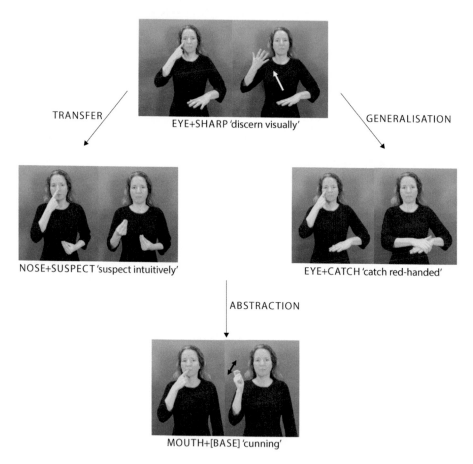

Figure 14. Semantic shifts in IsraelSL signs with sense prefixes
(photographs based on Aronoff, Meir & Sandler, 2005)

The loss of specific semantic content in forms that participate in grammaticalisation processes is referred to by theoreticians as desemanticisation (Heine & Narrog, 2010). Typically, the element in question assumes a more general, abstract meaning, and loses its original literal meaning. In this case, the meaning of the sense prefix becomes dislodged from physical sensory perception, becoming more abstract and non-embodied (as in 'smell' to 'intuition' in NOSE+SUSPECT), or becoming generalised (e.g. from 'visual evidence' to 'any kind of evidence' in EYE+CATCH).

In addition to semantic changes, a range of other changes typically associated with grammaticalisation processes are also in evidence in signs that have sense prefixes. These characteristics are phonological, morphological, and grammatical. At the phonological level, it is evident that the sense prefixes, consisting merely of brief initial contact with the index finger, are phonologically reduced in comparison with signs that are free forms. Morphologically, the initial index finger tap becomes a bound morpheme, and the resulting sign is morphologically complex. Moreover, the sense prefixes constitute a closed class of five items, each with their own distributional restrictions in terms of which stems they can combine with. In other words, we see a paradigm formation, and this is typical of grammaticalisation processes. The five prefixes are EYE, EAR, NOSE, MOUTH, and HEAD, the last one participating in the same paradigms with the same characteristics even though its meaning is related to cognition and does not involve sensory perception.

Sometimes the same stem can co-occur with several different sense prefixes. This may result in different meanings of the morphologically complex signs, while in other cases, there is no clear difference in meaning. For example, the last sign in Figure 15 MOUTH+[BASE] 'cunning' has another counterpart with the same stem, but a different prefix HEAD+[BASE], meaning 'smart'. On the other hand, NOSE+SUSPECT and EYE+SUSPECT seem to have no obvious difference in meaning.

Forms looking very much like the IsraelSL sense prefixes are also found in other sign languages. For example, the sign CHECK has an EYE prefix in ASL (USA/Canada), LIBRAS (Brazil), TİD (Turkey), LGP (Portugal), BSL (Britain), and ISL (India), and a NOSE prefix in CzSL (Czech Republic), ÍTM (Iceland), and PJM (Poland). It would clearly be worthwhile to undertake a systematic survey of these signs across a larger number of sign languages. At the moment, no such data are available.

4.3   Cross-linguistic patterns in perception metaphors in sign languages

Based on the data observed within this study, there are several recurring patterns with respect to semantic correspondences that one can observe. In addition to the above-mentioned *seeing to knowing* and *hearing to knowing* transfers – which are also common across spoken languages – several other patterns are repeatedly attested in the data under consideration here. The metaphorical extension from smelling (source domain) to intuition (target domain), mentioned earlier in this section, is attested in several sign languages, and fits well with similar correspondences in spoken languages. These examples belong to the single-stage metaphor type (SLI → LS2). In LSF (French Sign Language), LGP (Portuguese Sign Language) and PJM (Polish Sign Language), the sign SUSPECT has a PoA at the nose. Similarly, tapping the tip of the nose with the index finger several times means 'to have a feeling about something' in Indian Sign Language. All of these are monomorphemic signs. The BSL sign SEEM discussed above also potentially belongs in this group. By contrast, in Israeli Sign Language, the index finger contact with the tip of the nose is a prefix, as discussed in Section 4.2.

Another common semantic extension goes from spoken communication to general communication. These signs are articulated at or near the mouth, often with a movement away from the mouth to evoke the concept of a message moving from a sender to an addressee. Although these signs do not fall under the category of sensory perception, they are included here because of similarities in the underlying logic.

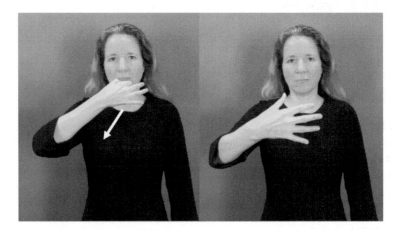

Figure 15. NEWS/INFORM (TİD, GSL)

In TİD and Greek Sign Language (GSL), for example, the sign NEWS/INFORM moves outward from the mouth (see Figure 15). In SKSL, the sign GOSSIP is also articulated near the mouth. Just as in the case discussed above where news/information is iconically linked to hearing (Figure 8), in these cases, signs with a meaning of communication use the mouth as PoA, despite the fact that deaf signers generally do not communicate vocally, but convey information via the visual-gestural channel. In many sign languages, signs meaning 'telling', 'talking' and the like, have movements that start at the mouth. Therefore, there is a semantic abstraction from communication in spoken language to communication in general.

Another similar semantic extension that falls in the domain of sensory perception is the abstraction from 'experiencing via a specific sense' to 'experiencing in general'. For example, the BSL sign CHECK begins with brief contact just under the eye (see Figure 16), suggesting visual checking. However, CHECK is also used in contexts where other senses are involved, not just in the case of visual checking. For example, in order to say that one needs to taste whether the soup has enough salt in, or feel whether the bathwater is the right temperature, the same sign CHECK can be used.

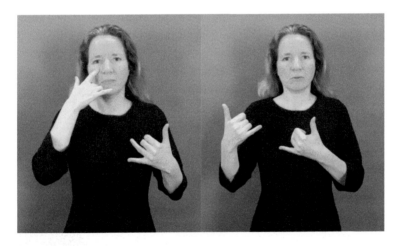

Figure 16. CHECK (BSL)

A sign meaning 'uncomfortable' in BISINDO is another semantic extension, although in this case the previous specific sense was taste rather than sight. The sign comprises an indexical point to the mouth, followed by a negative suffix based on a negative handshape. It meant 'bad taste', and has extended to refer to 'something that feels bad'. A sign in BSL deploys a similar metaphor, which can best be translated using the English idiom 'leave a bad taste in the mouth'.

Figure 17. TASTE-BAD / UNCOMFORTABLE (BISINDO)

From the limited data available for this chapter, there seems to be some preliminary evidence showing that visual perception is prioritised over the other senses in the domain of perception metaphors. Table 3 shows some cross-linguistic examples of the same meaning expressed in different sign languages. The table highlights which of the senses is involved in the metaphor, but conflates the various semantic and morphological subtypes discussed in Sections 4.1 and 4.2. The aim is merely to identify which of the senses is involved in the metaphor, irrespective of its formal realisation in individual languages.

Although Table 3 is not in any way a systematic compilation, there is a suggestive pattern in that the visual sense metaphor is the only one that appears with each meaning. While each meaning covers more than one sense metaphor, visual perception as the source domain is the only channel that is always an option for generating a sensory metaphor. Further research is needed in order to ascertain whether this is a robust pattern, or whether the predominance of visual perception metaphors in these examples is a coincidence. This pattern accords well with the frequent characterisation of sign communities as prioritising the visual channel, and deaf people, in particular those born deaf, as "visual people", that is, making use of visual perception both for linguistic and non-linguistic purposes to a greater extent than hearing people (MacSweeney et al., 2002; Bottari et al., 2011; see also the discussion in Takashima, this volume). However, as visual perception is also a very common source domain for metaphors in spoken languages, it is not yet clear whether this pattern is related to the visual modality of sign languages.

At the same time, for some of the examples above, in some instances the physical realities of visual perception and communication among deaf people are actively

Table 3. Senses involved in metaphorical extensions across sign languages

target meaning	relevant formational aspect	eye / seeing	ear / hearing	nose / smelling	mouth/ throat/ tasting	instantiated in sign languages
IGNORE/ DISREGARD	Outward movement away from sense organ			X		ASL, LIBRAS, ÖGS
		X				NS
			X			BSL, ISL, PJM
CHECK	Sense prefix	X				ASL, BSL, ISL, IsraelSL, LIBRAS, PGL, TİD
				X		CzSL, İTM, IsraelSL, PJM
			X			IsraelSL
	PoA at sense organ	X				ZGS, SKSL
CURIOUS	PoA at sense organ			X		CzSL, DGS, ESL, İTM, LGP, LIS, LSE, LSF, LSL, ÖGS, STS
		X				LIBRAS, NS
GREED / GREEDY	PoA at sense organ				X	ISL, İTM
		X				LIBRAS, TİD
SUGGEST	Sense prefix	X				IsraelSL
					X	IsraelSL

disregarded in the corresponding perceptual metaphor (see the signs meaning 'news', 'information', 'telling', 'talking', etc). In this regard, the sign in Figure 18 from Indian Sign Language is worth consideration. Like its counterpart in Figure 9, this sign means 'news, information' but with an explicit focus on the visual channel, as the PoA is on the eye and not on the ear. This is an example of re-metaphorisation, where the auditory perception metaphor is replaced with the visual perception metaphor. This sign is a recent innovation and is used by younger signers in India. Takashima (this volume) reports a similar example from Japanese Sign Language, where a sign meaning 'go in one ear and out the other' in the sense of 'receive information but not retain it' has been changed by younger signers: instead of articulating the sign at the ears, in line with the idiom also found in spoken Japanese, the sign is articulated at the eyes, so as to say 'go in one eye and out the other'.

While Table 3 deals with seeing, hearing, smelling and tasting, we have said next to nothing in this chapter about the fifth sense, touch. There is evidence of a

Figure 18. '(Visual) news, information' (ISL)

Figure 19. SENSITIVE (BSL)

small number of signs that are linked with touch, including SENSITIVE in BSL, which is articulated by delicately making contact with the middle finger of one hand on the back of the other (Figure 19). Here, a sign that indicates sensitive skin has come to refer to the quality of sensitivity in general (for example, a person who is sensitive to bright light, or sensitive in a psychological sense). The relative lack of touch-based metaphors compared to other senses can perhaps partly be explained by the absence of a single PoA associated with touch. As mentioned in Section 1, the sense of 'touching/feeling' can be associated with a number of different PoAs.

5. Conclusion

This chapter has provided ample evidence that the topic of perceptual metaphor is a rich ground for research and discoveries in sign languages. Certainly, a more in-depth systematic review across a larger number of sign languages would be very welcome.

The data show some parallels with spoken languages, such as the well-known HEARING TO KNOWING and SEEING TO KNOWING metaphorical transfers from a sensory source domain to a more abstract, cognitive target domain (e.g., Sweetser, 1990; Evans & Wilkins, 1998; Vanhove, 2008). At the same time, it is very clear that by virtue of their modality, sign languages behave very differently from spoken languages in some respects. This is mainly due to the Transparency Principle, i.e., the fact that unlike words in spoken languages, signs in sign languages "look like what they mean". As has been argued in this chapter, this has radical consequences for the use of metaphors that are based on sensory perception. In particular, sign languages have two types of metaphors for sensory perception, called single-stage and double-stage metaphors here, both of which are different from what we find in spoken languages due to the role of sublexical iconicity in these signs. The parallels and modality-related differences are typical of other research findings in Sign Language Typology (Zeshan et al., 2013; Palfreyman, Sagara & Zeshan, 2015; Zeshan & Palfreyman, 2017).

Finally, it is striking to observe the relative absence of perception metaphors in sign languages that have cognition as their target domain. In our data, the examples with signs meaning 'news, information' and the like are rare and certainly not nearly as frequent as equivalent metaphors in many spoken languages. This may be due to the fact that across sign languages, there is a strong tendency for the semantics of cognition to use a separate metaphor, namely the head as PoA. For the entire semantic domain of cognition, including notions such as thinking, knowing, remembering, and forgetting, as well as qualities such as smart, stupid, etc., the head (in particular the temple) is a widely preferred PoA. Some sign languages, in particular in East Asia, use the torso instead, which is based on a different metaphor. The existence of ready metaphors for cognition across sign languages seems to act as a barrier to employing sensory perception metaphors in this domain.

Acknowledgements

We are very grateful to the deaf sign language users who have generously shared information about their sign languages with us: Hasan Dikyuva, Kang-Suk Byun, Qian Sun, Sibaji Panda, Muhammad Isnaini. We would like to thank Deepu Manavalamamuni and Jagdishkumar Choudhari for help with some of the pictures.

References

Aronoff, M., Meir, I., & Sandler, W. (2005). The paradox of sign language morphology. *Language*, 81(2), 301–344. https://doi.org/10.1353/lan.2005.0043

Aronoff, M., Meir, I., Padden, C., & Sandler, W. (2005). Morphological universals and the sign language type. In G. Booij & J. van Marle (Eds.), *Yearbook of Morphology 2004* (pp. 19–39). The Netherlands: Springer. https://doi.org/10.1007/1-4020-2900-4_2

Bottari, D., Caclin, A., Giard, M-H., & Pavani, F. (2011). Changes in early cortical visual processing predict enhanced reactivity in deaf individuals. *PLoS ONE*, 6(9), 1–10. https://doi.org/10.1371/journal.pone.0025607

Brentari, D. (1998). *A prosodic model of sign language phonology*. Cambridge, MA: MIT Press.

Cormier, K. (2007). Do all pronouns point? Indexicality of first person plural pronouns in BSL and ASL. In P. Perniss, R. Pfau & M. Steinbach (Eds.), *Visible variation: Comparative studies on sign language structure* (pp. 63–101). Berlin: De Gruyter.

Cuxac, C. (2000). *La langue des Signes Française (LSF), Les voies de l'iconicité*. Paris: Ophrys.

Cuxac, C. (2004). Phonétique de la LSF: une formalisation problématique. *Silexicales, Actes du Colloque, Linguistique de la LSF: recherches actuelles*, 93–113.

Evans, N., & Wilkins, D. (1998). *The knowing ear. An Australian test of universal claims about the semantic structure of sensory verbs and their extension into the domain of cognition*. Köln: Institut für Sprachwissenschaft, Universität zu Köln.

Fischer, S. D., & Gong, Q. (2010). Variation in East Asian sign language structures. In D. Brentari (Ed.), *Sign languages* (pp. 499–518). Cambridge: Cambridge University Press. https://doi.org/10.1017/CBO9780511712203.023

Frishberg, N. (1975). Arbitrariness and iconicity: Historical change in American Sign Language. *Language*, 51, 696–719. https://doi.org/10.2307/412894

Heine, B. (1997). *Possession: Cognitive sources, forces, and grammaticalization*. Cambridge: Cambridge University Press. https://doi.org/10.1017/CBO9780511581908

Heine, B., & Kuteva, T. (2002). *World lexicon of grammaticalization*. Cambridge: Cambridge University Press. https://doi.org/10.1017/CBO9780511613463

Heine, B. & Narrog, H. (2010). Grammaticalization and linguistic analysis. In: Heine, B. & Narrog, H. (Eds.) *The Oxford handbook of linguistic analysis*. Oxford: Oxford University Press, 407–428.

Hopper, P. J., & Traugott, E. C. (1993). *Grammaticalization*. Cambridge: Cambridge University Press. https://doi.org/10.1017/CBO9781139165525

Johnston, T. (2008). Corpus linguistics and signed languages: no lemmata, no corpus. Proceedings of the 3rd Workshop on the Representation and Processing of Sign Languages: Construction and Exploitation of Sign Language Corpora. Marrakech, Morocco, June 2018.

Kisch, S. (2008). "Deaf discourse": The social construction of deafness in a Bedouin community. *Medical Anthropology*, 27(3), 283–313. https://doi.org/10.1080/01459740802222807

Lakoff, G., & Johnson, M. (2003). *Metaphors we live by*. Chicago: University of Chicago Press.

MacSweeney, M., Woll, B., Campbell, R., McGuire, P. K., & David, A. S. (2002). Neural systems underlying British Sign Language and audio-visual English processing in native users. *Brain*, 125(7), 1583–1593. https://doi.org/10.1093/brain/awf153

Palfreyman, N. (2017). *Variation in Indonesian Sign Language: A typological and sociolinguistic analysis*. Lancaster: Ishara Press and Berlin: De Gruyter Mouton.

Palfreyman, N., Sagara, K., & U. Zeshan (2015). Methods in carrying out language typological research. In E. Orfanidou, B. Woll, & G. Morgan (Eds.), *Research methods in sign language studies* (pp. 173–192). Chichester: Wiley Blackwell.

Pfau, R., & Steinbach, M. (2011). Grammaticalization in sign languages. In H. Narrog, & B. Heine (Eds.), *The Oxford handbook of grammaticalization* (pp. 681–693). Oxford: Oxford University Press.

Sandler, W., Aronoff, M., Meir, I., & Padden, C. A. (2011). The gradual emergence of phonological form in a new language. *Natural Language and Linguistic Theory*, 29(2), 503–543. https://doi.org/10.1007/s11049-011-9128-2

Schembri, A., & Johnston, T. (2012). Sociolinguistic aspects of variation and change. In R. Pfau, M. Steinbach, & B. Woll (Eds.), *Sign language: An international handbook*, (pp. 788–816). Berlin: De Gruyter. https://doi.org/10.1515/9783110261325.788

Steinbach, M., & Pfau, R. (2007). Grammaticalization of auxiliaries in sign languages. In P. Perniss, R. Pfau, & M. Steinbach (Eds.), *Visible variation: Comparative studies on sign language structure* (pp. 303–339). Berlin: Mouton De Gruyter.

Sweetser, E. E. (1990). *From etymology to pragmatics. Metaphorical and cultural aspects of semantic structure.* Cambridge: Cambridge University Press. https://doi.org/10.1017/CBO9780511620904

Vanhove, M. (2008). Semantic associations between sensory modalities, prehension and mental perceptions. In M. Vanhove (Ed.), *From polysemy to semantic change: Towards a typology of lexical semantic associations* (pp. 341–370). Amsterdam: John Benjamins. https://doi.org/10.1075/slcs.106.17van

Wilbur, R. B. (2000). Phonological and prosodic layering of nonmanuals in American Sign Language. In K. Emmorey & H. Lane (Eds.), *The signs of language revisited: Festschrift for Ursula Bellugi and Edward Klima* (pp. 213–244). Mahwah, NJ: Lawrence Erlbaum.

Zeshan, U. (2003). Towards a notion of 'word' in sign languages. In R. M. Dixon, & A. Y. Aikhenvald (Eds.), *Word: A cross-linguistic typology* (pp. 153–179). Cambridge: Cambridge University Press.

Zeshan, U. (2006). *Interrogative and negative constructions in sign languages.* Sign Language Typology Series No. 1. Nijmegen: Ishara Press. https://doi.org/10.26530/OAPEN_453832

Zeshan, U. & Perniss, P. (2008). *Possessive and existential constructions in sign languages.* Sign Language Typology Series No. 2. Nijmegen: Ishara Press.

Zeshan, U. & Palfreyman, N. (2017). Sign language typology. In A. Y. Aikhenvald, & R. M. W. Dixon (Eds.), *The Cambridge handbook of linguistic typology* (pp. 178–216). Cambridge: Cambridge University Press.

Zeshan, U., & Sagara, K. (Eds.). (2016). *Semantic Fields in Sign Languages: Colour, Kinship and Quantification.* Sign Language Typology Series No. 6. Berlin: De Gruyter and Lancaster: Ishara Press. https://doi.org/10.1515/9781501503429

Zeshan, U. & De Vos, C. (2012). *Sign languages in village communities: Anthropological and linguistic insights.* Berlin/New York: De Gruyter Mouton & Lancaster: Ishara Press.

Zeshan U., Escobedo Delgado, C.E., Dikyuva, H., Panda, S. & De Vos, C. (2013). Cardinal numerals in village sign languages: Approaching cross-modal typology, *Linguistic Typology* 17(3): 357–396.

CHAPTER 15

Metaphors of perception in Japanese Sign Language

Yufuko Takashima

Japan Society for the Promotion of Science & Tokyo Gakugei University

Perception metaphors have been examined by analysing the polysemy of perception verbs in spoken languages. This chapter explores instantiations of metaphors of perception in Japanese Sign Language (JSL). Here I propose that the
locations of articulation of signs be considered meaningful units and analyse
signs articulated on or near to the signer's eyes, ears, and nose in JSL. There are
some potentially polysemous signs that illustrate meaning extensions from vision
to intellection, where signs articulated on the perceptual organs are understood
through metaphor. These conceptual metaphors in JSL are compared to the polysemy of perception expressions in the dominant spoken language, Japanese.

Keywords: perception verbs, sign languages, Japanese Sign Language, conceptual
metaphor, polysemy, iconicity, Deaf culture

1. Introduction

According to Conceptual Metaphor Theory, the omnipresence of conceptual metaphor observed in languages is based on our cognitive system (Lakoff, 1993a), and
conceptual metaphors can be observed in the linguistic system of a sign language
as well as in a spoken language. In this chapter, I explore perception metaphors in
Japanese Sign Language (JSL) by examining the locations of articulation as meaningful units. I expect that conceptual metaphors of perception are found by examining the signs articulated on the eyes, ears, nose, and mouth. After identifying
metaphors relevant to each sensory modality, I discuss the influence of Deaf culture
on sign language by comparing these metaphors with perception metaphors of the
dominant spoken language, Japanese.

Several studies have been conducted on conceptual metaphors as they appear
in the location and movement of articulation in American Sign Language (ASL)
and Catalan Sign Language (LSC) (Jarque, 2005; Taub, 2001; P. Wilcox, 2004). These
studies claim that both iconic and metaphoric mappings lead to the construction of

https://doi.org/10.1075/celcr.19.15tak

signs. Concerning the poverty of polysemy of some signs, Meir (2010) proposed the double mapping constraint (DMC) that states an iconic sign cannot be extended to an abstract meaning based on a conceptual metaphor when the conceptual structure in the abstract domain does not correspond with the structure of the iconic form. DMC may also explain the poverty of extended meanings in the realm of basic perception verbs. Here we are not concerned with the particular details of DMC because previous studies suggest that the location of articulation by itself is not iconic enough to restrict double mapping. Nevertheless, studies have indicated that the locations of articulations of signs have meanings based on iconicity and metaphoric extension (Cates et al., 2013; P. Wilcox, 2004). Yet, there are no previous studies outside this volume that explore if and how the perception metaphors observed in spoken languages manifest themselves in sign languages (cf. Zeshan & Palfreyman, this volume).

1.1 Conceptual metaphors of perception

In Conceptual Metaphor Theory, metaphorical mapping is defined as a conceptual mapping from a more concrete source domain to a more abstract target domain (Lakoff & Johnson 1980, among others). Lakoff noted, "Metaphor allows us to understand a relatively abstract or inherently unstructured subject matter in terms of a more concrete, or at least a more highly structured subject matter" (1993a, p. 244–245).

Previous studies suggest the domain of perception can be both the source and target domain of metaphor. The focus here is on the former type of metaphor: perception as the source domain. For example, visual perception terms can describe cognitive and intellectual activities in the conceptual metaphor UNDERSTANDING IS SEEING (based on a conceptual mapping from perception to cognition) in linguistic expressions such as "I see what you mean." (Lakoff, 1993b; Sweetser, 1990).

It is also worth considering the view that source domains in metaphor tend to be concrete and intersubjective (Dancygier & Sweetser, 2014; Lakoff, 1993a). Taking this view into consideration, the degree of possibility to be a source domain is potentially similar in visual, auditory, and olfactory sensory modalities (in hearing communities), given that multiple people can take part in the perception event at the same time. Taste and touch are different from the other three modalities (vision, audition, and olfaction) with respect to the degree of intersubjectivity requiring personal physical/visible contact with stimuli. To simplify, I limit my discussion to vision, audition, and olfaction here, though there is a debate as to whether olfaction is a proximal or distal sensory modality (for further discussion, see Speed & Majid, 2017).

Additionally, metaphorical mapping is based on culture-specific behaviour and construal of our interaction with the environment (Kövecses, 2011). Regarding culture, there are at least two aspects that we should consider: deaf people are usually surrounded by hearing people, as well as engaged with specific aspects of Deaf identity. When examining the cultural basis of signs, one must take into account that the "signed languages of deaf communities are not based on spoken languages, but they may, in fact, be significantly affected by the language of the surrounding community" (Johnston & Schembri, 2007, p. 13). On the other hand, Deaf signing people in Japan consider themselves a linguistic minority who share JSL and Deaf culture. They recognise the fact that deaf people are individuals who do not hear, but they do not consider the lack of hearing a disability. Deaf culture is grounded in the fact that the majority of the sign language users are Deaf people who are not able to hear or are hard of hearing. It is possible then that some culture-specific behaviour of Deaf people could play a role in metaphors of audition in JSL. I explore this possibility by comparing audition metaphors in JSL with those in spoken Japanese. Deaf people may also prefer to consider themselves as "visual people" (Lane, Pillard, & Hedberg, 2011). However, even though this conceptualisation could be relevant it is hard to interpret since vision verbs have been shown to be more frequently talked about in conversation than other sensory verbs in a comparative study of 13 spoken languages (San Roque et al., 2015).

1.2 Iconic and metaphorical mapping in sign languages

Iconic and metaphorical double mapping found in sign languages (Jarque, 2005; Taub, 2001) occur in different domains. Iconic mapping is based on a relationship between perceptual images of the world-out-there and phonology (Taub, 2001; S. Wilcox, 2004). For example, the sign meaning 'cat' in ASL resembles whiskers of a cat, and 'cat' in JSL resembles a cat's behaviour of licking a paw. These are conventionalised lexical items in each language based on a specific part of the cat's appearance or behaviour. Metaphorical mapping, in contrast, is defined as a cross-domain mapping. In sign language, we observe double mapping. For example, Taub (2001) analysed communication verbs in ASL, such as I-INFORM-YOU, and showed that the sign is articulated from the forehead and indicates sending an object away from the signer, based on the conceptual metaphor COMMUNICATION IS SENDING. This transfer is (1) iconically mapped because the form of the sign resembles actual physical transfer, and (2) metaphorically mapped because the sign does not indicate physical transfer, but transfer of information. Accordingly, we can analyse the movement and location of articulation of signs, such that parts of the form belong to the source domain of a conceptual metaphor.

1.3   Sign language phonology and location of articulation

Sign language phonology consists of handshape, location, and movement of articulation. Each of these parameters has been described as an arbitrary building block from the structuralist viewpoint (see Sandler & Lillo-Martin, 2006, Chapter 8 for a review; Stokoe, 1980). On the other hand, some researchers have argued that each parameter of articulation is meaningful (Cates, et al., 2013; Pietrandrea, 2002).

When one can see a correspondence between the meaning and form of a sign, one can say that they are iconically related. It seems harder to determine how much the location of articulation is related to abstract meanings. Take a set of signs articulated on the wrist in JSL as an example. Consider their meanings: 'skill', 'practice', 'acquire', 'be good at', 'be bad at', and 'time'. In this list of meanings, 'time' appears to have a clear motivation: a wrist watch. The remaining cases reveal a meaning cluster related to 'skill', but the motivation for this conceptual metaphor is not clear. One could argue that one of the signs just happened to be conventionalised on that location, and then similar signs were motivated by the first one. It is important to note, however, that in spoken Japanese there is a set of expressions that are based on the conceptual metaphor SKILL IS LOCATED ON ONE'S ARM. So, arguably, the JSL examples are calqued from the surrounding spoken language.

P. Wilcox (2000; 2004) and S. Wilcox and P. Wilcox (2013) state that ASL has lexical items related to the mind that are articulated on the temple and around the head. In addition to that, idiosyncratic, newly created expressions related to memory and thought are also articulated around the head. These studies provide evidence that the location of articulation not only has an iconic meaning (e.g., mouth is the location of tasting), but are also construed as a source domain of conceptual metaphor on which the sign is based (e.g,. mouth is the location of the sign for 'favourite' based on SOMEONE'S PREFERENCE (FAVOUR) IS SOMEONE'S TASTE). What seems to be lacking is an investigation of a set of signs based on different related locations of articulation in order to identify their motivation. Therefore, it is worth examining the signs articulated around the three perceptual organs to examine possible metaphorical mappings.

2. Data and methodology

2.1 Language profiles

2.1.1 *The language profile of JSL*

Japanese Sign Language (JSL, also termed *Nihon-shuwa* or NS) is a natural sign language that is used by Deaf people in Japan. The language community mainly consists of graduates from roughly 100 deaf schools. The signing population of JSL is considered to be approximately 60,000 when counting the number of graduates from deaf schools (Ichida, 2010). Since the 1990s, young Deaf people in Japan learned about Deaf activism in the United States, and consequently identified themselves as a linguistic and cultural minority, calling themselves *rousha*, following the concept of capital D "Deaf" in the United States (Kimura & Ichida, 1995; Padden & Humphries, 1988). They recognise that the system of their language is different from spoken Japanese.

Other members of this language community are children of Deaf signing adults and second language learners. There are some congenital deaf, late deaf, and hard of hearing people who learn JSL later in life who never attend deaf schools, or attend deaf schools where the teachers and students do not use sign language. Some of them also identify themselves as members of the Deaf community. Some other deaf people do not agree with the imported concept of "Deaf", regardless of whether they use JSL or signed communication similar to JSL (Kimura & Ichida, 1995; for further discussion, see Nakamura 2006). There are also hearing learners who work as interpreters or communicate with deaf people. Some learners can only use signed Japanese based on the grammar of spoken Japanese (Ichida 2010).

Although the language has tremendous regional variation, the origin of modern JSL can be traced back to 1878 when the first deaf school was established, after which teachers and students spread the language to other deaf schools established across the country over the course of a decade. It is not clear if there was contact between the people in deaf schools and local, small deaf communities before the advent of deaf schools. With respect to history, under the Japanese occupation, educators introduced JSL to Korea and Taiwan. Therefore, Korean Sign Language and Taiwan Sign Language are sister languages of JSL.

Since the core of the language has emerged and been maintained mostly by the education system, even though educators had banned the use of sign language at schools previously (during the 1930s–1990s), JSL is categorised as an urban sign language. In fact, students at the deaf schools kept using sign language in their residential school lives even though it was banned in classrooms. Today, most deaf schools have introduced a kind of signed Japanese in order to teach spoken Japanese.

There has been little pressure to standardise JSL in education or broadcast media. For the purposes of this study, however, it is necessary to choose one regional variety to find coherent metaphorical extensions. As a result, this study is based on the regional variety of JSL used in Tokyo.

2.1.2   *The language profile of Spoken Japanese*

Spoken Japanese is used as a first language by around 130 million people in Japan, almost the same number as the country's total population. Although there are dialectal variations in the isolated island country, most people under the age of 70 can read, write, listen, and speak in so-called standard Japanese. Japan can be considered a monolingual country if you ignore the minority languages: the Ryukyuan languages, Ainu, dialects, and sign languages. Every speaker of a minority language needs to learn spoken Japanese when they go to elementary school.

Spoken Japanese is physically isolated from other languages, and there are no known related languages other than the Ryukyuan languages. Japanese people usually learn English as their second language at junior high school, from the age of 12, all the way through to higher education. Even though most speakers have studied English, the Japanese language is thought to not be considerably affected by English (except for the growing number of borrowed words).

2.2   Data collection

2.2.1   *Collection of JSL signs*

The first step involved locating signs articulated around the eyes, ears, and nose in the largest dictionary of JSL edited by the Japan Federation of the Deaf (Nihon-Shuwa-Kenkyuujo, 2011). As is often the case in any deaf community, an edited dictionary is not a sufficient resource for learning a sign language since there is considerable variation between signers (Lucas, 2003). This dictionary contains illustrations of each sign, but the location of articulation is often not clear. To find examples of real usage, I checked the relevant lexical items listed in the dictionary with one native Deaf signer and one Deaf signer who had learned sign language as a child at a residential school for the deaf. They added and removed some of the items, when the location of the sign was not related to the perceptual organs, according to the signer's intuitive judgment. In addition, other items were removed if the signer was not familiar with them.

Based on this procedure, it appears that the judgement of the locations of articulations is subjective. For example, some signs are located next to the body, but the Deaf signers confirm that the signs are related to the ear because they are directed to the ear. Some signs were not articulated in front of the eyes but under the eye (on the cheek, to be precise). The cheek was sometimes judged to be a distinct location of articulation. Therefore, the location of articulation is not something that can be objectively observed by non-signers, but appears to be subjectively construed by signers.

By examining these signs, I identified simple perception verbs for the visual, auditory, and olfactory modalities. I then analysed the use of these basic perception verbs with language consultants by eliciting in JSL possible conceptual metaphors found in spoken Japanese and other languages. I also examined other signs, with meanings such as mental perception, knowing, understanding, and cognition. I then also identified synonyms, related words, and idioms. If I could not find similar lexical items in JSL and spoken languages, I explored possible motivations for the signs I did find. The signs which could not be interpreted as influenced by spoken Japanese conceptual metaphors, were considered as candidates for having their basis in Deaf culture.

2.2.2 *Conceptual metaphors in spoken Japanese*

Spoken Japanese has been well described by linguists for over two hundred years, and many cognitive linguists have studied conceptual metaphors in Japanese (e.g., Kusumi, 2007; Nabeshima, 2011: Seto, 1995; Yamanashi, 1988). I mainly make use of data from my previous studies on Japanese perception expressions (Takashima, 2013) to use as the basis for comparison with JSL. In this study, conceptual metaphors are found by analysing polysemy of basic perception verbs, their compound verbs, and idioms related to perceptual organs: eyes, ears, and nose.

3. Vision verbs and signs articulated around the eyes

3.1 Basic vision verbs

I will first examine several types of basic visual perception verbs meaning 'see' that literally express visual perception. I will explore their iconic forms (based on the act of "seeing") and their meanings.[1]

---

1. JSL signs have conventional labels in spoken Japanese. Deaf people sometimes add the label in mouthing when articulating the sign. In some cases, they add several labels to one sign in mouthing to distinguish meanings. The meaning of a spoken Japanese word corresponding to a sign is similar to the meaning of the sign. Notice that the meaning of the label is not necessarily the same as the meaning of the sign (cf. Penner, 2013).

3.1.1   *SEE as movement of the eyeball and line of eye gaze*

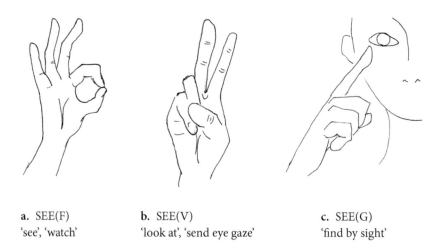

a. SEE(F)	b. SEE(V)	c. SEE(G)
'see', 'watch'	'look at', 'send eye gaze'	'find by sight'

Figure 1. Variations of SEE

JSL has three types of 'see' verbs, all labelled *miru* (a transitive verb meaning 'see' in spoken Japanese): SEE(F) with an F handshape in front of the signer's eye (Figure 1a); SEE(V) with a V handshape moving from the signer's eye to a perceived object (Figure 1b); and SEE(G) with a G handshape and an abrupt movement from the signer's eye to a perceived object.

SEE(F) is articulated using the F handshape, making a round shape with the index finger and thumb, and is located in front of the signer's eye on the dominant hand side (Figure 1a). This form represents the shape of the eyeball as one can easily guess; and the Deaf consultants agreed with this interpretation.

SEE(V) accounts for the eye gaze with the index and middle fingers directed towards the object at which the signer is looking. The meaning is similar to 'look at' and 'glance at' in English, although spoken Japanese does not have different words to express the difference between 'see' and 'look at'.

SEE(G) is articulated via the index finger moving toward the object with an abrupt movement. Whereas SEE(V) can be articulated without moving the hand from the eyes towards the object but merely by directing the fingertips towards the object, SEE(G) requires an abrupt motion that expresses the punctual aspect of SEE(G), namely to 'find by sight'.

I maintain that these signs are iconically motivated by the image of visual attention and the location and shape of the eyeballs. Even though it is debatable whether eye gaze can be expressed as lines from the eyes towards the perceived object, the interpretation is intuitive both for hearing and Deaf Japanese people.

3.1.2 Transfield mapping from vision

I also examined how vision verbs are semantically extended, in particular, focusing on transfield meaning extensions from visual perception to cognition, as this has been an extension documented in many languages (Sweetser, 1990). Meaning extensions of vision verbs were examined with Deaf consultants by translating the known uses of basic vision verbs from spoken Japanese to JSL.

In contrast to what has been documented in many languages, the three basic vision verbs are not extended to cognition meanings – although they can be modified and acquire a cognition meaning, a point discussed further below. There were, however, metonymic extensions of these verbs. For example, both SEE(F) and SEE(V) can express 'to keep an eye on'. If one is asked to look after something (such as luggage), one should keep an eye on it; should one suspect that others may steal the luggage, one should hold on to it. While *miru* 'see' in spoken Japanese has the metonymic extension of both 'to keep an eye on something' and 'take care of someone', the basic vision verbs in JSL lack the latter meaning extension.

In summary, the three vision verbs in JSL do not have transfield extended meanings, without modification.

3.1.3 Modification

The above-mentioned vision verbs are iconic because the forms of the signs show a similar relationship to the way humans see using their eyes. I now turn to the modification of basic vision verbs.

While SEE(F) is articulated statically in front of the eye, this sign has three modified variants with different movements. First, when a signer moves the F handshape from the location of the eye to his or her side and returns it abruptly, the sign means 'peep at'. The sign can thus be modified to express a manner of seeing, while still remaining in the vision domain. Second, the sign SEE-ONESELF using the F handshape articulated by moving both hands from the eyes to the chest while drawing a downward arc (Figure 2) means to 'see oneself' and 'think about oneself'. The former meaning is still in the domain of vision, but the latter is in the domain of cognition. Third, JSL has the modified SEE(F) meaning SEARCH in which movement is circular on the vertical plane parallel to the signer in front of the eye. This sign can be used in the domain of not only vision and space, but also in an abstract conceptual domain of intellection, such as 'search for information'.

There are also compound verbs formed with the vision verb *miru* in spoken Japanese corresponding to the modified signs in JSL: *nusumi-miru* 'steal-see: peep at'; *kaeri-miru* 'return-see: think about (see) oneself'; and *mi-tuskeru* 'see-put: search to find out'. *Nusumi-miru* 'steal-see: peep at' remains in the domain of vision like the modified sign 'peep at' in JSL.

Figure 2. SEE-ONESELF

Comparing *kaeri-miru* 'return-see' in spoken Japanese and SEE-ONESELF in JSL, the spoken Japanese word rarely means 'looking back' or 'see oneself' in the domain of vision, but rather means 'thought about one's past experience or action'; however, the sign in JSL can literally mean 'see oneself' in the domain of vision. For example, when you notice that everyone looks at you, you can 'see yourself' in JSL, but speakers do not use *kaeri-miru* 'return-see' in spoken Japanese.

There are a few ways to express 'search' in spoken Japanese, as possible counterparts to the JSL sign SEARCH (SEE(F) modified by circular movement). For instance, *mi-tsukeru* 'see-put' is a fully conventionalised transitive compound verb that has an intransitive counterpart, *mitukaru*, which cannot be broken into two verbs. Another possible counterpart of the sign SEARCH is *sagasu* in Japanese, which does not have any relationship to vision. So compared with these spoken Japanese words which are not tightly connected with vision, SEARCH in JSL implies searching by seeing.

Turning to SEE(V), we did not find any transfield mappings, but the sign can occur with a modification. SEE(V) is a so-called agreement verb that can be articulated backward to the signer to mean 'be looked at'. Although it can be modified, it remains in the domain of vision (in the passive voice). Finally, the only modification of SEE(G) which occurred was with TRY, discussed below. TRY and SEE(G) share the same handshape, but there is not a strong connection between the two in terms of their meaning.

In sum, one of the basic vision verbs in JSL can be modified, and some of them can acquire a meaning outside of the vision domain via transfield mapping. The corresponding compound verbs in spoken Japanese show some similarities and differences. In some respects, the process of modification in JSL is similar to that of verb compounding and idiom formation in spoken Japanese.

3.2   Vision to cognition

In this section, I examine signs articulated around the eyes, where the JSL consultants did not consider the sign to be a modified version of the basic perception verb. These signs relate to the conceptual metaphor UNDERSTANDING IS SEEING (Lakoff & Johnson, 1980; Sweetser, 1990).

3.2.1   *EXAMINE and FIND*

First, the cognitive activities EXAMINE and FIND_OUT are articulated in front of the signer's eyes using the dominant hand with the handshape of a bent V. The movement for EXAMINE involves shaking, and FIND_OUT is moved once from in front of the eyes to away from them. Each movement seems related to the temporal aspect of each event. As EXAMINE means a process of inspection, the movement is prolonged. FIND_OUT describes the achievement of the inspection, and the movement is, therefore, punctual. One can EXAMINE something both visually and without visual input, and one can FIND_OUT something both visually and without visual input. Compared with SEE(G) above, which means 'find by sight', in the domain of vision, FIND_OUT can be used in the field of cognition, e.g., 'notice'.

3.2.2   *TRY*

TRY is articulated using the G handshape and pointing several times below the dominant eye. Another version of TRY is articulated below the dominant eye with an F handshape. In spoken Japanese, *miru* 'see' is grammaticised to function as the explorative auxiliary verb *te-miru*, which means 'try to do'. By contrast, TRY in JSL has a form that differs from the basic vision verbs in JSL, but it is still articulated close to the eye. In fact, TRY(G) with a G handshape shares the handshape with SEE(G), and the location of articulation is similar in both signs. TRY(F) shares the handshape with SEE(F) but the location of articulation of TRY(F) is further below, and the hand orientation is different from SEE(F). Both types of TRY have different hand orientations and movements from the corresponding basic vision verbs in JSL.

As the concept *trying* is not related to *seeing* directly, it is difficult to assess if the location of the sign TRY in JSL happens to be close to the eye. But we can observe the similarities between the meaning extension of 'see' to 'try' in spoken Japanese and the sign articulated under the eye through the metaphorical extension TRYING IS SEEING. In the next section, I will examine further examples which indicate that the location of articulation is meaningful from the viewpoint of conceptual metaphor.

3.2.3   *LEARN, BE_INTERESTED, CONCENTRATED ON*

Other signs articulated around the eyes that are related to cognition include LEARN, KEEN, BE_INTERESTED, CONCENTRATE_ON and BE_SURPRISED. These signs do not necessarily involve literal meanings of visual perception. For example, it is possible to LEARN without seeing. In spoken Japanese, for instance, *manabu* 'learn' is not related to seeing, nor are any vision verbs and idioms related to learning. Similarly, CONCENTRATE_ON is articulated around the eyes, but the counterpart in spoken Japanese is not related to visual attention.

On the other hand, in the case of BE_INTERESTED, examining other related expressions in spoken Japanese, I found a similar idiom including *me* 'eye' to 'be interested in'. The idiom is *(something)-ni-me-o-ubawareru* which literally means '(my) eyes are stolen by something' and can be translated to 'be attracted by something'. It is based on the same image that when someone is interested in or attracted by something, they cannot stop paying attention to it.

If the location of articulation is a meaningful unit, we can say that the eyes provide a locus of cognitive attention and a window which enables us to access conceptual information. From the viewpoint of Conceptual Metaphor Theory, these signs can be viewed as being broadly based on the metaphorical mapping from vision to cognition.

3.3   Semantic networks of meaning extension of vision verbs in spoken Japanese and signs around eyes

Now I consider in more detail the similarities and differences of the meaning extensions of vision verbs between spoken Japanese and JSL. After introducing the polysemous meaning network of basic vision verbs in spoken Japanese, I draw a similar network based on the signs in JSL articulated around the eyes, and in the space above them, as a point of comparison.

According to previous studies, the basic spoken Japanese vision verb *miru* has at least eight meanings, as presented in Figure 3a (Takashima, 2013; Tanaka, 1996). This network is based on metaphorical and metonymic extensions. The metaphoric extensions are mapped from the perceptual domain to the cognitive domain in 'to look at' to 'to examine/acquire information' or 'to see+know accidentally' or 'to have (unexpected) experience'. Other extensions are based on pragmatic connotations. For example, the meaning 'try' applies in cases like seeing objects to buy, such as clothes or bags, and examining them visually. If you see someone, sometimes you examine her appearance and condition. If you then find a problem, and happen to have the skill to solve it, you need to resolve the problem, leading to the 'take care' meaning extension (cf. Tanaka, 1996, p. 136).

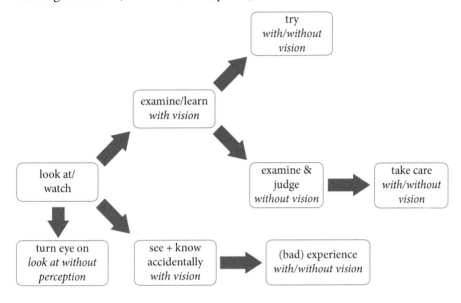

a. Meaning extensions of the vision verb *miru* 'see' in spoken Japanese

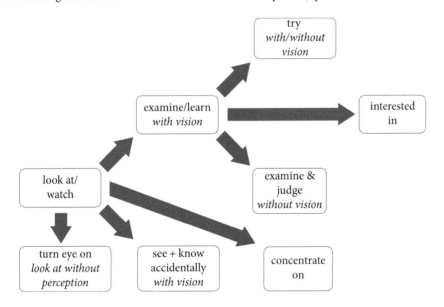

b. Meanings of signs articulated around the eyes in JSL

Figure 3. Meanings of 'see' in spoken Japanese and signs around the eyes in JSL

The meanings of signs articulated around the eyes in Figure 3b are arranged in correspondence with those in Figure 3a. When comparing Figure 3b to Figure 3a, we can observe that JSL lacks the following extended meanings that appear in spoken Japanese: 'take care' and 'have a bad experience'. On the other hand, 'be interested in' and 'concentrate on' are not included in the spoken Japanese meaning network. Further study is needed to clarify the semantic network of the conceptualisation of seeing and other related concepts that appear to be related to the eyes, vision, and vision as cognition in JSL.

As mentioned in 3.2.3, I also found an idiom corresponding to the sign INTERESTED_IN, but these idiomatic expressions of spoken Japanese are not included in Figure 3a. Further research on the comparison between idioms in spoken Japanese and signs in JSL would clarify the correspondence between the two languages.

In summary, vision verbs and signs articulated around the eyes in JSL share aspects of the semantic network of spoken Japanese's basic vision verb and its polysemous meanings. While JSL lacks some concepts articulated around the eyes that are expressed in the meaning extensions in spoken Japanese's vision verb, JSL has additional concepts that are not related to vision in spoken Japanese.

4. Audition and signs around the ears

4.1   The basic auditory signs

Signs expressing auditory perception in JSL are articulated around the ears. The directions of these signs include movement away from the body to the ear using a G handshape (HEAR(G): Figure 4a), or hand closing (HEAR(B→C): Figure 4b); there is also a static sign which involves putting the flat B hand behind the ear (HEAR(B): Figure 4c).

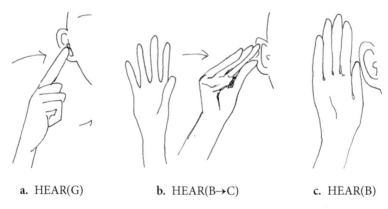

a. HEAR(G)   b. HEAR(B→C)   c. HEAR(B)

Figure 4. Variations of HEAR

The direction, location, and handshapes of the signs are intuitive for hearing Japanese people. Some people expect that a sign language lacks lexical items of auditory perception because they assume that deaf people have never experienced auditory perception and a language cannot describe anything which the users have never experienced. These assumptions are not true. Some signers are not congenitally deaf. In fact, many congenitally deaf people are not completely deaf although their auditory experience is still different from that of hearing people. More to the point, people can express things that they have never experienced. Therefore, it is not surprising that Deaf people have lexical items to describe auditory perception. However, we need to examine just what these basic auditory verbs mean precisely. Let us consider the meanings from four perspectives: (1) literal meaning as auditory perception, (2) receiving information without sound, (3) metonymic extension from 'hear' to 'obey' and 'ask', and (4) other signs articulated around the ears.

First of all, let us consider the meaning of HEAR to describe audition for both Deaf and hearing people in JSL. According to one Deaf consultant, it is appropriate for a hearing person to utter (1a), meaning 'I heard a car horn'. On the other hand, when a Deaf person, who is assumed as deaf, signs the situation, they need to add UNDERSTAND after HEAR to describe the same situation, as in (1b). This is because Deaf people usually do not utter 'I heard the sound'; if the Deaf person could 'hear' the sound, it would be an unusual situation. The irregular event needs to be marked by additional elements; one way to do that is to use UNDERSTAND.

(1) a. (hearing person) CAR HORN HEAR
    b. (Deaf person)   CAR HORN HEAR UNDERSTAND
    'I heard a car horn.'

Notice that the sign is not based on the embodied experience of perception of Deaf people, but that the sign relies on the experience of hearing people who "hear" the sound and receive spoken information via their ears.

Second, let us examine a common meaning extension of basic hearing verbs, namely 'receive information', regardless of whether you hear it or not. The basic auditory verbs above can mean 'receiving information from others' in both spoken and signed languages. For example, a Deaf person can say 'I heard it from my friend that Mr. A married Ms. B. Don't you know that?' based on his previous conversation with his Deaf friend in signing. A similar usage of HEAR in ASL is provided in a previous study on reported speech, where a signer HEARD 'received' information from someone who signed it to her (Shaffer, 2012).

Third, one can find that 'hear' has a metonymically extended meaning of 'obey/heed' and 'ask' in spoken languages (Sweetser, 1990; Vanhove, 2008), including in spoken Japanese. These are metonymic extensions based on the event sequence centred on 'to hear': if someone wants to hear information, they need to ask; if someone heard an order or advice, s/he might obey the order or advice. HEAR in JSL does have the extended meaning of 'obey', but not the meaning of 'ask'. It is also interesting that ASK is articulated on the cheek, the location related to speaking in JSL.

Examining metaphorical meaning, I did not find any other metaphoric meaning extensions of the basic auditory verbs mentioned above. Therefore, let us look at other signs articulated around the ears beyond the basic auditory verbs.

I found a limited number of signs articulated around the ear, that included signs such as INFORMATION and RUMOUR. It is striking that although deaf people obtain information mainly through the visual modality – visual image, sign and written language – the sign for INFORMATION is articulated around the ears. Usually, Deaf people are annoyed by the amount of information which is shared in the hearing community by means of gossip through whispering, unofficial chats in the staff kitchen, and the like.

These findings lead us to the conclusion that even though JSL is mainly used by Deaf people, the signs of audition are close to hearing people's conceptualisation of hearing. One may infer that these expressions are selected under the circumstance that Deaf people are always surrounded by hearing people. An alternative possibility is that this reflects Deaf people's actual experience of hearing. Most deaf and hard of hearing people can still hear or sense some sounds. In addition, they might have experience hearing with hearing aids. They have also learned how to concentrate on audition in detail.

4.2   Young Deaf people change the location of articulation of idiomatic phrases from the ears to the eyes

To examine Deaf people's recognition of location of articulation and the influence of spoken Japanese and Deaf culture, it is worth introducing the location change of a JSL sign which means 'go in through one ear and out the other' in English. The old sign is RIGHT EAR TO LEFT EAR (Figure 5a). I surmise that this sign was created based on a spoken Japanese idiom *migi kara hidari e nagasu* 'something flows from the right (ear) to the left (ear)'. The idiom means a person hears something but does not retain the information.

A Deaf consultant aged 50 said the old sign is not used by signers who are 70 years old or older. These older signers tend not to have skills in speaking, reading, and writing in spoken Japanese because of their education; thus, their language is less influenced by spoken Japanese. Accordingly, one can assume the sign was borrowed from the spoken Japanese idiom in the last 50 years.

Furthermore, young signers prefer to use a modified eye-related form of the sign FRONT TO BACK (Figure 5b). It means exactly the same thing as the old sign, namely that a person seems to perceive something but does not retain the relevant information.

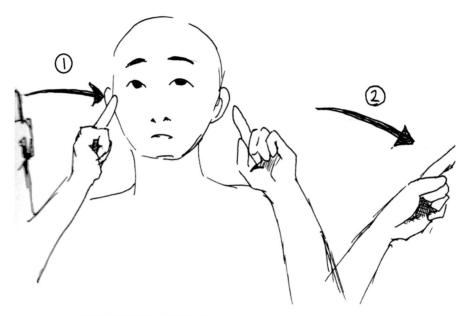

a. old sign: RIGHT EAR TO LEFT EAR

b. newly modified sign: FRONT TO BACK (eye related)

Figure 5. Change of location of articulation of a sign meaning 'go
in through one ear and out the other'

My consultants explained the change as a result of the establishment of the identity of "Deaf" as I mentioned in 2.1.1. When the concept of Deaf culture was adopted around 1990 from the US, Deaf people in Japan re-examined their identity. Due to the affirmation of Deaf-ness, younger Deaf people did not keep using the hearing people's metaphor but changed the location of the sign to suit their intuition and culture.

5. Smelling and signs on the nose showing negative evaluation

5.1   The basic verbs for smelling

The basic verbs indicating 'to smell' in JSL describe the emanation of a smell from the source to the signer's nose (Figure 6). The hand indicates the emanation of the smell towards the nose. When the smell is good, the signer's facial expression shows a positive reaction with relaxed eyebrows and a smile on the lips. By contrast, bad smells are indicated by furrowed eyebrows and a tightly closed mouth.

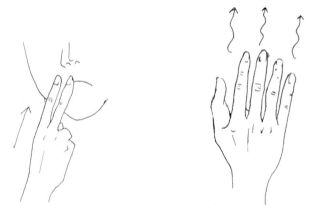

a. SMELL(V)   b. SMELL (bent open 5 fingers wiggling)

Figure 6. Variations of SMELL

Let us examine the extended meanings by comparing JSL with spoken Japanese. In spoken Japanese, olfactory verbs *kagu* (transitive verb: 'someone smells/sniffs something'), *niou* (intransitive verb: 'something smells/is stinky'), extend to mean 'to search for hidden information', and 'to catch dubious information'. In that sense, someone can 'smell out' dubiousness (e.g. *kare-wa hanzai no nioi o kagi-tsuke-ta* 'he smells out a scent of a crime'). In JSL, the Deaf consultants and I did not find a similar meaning extension, namely 'to smell out abstract or shady information' in JSL.

Next, I examined bodily-anchored lexical items articulated on the nose. I found many adjectives which are evaluative. Some signs can be explained by the idiomatic origin that is shared with spoken Japanese. Others cannot be explained by either hearing-Japanese culture, nor Deaf culture. I will examine them in the section below.

An example of an evaluative expression that is similar to a spoken Japanese idiom includes BE-GOOD-AT (BE PROUD OF) which is articulated with a Y handshape with the thumb on the nose and the pinky finger pointing upwards. The articulation of the sign corresponds to the Japanese idiomatic phrase *hana-ga-takai* '(my) nose is high', which means 'be proud of'. If one changes the sign by orientating the pinky downwards, it means LOSE ONE'S PRIDE, which has a similar meaning to *hana-ga-oreru* 'nose-GEN-break: nose is broken' in spoken Japanese. Similarly, BE EMBARRASSED and HUMBLE are articulated on the nose in JSL. In summary, the former two signs seem to share the conceptual metaphor HIGH PRIDE IS HIGH NOSE with spoken Japanese, while the other two are related to characteristics of pride as well.

5.2 Is the nose the location of evaluation?

Turning now to signs on the nose which cannot be explained by either hearing Japanese culture nor Deaf culture intuitively, there are some basic abstract evaluation adjective signs that occur on the nose; for example, GOOD, OLD, and SO-SO.

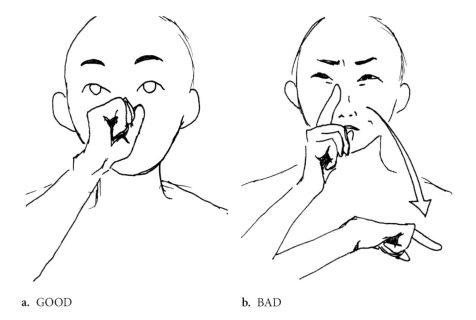

a. GOOD   b. BAD

Figure 7. Examples of signs of evaluation articulated on the nose

By categorising these evaluation signs, one can find antonymous pairs:

i.   negative evaluation articulated on the nose with its antonym, positive evalua-
     tion, articulated in neutral space (in front of the upper body);
ii. positive or neutral evaluation articulated on the nose, with its antonym artic-
     ulated in neutral space; and
iii. both negative and positive evaluation antonyms articulated on the nose (see
     Table 1).

Table 1. Evaluation signs: Antonymous pairs and their location of articulation

Negative signs articulated around the nose	The antonym (location of articulation)
OLD	NEW (neutral space)
DIRTY	CLEAN (neutral space)
COUNTRYSIDE (rural, not-fashionable)	URBAN (neutral space)
RUDE	POLITE (forehead); SOFT (neutral)
LAZY	SERIOUS (chest; eye height)
Neutral signs articulated around the nose	The antonym (location of articulation)
MODEST	AGGRESSIVE (cheek)
UNCONCERNED	CARE, BE-INTERESTED (eyes)
RELIEF	STRESSED (chest)
Evaluation pairs articulated around the nose	
SUCCESS/FAIL, PRIDE/SHAME, GOOD/BAD, BE-GOOD-AT/BE-BAD-AT, SO-SO,	

By judging from the list above, the signs articulated around the nose are more
closely related to negative evaluations than to positive ones. Considering the viewpoint of conceptual metaphor, the domain of olfactory perception can be considered the source of the metaphorical mapping, reflecting the importance of smell
for the human body; a bad smell has a critical meaning for the human body, unlike
a pleasant scent. Thus, I propose that the conceptual metaphor NEGATIVE EVALUA-
TION IS BAD SMELL (cf. Ibarretxe-Antuñano, this volume) to express bad evaluations
is first articulated on the nose, after which the negative connotation faded away and
EVALUATION IS SMELL appeared. To examine this hypothesis, we require diachronic
data, but it is difficult to look up philological data in the field of sign language
studies. So, this is just one possible interpretation. However, further supported
evidence is provided from experimental psychology that smell naming is based on
pleasantness (Yeshurun & Sobel, 2009). Therefore, the conceptual metaphor can
be based on the human (in)ability to name smells and the fact that humans tend to
focus on the pleasantness (good) or unpleasantness (bad, disgusting) of smells in
linguistic expressions as related to the target domain of the metaphor as evaluation
(for further discussion, see Winter, this volume).

Turning now to examine these signs by comparing them to signs articulated on other sensory organs, adjectival signs articulated around the eyes are limited to the realm of vision (VIVID, OBSCURE, and DARK). In addition, many verbs associated with vision and intellect are articulated around the eyes. On the other hand, signs articulated around the nose in JSL are not necessarily related to smelling or to the nose. Although only a few verbs appear around the nose, comparatively more adjectives are articulated in this position. Hence, we can interpret that the dynamic nature of vision does not allow for adjectival metaphorical extension to the eyes, while the nature of olfaction, which involves passively receiving and evaluating smells, accepts adjectives outside of the domain of olfaction, namely evaluative adjectives.

6.   Discussion and conclusion

This chapter shows that the location of articulation of perception expressions in a signed language can be related to conceptual metaphors. First, one characteristic of perception expressions is that the location of articulation is determined by the perception organs involved. For example, signs regarding visual perception have the eyes as their location of articulation. Other signs made on or around the relevant organs of perception, beyond cases of basic perception verbs, can be construed as meaningful clusters that we understand based on conceptual metaphors of perception. Though the basic perception verbs seldom have extended meanings, I found evidence indicating the existence of conceptual metaphors in JSL such that modified ones have meanings both in the domain of perception and cognition. I conclude that the locations of articulation not only provide an iconic basis for perception verbs but are understood as a source domain of conceptual metaphor, and thus make semantic clusters of signs similar to idiomatic expressions in the surrounding spoken language. In addition, I showed evidence that signers recognise the location of articulation as a meaningful unit related to the change in the location of the sign among younger speakers which means 'go in through one ear and out the other', examined in 4.2 above.

With regard to culture and behaviour, differences in conceptual metaphors between JSL and spoken Japanese are found in signs articulated around the eyes and ears. Many signs with meanings of intellection are articulated around the eyes and some signs' meanings are not found in the polysemy of vision verbs and other expressions related to vision in spoken Japanese. On the other hand, the vision verb in spoken Japanese has an extended meaning of 'to take care' which cannot be found among signs articulated around the eyes in JSL. So, signs related to eyes in JSL do not have broader meanings as words and idioms in spoken Japanese do, but rather, they have different distributions.

A small number of signs that are articulated around the ears are related to audition, as opposed to the other two sensory modalities. Also, signs articulated on the nose have evaluative meanings. This semantic cluster can be construed as the extension from a bad smell to a bad evaluation. Alternatively, we can think of the location of the nose as being at the centre of the face. The central location of the face can then be interpreted as a neutral location, and as such, not related to smell, per se. Further research could distinguish these accounts.

Acknowledgements

I would like to thank Mr. Ryutaro Sano and Ms. Eikoh Kuroda for their help. I am also grateful to the editors for their comments and encouragement. This work was supported by JSPS KAKENHI Grant-in-Aid for JSPS Research Fellow Numbers JP13J10373, and JP17J40245.

References

Cates, D., Gutiérrez, E., Hafer, S., Barrett, R., & Corina, D. (2013). Location, location, location. *Sign Language Studies*, 13(4), 433–461. https://doi.org/10.1353/sls.2013.0014

Dancygier, B., & Sweetser, E. (2014). *Figurative language*. Cambridge: Cambridge University Press.

Ichida, Y. (2010). Introduction to Japanese Sign Language iconicity in language. *Studies in Language Sciences*, 9, 3–32.

Jarque, M. (2005). Double mapping in metaphorical expressions of thought and communication in Catalan Sign Language. *Sign Language Studies*, 5(3), 292–316. https://doi.org/10.1353/sls.2005.0008

Johnston, T. A., & Schembri, A. C. (2007). *Australian Sign Language (Auslan): An introduction to sign language linguistics*. Cambridge: Cambridge University Press. https://doi.org/10.1017/CBO9780511607479

Kimura, H., & Ichida, Y. (1995) Rou bunka sengen: gengoteki shosusha to shite no rousha [A declaration of deaf culture: Deaf people as a linguistic minority], *Gendai Shiso* 23(3), 354–399.

Kövecses, Z. (2011). Recent developments in metaphor theory. *Review of Cognitive Linguistics*, 9(1), 11–25. https://doi.org/10.1075/rcl.9.1.02kov

Kusumi, T. (Ed.). (2007). *Metaphor kenkyu no saizensen* [Frontier of research on Metaphor]. Tokyo: Hitsuji-shobo.

Lakoff, G. (1993a). The contemporary theory of metapor. In A. Ortony (Ed.), *Metaphor and thought* (pp. 202–251). Cambridge University Press. https://doi.org/10.1017/CBO9781139173865.013

Lakoff, G. (1993b). The metaphor system and its role in grammar. In K. Beals, G. Cooke, D. Kathman, S. Kita, K.-E. McCullough, & David Testen (Eds.), *CLS29: Volume 2* (pp. 217–241).

Lakoff, G., & Johnson, M. (1980). *Metaphors we live by*. The University of Chicago Press.

Lane, H., Pillard, R. C., & Hedberg, U. (2011). *The people of the eye: Deaf ethnicity and ancestry*. Oxford: Oxford University Press.

Lucas, C. (2003). The role of variation in lexicography. *Sign Language Studies*, 3(3), 322–340. https://doi.org/10.1353/sls.2003.0009

Meir, I. (2010). Iconicity and metaphor: Constraints on metaphorical extension of iconic forms. *Language*, 86(4), 865–896. https://doi.org/10.1353/lan.2010.0044

Nabeshima, K. (2011). *Nihongo no metaphor* [Metaphor in Japanese]. Tokyo: Kuroshio-shuppan.

Nakamura, K. (2006). *Deaf in Japan: Signing and the politics of identity*. Ithaca, New York: Cornell University Press.

Nihon-Shuwa-Kenkyuujo (Social Welfare Corporation National Sign Language Training Center) (Ed.). (2011). *Shin Nihongo-Shuwa Jiten* [New Japanese-Japanese Sign Language dictionary]. Tokyo: Chuo Houki Shuppan.

Padden, C., & Humphries, T. (1988). *Deaf in America: Voices from a culture*. Cambridge, MA: Harvard University Press.

Penner, M. (2013). The mouthing of verbs in Japanese Sign Language. M.A. thesis, University of North Dakota, Grand Forks.

Pietrandrea, P. (2002). Iconicity and arbitrariness in Italian Sign Language. *Sign Language Studies*, 2(3), 296–321. https://doi.org/10.1353/sls.2002.0012

San Roque, L. S., Kendrick, K. H., Norcliffe, E., Brown, P., Defina, R., Dingemanse, M., Dirksmeyer, T., Enfield, N. J., Floyd, S., Hammond, J., Rossi, G., Tufvesson, S., Van Putten, & Majid, A. (2015). Vision verbs dominate in conversation across cultures, but the ranking of non-visual verbs varies. *Cognitive Linguistics*, 26(1), 31–60. https://doi.org/10.1515/cog-2014-0089

Sandler, W., & Lillo-Martin, D. (2006). *Sign language and linguistic universals*. Cambridge, MA: Cambridge University Press. https://doi.org/10.1017/CBO9781139163910

Seto, K. (1995). *Metaphor shikou* [Metaphorical thought]. Tokyo: Kodansha.

Shaffer, B. (2012). Reported speech as an evidentiality strategy in American Sign Language. In B. Dancygier & E. Sweetser (Eds.), *Viewpoint in language* (pp. 139–155). Cambridge, MA: Cambridge University Press. https://doi.org/10.1017/CBO9781139084727.011

Speed, L. J., & Majid, A. (2017). Dutch modality exclusivity norms: Simulating perceptual modality in space. *Behavior Research Methods*. https://doi.org/10.3758/s13428-017-0852-3

Stokoe, W. C. (1980). Sign language structure. *Annual Review of Anthropology*, 9, 365–390. https://doi.org/10.1146/annurev.an.09.100180.002053

Sweetser, E. (1990). *From etymology to pragmatics: The mind-body metaphor in semantic structure and semantic change*. Cambridge, MA: Cambridge University Press. https://doi.org/10.1017/CBO9780511620904

Takashima, Y. (2013). Gengo no Shintai-sei to Shukan-sei ni kansuru Kankaku-Chikaku Hyougen no Ninchi-teki Kenkyuu [A cognitive approach to sensory-perception expressions from embodiment and subjectivity of natural language]. PhD dissertation, Kyoto University, Kyoto.

Tanaka, S. (1996). The polysemic structure of "miru (see)". *Gengo Kenkyu*, 110, 120–142.

Taub, S. F. (2001). *Language from the body: Iconicity and metaphor in American Sign Language*. Cambridge: Cambridge University Press. https://doi.org/10.1017/CBO9780511509629

Vanhove, M. (2008). Semantic associations between sensory modalities, prehension and mental perceptions. A cross-linguistic perspective. In M. Vanhove (ed.), *From polysemy to semantic change: Towards a typology of lexical semantic associations* (pp. 163–215). Amsterdam: John Benjamins. https://doi.org/10.1075/slcs.106.17van

Wilcox, P. P. (2000). *Metaphor in American Sign Language*. Washington, DC: Gallaudet University Press.

Wilcox, P. P. (2004). A cognitive key: Metonymic and metaphorical mappings in ASL. *Cognitive Linguistics*, 15(2), 197–222. https://doi.org/10.1515/cogl.2004.008

Wilcox, S. (2004). Cognitive iconicity: Conceptual spaces, meaning, and gesture in signed language. *Cognitive Linguistics*, 15(2), 119–147. https://doi.org/10.1515/cogl.2004.005

Wilcox, S., & Wilcox, P. P. (2013). Cognitive linguistics and signed languages. *International Journal of Cognitive Linguistics*, 3(2), 127–151.

Yamanashi, M. (1988). *Hiyu to rikai* [Metaphor and understanding]. Tokyo: Tokyo Daigaku Shuppankai.

Yeshurun, Y., & Sobel, N. (2009). An odor is not worth a thousand words: From multidimensional odors to unidimensional odor objects. *Annual Review of Psychology*, 61, 219–241. https://doi.org/10.1146/annurev.psych.60.110707.163639

CHAPTER 16

Perception and metaphor
The case of smell

Zoltán Kövecses
Eötvös Loránd University

The general issue I address in the paper is this: How is the concept of smell linguistically coded in English, as examined from a cognitive linguistic perspective? I break down this larger theoretical issue into three sub-issues: One sub-issue concerns what the lexis of smell in English reveals about the conceptual organisation of smell. What is the conceptual prototype of smell? Another has to do with which lexical items are used from the domain of smell to structure other, more abstract concepts. Indeed, I show, partly based on previous work by others, that there are several conceptual metaphors that involve the concept of smell as their source domain. However, and this is the third sub-issue, I also argue that smell can also occur as a target domain in conceptual metaphors. This possibility presents a challenge to conceptual metaphor theory, which claims that perceptual experiences (and the concepts corresponding to them) are understood in a direct, literal way and that concepts that are not based on perceptual experiences (i.e., are not concrete) are understood figuratively by making use of such direct, literal conceptualisations. I conclude that smell is a fairly richly coded concept in English, but whose degree of "linguistic codability" can only be established relative to counterpart concepts in other languages and relative to other sense modalities in studies conducted by means of the same methodology and cognitive linguistic machinery as employed in the present one.

Keywords: metaphor, smell, smell metaphors, linguistic codability, conceptual structure of smell, smell as source, smell as target, conceptual metaphor theory, smell and emotion, prototype of smell as a concept

1. Introduction

The general goal and the general issue I would like to pursue here is to characterise how the sense modality of smell is linguistically coded in English. I break down this general goal into three more specific ones, corresponding to three sub-issues.

https://doi.org/10.1075/celcr.19.16kov
© 2019 John Benjamins Publishing Company

First, following a large body of traditional research into synaesthetic metaphors, researchers in conceptual metaphor theory (e.g., Kövecses, 2002/2010; Lakoff & Johnson, 1980, 1999) revealed systematic correspondences (conceptual metaphors) between domains of perception, or "the senses" for short, and other, more abstract domains (see Evans & Wilkins, 2000; Ibarretxe-Antuñano, 1999; Neagu, 2013; Sweetser, 1990). For example, Sweetser (1990) found systematic mappings between the domain of vision and that of knowing both across languages and in diachrony (i.e., the conceptual metaphor KNOWING IS SEEING). In more recent years, researchers found that conceptual metaphors are also formed between the various sense modalities, such as between the visual and auditory modalities (yielding SEEING IS HEARING, as in *a **loud** colour*) (see, e.g., Barcelona, 2000). It was also observed that vision /seeing itself as a domain undergoes metaphorical conceptualisation (cf. the metaphor SEEING IS TOUCHING, as in *I can't **take** my eyes **off** her*); that is, it can function as a target domain (Lakoff & Johnson, 1980). Following the work by others, here I continue to explore the sub-issue of the use of sense perceptions as source domains in conceptual metaphors in English. This is one of my goals in the present chapter.

Second, it can be proposed that the basic sense domains, such as smell, function as target domains for a rich system of generic metaphors. This rich metaphorical system ties the conceptualisation of perception to the conceptual system at large. In the paper, as my further goal, I examine this proposal in more detail in relation to smell and ask why such metaphorical conceptualisation is a necessary phenomenon, and not something that should not occur (as conceptual metaphor theory (CMT) would predict on the grounds that directly meaningful concepts are understood in a literal way).

Third, I am also interested here in the structure of the conceptual category of smell. What I mean by this is the internal organisation of the concept: which conceptual entities and relations make it up, how the entities fit together, and the issue of what might be a prototype of the category (see Rosch, 1978), as these terms are used by cognitive linguists (see, e.g., Kövecses, 2006; Lakoff, 1987; Langacker, 1987). As we will see, the notion of frame plays a major role in answering these questions, as it is defined by Fillmore (1982) in cognitive linguistics. "Frame" goes under a variety of different names in cognitive science, including scene, scenario, model, domain, and even folk theory, just to mention a few. I will use frame in the sense of Fillmore in which it is any coherent area of human experience. I take this to be the common denominator to the various usages. More specifically, a frame, on this view, is an idealisation and schematisation of human experience with respect to which words have a meaning. We understand the word 'buy' with respect to a commercial event frame, which also includes the buyer, the seller, the goods, and the money that changes hands.

All three goals above hang together, as I see the sub-issues. As mentioned above, the larger theoretical issue that interests me is how the sense modality of smell is coded linguistically (see, Levinson & Majid, 2014). What do the three previously mentioned sub-issues have to do with linguistic codability? The structure of concepts (conceptual categories) consists of a variety of aspects. One of them is the prototype of a concept, which is represented by a conceptual frame. Frames comprise entities and relations that are organised into a structured whole. The conceptual entities and relations are linguistically revealed (and coded) by means of lexical items and their grammatical relations. Which and how many entities and relations are coded in a language relative to a concept is one measure of its linguistic codability. A second way in which we can assess codability is to examine such aspects of a concept as the semantic dimensions that characterise them (e.g., size, intensity, brightness, duration – see Levinson & Majid, 2014). These are also revealed by lexical items, and are often metaphorical. In this case, the concept in question with its dimensions would serve as a target domain, and the metaphorical lexical items would come from some source domain. Similarly, a third measure of linguistic codability may be the opposite of the previous situation; that is, where the concept in question would function as a source domain with respect to a target. The particular lexis of a concept in question that is used to structure a target metaphorically would further indicate how the concept is linguistically coded. I will examine these three ways in which the concept of smell is coded in English.

All in all, then, I do not think of linguistic codability simply as the question of whether a sensation of any kind, such as smell, can or cannot be expressed in a language (by a particular lexical item). If it can be expressed by a lexical item, I think of linguistic codability in terms of the various conceptual distinctions that characterise the sensation for speakers of the language. In other words, I take linguistic codability to be the degree of conceptual complexity that constitutes the concept, as revealed by its conventional lexis.

Finally, the reason for choosing the concept of smell for investigation is that smell can be seen as a fairly ineffable percept and concept (at least in relation to some other percepts, like colours in English). Levinson and Majid define ineffability in the following way: it is "the degree to which percepts or concepts resist linguistic coding" (Levinson & Majid 2014, p. 407). In order to see how *ineffable* smell is, I suggest, with Levinson and Majid (2014), that (a) we have to try to describe how it is linguistically coded in one language (say, in English), (b) study how it is linguistically coded in other languages, and (c) compare its "codedness" with that of other sense modalities. It is the first task that I attempt to carry out here, with the help of the machinery of cognitive semantics. I suggest that the study of the three sub-issues briefly outlined above (smell as source domain, smell as target domain, and the conceptual structure of smell) can greatly help us to begin to describe the concept of smell on the basis of which the precise degree of its ineffability (in relation to other modalities and other languages) can be explored in future work.

In other words, I regard the present enterprise, and several others in this volume, as complementing studies that deal with the larger, sociological and cultural-historical importance and function of smell, such as in the work of Classen, Howes and Synnott (1994). While their approach examines the "macroscopic" social and cultural aspects of smell throughout the ages in several societies, the present one focuses attention on its "microscopic" cognitive structure and conceptualisation at the present time in a single language – English.

2. Methodology

The linguistic study of metaphor depends, in part, on our goals: whether we want to characterise how individual speakers use metaphors in context (corpus linguistics, discourse analysis) or whether we are interested in making hypotheses concerning our shared metaphorical conceptual system (lexical approach). The former can be regarded as a "bottom-up" approach, while the latter the "top-down" one (see Kövecses, 2011). In my view, both are legitimate enterprises and both are necessary for the study of conceptual metaphors related to a particular topic area, such as smell.

For the purposes of the present paper I use what can be called the "lexical method," or the "lexical approach" (see Kövecses, 1986, 2015a, Kövecses, et al., in press). Given this method, we search for various lexical items or other types of information that are related to the perceptual category of SMELL. The best sources for these are dictionaries: monolingual and bilingual dictionaries, thesauri, collocation dictionaries, idiom dictionaries of various sorts, and, in general, any collections of words and phrases related to a concept. The various lexical items that belong to a particular concept, or, as it is commonly referred to in CMT, a domain, are *types*, not tokens. The types provided by the dictionaries represent the most conventionalised linguistic items of a language related to a domain. The types are *decontextualised lexemes*, as opposed to *contextualized linguistic expressions* (i.e., the tokens).

3. The conceptual structure of smell

By the conceptual structure of a conceptual category, I mean the conceptual elements (entities and relations between them) that make up the category and the particular causal and temporal organisation of these elements. The most common term for such a constellation of elements and their organisation is that of frame in the sense it was discussed above (see, e.g., Fillmore, 1982).

Let us first consider the five senses of *smell* as a noun and its five senses as a verb in WordNet (http://wordnet.princeton.edu). On its webpage, WordNet is described in the following way: "WordNet® is a large lexical database of English. Nouns, verbs, adjectives and adverbs are grouped into sets of cognitive synonyms (synsets), each expressing a distinct concept. Synsets are interlinked by means of conceptual-semantic and lexical relations". Below are the results for the search term "smell":

Noun

- **smell**, odor, odour, olfactory sensation, olfactory perception (the sensation that results when olfactory receptors in the nose are stimulated by particular chemicals in gaseous form) *"she loved the smell of roses"*
- olfactory property, **smell**, aroma, odor, odour, scent (any property detected by the olfactory system)
- spirit, tone, feel, feeling, flavor, flavour, look, **smell** (the general atmosphere of a place or situation and the effect that it has on people) *"the feel of the city excited him"*; *"a clergyman improved the tone of the meeting"*; *"it had the smell of treason"*
- **smell**, sense of smell, olfaction, olfactory modality (the faculty that enables us to distinguish scents)
- **smell**, smelling (the act of perceiving the odor of something)

Such definitions of the senses of the noun make it clear that smell is regarded in English as a sensation, a property, a faculty, and an act. These are literal senses of the word, and they jointly constitute elements of a frame in the sense of Fillmore (1982), as I show below. The third sense, "general atmosphere", is metaphorical and is not part of this frame. I will return to it in the next section on the metaphorical aspects of smell.

Verb

- **smell** (inhale the odor of; perceive by the olfactory sense)
- **smell** (emit an odor) *"The soup smells good"*
- **smell** (smell bad) *"He rarely washes, and he smells"*
- smack, reek, **smell** (have an element suggestive (of something) *"his speeches smacked of racism"*; *"this passage smells of plagiarism"*
- **smell**, smell out, sense (become aware of not through the senses but instinctively) *"I sense his hostility"*; *"I smell trouble"*; *"smell out corruption"*

The senses of the verb are glossed by *WordNet* as "inhale the odor of", "emit an odor", "smell bad", "have an element suggestive (of something)", and "become aware of not through the senses but instinctively". These senses, like the senses of the noun, are also elements of a frame connected to smell, except for the last two metaphorical senses (to which I return later).

I suggest that, given the definitions above, we can distinguish two conceptual frames associated with smell: a passive and an active one (for a similar distinction, see also Ibarretxe-Antunano, 1999). Since prototypes for categories are conceptually represented as frames (see, e.g., Lakoff, 1987, who calls them "idealized cognitive models"; Barsalou, 1999), we can think of the two frames as two prototypes of the conceptual category of smell. Lexically, the two prototypes are based on the verbs *emit* (odour) and *sniff* (at something). Or, alternatively, since in most cases conceptual categories are represented by just one prototype for a category (such as a particular kind of red for the category of red or a particular kind of chair for the category of chair; see, e.g., Lakoff, 1987), we can take just one of them as the prototypical case and the other as a deviation from the prototype, a non-prototypical member of the category of smell. I return to this issue below.

The "passive" frame for smell includes a number of conceptual elements; namely, that smell has an *origin*, has a *cause*, that the origin *produces* the smell, the *smell* itself, the *organism* with the faculty of smell, the *faculty* itself, and the experience of *perceiving* the smell. In this frame of smell, the organism with the faculty of smell functions in the role of patient or experiencer; the experience of smell occurs to the organism. We can represent this as a series of events, a dynamic frame (or scenario) (see Figure 1). In the representations of frames that follow, the dashes indicate an entity and an event and the arrow indicates a causal and/or temporal relationship between the two events. In the passive prototypical frame, the origin and the cause coincide, but this need not be the case.

origin/cause of smell – emits smell → organism with the faculty of smell (experiencer) – perceives the smell

Figure 1. Passive frame for smell

The "active" frame has somewhat different conceptual elements. They include an *object* as the source of smell, the *smell* as a property of the object, the object *having* smell, an *agent* with the faculty of smell, the agent *performing the action* of smelling, and the agent *perceiving* the smell (see Figure 2).

the object as source – has property of smell → agent (with faculty of smell) – performs act of smelling – agent perceives smell

Figure 2. Active frame for smell

As regards the distinction between passive and active smell, as mentioned above, it could probably be also argued that there is only one prototype for the category, as is usually the case (see, e.g., Rosch, 1978). Would it be the passive or the active version? I will argue in the next section that it might be the passive one.

4. A comparison with emotion

In order to see why we have some grounds for making the suggestion that the prototype of smell is the passive version of the smell frame, I turn to a comparison of smell with emotions. The comparison might be useful since emotion and perception are correlated in many ways (see, e.g., Chu & Downes, 2000; Soudry, et al, 2011; Willander & Larsson, 2007) and exhibit several similarities. As a matter of fact, Prinz (2006) goes so far as to suggest that emotion is a form of perception. We do not have to follow Prinz to this conclusion (offered as an expert theory), but we can observe certain features that perception and emotion share, at least at the level of language-based folk theories (see Holland & Quinn, 1987), as we shall see below. Thus making use of work on emotion might reveal important (folk-theoretical) commonalities and differences between emotion and smell. And in the next section, I propose that the most obvious relationship between smell and some other sense modalities like touch and taste, on the one hand, and emotion, on the other, is that the former are used to metaphorically conceptualise the latter. This yields the general conceptual metaphor EMOTION IS PERCEPTION to which I return in the next section, where I discuss smell, touch and taste as potential source domains for the emotions.

In a paper on the emotion of surprise, based on lexical evidence I identified the following schematic conceptual structure (or frame) for the concept of surprise (Kövecses, 2015a) (see Figure 3). In this and the next figure, the vertical line indicates that the loss of control over surprise manifests itself in certain bodily or expressive effects, or responses.

cause (of surprise) – causes surprise → loss of control (i.e., self – loses control)

|

effects of surprise

Figure 3. The frame for the concept of surprise

This schematic structure partially coincides with that of some basic prototypical emotions, such as anger, fear, joy, sadness (see, e.g., Ekman, 1992), in that there is a cause that provokes the emotion to come into existence. On the other hand, the basic prototypical emotions are also characterised by an elaborate "control" aspect and an "action" component (indicated in bold in Figure 4 below), as suggested by a number of researchers in the cognitive linguistic study of emotions (Lakoff & Kövecses, 1987; Kövecses, 2000; Soriano, 2005; Yu, 1998).

cause (of emotion) – causes emotion → **control** of emotion → **action**

|

effect of emotion

Figure 4. The schematic structure of prototypical emotions represented as a frame

The control aspect of prototypical emotions typically consists of several stages: attempt at control, loss of control, and lack of control. But in surprise there is an immediate loss of control and there is no attempt to resist the emotion. In prototypical emotions, there is also a loss of emotional control that is preceded by an attempt to control the emerging emotion. This is one reason why the schematic folk theory of surprise is different from that of prototypical emotions. Another reason is that it does not have a clear action tendency (the action aspect, such as revenge for anger or flight for fear) that prototypical emotions are characterised by (see, e.g., Frijda, 1986). For these reasons, surprise can be regarded as a non-prototypical emotion (in contrast to anger, fear, etc.).

I suggest that smell and the other sense modalities are more like the non-prototypical emotion of surprise than the prototypical basic emotions. The conceptual structure of the various sense modalities do not have an elaborate control aspect and an action component comparable to those found in prototypical emotions. The perception of smell arises without the possibility of controlling the resulting sensation; there is no "attempt at control". The experiencer of smell immediately experiences the sensation, whether he/she wants to or not. In this respect, smell is like the non-prototypical emotion of surprise. The only difference is that in the case of surprise the experience is primarily cognitive, while in the case of smell it is primarily perceptual.

It is for this reason that I propose that the prototypical frame for smell (and perhaps the other sense modalities in general) is constituted by the passive version of smell outlined above – not the active one. In the passive version, if the smell is emitted by a source, the experiencer will perceive it – without the possibility of having any control over the perception. In the active version, the person actively "seeks out" the smell (by sniffing). Because of this, the experience of the smell sensation is, in this sense, under his/her control. The passive version of smell is also probably more common than the active one (whenever we breathe, we smell). Thus, the prototype for smell is probably more like an unintentional and uncontrolled sensation, and not an intentional and controlled act.

5. Smell as a source domain

Smell is an interesting concept from a conceptual metaphor theory perspective, since it can function in metaphors not just in one but two ways: either as a source domain or as a target domain.

Let us start with smell as a source. There are many conventional metaphorical linguistic expressions involving smell, such as the following:

1. I smell a rat here.
2. The movie stinks.
3. He could always smell out fear.
4. It had the smell of treason.

On the basis of such and similar metaphorical expressions, we can identify the following four different conceptual metaphors:

1. SUSPICION IS SMELLING
2. BAD IS SMELLY
3. BECOMING INSTINCTIVELY AWARE OF/GUESSING SOMETHING IS SMELLING SOMETHING
4. THE GENERAL ATMOSPHERE OF SOMETHING IS AN OLFACTORY PERCEPTION

The first three are well-known conceptual metaphors in the literature (see, e.g., Ibarretxe-Antunano, 1999; Neagu, 2013; Sweetser, 1990). However, the fourth is not commonly discussed.

Actually, the metaphor THE GENERAL ATMOSPHERE OF SOMETHING IS AN OLFAC-TORY PERCEPTION forms a part of a more general pattern of metaphors. Consider the following cases that all involve a form of perception, where the description of the target domain and most of the examples come from *WordNet* (see the third sense of smell as a noun in the section on the conceptual structure of smell):

1. Smell
   THE GENERAL ATMOSPHERE OF SOMETHING IS AN OLFACTORY PERCEPTION: "It had the smell of treason."
2. Sound
   THE GENERAL ATMOSPHERE OF SOMETHING IS AN AUDITORY PERCEPTION: "A clergyman improved the tone of the meeting."
3. Touch
   THE GENERAL ATMOSPHERE OF SOMETHING IS A TACTILE PERCEPTION: "The feel of the city excited him."

4. Taste

    THE GENERAL ATMOSPHERE OF SOMETHING IS A GUSTATORY PERCEPTION: "Her performance adds flavor to the show." "The conversation left a bad taste in my mouth."

5. Vision

    THE GENERAL ATMOSPHERE OF SOMETHING IS A VISUAL PERCEPTION: "I don't like the looks of this."

6. Spiritual perception

    THE GENERAL ATMOSPHERE OF SOMETHING IS A SPIRITUAL PERCEPTION: "the spirit of the times"

I included "spiritual perception" in this list and coined the term "spiritual perception" on the analogy of Sweetser's (1990, p. 40) term "spiritual vision". Spirituality is of course not a basic sense perception unless we take it to be metaphorically as such. It was included here nonetheless, since it neatly fits the pattern of perception-related metaphors.

Overall, it seems that the basic sense perceptions can all be used to metaphorically conceptualise the general atmosphere of a situation or event. It is an open question what makes such sense perceptions appropriate vehicles to conceptualise our vague, hard-to-pin-down impressions of certain situations or events. What is it in the epistemological structure of smell, taste, sound, and vision that makes them excellent (and perhaps the only) source domains of this quality of human experience? I do not attempt to answer this question here.

In all probability, there are more conceptual metaphors in which smell functions as a source domain (in addition to suspicion, badness, guess, and general atmosphere as target domains). However, these are difficult to find with the methodology I am employing here. This job could be done by extensive corpus-based studies. But even the lexical method allows us to discover some of these cases. Take the example "the sweet smell of success" from the *Oxford Learner's Dictionary* (http://www.oxfordlearnersdictionaries.com/definition/english/success). The phrase is rendered in the dictionary as follows: "(informal) the pleasant feeling of being successful." Here, the feeling that arises from success is conceptualised metaphorically as SMELL, yielding the metaphor EMOTION IS SMELL, or more generally, EMOTION IS PERCEPTION.

As a matter of fact, the EMOTION IS PERCEPTION general conceptual metaphor includes one of the major metaphors for emotions: EMOTION IS FEELING/TOUCH. This is a basic metaphorical conceptualisation of the emotions, with linguistic examples such as *feel* (e.g., *I felt sorry for him, I was deeply touched*) and *feeling* (e.g., *I know the feeling*), as well as *hit* and *hurt* (e.g., *The news hit me, She was hurt*). The EMOTION IS TOUCH conceptual metaphor was noticed by Lakoff and Johnson (1980) under the heading EMOTIONAL EFFECT IS PHYSICAL CONTACT and by Kövecses

(1990) under the heading EMOTION IS FEELING. By contrast, SMELL does not appear to be a common way to conceptualise emotion although this is what we find in the example above.

Further, emotion is also conceptualised as taste in the example under discussion ("the sweet smell of..."). Although the word *sweet* apparently modifies smell, it actually qualifies emotion / feeling (the real target domain of smell in the example), which is, as the dictionary definition of the phrase above shows, part of the implicit meaning of the phrase. Since the property of sweetness is a characteristic of taste, we can suggest another conceptual metaphor for emotions: EMOTION IS TASTE. Thus, we get the following sense-perception-based conceptual metaphors for emotion (see Figure 5).

EMOTION IS PERCEPTION

EMOTION IS TOUCH   EMOTION IS TASTE   EMOTION IS SMELL

Figure 5. The sense-perception-based conceptual metaphors for emotion

Intuitively, there is probably a rank order between these conceptual metaphors: EMOTION IS TOUCH seems to be more common, conventional, and significant in the conceptualisation of emotions than EMOTION IS TASTE, which in turn seems to be more common, conventional, and significant than EMOTION IS SMELL. However, without corpus-linguistic data this idea remains a hypothesis to be tested.

What provides the grounds for the existence of these conceptual metaphors? What links the source domains to the target domains? It seems to me that the three conceptual metaphors are not grounded in the same way, that is, they do not have the same experiential, or bodily, basis (or grounding) (see, e.g., Lakoff & Johnson, 1980; Kövecses, 2002/2010). In conceptual metaphor theory, conceptual metaphors can be grounded or 'motivated' in essentially two ways (Grady, 1999): by resemblance (source resembles target) or by correlation (source is correlated with target). Emotion resembles perception (cf. Prinz, 2006), but it is also different from it. Resemblance between the two is sufficient to explain why emotion is a form of perception, but it is not sufficient to explain why EMOTION IS TOUCH definitely appears to be, or 'feels' like, a conceptual metaphor, and not a literal relationship. In the case of touch, the experiential basis for the metaphor may be that the same body organs and bodily sensations that can be found in touch (e.g., skin, change in temperature, pain) can be found in emotions (such as anger, fear). In the case of taste and smell, the experiential basis for the metaphor may be that the same brain structures that participate in taste and smell (e.g., the amygdala) also play a role in emotions in general (see Winter, 2016). This would mean that in all three cases we have certain correlations between certain sense perceptions and emotions that serve as the bodily basis for the metaphors.

But I believe that there is a difference between the cases of taste and smell. It appears to me that taste, especially in its evaluative function (sweet, bitter, bad), has a much wider scope of application (see Kövecses, 2000/2010) than smell. Sweet applies to not only emotional feelings (cf. sweet feeling of success) and particular emotions (sweet revenge) but also to anything positively evaluated. This situation would give rise to a broader metaphor than EMOTION IS TASTE; it would be PLEASANT IS SWEET (UNPLEASANT IS BITTER/SOUR/BAD TASTING) with a wide scope of application to pleasant experiences in general. (For further complications to this analysis, see Winter, this volume). It should be noticed, however, that both the emotion-related and the general application of the 'sweet taste' source domain is only conceivable as a result of a schematisation process that occurs to sweet (taste) in its literal sense. In the course of the process the literal sense of sweet is schematised, it is semantically bleached out, giving rise to general 'pleasantness', which is not limited to taste. In this case, a domain (such as sweetness-taste) that becomes the source gives rise to a target (such as pleasant) through the schematisation of the original domain. In another publication (Kövecses, 2015b), I propose schematisation as an additional way (besides resemblance and correlation) for the emergence of metaphors.

We may also wonder if the sense modalities of vision and hearing are also used to conceptualise emotions metaphorically – together with touch, taste, and smell. Given the very limited database I worked with, this was not the case. Assuming that this is the correct conclusion to draw, we can ask why vision and hearing are not used to conceptualise emotions metaphorically. The reason may be that, as Winter (2016) suggests, the brain structures that are implicated in both taste and smell, on the one hand, and emotion, on the other, are not implicated in the case of vision and hearing. However, such a claim can only be made very tentatively at the present stage of research.

6.   Smell as a target domain

The sense of smell is perhaps one of the most basic ways in which humans (and animals) gather information about reality. For this reason it serves as a perfect source domain, very much in line with what we would expect. For instance, the concept of suspicion is conventionally conceived of as smell, hence the conceptual metaphor SUSPICION IS SMELL (as in, *I can smell trouble*). Immorality and, more generally, badness is conceptualised as (bad) smell (as in, *The movie stinks*), yielding BAD IS SMELLY. And the vague and loose concept of "general atmosphere of something" is understood in terms of smell (as in, *What he did smells of fraud*), giving us the conceptual metaphor THE GENERAL ATMOSPHERE (OF SOMETHING) IS SMELL. In all of these cases, there is a sensory domain (smell) and a more abstract, subjective, evaluative, and complex domain. The latter functions as a target, the former as a source domain. The two are in a relationship of correlation, which means that the sensory domain is correlated with the non-sensory one in bodily experience.

Thus we assume that smell is an ideal source domain. Given this, we would *not* expect it to be understood metaphorically, that is, as functioning as a *target domain*. We are likely to think that it can be directly and straightforwardly comprehended without any metaphors. But it is in fact conceptualised metaphorically as a target. How is this possible? The reason, I suggest, is that smell like any other concept is characterised by a number of conceptual dimensions, or to put it in the framework of Langacker (1987), it is part of a domain matrix. Thus the concept of smell is connected to the idea that it is something that exists, that it is something that can have various degrees of intensity, that it is something that the perceiver, or experiencer, cannot help perceiving, that is, that he or she has no control over whether or not s/he perceives it. In other words, we can identify at least the following three dimensions for the concept of smell: EXISTENCE, INTENSITY, and LACK OF CONTROL.

In a "domain matrix" view of the conceptual system, the three dimensions are high-level, generic concepts that characterise many concepts, concrete and abstract alike. They are generic in the sense that they are superordinate concepts, which include specific cases. For instance, intensity may be realised as intensity of motion, intensity of pain, intensity of emotion, intensity of light, intensity of exercise, and, of course, intensity of smell. The superordinate concept is intensity. Such superordinate concepts function as shared dimensions of more specific concepts. Existence, intensity, and (lack of) control are concepts that form an integral part of many domains, including that of smell. Levinson and Majid (2014) discuss a number of such dimensions for various sense modalities. Further dimensions of concepts can be found in, for instance, Lakoff's (1993) Event Structure metaphor (Lakoff discusses, among others, state, change, cause, manner, and purpose). As a matter of fact, we can also regard the concept of pleasantness (or positive evaluation) that was discussed above as a dimensional concept ranging over many domains, not just smell.

An important property of these dimensional concepts is that they are all generic-level ones and abstract. As such, they easily lend themselves to metaphorical conceptualisation. The question is what kinds of conceptual metaphors are formed by making use of them in relation to smell.

6.1 Existence

Let us begin with existence. Consider some examples for how the existence of smell is presented by the *Online Oxford Collocation Dictionary* (http://oxforddictionary. so8848.com/search1?word=smell):

Verb+smell:

1. be filled with, have: "The air was filled with a pervasive smell of chemicals." "The cottage had a musty smell after being shut up over the winter."
2. give off: "The skunk gives off an unpleasant smell when attacked."
3. catch, detect: "As she walked into the house she detected the smell of gas."

The examples indicate a variety of ways in which the existence of smell can be conceptualised. In the case of *fill*, the smell is viewed as a substance and the object or location with the smell is viewed as a container, and the existence of the smell as the substance being in the container. In the case of *have*, existence of the smell corresponds to the possession of an object that is the property of smell itself. In the case of *give off*, causing smell to come into existence is the transfer of an object and the source of the smell is a surface. Finally, *catch* and *detect* are not dedicated to denoting the existence of smell; they simply assume its existence.

The examples and their construals of the existence of smell they reveal point to the following conceptual metaphors:

filled with:

1. SMELL IS A SUBSTANCE
2. THE OBJECT / LOCATION THAT HAS THE SMELL IS A CONTAINER
3. THE EXISTENCE OF SMELL IS FOR THE SUBSTANCE TO BE IN THE CONTAINER

have:

1. SMELL IS AN OBJECT
2. THE EXISTENCE OF SMELL IS THE POSSESSION OF AN OBJECT

give off:

1. SMELL IS AN OBJECT
2. CAUSING SMELL IS TRANSFERRING THE OBJECT
3. SOURCE OF SMELL IS A SURFACE

The three cases conceptualise the experience of smell as the existence of a state. The state is either a substance or an object. Existence is viewed as a substance being in a container, as possessing an object, and as transferring an object. The three specific cases of existence metaphors for smell are thus instances of three generic-level metaphors for existence:

1. EXISTENCE IS BEING IN A CONTAINER
2. EXISTENCE IS POSSESSION
3. (CAUSING) EXISTENCE IS TRANSFER

Generic-level and specific-level metaphors can be arranged in a schematicity hierarchy, where the specific-level metaphors are instances of the generic-level ones (see Kövecses, 2017). For example, the metaphor THE EXISTENCE OF SMELL IS FOR THE SUBSTANCE TO BE IN THE CONTAINER is an instance of the EXISTENCE IS BEING IN CONTAINER metaphor. These latter kind of conceptual metaphors apply to a large number of specific-level instances of existence of any kind, not just to the existence of smell.

6.2   Intensity

Another generic-level concept that is linked to smell is intensity, as Levinson and Majid (2014, p. 413) also suggest: "Intensity is another candidate cross-modal dimension. Lights, sounds, smells, tactile pressures, tastes, pains, emotions can all have low or high intensities." In the case of smell, intensity involves a scale of values from weak to strong. Collocation dictionaries give us a good idea of this notion in relation to smell. Consider the following collocations for smell from the *Online Oxford Collocation Dictionary* (http://oxforddictionary.so8848.com/search1?word=smell):

Adjective:

1. overpowering, pervasive, pungent, rich, sharp, strong: "There was an overpowering smell of burning tyres."
2. faint, distinct, distinctive, particular, unmistakable, funny, peculiar, strange, unusual: "What's that funny smell?"
3. familiar, lingering, aromatic, delectable, delicious, fragrant, fresh, lovely, nice, savoury, sweet, wonderful: "the aromatic smells of a spring garden full of herbs"
4. warm, appalling, awful, bad, evil, horrible, nasty, offensive, terrible, unpleasant, vile, acrid, nauseating, putrid, rank, sickly: "An acrid smell filled the air."
5. damp, dank, musty, rancid, sour, stale: "the sour smell of unwashed linen"
6. earthy, fishy, masculine, metallic, musky, oily, smoky, spicy, cooking: "Cooking smells drifted up from the kitchen."

Many of these adjectives deal with different kinds of smell, but some of them denote the intensity aspect of smell. These latter adjectives (and the verb *fill* in the example) appear to be based on several different conceptual metaphors – in some cases, on etymological grounds:

1. *overpowering, strong, faint*: INTENSITY OF SMELL IS STRENGTH OF EFFECT
2. *sharp, pungent*: INTENSITY OF SMELL IS SHARPNESS OF AN OBJECT
3. *vaguely*: INTENSITY OF SMELL IS DEGREE OF BRIGHTNESS OF LIGHT
4. *pervasive, fill*: INTENSITY OF SMELL IS QUANTITY OF A SUBSTANCE

These conceptual metaphors that relate to the intensity aspect of smell also have their generic-level variants:

1. *overpowering, strong, faint*: INTENSITY IS STRENGTH
2. *sharp, pungent*: INTENSITY IS SHARPNESS
3. *vaguely*: INTENSITY IS BRIGHTNESS
4. *pervasive, fill*: INTENSITY IS QUANTITY

As can be seen from these examples of metaphors, the intensity of smell can be metaphorically conveyed by another sense modality, as in the case of INTENSITY OF SMELL IS SHARPNESS OF AN OBJECT or INTENSITY OF SMELL IS THE DEGREE OF BRIGHTNESS OF LIGHT. These cases might point to such cross-modal conceptual metaphors as SMELL IS TOUCH/FEELING and SMELL IS VISION, respectively. However, it may well be that these metaphors do not extend (do not apply) beyond the dimension of intensity.

6.3   Lack of control

The issue of control is also relevant to smell (and maybe also perception in general). A curious property of perceptual experience, especially smell, is that we do not have control over whether we perceive (we must breathe) or over what we perceive – unless, of course, we deliberately seek out a particular perceptual sensation (that is, in the default case, smell, and maybe sense perception in general, is passive, as suggested at the beginning of the paper). If our sense organs are normal and no external circumstance blocks perception, we perceive any existing perceptual stimulus. This is also often rendered in metaphorical ways – one of the chief ways among them (according to dictionary information) is by means of the verb *hit* in the case of smell. Consider the example taken from the *English Collocations Dictionary* online (https://www.ozdic.com/collocation-dictionary/smell): "Then the pungent smell hit us – rotting fish and seaweed." We can analyse the metaphorical use of *hit* as follows:

1. SMELL IS A PHYSICAL FORCE
2. INTENSE SMELL IS A STRONG PHYSICAL FORCE
3. SENSING AN INTENSE SMELL IS COMING INTO CONTACT WITH A STRONG PHYSICAL FORCE

The three basic conceptual metaphors above can be combined into a complex one that describes the metaphorical conceptualisation of the perceptual experience of strong smell: THE EXPERIENCER OF AN INTENSE SMELL IS A PERSON COMING INTO ABRUPT PHYSICAL CONTACT WITH A STRONG PHYSICAL FORCE. But most importantly, the main point is, as before, that the specific-level conceptual metaphors are licensed by corresponding generic-level ones:

1. CAUSES ARE FORCES
2. INTENSITY IS STRENGTH
3. SENSING IS CONTACT

Again, these generic-level metaphors pervade the conceptual system and allow us to conceptualise various kinds of causes, intensity, and sensation, and not just smell as a cause, not just the intensity of smell, and not just sensing smell. In other words, smell as an extremely basic and direct experience has aspects to it that lend themselves to metaphorical conceptualisation.

7. Conclusions

In the paper, I showed that smell has an elaborate conceptual structure, which is, essentially, a language-based folk theory of smell. On the basis of lexical evidence from English, I identified two frames that stand out among the many versions of smell as a conceptual category: a passive and an active frame. I argued that it is the passive version of smell that probably best represents the conceptual prototype of smell. The suggested or hypothetical prototype shows which conceptual elements of smell are linguistically coded.

The category of smell also comes with an elaborate metaphorical structure (see also Anderson, this volume). Smell can function as both a source domain and a target domain. As was pointed out by previous research, in English smell is used to conceptualise several abstract concepts, such as suspicion, badness, and guessing. The present study found that smell is employed to metaphorically comprehend two additional target concepts: general atmosphere (of a state or event) and emotion. The metaphorical conceptualisation of emotions by smell appears to be marginal in importance – at least based on the lexical evidence that was used in the present study. But it may well be that another methodology (such as a corpus-based study) would bring different results.

However, other sense modalities appear to play a major role in the metaphorical conceptualisation of emotions. In particular, touch and taste figure importantly in this. Touch is a metaphorical source domain that functions in a constitutive role in conceptualising emotions. Its basicness and importance is shown by the fact that probably the most common synonym for emotion, *feeling*, is based on this metaphor. The conceptual role of taste is not constitutive in the way touch is, but it captures a basic dimension of emotions: their positive or negative polarity.

The idea that smell, an extremely basic kind of experience, functions as a target domain in metaphorical conceptualisation presents a challenge to conceptual metaphor theory, which assumes that basic experiences, such as smell, are the best source domains in conceptualising more complex abstract concepts and that they require no metaphorical conceptualisation. It seems that smell can also function as a target that needs to be comprehended metaphorically. This is because it has conceptual dimensions, such as existence, intensity, and lack of control, that are complex and abstract enough to call for metaphorical conceptualisation. The conceptual metaphors used for this purpose (e.g., EXISTENCE IS BEING IN A CONTAINER, INTENSITY IS STRENGTH, CAUSES ARE FORCES) are all generic-level ones that pervade the conceptual system. Such generic metaphors appear to characterise not only complex and abstract concepts (such as emotion concepts) but also our most mundane and perception-based ones, such as smell.

The conceptual status of smell as both source and target domain shows further aspects of how smell is linguistically coded. In addition to the elements that make up the frames that constitute the concept, the frames have certain dimensions, such as positive-negative polarity, existence, intensity, and (lack of) control that are also revealed by the lexis that is used about smell. Further studies along the same cognitive linguistic lines as the present one, and on languages other than English and on other sense modalities will have to be conducted to be able to judge the relative degree to which smell is linguistically coded.

Acknowledgements

I gratefully thank the editors of this volume for their many constructive comments on an earlier version of my paper and for inviting me to the workshop on perception metaphors.

Online sources

English Collocations Dictionary online. https://www.ozdic.com/collocation-dictionary/smell
Online Oxford Collocations Dictionary. http://oxforddictionary.so8848.com/search1?word= smell
Oxford Learner's Dictionary. http://www.oxfordlearnersdictionaries.com/definition/english/ success
WordNet. http://wordnetweb.princeton.edu/perl/webwn?s=smell&sub=Search+WordNet&o2= &o0=1&o8=1&o1=1&o7=&o5=&o9=&o6=&o3=&o4=&h

References

Barcelona, A. (2000). On the plausibility of claiming a metonymic motivation for conceptual metaphor. In A. Barcelona (Ed.), *Metaphor and metonymy at the crossroads* (pp. 31–58). Berlin & New York: Mouton de Gruyter. https://doi.org/10.1515/9783110894677.31

Barsalou, L. W. (1999). Perceptual symbol systems. *Behavioral and Brain Sciences*, 22, 577–609.

Chu, S. & Downes, J. J. (2000). Odour-evoked autobiographical memories: psychological investigations of Proustian phenomena. *Chemical Senses*, 25(1), 111–116. https://doi.org/10.1093/chemse/25.1.111

Classen, C., Howes, D. & Synnott, A. (1994). *Aroma: the cultural history of smell*. London and New York: Routledge.

Ekman, P. (1992). An argument for basic emotions. *Cognition and Emotion*, 6 (3/4), 169–200. https://doi.org/10.1080/02699939208411068

Evans, N. & Wilkins, D. (2000). In the mind's ear: The semantic extensions of perception verbs in Australian languages. *Language*, 76(3), 546–592. https://doi.org/10.2307/417135

Fillmore, C. J. (1982). Frame semantics. In the linguistic society of Korea (ed.), *Linguistics in the Morning Calm* (pp. 111–137). Seoul: Hanshin.

Frijda, N. (1986). *The emotions*. Cambridge: Cambridge University Press.

Grady, J. (1999). A typology of motivation for conceptual metaphors: Correlations vs. resemblance. In R. W. Gibbs & G. J. Steen (Eds.), *Metaphor in Cognitive Linguistics* (pp. 79–100). Amsterdam and Philadelphia: John Benjamins. https://doi.org/10.1075/cilt.175.06gra

Holland, D. and Quinn, D. (Eds.). (1987). *Cultural Models in Language and Thought*. New York: Cambridge University Press.

Ibarretxe-Antuñano, I. (1999). Metaphorical mappings in the sense of smell. In R. W. Gibbs & G. J. Steen (Eds.) *Metaphor in cognitive linguistics* (p. 29–45). Amsterdam: John Benjamins. https://doi.org/10.1075/cilt.175.03iba

Kövecses, Z. (1986). *Metaphors of anger, pride, and love*. Amsterdam: John Benjamins. https://doi.org/10.1075/pb.vii.8

Kövecses, Z. (1990). *Emotion Concepts*. New York: Springer Verlag.

Kövecses, Z. (2000). *Metaphor and emotion*. Cambridge and New York: Cambridge University Press.

Kövecses, Z. (2002/2010). *Metaphor: A practical introduction*. (Second edition 2010) Oxford and New York: Oxford University Press.

Kövecses, Z. (2011). Methodological issues in conceptual metaphor theory. In S. Handl & H-J. Schmid (Eds.), *Windows to the mind: Metaphor, metonymy and conceptual blending* (pp. 23–39). Berlin/New York: Mouton de Gruyter. https://doi.org/10.1515/9783110238198.23

Kövecses, Z. (2015a). Surprise as a conceptual category. *Review of Cognitive Linguistics*, 13(2), 270–290. https://doi.org/10.1075/rcl.13.2.01kov

Kövecses, Z. (2015b). Metaphor and emergentism. In B. MacWhinney & W. O'Grady (Eds), *The handbook of language emergence* (pp. 147–162). Oxford: Wiley-Blackwell.

Kövecses, Z. (2017). Levels of metaphor. *Cognitive Linguistics*, 28(2), 321–347. https://doi.org/10.1515/cog-2016-0052

Kövecses, Z. & Ambrus, L. & Hegedűs, D. & Imai, R. & Sobczak, A. (in press). The lexical vs. the corpus-based method in the study of metaphors. In M. Bolognesi & K. Despot & K. Štrkalj & M. Brdar (Eds.), *Fantastic metaphors and where to find them: traditional and new methods in figurative language research*. Amsterdam: John Benjamins.

Lakoff, G. (1987). *Women, fire, and dangerous things*. Chicago: The University of Chicago Press. https://doi.org/10.7208/chicago/9780226471013.001.0001

Lakoff, G. (1993). The contemporary theory of metaphor. In A. Ortony (Ed.), *Metaphor and thought* (pp. 202–251). Cambridge: Cambridge University Press. https://doi.org/10.1017/CBO9781139173865.013

Lakoff, G. & Johnson, M. (1980). *Metaphors we live by*. Chicago: The University of Chicago Press.

Lakoff, G. & Johnson, M. (1999). *Philosophy in the flesh*. New York: Basic Books.

Lakoff, G. & Kövecses, Z. (1987). The cognitive model of anger inherent in American English. In D. Holland & N. Quinn (Eds.), *Cultural models in language and thought* (pp. 195–221). Cambridge and New York: Cambridge University Press. https://doi.org/10.1017/CBO9780511607660.009

Langacker, R. (1987). *Foundations of cognitive grammar*. Vol. 1. Stanford: Stanford University Press.

Levinson, S. C. & Majid, A. (2014). Differential ineffability and the senses. *Mind and Language*, 29(4), 407–427. https://doi.org/10.1111/mila.12057

Neagu, M. (2013). What is universal and what is language-specific in the polysemy of perception verbs? *Revue roumaine de linguistique LVIII 3*, 329–343.

Prinz, J. J. (2006). Is emotion a form of perception? *Canadian Journal of Philosophy*, Volume 36, Supplement [vol. 32], 137–160. https://doi.org/10.1353/cjp.2007.0035

Rosch, E. (1978). Principles of categorization. In E. Rosch & B. B. Lloyd (Eds.), *Cognition and Categorization* (pp. 27–48). Hillsdale, NJ: Lawrence Erlbaum.

Soriano, C. (2005). The Conceptualization of anger in English and Spanish: A Cognitive Approach. Unpublished PhD thesis, University of Murcia.

Soudry, Y. & Lemogne, C. & Malinvaud, D. & Consoli, S.-M., & Bonfils, P. (2011). Olfactory system and emotion: Common substrates. *European Annals of Otorhinolaryngology, Head and Neck Diseases*, 128(1), 18–23. https://doi.org/10.1016/j.anorl.2010.09.007

Sweetser, E. (1990). *From etymology to pragmatics*. New York: Cambridge University Press. https://doi.org/10.1017/CBO9780511620904

Willander, J. & Larsson, M. (2007). Olfaction and emotion: The case of autobiographical memory. *Memory & Cognition*, 35(7), 1659–1663. https://doi.org/10.3758/BF03193499

Winter, B. (2016). Taste and smell words form an affectively loaded and emotionally flexible part of the English lexicon. *Language, Cognition and Neuroscience*, 31(8), 975–988. https://doi.org/10.1080/23273798.2016.1193619

Yu, N. (1998). *The contemporary theory of metaphor. A Perspective from Chinese*. Amsterdam: John Benjamins. https://doi.org/10.1075/hcp.1

CHAPTER 17

Perception verbs in context
Perspectives from Kaluli (Bosavi) child-caregiver interaction

Lila San Roque and Bambi B. Schieffelin
Radboud University / New York University

Perceptual language is a rich site of polysemous meaning and pragmatic extension. In this chapter, we explore the question of how children learning a language
come to grips with this complexity, focusing on basic perception verbs as used in
child-caregiver interaction in the language Bosavi, spoken in Papua New Guinea.
We discuss creative and routinised instances of perception verb use in these interactions, and comment on connections to recognised cross-linguistic patterns
of polysemy. Finally, we suggest ways that Christian missionisation and literacy
practices may have influenced shifting uses of the language of sight and audition
in the Bosavi context.

Keywords: polysemy, language socialisation, Papua New Guinea

1. Introduction

As we learn more about sensory language around the world, it seems that perception
terms are nearly always more than first meets the eye or ear. Perceptual language is a
rich site of polysemous meaning and metaphorical extension, for example, a word to
do with taste may be used in reference to sound (e.g., Williams, 1976), or a word that
refers to hearing may also have a meaning to do with understanding (e.g., Vanhove,
2008). How do children learning a language come to grips with this complexity of
meaning and function? It has been suggested that children typically over-extend the
possible meanings of polysemous terms (Rabagliati, Marcus & Pylkkänen, 2010),
and it is not always clear that literal, modality-specific perceptual meanings will be
uppermost in a child's mind as he or she starts to respond to and use such words.

For example, an early study by Edwards and Goodwin (1985) noted that for
children acquiring English, the vision verb *look* may be learnt more as part of an
attention-directing routine than as a reference to visual experience. These authors
discuss how, for one child, her initial uses of *look* (as well as those of her caregivers)
tend to be restricted to particular pragmatic routines that employ imperative forms,

https://doi.org/10.1075/celcr.19.17san

functioning almost exclusively to perform 'nominations' (i.e., direct attention to something in the environment). The child's first uses of *look* generalise from one situation (directing attention to herself) to more general nominations (directing attention to other things) and finally to describing visual experience (e.g., saying that someone else is looking at something). As well as stressing the potential importance of pragmatic function as a precursor to semantic content for the term *look*, Edwards and Goodwin (1985) further propose that the acquisition of *see* may relate to the awareness of mental experience, and thus metacognitive abilities. This proposal connects to one of the most well-known perceptual metaphors, that is, the semantic association of vision terms with cognition, found in a range of the world's languages, (see, e.g., Sweetser, 1990; Aikhenvald & Storch, 2013) although not necessarily a strict universal (e.g., Evans & Wilkins, 2000).

Picking up on the theme of non-perceptual meanings of *see* in English, Johnson (1999) suggests that in first language acquisition this verb may initially be understood as having a complex of semantics from the domains of vision, attention, cognition and sociality, and that it is by no means clear that children recognise vision as the primary core meaning. Johnson (1999) generalises this possibility to polysemy more broadly, proposing that a theory of 'conflation' (i.e., the child conflates what might be distinct adult senses) is just as viable as a theory of 'metaphor' (i.e., the child acquires a single concrete sense that is then metaphorically extended). The studies of Edwards and Goodwin and of Johnson agree in suggesting that an English child's initial learning of basic vision verbs may be less concerned than one might expect with literal descriptions of visual experience.

In this chapter, we take a selection of extended meanings of perception verbs that are relatively well-attested cross-linguistically (cf. San Roque, Kendrick, Norcliffe & Majid, 2018), and present examples of how these meanings might be supported interactionally between young children and their caregivers in Bosavi (Kaluli), a language of Papua New Guinea. We extend knowledge about perceptual metaphor in child-caregiver conversation in two ways. Firstly, by exploring semantic associations in a language other than English (although we note that children's acquisition of perception-related metaphors in other languages has been investigated from experimental perspectives, see, e.g., Shayan, Ozturk, Bowerman & Majid, 2014). And secondly, by examining not just child and caregiver uses of vision verbs, which have been a focus of earlier research, but also audition and (to a much more limited extent) touch, taste and smell terms. We comment on vision-attention and vision-knowledge associations in the Bosavi data, as well as briefly visiting a few other semantic associations that have been identified as cross-linguistically relevant, including visual and attemptive meanings (e.g., 'see' > 'try', Foley, 1986; Voinov, 2013), hearing and obedience (e.g., Sweetser, 1990; Evans & Wilkins, 2000; Vanhove 2008), touch and affectedness (Ibarretxe-Antuñano, 2006), taste and evaluation (e.g., Sweetser, 1990), and smell and deduction (e.g., Ibarretxe-Antuñano, this volume; 1999).

At this early stage of investigation, we aim to present examples from Bosavi where the conversational context creates potential for particular associations of perception verbs (see also Wilkins, 1981; Majid, 2013), thus showing that such potential can be present in children's early linguistic encounters even in diverse cultures. Subsequent research may give opportunities to further draw conclusions concerning the trajectory of development of 'extended meanings' of perception verbs for Bosavi child learners, and even concerning the genesis of particular polysemies in interaction (see San Roque, Kendrick, Norcliffe & Majid, submitted).

The following section (Section 2) provides background on the Bosavi, including introducing Bosavi perceptual language and the corpus of data on which the chapter is based. Then, moving from sight (Section 3), to sound (Section 4), to touch (Section 5), to taste and smell (Section 6), we discuss examples of perception terms in data from child-caregiver interaction, including creative and routinised instances of perception verb use, and comment on connections to recognised cross-linguistic patterns of polysemy. In Section 7 we summarise the semantic associations discussed and, as a parting note, suggest ways that Christian missionisation and literacy practices have influenced shifting uses of the language of sight and audition in the Bosavi context.

2. Language background

The Bosavi language (classified as Trans New Guinea, see, e.g., Ross, 2005) is spoken by approximately 2000 people living in Papua New Guinea. Bosavi lands lie within the Great Papuan Plateau, north of Mt Bosavi (Schieffelin & Feld, 1998, p. ix). The name 'Bosavi' is used indigenously to refer to a group of four dialects or language varieties: Kaluli, Wisesi, Walulu and Ologo. The material we discuss here relates especially to the Kaluli variety.

At the time the data discussed here were recorded, Bosavi people were living a largely subsistence lifestyle, with fairly limited contact with non-indigenous outsiders, and were mostly monolingual and non-literate. Traditionally, Bosavi people lived mostly in villages, in large longhouses, which accommodated up to about 100 people. They also spent time in smaller dwellings with members of their extended families. Young children spent a lot of time with their mothers, but also with siblings, cousins, grandparents, and other family members. Subsistence practices were mainly garden and game-based, with the forest environment and water features of the area providing a major cosmological focus, especially in relation to avian wildlife (Feld, [1982]2012, 1996; see also, e.g., E. Schieffelin, 1976; Schieffelin, 1990; E. Schieffelin & Crittenden 1991 for further background on the history, lifestyle, culture and concerns of Bosavi peoples at the relevant time).

The examples we discuss in this chapter were recorded by Schieffelin from 1975 through 1976 in a village called Sululib. During this period, Schieffelin was resident in the village and (among other research) created a child language corpus of audio recordings and detailed contextual notes that focused on one girl, Ma:li, and on two boys, Abi and Wanu, from when they were around 2 years old until they were nearly 3. These three children were recorded in everyday interaction with caregivers and other family members roughly every five weeks, for a couple of hours at a time. The interactions were transcribed by Schieffelin in consultation with the children's mothers and other members of the community. Detailed information on the families, methods, and contexts can be found in Schieffelin (1990). For this chapter, we have selected examples that we found to be especially illustrative of certain potential meanings, after going through the corpus to identify occurrences of perception verbs more generally.

Like most Trans New Guinea languages, Kaluli is verb-final. Argument noun phrases can be elided if recoverable from context, so that verb-only sentences are common in connected discourse. An important point about Kaluli verbs, especially in reference to children's acquisition of the language, is the high amount of irregularity. Verbs can be described as having four different stems that are used in different morphological operations. For some verbs the stems are similar, but for others there is little to no crossover in form (Table 1).[1] For example, the verb 'take' is quite regular, with the same stem *di* occurring across the four main categories. However, the verb 'eat' shows little to no regular correspondence. The two main perception verbs that we look at in this chapter, *bo:ba* 'see/look (at)', and *dabuma* 'hear/listen (to)' show some regular and some less predictable stem changes. Children need to learn these irregularities to correctly use these verbs.

The imperative stems of basic verbs of perception in Bosavi for the five senses, based on Viberg's (1983) classic framework, are shown in Table 2. The first three

---

1.   In this chapter we follow the Bosavi orthography largely as proposed by Rule (1964) and described in Schieffelin and Feld (1998). Most sound-letter correspondences are reasonably similar to the IPA equivalents, the main exceptions being: y = [j], $a:$ = [ɛ] or [æ], $o:$ = [ɔ] or [ʋ]. For the sake of space and simplicity, we show the interlinear gloss of *bo:ba* in examples as 'see' (rather than the more comprehensive translation 'see/look.at') and of *dabuma* as 'hear' (as opposed to 'hear/listen.to'). Furthermore, in multi-line examples, we give interlinear glosses only for those lines that include a relevant perception verb. Glossing conventions generally follow the Leipzig glossing rules, with the following additions: EMPH 'emphatic', HAB 'habitual' (Bosavi has two habitual inflections, distinguished here by subscript numbers; see Grosh & Grosh, 2004, pp. 17–18, for further information), HORT 'hortative', NEUT 'neutral/absolutive', PURP 'purposive', SEQ 'sequential', SNS 'sensory evidential'. Notes about accompanying actions that help to understand the context of the utterance are shown in double parentheses. Annotations in single parentheses following examples show the target children's approximate ages (where relevant) in months (m) and weeks (w), and identify Schieffelin's original recording.

Table 1. Some examples of Bosavi verbs, showing stem forms

	IMPERATIVE	FUTURE IMPERATIVE	FUTURE	PAST
'take'	*di-ma*	*di-ya:bi*	*di-a:no:*	*di*
'eat'	*maya*	*na:bi*	*ma:no:*	*mo:no:*
'see, look (at)'	*bo:ba*	*ba:da:bi*	*ba:ba:no:*	*ba:ba:*
'hear, listen (to)'	*dabuma*	*da:da:bi*	*da:ba:no:*	*dabu*

verbs are simple forms: *bo:ba* 'see, look (at)', *dabuma* 'hear, listen (to)' and *golóma* 'touch'. These are 'activity' and/or 'experience' verbs in that the perceiver is encoded as the subject. However, unlike in English, there is no lexical distinction between active direction of the senses (e.g., as in English *listen*) as opposed to receptive experience (English *hear*). Active or experiential smell and taste (e.g., as in an English sentence such as *I tasted the soup*) are described with complex expressions using the vision verb *bo:ba* in the case of taste, and the hearing verb *dabuma* in the case of smell. Smell is described using either *mun* 'odour' or *migi* 'nose' (marked for instrumental case) in combination with *dabuma* 'hear' (see also Feld, 1996).[2] Active taste can be expressed using *bo:ba* 'see, look (at)' in combination with the term *nola* (not otherwise known to be an independent verb or noun). Beyond this dedicated phrase, active taste can also be described using productive multi-verb attemptive constructions such as *dabe bo:ba* 'lick/slurp+see, try to lick/slurp' and *nudo: bulu bo:ba* 'try to tell the taste' (*bulu bo:ba* = try to hunt/catch). For source-based expressions (e.g., as in English *the soup looks nice but it tastes odd*), taste is encoded by the verb *nudab*, but the other senses lack dedicated verbs (cf. also Evans &Wilkins 2000 concerning the lack of source-based verbs in many Australian languages). Basic expressions for source-based sight, hearing, touch and smell thus remain a topic for further investigation.

Table 2. Basic perception expressions in Bosavi

	Activity/experience	source
sight	*bo:ba* 'see, look (at)'	
hearing	*dabuma* 'hear, listen (to)'	
touch	*golóma* 'touch'	
smell	*mun dabuma* 'smell a smell'	
	migi-ya: dabuma 'smell something' (nose-INSTR hear)	
taste	*nola bo:ba* 'taste, test food to see if cooked'	*nudab* 'taste'

---

2. Some varieties of Tok Pisin, a major lingua franca of Papua New Guinea (although not widely spoken in the Bosavi community at the time of recording), express olfaction using a similar verb + noun combination, *harim smel* 'hear/sense (a) smell' (Mihalic, 1971, p. 95); see also Viberg (1983, p. 141–142) regarding similar constructions cross-linguistically.

Of course, the basic perception verbs and predicates in Table 2 are not the only way of encoding perceptual experience in Bosavi. While it is beyond the scope of this chapter to discuss these terms, the language includes more complex and specific perceptual vocabulary (encompassing verbs, nouns, adjectives, ideophones, and complex predicates), a few examples of which are shown in Table 3. In addition, Kaluli encodes perceptual experience grammatically through evidential markers that indicate visual and non-visual sensory experience of an event or object (see Rule, 1964; Schieffelin, 1996; San Roque & Loughnane, 2012a, 2012b). Thus, the sensory world is encoded in a variety of ways beyond basic verbs, deserving of further detailed investigation. For our current purposes, the more general perception verbs offer us one tractable way to explore children's early encounters with the linguistic encoding of perceptual experience, and how concepts of perception connect to other semantic domains.

Table 3. Examples of specific sensory expressions (Schieffelin & Feld, 1998)

SOUND	SMELL	TASTE
fefelab 'flapping or flicking sound of breast cape or wings of bird of paradise'	*hesen* 'bad smell'	*nafa nudab* 'taste good' (*nafa* = 'good, clean, nice')
gige 'cracking sound, like breaking a bird eggshell'	*ko:lo:n* 'stink, very bad smell'	
	kugudo: 'oily smell of cooking pig'	*mogagi nudab* 'taste bad' (*mogagi* = 'badly, carelessly')
sololo 'sounds of small things slinking along the ground at night'	*kuk* 'smell of things decomposing, like a dead body'	*halab* 'taste bitter'
tubu 'sound of very large rock thrown or plunged into water'	*huf* 'crinkle top of nose; sniff a stink'	

3. Sight

We turn now to examples of basic perception verbs in interaction. We begin with *bo:ba* 'see, look (at)', the vision verb, which is the most frequent and flexible perception verb in the Bosavi child language corpus, found in a range of contexts. Our main focus here is on three types of occurrence. We first present examples of *bo:ba* in both literal and playful sequences that focus on visual experience and attention, and then instances that highlight a relationship of vision to knowledge. Finally, we discuss constructional uses of *bo:ba* that have an attemptive sense, meaning something like 'try' or 'see if you can…'.

In the Bosavi conversations, attention to and verbal expression of what one saw was encouraged at an early age, and by 26 months, the three children are all recorded using several forms of *bo:ba*. A simple example is shown in (1), a question-answer sequence that focuses attention on whether or not the addressee (Ma:li, here 26 months) had seen a particular person during a visit to another household. Here, Ma:li's use of the correct verb form is potentially cued by her mother's question.

(1) Mo: *Yabe-yo:*   *ge*   *ba:ba:-yo:*?
        Yabe-NEUT 2SG see.PST-Q
        'Did you see Yabe?'
      Ma:li: *ba:ba:*
        see.PST
        '[I] saw [him].'   (26m MIII 2–1)

In the recorded family interactions, the verb often occurs as a present question, *ba:daya* 'do you see?' or *a:no: ba:daya?* 'do you see that?' throughout talk to direct others to notice something. While instances of *bo:ba* were scattered throughout interactions, a particularly striking feature across all three households was the saturated use of verbs of seeing in activities where novel objects were the focus of intense scrutiny and talk. For example, a bar of soap with a little person etched on it elicited detailed naming and discussion of the body parts that were visible, including contributions from 2-yr-old Wanu (2).

(2) *do*   *gib-o:*   *we* *ba:d-a-ya?*
      1SG.POSS.father foot-NEUT this see-2.PRS-Q
      'My father, do you see this foot?'   (25m1w WII 3–1)

Such examples show similarities to the central 'nominating' function of English *look* as discussed by Edwards and Goodwin (1985), suggesting the important role of vision verbs in establishing joint attention. However, in the Bosavi interactions, a question format was favoured, and an imperative form of *bo:ba* 'see, look(at)' was rarely used by adults or children (except as part of the attemptive construction, discussed below).

  Novel objects also triggered playful sequences with a focus on visual experience (and visual technologies), as in the more extended Extract (3). In this sequence, the play is based on imitating the photographic endeavours of the local missionary, using an old adhesive tape dispenser as a pretend camera to look through and 'take pictures'. Ma:li's mother uses the second person present question *ba:daya*, 'do you see?' as she looks through the hole in the tape dispenser and playfully asks Ma:li to look at her. Ma:li responds using *bo:do:l* 'I see' (3b). However, when she tries to express her desire to look at or through the tape dispenser herself, also employing a final emphatic marker, she incorrectly selects a third person verb form (shown preceded by an asterisk), in (3c). Following Ma:li's assertion, Ma:li's mother offers the tape dispenser with the imperative *bo:ba*, asks her if she sees (*ba:daya*), and then if she has seen (*ba:ba:ya*) providing three different verb forms in quick succession. She subsequently explicitly models Ma:li's utterance with the correct verb form, which Ma:li repeats in response (3g).

(3) a. Mo: *Ma:li, giyo: ne ba:d-a-ya?*
              Ma:li 2SG 1SG see-2.PRS-Q
              'Ma:li do you see me?' ((Ma:li is reaching for dispenser, whining))

     b. Ma:li: *niyo: no gelo bo:d-o:l*
                 1SG and 2SG see-1.PRS
                 'I and, I also see you.

     c.   *no:*   *nelo: *ba:d-ab-a: *ba:d-ab-a:*
                1SG.POSS.mother 1SG see-2/3.PRS-EMPH see-2/3.PRS-EMPH
                ba:d-ab-a:!
                see-2/3.PRS-EMPH
                Mother I *see! I *see, I *see!' ((Mother is holding up dispenser to
                Ma:li so she can look through the hole))

     d. Mo: *go:no: bo:ba,   giyo: ne ba:d-a-ya?*
              2SG look.IMP 2SG 1SG see-2.PRS-Q
              ba:d-a-ya? ba:d-a-ya?
              see-2.PRS-Q see-2.PRS-Q
              'You yourself look, do you see me? Do you see? Do you see?

     e.   *Ma:li o: gi ba:ba:-ya?*
                Ma:li   and 2SG see.PST-Q
                Ma:li, and did you see?

     f.   *niyo: no:no: bo:d-o:l a:la: sa:l-an*
                1SG 1SG   see-1.PRS like.that say-HAB$_1$
                I myself see, one says like that.'

     g. Ma:li: *o: niyo: no:no: bo:d-o:l*
                 and 1SG   1SG   see-1.PRS
                 'And I myself see.'   (26m MIII 3–2)

As well as interactions involving *bo:ba* that explore visual experience (both literally and playfully), we see situations in the data which highlight a connection between vision and intellection. In regard to other languages, such a connection has been described as an instance of metaphorical meaning, extending the physiological experience of seeing to mental experience (see also Proos, this volume), and is argued to be enshrined in cross-linguistic patterns of polysemy (e.g., Sweetser, 1990). While we do not claim that Bosavi speakers necessarily understand *bo:ba:* as polysemous in this way, we note that certain uses of this verb indicate a semantic association between seeing and knowing, or, in this case, between *not* seeing and *not* knowing.[3] Searching for missing objects such as net bags and axes or knives in the dark smoky longhouse was a regular activity. Questions about the location of an object were most often responded to with *nelo: mo:ba:ba:* 'I did not see it'; in other words, I don't know where it is. The three children appear to be competent users of this 'denial' strategy from around 30 months. An example is shown in (4), where Ma:li's mother questions her about the location of some salt, implying that Ma:li must be the one who put it wherever it is. However, Ma:li denies having even seen it (4d). In this interaction Ma:li seems to be at least implicitly aware that *bo:ba* is relevant to issues of knowledge and responsibility.

(4) a. Mo: *so:luwo: aba da:laba:le?*
             'I wonder where is the salt?
    b.   *so:luwo: so:lu ina:lilo: dimiyalo:*
             Salt, the salt that was given the day before yesterday.
    c.   *gilo: sa:lisalo aba difa:yo:?*
             You were holding it, where did you put it?'
    d. Ma:li: *ah!*   **ne-lo:**   **mo:-ba:ba:.**   **mo:-ba:ba:**
             no   1SG-NEG   NEG-see.PST   NEG-see.PST
             'No! I didn't see it. Didn't see it.'   (32m2w MVIII 23–1)

Other interactions suggest that visual experience is equated with knowledge in the sense of familiarity. When Ma:li fails to recognise the object that her mother is pulling from the fire – a sweet potato – her mother responds in disbelief with a rhetorical question, 'Don't you usually see it?', suggesting 'How can you not know what this is?' (5).

(5) Mo: *ge mo:-**ba:da:**-sen-o:?!*
         2SG NEG-see-HAB$_2$-Q
         'Don't you usually see it?!'   (28m3w MV 14–1)

As well as occurring as a simple main verb, *bo:ba* is used with the word *se* 'just, only' and another verb root to express attemptive meaning, so that *se* V *bo:ba* means something like 'try to V', or 'see if you can V'. There is also a contracted variant of this construction, where *bo:ba* is reduced to *ba* (glossed in the relevant examples as '(see).IMP'). Example (6) shows an utterance from Ulahi to her daughter, Mobiya (age 8). The verb *keda:i* 'search for' preceded by *se* and followed by the imperative *bo:ba* to mean 'try to search'. (However, as searching typically involves looking, this

---

3. *Bo:ba* 'see' is also associated with intellection in the complex predicate *á:la: bo:ba*, literally, 'two see/look', which is defined in the Bosavi dictionary as: "put two ideas together to see how they add up; realise that different things you see or hear join together to make a larger story" (Schieffelin & Feld, 1998, p. 3).

could potentially be interpreted as a transitional example, where both visual and attemptive meanings are active.)

(6) *bolo se   keda:i   **bo:ba***
     ball just search.for see.IMP
     'Try to search for the ball.'   (AIII 6–1)

Examples (7) and (8) show other situations where children use or encounter the *bo:ba* attemptive construction, in both full and contracted form. In these examples, visual semantics are no longer an obvious interpretation. In (7), Abi's elder sister, 5-year-old Yogodo, first tells her mother to 'eat' using the simple imperative (*maya:*), but then reformulates this directive using the attemptive construction (*na:i bo:ba*).

(7) Yog: *we   maya:.   no:,   se   na:i **bo:ba***
          this eat.IMP.EMPH 1SG.POSS.mother just eat see.IMP
          'Eat this. Mother, see if you can eat this.'   (AIV 7–1)

Example (8) shows an occasion where Ma:li (30 months, 2 weeks) and Mama (3 years, 7 months) have been doing extended sound play, no longer producing referential language. However, there are cultural prohibitions on such vocalisations, (the children sound like birds, the spirits of the dead) and Ma:li's mother thus urges the children to speak properly.

(8) *wai! to   nafa se   sa:la:i **ba!**   we   o:ba: to!*
     hey talk good just speak (see).IMP this bird talk
     'Hey! Try to speak good language. This is bird language!'   (MVI 19–2)

The use of a vision verb to express attemptive modality, as in Bosavi, is widespread in Papuan languages (Foley, 1986) and found in unrelated languages around the world (Matthieu-Reeves, 2009; Voinov, 2013). In a study of this phenomenon, Voinov (2013) suggests that this can be traced to the metaphor 'seeing is touching' as proposed by Lakoff and Johnson (1980), or, more generally, the 'mind-as-body' metaphor discussed by Sweetser (1990). That is, vision is equated with physical manipulation, and the idea of manipulating objects is further extended to manipulating events; to see an action relates to "the process of controlling an action in an attempt to perform it" (Voinov, 2013, p. 73). If this is so, we would perhaps expect to find cases of transitional meaning in interaction, where a vision verb could be interpreted as having visual, control, and/or attemptive semantics simultaneously. To date we have not noted any such cases, but it is something to keep in mind for further work.[4] An alternative proposal is that of Mathieu-Reeves (2009, pp. 27–28), who suggests that attemptive meanings for 'see' stem from the concept of mentally 'envisioning' or imagining an event.

Overall, it remains very much an open question whether Kaluli child learners draw a connection between the attemptive construction and *bo:ba* used as a main verb (and thus experience any semantic conflation of 'seeing' and 'trying'). The construction appears to be quite formulaic, nearly always occurring as an imperative, and there is little opportunity to observe creative use. While very young children heard many attemptive utterances in family interactions, their own production was relatively rare. The earliest recorded uses of this construction are in fact with the verb 'see', as seen in (9) and (10). However, in these examples Abi uses the contracted form *ba* rather than the full form *bo:ba* (glossed in these examples as '(see).IMP'), and it seems reasonably likely that he is unaware of any co-identity between the forms.

(9) *so:wa la:su niyo:*   *se* **ba:da:i ba**
     baby   1SG.POSS just see   (see).IMP
     'Try to look at my baby.'   (33m2w AVIII 22-2)

(10) *a:no: se*   **ba:da:i ba**
     that just see   (see).IMP
     'Try to look at that.' ((hiding his hand in a tin))   (35m2w AIX 29–1)

Children's awareness of any possible connection between 'seeing' and 'trying' may further relate to their competence in complex predication more generally, for example, whether they understand multi-verb strings as productive constructions or use them as rote-learned forms.[5]

Summing up, the young Bosavi children in the corpus hear and produce the vision verb *bo:ba* in a range of contexts, including literal and playful sequences that focus on visual experience, as well as situations that highlight the connection between sight and knowledge. Children are also exposed to a specialised use of the vision verb (or a contracted form of it) to mark attemptive modality, and make some attempts to use this construction.

---

4. As a possible counter-argument to Voinov's hypothesis, however, we note that for many languages of the region visual semantics (as encoded by evidentials) can also be associated with a *lack* of control (see Rule, 1977 on Foe; San Roque, 2008; San Roque & Loughnane 2012a, 2012b).

5. The recorded children's earlier multi-verb predications tend to be purposive constructions in which *bo:ba* features heavily as a non-final form, such as *ba:ba:-ni ho:n-o:l* (see-PURP go-1PRS), 'I am going in order to see'. This shows quite a different temporal and causal relationship to that in the attemptive construction.

4. Hearing

The verb *dabuma* 'hear, listen (to)' had very limited use by children and adults in the corpus, with the exception of one highly routinised utterance, *ge siyo:wo: da:daya?*, 'do you hear what I said?'. This phrase is typically uttered after a request that has not been complied with and is part of the extensive repertoire of rhetorical questions that Bosavi speakers, adults and children alike, use not only to tease, shame and challenge (see Schieffelin, 1990) but also to assert their desires and authority. This was especially salient in the speech of caregivers and older children, who used it to try to verbally compel others to act. The implication of the use of *dabuma* here is that the speaker must not have heard, otherwise, compliance would be of course forthcoming. This speech formula thus shows links to concepts of heeding and responsiveness: to hear is to understand and comply (see, e.g., Sweetser, 1990; Vanhove, 2008).

Excluding prompting through *a:la:ma* 'say it' routines (see Schieffelin, 1990), the first spontaneous child usage of *dabuma* was Ma:li (at 24 months 3 weeks), shown in (11). Earlier in this interaction, Ma:li's mother had offered her ripe banana, which she refused. Her mother began cooking and talking with other women, and about 10 minutes later, Ma:li initiated a series of requests for banana, to which she received no response. Raising the volume, varying the request format, and adding emphatic markers to each successive request, Ma:li was starting to cry.

(11)   Ma:li: *no: magu geno: ma:*
             'Mother give (me) ripe banana
             ge   siyo:-wo: da:d-a-ya?   no:wo:!
             2SG   say.PST-NMLZ hear-2.PRS-Q 1SG.POSS.mother
             Do you hear what I said? Mother!'
     Mo: *wengaba:?*
             'Why are you doing this?!'   (24m3w MII 2–2)

Ma:li's use of 'do you hear what I said?' elicited a verbal response from her mother, a rhetorical question meaning, 'Stop what you are doing! There is no reason for your behaviour!'. Over the next several months Ma:li regularly used 'do you hear what I said?' to challenge her mother after her repeated requests for food or to nurse were ignored. Her mother never directly refused her, a cultural preference, but rather used talk to redirect her attention to something else.

In contrast to Ma:li, the two young boys in the study were rarely refused anything due to gender-based differences in child socialisation, and did not produce this formulaic utterance in request sequences. Nonetheless, they heard this expression used by their mothers and older sisters in a confrontational tone, and occasionally used it themselves in teasing or challenging routines to add force to their assertions. One of the most extensive sequences in which it was used in verbal play, over 10 minutes of nonstop talk among three participants. This interaction highlights how routinised and formulaic utterances from any sensory domain can be mobilised for verbal play for a particular pragmatic effect that is very salient in Kaluli family interactions.

Abi's mother has gone outside the house, leaving Abi (now aged 30 months) with his two sisters, Waye, age 7 and Yogodo, age 5. The two girls are trying to cook sweet potatoes in the fire, and Abi has been messing it up. Yogodo yells at him to stop, and her older sister immediately says to Abi 'Do you hear what I said?!', which is repeated by the younger sister. Abi repeats it twice and over many exchanges his two sisters verbally challenge Abi who also responds with 'Do you hear what I said?!' as he strikes at them with a stick, kicks embers, and generally creates a scene. He utters the phrase 14 times in addition to many fragments of it. His sisters phonologically vary and distort this phrase as a way of teasing Abi and also use other formulaic teasing routines with each other and Abi to intensify the key and encourage his behaviour (which their mother would have stopped). Here the poetic and pragmatic functions of this routinised metalinguistic formulation go beyond any literal use of the sensory verbs.

Less commonly, we encounter the verb *dabuma* in information-seeking questions. Example (12) highlights how children can be directed to attend to the aural environment for information, although again this is through questions rather than commands. Here, Ma:li's mother uses the interrogative *da:daya* to direct Ma:li's attention to talk that is going on outside, before offering an explanation for the source of this talk, in this case a foreign visitor.

(12) Mo: *to-wo:*   *o:dowa-yo:m   ge   da:d-a-ya?*
             talk-NEUT be.3.PRS-SNS 2SG hear-2.PRS-Q
             'Do you hear the talk going on?'
       Ma:li: *o:ba:?*
             'What?'
       Mo: *towo: o:dowayo:ka: anasowo:*
             'There's talk going on, the white man.'   (27m3w MIV 9–2)

Example (13) shows a rare example of an imperative utterance with *dabuma*. In this case, the hearing verb is used in an attemptive construction in combination with a reduced form of *bo:ba* (as discussed above). Here, Ma:li's mother urges her to pay close attention to her (the mother's) speech as she directs Ma:li to repeat an earlier utterance.[6]

(13)   Ma:li: *no: Babiyo: na:sena:le?*
                'Mother, I wonder does Bambi usually eat [this type of taro]?'
        Mo: *se   da:da:i **ba**,   ge   na:-sen-o:?   a:la:-bo*
                just   hear   (see).IMP 2SG   eat-HAB$_2$-Q   like.that-?
                'Just try to listen, do you usually eat? One says like that.'

                                                          (31m2w MVII 21–2)

While the basic verb of hearing is itself quite restricted in both literal and extended use, the Kaluli attention to the aural environment, explored in great detail in Steven Feld's work (e.g., 1982 [2012], 1996) is nevertheless very present in the interactional corpus, as it is common for adults and children to comment on and attempt to decipher sounds and their sources. However, such talk rarely employs the perception verb *dabuma*, but uses a range of other resources, such as the sound ideophones exemplified in Table 3, deictic elements, and/or nominal reference (Schieffelin & San Roque, 2017). Overall, the most salient use of *dabuma* for children appears to be in relation to listening to talk only (cf. San Roque et al. 2015; Sweetser 1990), and especially in a routinised question that highlights responsiveness and heedfulness to linguistic communication. This routinised formula illustrates how semantic associations that have been identified more generally in the world's languages (often on the basis of survey and dictionary data) can be emergently relevant in interaction between children and their caregivers in one particular society.

5.   Touch

Most occurrences of *golóma* 'touch' in the corpus are situations where the verb is employed in the sense of 'make contact' rather than the more sensory meaning 'feel'. With reference to the former type, Extract (14) illustrates how touch is employed in play and teasing, highlighting issues of control and prohibition. Here, the older girl Solia (8 yrs) challenges Ma:li to try and touch her mother's bag, using the phrase 'try and touch it' as a kind of dare – that is, there's no way you can touch this! Several different forms of the verb 'touch' follow in quick succession.

---

6.   The sequential situation here is complex. Ma:li has previously asked Bambi 'Do you eat this?' but received only a repair initiation ('What?') in response. This prompted Ma:li to ask her mother about Bambi's eating habits instead. However, rather than respond directly, Ma:li's mother urges Ma:li to repeat her original question to Bambi, which Ma:li subsequently does, finally receiving an answer from Bambi herself.

(14) Solia: *ni*   *no:-wa:*   *bida:liya-yo:* *giyo:* *se* *gola:i*
         1SG.POSS 1SG.POSS.mother-POSS bag-NEUT   2SG just touch
         ba.   *bida:liya-yo:.*
         (see).IMP bag-NEUT
         'My mother's bag, you just try to touch it. The bag!'

     Ma:li: *o:ke* ((pointing to one of several))
         'Right there.'

     Solia: *o:mba. niyo: nowo: we. no ko:lo: no:wa:no:*
         'Not that one. Another of mine here. And that's my mother's.'

     Ma:li: *o:ke! a:no:* ***golo:***   ((Ma:li reaches for bag but doesn't touch it))
         here that   touch.PST
         'Right here! I touched that.'

     Mo: *Ma:li! ge* ***mo:-gom-a:ib.***
         Ma:li 2SG NEG-touch-2/3.FUT
         'Ma:li! You will not touch.'

     Solia: *o: ge dimido: ko:lo:* ***gol-an-o:?***   ((teasing))
         and 2SG make.PST so   touch-HAB$_1$-Q
         'And did you make it so you can touch it?'

     Ma:li: ***mo:-gol-an***
         NEG-touch-HAB$_1$
         'One doesn't touch.'   (32m2w MVIII 25–2)

The exchange between the children, as well as the mother's assertion ('You will not touch!') draw a connection between touching, ownership and permission, relating more broadly to Ibarretxe-Antuñano's (2006) finding that verbs of touch may be commonly extended with 'affect' meanings. The exchange in (14) propagates the notion that one may have the right to touch (affect) objects that belong to oneself or one's family, but not those of others.

     One or two instances in the data alternatively highlight touch as a sensory channel for learning about the world. One of these is shown in (15), an attemptive construction, followed by a plain imperative, addressed to Ma:li. In this case, Ma:li is being urged to test the temperature of water that is being heated.

(15) Mo: *giyo: se* ***gola:i ba.***   *ho:no:* ***golóma***
         2SG just touch (see).IMP water touch.IMP
         'You try and touch it. Touch the water.'   (30m2w MVI 18–1)

Example (15) shows a situation where *golóma* is used in a similar way to the English tactile verb *feel* to talk about tactile temperature (cf. Koptjevskaja-Tamm, 2015). However, unlike *feel* (which has a very broad range of meanings), the Bosavi form cannot also refer to internal sensation, emotion, and suchlike.

6. Taste and smell

The senses of taste and smell were only rarely spoken of in the Bosavi child inter-actions. We discuss two examples here to give at least a glimpse of gustatory and olfactory talk as used with young children. Example (16) shows an instance of the verb *nudab* 'taste' (where the stimulus is the subject of the verb, as in English *this tastes funny*). In this sequence Abi is trying to nurse, but his mother is trying to discourage him. One of the tactics she uses is to try and distract him into talking rather than drinking, in this case by suggesting he assess the taste of the milk.

(16)   *bo ibo: ha:nabike na:la:ya? wa? aundo:ma. aundo:malo:*
        'Are you drinking the breast milk that is going? Huh? There is none. There is really none. ((he keeps nursing))
        nafa **nud-ab**-*a?*   *mogagi* **nud-ab**-*a?*
        good taste-3.PRS-Q bad   taste-3.PRS-Q
        Does it taste good? Does it taste bad?
        Abi! nafa **nud-ab**-*a,*   *bo-wo:?*
        Abi   good taste-3.PRS-Q breast-NEUT
        Abi! Does it taste good, the breast?'   (31m2w AVI 16–1)

While the use of *nudab* 'taste' in (16) is quite literal, we can also see how it relates to notions of evaluation that are often relevant to taste metaphors. That is, talking about the taste of something is often linked to the subjective assessment of that item (e.g., as good or bad), and in some languages taste vocabulary can thus be extended to the expression of subjective assessment beyond the domain of food and flavour (e.g., Sweetser, 1990; King, 2015).

The basic smell predicate *mun dabuma* (which employs the verb *dabuma* 'hear') does not appear to be used at all in the Bosavi child corpus. However, there are some occasions where caregivers and children discuss smells in other ways, for example using *mun* 'odour' in a noun phrase, or employing the more specific verb *heseab* 'smell bad, stink'. In (17) Abi's elder sister, Yogodo (nearly 6 years old) comments on the presence of the smell of a just-lit match, using the nominal *mun*. The verb here is inflected with the non-visual sensory evidential -*o:m*, by which Yogodo indicates that she perceives this situation using a sense other than vision (see also Example (12), where the same marker occurs in relation to sound).

(17)   *masisi* **mun**   *dowa-yo:m*
        match odour be.3.PRS-SNS
        'The odour of matches is around.'   (AX 33–2)

In the interaction of which (17) is part, Yogodo is trying to figure out who it is that has matches and is lighting them. This highlights the relevance of smell to detection and deduction, a metaphorical extension that is present in some other languages (e.g., English *to smell a* rat, see Kövesces, this volume; Nunggubuyu, Evans & Wilkins, 2000, p. 576; Catalan Sign Language, Wilcox & Wilcox, 2012).

7. Summary and coda

We do not think of 'perceptual metaphor' as something high-minded that belongs to the literary domain or to elaborated verbal art, but rather as part of everyday meaning-making and language use. In Bosavi interactions between young children, their siblings, and caregivers, we observe potential for associating the linguistic encoding of perception with other semantic domains, including several that are known to be cross-linguistically relevant to perceptual vocabulary. To be clear, we are not making claims about a causal or inevitable relationship between our observations concerning Bosavi and cross-linguistic semantic associations: that is, we do not suggest that these extended meanings arise specifically and necessarily in child-caregiver interaction. Rather, we want to draw attention to the possibility that a link between these domains could have been present quite early for these Kaluli children. We have discussed the data as exemplifying possible connections between sight and knowledge; sight and trying; hearing and responsiveness or heeding; touch and control, permission, and affect; taste and evaluation; and smell and deduction.

Perhaps (some of) these meanings are not clearly distinguished as separate from literal perceptual senses, but 'come along for the ride' (or even shape the course) as children learn to talk appropriately about these domains. From a child's perspective, it may not be that a perception verb extends to accrue a metaphorical sense, but rather that it relates to a complex of overlapping verbalised experiences (as per Johnson, 1999), as seems possible for the verb *bo:ba* 'see, look (at)'. Furthermore, for some perceptual vocabulary, a child's early experience may be restricted to a particular pragmatic routine that is rich in social meaning but only weakly identifies literal sensory experience (as per Edwards & Goodwin, 1985), as for the audition verb *dabuma* 'hear, listen (to)' in the phrase 'do you hear what I said?'. Verbs of perception may further blur physical sensation with physical action, bundled up with social-pragmatic notions of permission and prohibition, as for *golóma* 'touch'.

A noticeable feature in this first study of perception verbs in the Bosavi corpus is the apparently dominant role of interrogatives as opposed to simple imperatives in directing the senses of others. Adults and children alike often choose a question format such as 'do you see?' to draw attention to perceptual experiences rather than a command such as 'look!'. Perhaps this aligns with a feeling that your senses are ultimately your own business, and that perceptual attention (like other aspects of socialisation) can be led but not forced. Overall, this stance would be in accord with the Bosavi cultural ideology that it is not appropriate to assert the private experiences and unexpressed internal states of others (Schieffelin, 2008; see also San Roque & Schieffelin, 2018). The use of sensory questions also highlights the potential for talk about perception to calibrate and confirm intersubjective alignment (Majid & Levinson, 2011; Kendrick, this volume; San Roque, Kendrick, Norcliffe & Majid, 2018). We further acknowledge that looking at basic verbal expressions of perception is only a small part of the Bosavi picture. Children are also learning to attend to and encode perceptual experience using more specific vocabulary from a range of word classes (e.g., as mentioned in Section 2), and even grammaticalised evidential forms (see also Schieffelin, 1985, pp. 568–588). These are exciting areas for further research.

What happens to sensory ideologies in the face of radical change? In the early 1970s, two Australian missionaries from the Unevangelised Fields Mission established a small mission station outside of the villages, and introduced their own practices of listening and looking. These would add new dimensions to the use and understanding of two sensory verbs, see/look and hear/listen, that would be evident in sermons, bible reading, and literacy practices.

Like their fellow missionaries working in nonliterate communities, they used a mission primer template and produced a set of short primers, designed to be used for early vernacular literacy instruction for adults or children. Ma:li's parents were among the first Kaluli to take an interest in Christianity, and the only adults in Sululib village pursuing literacy. These primers also provided a new context and a novel object for visual attention, and Ma:li's curiosity about what her mother was doing when she looked at and named drawings in the primers, as in Extract (18), was clear.

(18)   Ma:li: *no:*   *nelo:* *bo:d-o:l-e?*   *ba* *a:no:*
             1SG.POSS.mother 1SG   see-1.PRS-Q.EMPH just that
             nelo: *bo:d-o:l-o?*
             1SG   see-1.PRS-Q
             'Mother can I see? Can I just see that?'
       Mo: *dinafa*   *ba:da:bi*
              carefully look.FUT.IMP
              'Look carefully.'   (27m3w MIV 9–2)

In terms of sensory verb use, the Kaluli Primer Book 2, which consists of 22 pages each with a short 2–3 word sentence, has 11 tokens of *bo:ba* 'see/look', 9 of which are imperatives, with the remaining two being second/third person present forms. With the exception of the names of the characters, *bo:ba* is the most repeated word in the text.

Since it was introduced by the mission, reading in Bosavi was always done aloud, whether it was scripture in Tok Pisin, or a vernacular literacy text about malaria. Schieffelin's research (1996, 2000) on adult literacy lessons and sermons led by Kaluli speakers shows that the verb 'see/look' is used to direct readers to look at the book or a particular page or picture in it. For example, in (19), Kulu, the instructor in a literacy class at the mission station (recorded by Schieffelin in 1984) uses three different imperative forms of *bo:ba* when directing a group of young men to look at a picture.

(19) *bikisayo:* **ba:da:bi.**   *bikisayo: se* **ba:da:i** *ha:n-a:bi,*   *a:no:* **bo:ba!**
      picture look.FUT.IMP picture just look   go-FUT.IMP that look.IMP
      'Look at the picture. Just go look at the picture, look at that!'

In addition, books were given a speaking voice, and those interested in becoming Christians were told that they had to 'hear/listen to' the Word in order to understand. While it is beyond the scope of this chapter to go into extensive detail, literacy lessons, and sermons, made explicit the new source of knowledge and truth, the Bible, which required that persons listen to this book that speaks. As Kulu himself as well as other Bosavi Christians put it:

(20) *buko: wena-milo: to   sa:l-ab   we **da:da:-sa:ga:***
      book this-LOC   word say-3.PRS this listen-SEQ
      asulu-ma:niki
      know/understand-HORT
      'Listening to what the words in this book say makes us know/understand.'

With the introduction of Protestant Christianity, and the elaborate language ideology that accompanied it, new forms of truth, and ways of hearing and listening to it, were introduced by Kaluli pastors into their vernacular.[7] As recently discussed by O'Meara and Majid (2016) in regard to the Seri smellscape and odour lexicon, cultural and linguistic practices are not timeless, but can be changed by contact with other regimes of organising worlds of knowing within a very short time span. Within a decade of when the Bosavi child corpus was recorded, there were many changes, including the ways in which seeing, looking, listening and hearing were talked about.

---

7. Even the domain of taste may be incorporated into this transformation: Schieffelin's recordings of sermons by Bosavi pastors include several instances where God's word is treated metaphorically as nourishing 'food' to be 'tasted'. We do not have evidence that understanding talk as food was also a robust pre-Christian metaphor, and it seems likely it was introduced through missionisation.

Acknowledgements

Thanks to the Sululib community and to the National Science Foundation and the Wenner-Gren Foundation for Anthropological Research for their generous support for Schieffelin's fieldwork in Bosavi. San Roque's contribution was supported by the Netherlands Organisation for Scientific Research (Veni award 275-89-024, 'Learning the senses: Perception verbs in child-caregiver interaction'). Thank you also to Asifa Majid, Carolyn O'Meara and Laura J. Speed.

References

Aikhenvald, A. Y. & Storch, A. (Eds.). (2013). *Perception and cognition in language and culture*. Leiden: Brill.

Edwards, D. & Goodwin, R. (1985). The language of shared attention and visual experience. A functional study of early nomination. *Journal of Pragmatics*, 9, 475–493. https://doi.org/10.1016/0378-2166(85)90017-7

Evans, N. and Wilkins, D. (2000). In the mind's ear: The semantic extensions of perception verbs in Australian languages. *Language*, 76(3), 546–592. https://doi.org/10.2307/417135

Feld, S. (2012) [1982]. *Sound and sentiment: Birds, weeping, poetics, and song in Kaluli expression*. Durham: Duke University Press. 3rd ed. https://doi.org/10.1215/9780822395898

Feld, S. (1996). Waterfalls of song: An acoustemology of place resounding in Bosavi, Papua New Guinea. In S. Feld & K. Basso (Eds.), *Senses of place* (pp. 91–136). Santa Fe: School of American Research.

Foley, W. A. (1986). *Papuan languages of New Guinea*. Cambridge: Cambridge University Press.

Grosh, A. & Grosh, S. (2004). Grammar essentials for the Kaluli language. Summer Institute of Linguistics, Papua New Guinea. [ms]

Ibarretxe-Antuñano, I. (1999). Metaphorical mappings in the sense of smell. In R. W. Gibbs, Jr. & G. J. Steen (Eds.), *Metaphor in Cognitive Linguistics: Selected papers from the 5th International Cognitive Linguistics Conference, Amsterdam, 1997* (pp. 29–46). Amsterdam/ Philadelphia: John Benjamins.

Ibarretxe-Antuñano, I. (2006). Cross-linguistic polysemy in tactile verbs. In J. Luchjenbroers (Ed.), *Cognitive linguistics investigations across languages, fields, and philosophical boundaries* (pp. 235–253). Amsterdam: John Benjamins. https://doi.org/10.1075/hcp.15.16iba

Johnson, C. (1999). Metaphor vs. conflation in the acquisition of polysemy: The case of *see*. In M. K. Hiraga, C. Sinha & S. Wilcox (Eds.), *Cultural, psychological and typological issues in cognitive linguistics: Selected papers of the bi-annual ICLA meeting in Albuquerque, July 1995* (pp. 155–170). Amsterdam/Philadelphia: John Benjamins.

King, P. (2015). Papua New Guinean sweet talk: Metaphors from the domain of taste. In E. Piirainen & A. Sherris (Eds.), *Language endangerment: Disappearing metaphors and shifting conceptualizations* (pp. 37–64). Amsterdam/Philadelphia: John Benjamins. https://doi.org/10.1075/clscc.7.02kin

Koptjevskaja-Tamm, M. (Ed.). (2015). *The linguistics of temperature*. Amsterdam/Philadelphia: John Benjamins. https://doi.org/10.1075/tsl.107

Lakoff, G. & M. Johnson. (1980). *Metaphors we live by*. Chicago: University of Chicago Press

Majid, A. (2013). Making semantics and pragmatics "sensory". *Journal of Pragmatics*, 58, 48–51. https://doi.org/10.1016/j.pragma.2013.09.019

Majid, A. & Levinson, S. C. (2011). The senses in language and culture. *Senses and Society*, 6(1), 5–18. https://doi.org/10.2752/174589311X12893982233551

Mathieu-Reeves, D. (2009). Reanalysis of serial verb constructions in Yimas, a Sepik-Ramu language of Papua New Guinea. MA dissertation, University of Oregon.

Mihalic, F. (1971). *The Jacaranda dictionary and grammar of Melanesian Pidgin*. Milton, Queensland: The Jacaranda Press.

O'Meara, C. & Majid, A. (2016). How changing lifestyles impact Seri smellscapes and smell language. *Anthropological Linguistics*, 58(2), 107–131. https://doi.org/10.1353/anl.2016.0024

Rabagliati, H., Marcus, G. F. & Pylkkänen, L. (2010). Shifting senses in lexical semantic development. *Cognition*, 117(1), 17–37. https://doi.org/10.1016/j.cognition.2010.06.007

Ross, M. (2005). Pronouns as a preliminary diagnostic for grouping Papuan languages. In A. Pawley, R. Attenborough, J. Golson & R. Hide (Eds.), *Papuan pasts: Cultural, linguistic and biological histories of Papuan-speaking peoples* (pp. 15–65). Canberra: Pacific Linguistics.

Rule, W. M. (1964). Customs, alphabet and grammar of the Kaluli people of Bosavi, Papua. Manuscript.

Rule, W. M. (1977). *A comparative study of the Foe, Huli, and Pole languages of Papua New Guinea*. Sydney: University of Sydney.

San Roque, L. (2008). An introduction to Duna grammar. PhD dissertation, Australian National University.

San Roque, L., & Loughnane, R. (2012a). The New Guinea Highlands evidentiality area. *Linguistic Typology*, 16, 111–167. https://doi.org/10.1515/lity-2012-0003

San Roque, L., & Loughnane, R. (2012b). Inheritance, contact and change in the New Guinea Highlands evidentiality area. *Language and Linguistics in Melanesia: Special Issue 2012 Part II*, 397–427.

San Roque, L., Kendrick, K. H., Norcliffe, E., Brown, P., Defina, R., Dingemanse, M., Dirksmeyer, T., Enfield, N. J., Floyd, S., Hammond, J., Rossi, G., Tufvesson, S., van Putten, S. & Majid, A. (2015). Vision verbs dominate in conversation across cultures, but the ranking of non-visual verbs varies. *Cognitive Linguistics*, 26, 31–60. https://doi.org/10.1515/cog-2014-0089

San Roque, L., Kendrick, K. H., Norcliffe, E. & Majid, A. (2018). Universal extensions of perception verbs are grounded in interaction. *Cognitive Linguistics*, 29(3): 371–406.

San Roque, L. & Schieffelin, B. B. (2018). Learning how to know: Egophoricity and the grammar of Kaluli (Bosavi, Trans New Guinea), with special reference to child language. In S. Floyd, E. Norcliffe & L. San Roque (Eds.), *Egophoricity*. (pp. 437–471). Amsterdam: Benjamins. https://doi.org/10.1075/tsl.118.14san

Schieffelin, B. B. (1985). The acquisition of Kaluli. In D. Slobin (Ed.), *The crosslinguistic study of language acquisition* (pp. 525–593). Mahwah, NJ: Lawrence Erlbaum.

Schieffelin, B. B. (1990). *The give and take of everyday life: Language socialization of Kaluli children*. Cambridge: Cambridge University Press.

Schieffelin, B. B. (1996). Creating evidence: Making sense of the written word in Bosavi. In E. Ochs, E. A. Schegloff & S. Thompson (Eds.), *Interaction and grammar* (pp. 435–60). Cambridge: Cambridge University Press. https://doi.org/10.1017/CBO9780511620874.010

Schieffelin, B. B. (2000). Introducing Kaluli literacy: A chronology of influences. In P. Kroskrity (Ed.), *Regimes of language: Ideologies, politics, and identities* (pp. 293–327). Santa Fe: School of American Research Press.

Schieffelin, B. B. (2008). Speaking only your own mind: Reflections on confession, gossip, and intentionality in Bosavi (PNG). *Anthropological Quarterly*, 81(2), 431–441. https://doi.org/10.1353/anq.0.0003

Schieffelin, B. B. & Feld, S. (1998). *Bosavi-English-Tok Pisin dictionary*. Canberra: Pacific Linguistics.

Schieffelin, B. B. & San Roque, L. (2017). Visual and auditory experiences in child-caregiver interaction: Insights from perception verbs in Bosavi (Kaluli). Paper presented at The 14th International Congress for the Study of Child Language (IASCL 2017), Lyon, 20 July.

Schieffelin, E. L. (1976). *The sorrow of the lonely and the burning of the dancers*. New York: St. Martin's Press.

Schieffelin, E. L. & Crittenden, R. (1991). *Like people you see in a dream*. Stanford: Stanford University Press.

Shayan, S., Ozturk, O., Bowerman, M. & Majid, A. (2014). Spatial metaphor in language can promote the development of cross-modal mappings in children. *Developmental Science*, 17(4), 636–643. https://doi.org/10.1111/desc.12157

Sweetser, E. (1990). *From etymology to pragmatics: Metaphorical and cultural aspects of semantic structure*. Cambridge: Cambridge University Press.
https://doi.org/10.1017/CBO9780511620904

Vanhove, M. (2008). Semantic associations between sensory modalities, prehension and mental perceptions. In M. Vanhove (Ed.), *From polysemy to semantic change: Towards a typology of lexical semantic associations* (pp. 341–370). Amsterdam/Philadelphia: John Benjamins.
https://doi.org/10.1075/slcs.106.17van

Viberg, Å. (1983). The verbs of perception: A typological study. *Linguistics*, 21, 123–162.
https://doi.org/10.1515/ling.1983.21.1.123

Voinov, V. (2013). Seeing is trying: The relation of visual perception to attemptive modality in the world's languages. *Language and Cognition*, 5(1), 61–80.
https://doi.org/10.1515/langcog-2013-0003

Wilcox, S. & Wilcox, P. P. (2012). Cognitive linguistics and signed languages. *International Journal of Cognitive Linguistics*, 3(2).

Wilkins, D. P. (1981). Towards a theory of semantic change. PhD dissertation, The Australian National University.

Williams, J. M. (1976). Synaesthetic adjectives: A possible law of semantic change. *Language*, 52(2), 461–478. https://doi.org/10.2307/412571

List of metaphors

Index